2016/17

Dear Terry,

Merry Christmas!
May this be a wonderful
New Year.

Love,
Rosie

# COLD
# FIRE

# JOHN BOYKO

# COLD
# FIRE

ALFRED A. KNOPF CANADA

PUBLISHED BY ALFRED A. KNOPF CANADA

Copyright © 2016 John Boyko

www.penguinrandomhouse.ca

Library and Archives Canada Cataloguing in Publication

Cold fire : Kennedy's northern front / John Boyko.

Includes bibliographical references and index.
Issued in print and electronic formats.

ISBN 978-0-345-80893-6
eBook ISBN 978-0-345-80895-0

1. Cuban Missile Crisis, 1962. 2. United States—History—1961–1969.
3. United States—Politics and government—1961–1963. 4. Kennedy, John F.
(John Fitzgerald), 1917–1963. 5. United States—Foreign relations—Canada.
6. Canada—Foreign relations—United States. 7. Canada—History—1945–1963.
8. Canada—Politics and government—1957–1963. 9. Diefenbaker, John G.,
1895–1979. 10. Pearson, Lester B., 1897–1972. I. Title.

E841.B69 2016            973.922            C2015-905781-7

Book design by Andrew Roberts
Cover images: (Lester Pearson and John Diefenbaker) © John McNeill / *The Globe and Mail* / The Canadian Press; (John F. Kennedy) © Paul Schutzer / The LIFE Picture Collection / Getty Images

Printed and bound in the United States of America

2 4 6 8 9 7 5 3 1

Penguin
Random House
KNOPF CANADA

This book is for Sue.

*Never has the task of finding the truth been more difficult.*

—JOHN F. KENNEDY, MONTREAL, DECEMBER 4, 1953

# CONTENTS

# PROLOGUE

THERE WAS NO CROWD AT THE AIRPORT. There were no reporters. Although the 1960 presidential election was three years away, Senator John F. Kennedy had been vigorously campaigning, and so he must have found his silent arrival in Toronto on that slate grey November afternoon either amusing or disconcerting. Throughout 1957 he had been a frequent and entertaining guest on American political chat shows. His office flooded newspapers and magazines with press releases and articles he had written or at least edited. He accepted 140 speaking engagements. The Herculean effort to render his already famous name even more so had spilled over the border, as these things do. By the time of his visit, Canadians knew of him and his ambition.

Twenty female University of Toronto (U of T) students certainly knew. They were waiting outside Hart House, where Kennedy was scheduled to participate in a debate. Since its opening in 1919, Hart House's lounges, library, and recreational facilities had become the university's social and cultural hub. The impressive Gothic revival building was a gift from the Massey family that had made its fortune in farm machinery. It was named for company founder Hart Massey and dedicated by his grandson, Vincent, who would later become the country's first Canadian-born governor general. He insisted on guidelines stipulating that within its stone, ivy-covered walls, Hart House would allow no studying, drinking, or women. The first two rules were often and flagrantly broken, but Margaret Brewin, Judy Graner, and Linda Silver Dranoff led a contingent hoping to end the third. They asked the Hart House warden to allow women to see the debate.

When rebuffed, they gathered friends, created placards, and greeted Kennedy with chants that alternated between "Hart House Unfair" and "We Want Kennedy."

Kennedy smiled but said nothing as he was escorted through the drizzling rain and noisy protesters. Beneath its towering, dark oak–panelled ceiling, the Debates Room could seat two hundred and fifty. It was packed. A scuffle interrupted introductions when a sharp-eyed guard noticed a guest's nail polish and removed three women who had snuck in disguised as men. With the women locked out, the men inside prepared to argue: "Has the United States failed in its responsibilities as a world leader?" Kennedy was given leave to present remarks from the floor in support of the team defending American actions.

Reading from a prepared text, he offered that Americans did not enjoy immunity from foreign policy mistakes but that the difference between statesmanship and politics is often a choice between two blunders. He expressed concern regarding the degree to which public opinion sometimes dictated sound public policy and admitted that the United States had misplayed some recent challenges in the Middle East and Southeast Asia. Regardless of these and other errors, he argued, American foreign policy rested on sound principles and his country remained a force for good.[1]

The address was well written but poorly delivered. Kennedy read in a flat tone and seldom looked up.[2] The student debaters tore him apart. Leading the team against him was a nineteen-year-old second-year student named Stephen Lewis. As a member of the four-man U of T debate team, he had competed at various Canadian and American universities and won accolades, including the best speaker award at a recent international competition.[3] Lewis argued that the United States consistently acted in ways that violated the tenets of its Constitution and Declaration of Independence. He accused America of trying to be "policeman, baby-sitter and bank to the world."[4] The audience offered good-natured ribbing throughout the debate. Cheers rewarded good points and witty rejoinders. Kennedy seemed to enjoy himself and was heckled along with the rest.[5]

The audience gasped in disbelief when adjudicators scored the debate 204 to 194 in favour of Kennedy's side. Afterwards, at a participants' reception, Lewis spoke with Senator Kennedy and expressed confusion as to why a Democrat such as he would defend the hawkish policies of the current Republican administration. Kennedy startled Lewis by confessing that he was a Democrat only because he was from Massachusetts and that if he were from a predominantly Republican state such as Maine, he would probably be a Republican.[6]

Kennedy was not through raising eyebrows. When leaving Hart House, a reporter asked his opinion of the women's demonstration. He smiled and said, "I personally rather approve of keeping women out of these places. . . . It's a pleasure to be in a country where women cannot mix in everywhere."[7] Although victorious, Kennedy had impressed few with his speech, fewer with his confession of political opportunism, and fewer still with his flippant dismissal of women and the concept of gender equality. His brief meeting with a small group of the protesting women the next morning changed no minds. Kennedy's Toronto flop was surprising; by 1957 he had become quite adept at handling gatherings that demanded a blend of political chops and charm.

He returned to his campaign and the students to their studies, but the brief visit had hinted at important questions soon to be asked in forums more significant than a student debate. On the day Kennedy visited Toronto, John G. Diefenbaker was Canada's prime minister and Lester B. Pearson was positioning himself to win the leadership of the opposition Liberals. The three leaders would soon meet at a crossroads—one that would determine the nature of Canada's independence, America's struggle against communist aggression, and the art and science of leadership itself in a new era of television and political celebrity.

The important decisions would be made while everything that had been certain for so long seemed to be changing. In 1957, economic growth on both sides of the border had fallen from a decade of 6 percent per year to an anaemic 1 percent. The good times that many had come to believe would never end were ending. Popular culture was changing. Rock 'n' roll and the Beat movement were leading many young people (and the young at heart) to question established values. Race relations were changing, as evidenced by America's non-violent civil rights protests and Diefenbaker's pledge to create a Bill of Rights and afford Native people the vote.

While the economic, cultural, and race challenges were confounding for many, the struggle between the United States and the Soviet Union was horrifying for all. They had been reluctant allies in the Second World War, but their struggle for ideological and imperial supremacy had begun before the war had even ended. Every civil war, coup, nationalist battle, or land reform effort became a proxy war with the communist Soviet Union backing one side and the democratic-capitalist United States the other.

The Soviet Union had been in possession of nuclear weapons since August 1949. On October 4, 1957, it launched Sputnik, the world's first artificial satellite. It was about the size of a beach ball, weighed 184 pounds, and circled the earth every ninety-eight minutes. A month later, Sputnik II rocketed into orbit. It was heavier and contained a dog named Laika. Every orbital beep was a braggart's boast: Soviet scientists had bested the Americans who, for two years, had been working on a satellite of their own.

A Canadian League of Nations delegate had observed in 1924, "We live in a fire-proof house, far from inflammable materials."[8] The ability of Soviet bombers to fly their terrifying payloads to North America had ended those halcyon days. Now, amid the already disconcerting social, political, and economic changes of the late 1950s, the technology that put Sputnik in space threatened to deliver nuclear weapons on intercontinental ballistic missiles (ICBMs) and turn every city into a pile of dry and brittle sticks ripe for flames. Every mother's child was now on the front line.

Canadians and Americans grew used to air-raid siren tests piercing quiet afternoons and emergency network drills interrupting their favourite television shows. Children practised curling up under their tiny desks and folding their hands over the back of their heads. Teachers assured the quivering kids that the multi-megaton bombs couldn't get them under there. Adults were less naive. Canadians could read a map. They knew that Canada lay between the Soviet Union and the United States and, should the Cold War turn hot, its first battles would occur in the Canadian sky.

Cold War fears led most Canadians to accept a basic fact: the United States might be threatening their sovereignty, but their security—in fact, their very survival—could depend on its protective umbrella. While this tension between needing and resenting America was not new, it had never been so perilous and urgent. Something had to give.

With the Cold War entering a new and dangerous phase and people afraid for their lives, the intelligent, ambitious, and determined Kennedy, Diefenbaker, and Pearson would each fight for his vision of what was best for his country and the world. More than a half century later, we still live with the consequences.

# O N E

---

# CHARACTER AND PRINCIPLES

## KENNEDY, PEARSON, AND DIEFENBAKER

"I have no first-hand knowledge of the depression," declared John Fitzgerald Kennedy, while campaigning for president in 1960. "My family had one of the great fortunes in the world and it was more than ever then. We had bigger houses, more servants, we travelled more . . . I really didn't learn about the depression until I read about it at Harvard."[1] John Kennedy was born into privilege. His grandfathers were successful businessmen, politically influential, and elected to municipal, state, and federal offices. His father, Joe, at age twenty-five, became America's youngest bank president. His shrewd investments, eye for profitable mergers, and work with Hollywood film studios quickly rendered him a multi-millionaire. His children grew up in large homes in New York and Palm Springs and took for granted the curiosity of photographers and reporters and the silent service of maids, nannies, and butlers while being chauffeured to school in their father's Rolls-Royce. John, Joe's second son whom everyone called Jack, never tried to hide or apologize for his family's wealth or the degree to which it isolated him from the experience of most Americans.

Kennedy's opulent beginnings distinguished him sharply from the two Canadian prime ministers whose years in power would intersect with his own. Like the much younger New Englander, Diefenbaker and

Pearson were complex men who defied expectation. Their origins, as well as the extraordinary circumstances that entangled the three men and their political legacies, rendered their meeting explosive and holds the key to appreciating the importance of those few but crucial years.

With trust funds guaranteeing his children's wealth, Joe Kennedy turned to politics. Franklin Roosevelt rewarded Joe's support by appointing him as the founding chair of the Securities and Exchange Commission— a fox enforcing henhouse rules. He was later appointed chair of the Maritime Commission and then, in December 1937, to the post he had been lobbying for: American ambassador to Great Britain. The appointment to the court of St. James was both his crowning achievement and downfall. He could not restrain himself from publicly criticizing Roosevelt and expressing views that contradicted American policies. As Nazi Germany goose-stepped Europe into war, Ambassador Kennedy argued that Hitler should be appeased and that Jewish groups were making things worse for themselves by protesting. He repeatedly said that if war came, America should do nothing because Britain had no chance of victory.[2] Unrepentant, he would eventually resign, in November 1940, and focus his energy and ambition on his children.

John had followed his older brother Joe Jr. to New England's prestigious Choate boarding school and then to Harvard. His father's money and influential network allowed the somewhat wild young man more interested in women than studies to grow up a little and develop a worldview through international travel. In 1937, John met with American ambassadors in France and Italy and was even honoured with a private audience with Pope Pius XI.[3] Two years later, despite having no official status, Kennedy met with foreign officials in France, Poland, Czechoslovakia, Romania, Turkey, Palestine, Greece, Syria, and the Soviet Union. He was President Roosevelt's representative at the coronation of the new pope.

He visited Nazi Germany in late August, just days before Hitler's invasion of Poland began the Second World War.

Ambassador Kennedy also arranged for John to have access to documents and people to help with his honours thesis. Entitled "Appeasement at Munich," it contended that in allowing its military power to wane, Britain had limited its ability to react to Hitler and so had indirectly helped cause the war. Only through building enormous military power and indicating a willingness to use it, Kennedy argued, could war be avoided. He wrote, "We must always keep our armaments equal to our commitments. Munich should teach us that; we must realize that any bluff will be called."[4]

Published in 1940 as *Why England Slept*, it attracted a wide and receptive audience. Learning to sell himself, Kennedy indulged newspaper and radio interviews, signed copies, and frequently telephoned bookstores to encourage and check sales. The book's success was the first step in repositioning the rapscallion as an intellectual. Its argument presaged ideas that informed his thinking for the rest of his life.

After failing the physical examination needed to join the navy, Kennedy endured months of a bland diet to quell stomach problems and a rigorous exercise program to strengthen his weak back. Finally, after a phone call from the ambassador to naval doctors, he was declared medically fit to serve and assigned a desk job in Washington. The twenty-four-year-old's torrid affair with former Miss Denmark Inga Arvad led to scandal. He was unaware that Arvad had been seen in Hitler's private box at the 1936 Berlin Olympics; suspecting she was a Nazi spy, the Federal Bureau of Investigation (FBI) had been following her and had bugged her apartment. FBI director J. Edgar Hoover and President Roosevelt were soon involved. Joe was called, and Navy Ensign Kennedy was expeditiously transferred to Charleston, South Carolina. The incident created the first entries in what became a thick FBI file that would later haunt him.

In July 1942, after months of treatment and convalescence for another serious illness, Kennedy was transferred to midshipman's school in Chicago and trained to command a patrol torpedo or PT boat. The plywood-hulled boats were eighty feet long and, when travelling at their top speed of about forty knots, provided a jolting ride for their thirteen-man crews. Kennedy had his grandfather pull strings, and in January 1943 he was transferred to active duty in the Pacific's Solomon Islands.

In the early morning of August 2, Lieutenant Kennedy's PT-109 was one of fifteen PT boats patrolling the Blackett Strait. Beneath a moonless sky, the Japanese destroyer *Amagiri* screamed out of the inky darkness and rammed Kennedy's ship. Two men were instantly killed and the others, some badly injured, bobbed in the waves amid the flames of burning gasoline. After gathering his crew back to what remained of the wrecked hull and holding on for nine hours, Kennedy led them on a perilous three-and-a-half-mile swim to a tiny island. With life-preserver straps clenched in his teeth, Kennedy pulled a wounded man to safety. The exhausted men took shifts swimming into the channel in vain attempts to signal American ships. Kennedy and a couple of others swam to a nearby island for food and water. When local men appeared in a rough-hewn canoe, Kennedy carved a note on a coconut and they took it to an American base. The battered crew was soon rescued.

The August 20, 1943, *New York Times* headline read: "Kennedy's Son Is Hero in Pacific as Destroyer Splits His PT Boat."[5] Newspapers across the country picked up the story and *The New Yorker* and *Reader's Digest* ran long articles. By November, a painful duodenal ulcer, the effects of malaria, and the return of intense back pain resulted in Kennedy earning an extended medical leave. He endured a painful operation for a ruptured disc. On March 1, 1945, he was placed on the navy's retirement list.

With the war's end, Kennedy considered a career in journalism, and his father arranged his assignment to William Randolph Hearst's *Chicago Herald-American*. His first project took him to San Francisco to cover the inaugural meeting of the United Nations (UN). As part of the large international press detail, he looked over the sea of delegates representing the fifty founding nations. Lester Pearson was there as a proud member of the Canadian delegation. John Diefenbaker was among the group of Members of Parliament observing the final debates and ratification of the 111 articles that would create the world's latest attempt to rid itself of war's scourge.

Lester Pearson travelled a very different road to San Francisco than John Kennedy. Twenty years older, he was born to a middle-class family of modest means in the village of Newton Brook, a few miles north of Toronto. His father, Edwin, was a second-generation Methodist minister and his mother, Annie Sarah, was the daughter of the Dufferin County sheriff. Moving from parish to parish, Pearson grew up the middle of three boys in a cloistered family in a series of small Ontario towns. He became a fine student who excelled at many sports in high school and then at the University of Toronto.

In April 1915, Pearson was among the thousands of Canadian boys stirred by the Great War's call of King and Empire and the ache for adventure. He enlisted as a member of the U of T hospital unit. The Macedonian region to which he was assigned was relatively quiet. While having abandoned illusions of war's glory, he yearned for greater service and excitement.[6] He requested a transfer and in spring 1917 was in England training first in an infantry unit and then with the Royal Flying Corps. His squadron commander promised to toughen him up by first giving him a tougher name, that of his cur dog—"Mike." The name stuck. He nearly finished the training program that would earn him a place among those doomed for short, glorious careers in the sky but was hospitalized due to injuries suffered in a bus accident on his way back to base from a night in blacked-out London. While recovering, he suffered what doctors called "generalized anxiety syndrome"—an emotional inability to carry on. It was shell shock without the shells. He was shipped home, where nightmares shredded his sleep. A slight stutter joined his persistent lisp.

Pearson completed his University of Toronto studies, articled for a time at a law firm, and even played a season of professional baseball in Guelph. For a year, he clerked at his uncle's Armour and Company in Chicago. He lodged at a dingy YMCA in the tough-as-nails south side of the city that was being ripped asunder by political corruption and criminal violence; weekends he enjoyed in the opulence of his uncle's estate and country club.

In 1921, the rich and well-connected Vincent Massey, who had led Pearson's U of T drill training squad, arranged an Oxford scholarship for the promising but professionally floundering young man. His father raised more money from friends and parishioners. Once back in England, Pearson played a number of sports and joined many other Canadians on the Oxford Blues' varsity hockey team. In a game against the Swiss national hockey team, German reporters were so impressed with Pearson's puck handling that they dubbed him "Herr Zig Zag." He observed post-war British politics first-hand and developed an admiration for British imperial power.[7] A summer at the University of Heidelberg kindled a fear of German militarism and the country's yearning for authoritarian efficiency.[8]

Upon graduation, in 1923, Pearson accepted Professor Hume Wrong's invitation to join the U of T history department. One of Pearson's students, Donald Fleming, would later serve in his Cabinet. Another, Maryon Moody, would become his wife. Maryon was bilingual, smart, and armed with an acerbic wit. She once suggested changing the old adage to "Behind every successful man is a surprised woman."[9] They married in August 1925.

While in the capital doing research, Pearson met respected scholar O.D. Skelton at an Ottawa Country Club luncheon. In 1925, Prime Minister Mackenzie King appointed Skelton undersecretary of state for external affairs and told him to hire the best minds available to build the size and professionalism of the tiny, sixteen-year-old department. In August 1928, Pearson became one of only fourteen external affairs staff. It marked the beginning of a long and impressive diplomatic career.

Pearson's first posting was a brief stint in Washington, but he was soon back in Ottawa where he worked for seven years on foreign policy and domestic assignments. In the fall of 1935, with Hitler terrorizing German Jews and preparing for war, Pearson was appointed first secretary in the Canadian High Commission in London. In 1938, his travels through Nazi Germany and France convinced him of the futility of British prime minister Neville Chamberlain's appeasement tactics. Pearson disagreed with American ambassador Joseph Kennedy that Britain could not win the war that everyone saw coming. Instead, he shared the opinion of Kennedy's son and urged Canadian and British officials to re-engage and rearm.[10]

In September 1939, twenty-eight-year-old John Kennedy was with his father and sister Kathleen in the British House of Commons public gallery when Chamberlain announced that Britain was at war. Pearson was a few blocks away at Canada House, listening in on a crackling radio. He gazed glumly through his office window at Trafalgar Square. Over the bustling crowds towered the monument to Lord Nelson, who had given his life the last time a megalomaniac tried to seize Europe. Ten days later, the Canadian Parliament followed Britain's lead and declared war. Washington remained silent.

Pearson sent his family home and remained at his post even through the German air raids that smashed London night after horrifying night. Demonstrating either courage or foolhardiness, Pearson once golfed through a daylight attack. On one tee his caddie advised him to slice as an unexploded bomb had buried itself on the fairway. He later claimed that wearing his helmet throughout the round had helped his swing by keeping his head down.[11]

With Skelton's death in January 1941, the external affairs department was shuffled and Pearson was reassigned first to Ottawa and then, in December, as minister-counsellor at the Canadian legation in Washington. He arrived shortly after Japan attacked Pearl Harbor and so experienced another capital adjusting to war. Three years later Pearson was appointed Canada's ambassador to the United States—the legation had become a full embassy months before. He admired American ideals but was often frustrated with politicians and reporters whose understanding of Canada betrayed stereotypes, rumours, or outright falsehoods, and even more so with those who harboured no curiosity at all regarding their neighbour.[12] He responded with soft politics and charm. He established close relationships with a number of reporters, bureaucrats, and public figures.[13] To keep Canada in the minds of those at the State Department, he organized softball games between the staff there and his own people.

Like many of his colleagues in External Affairs and the Canadian Foreign Service, Pearson believed that as an emerging middle power, Canada needed to adjust its role in the world to better reflect its growing independence from Britain and contributions to the current and last world wars. He believed in functionalism; rather than big powers making all the decisions all the time, if a state has a particular capacity and willingness to make military, diplomatic, or economic contributions to an issue or region, then it deserves a voice in determining policy. Linked to that idea was internationalism, which was the urge to exert influence over great powers by working with other countries and through multilateral organizations. Canada should no longer, as Mackenzie King had for so long been willing to do, simply watch in teeth-grinding silence as great powers acted on their own or only with other great powers. These beliefs led Pearson to see the creation of multilateral organizations as integral to raising Canada's voice and pursuing its interests.[14] If Canada was going to protect and promote what it thought mattered during the war and then in the post-war world, it needed a place at the grown-ups' table. Step one involved helping to construct as many of those tables as possible.

Pearson involved himself in the late-war effort to replace the discredited League of Nations with a new and better United Nations. Preliminary UN conferences had not gone well. At the 1943 international conference addressing food and agriculture, for instance, Pearson and delegates from a number of countries cringed as the American chair began with a singing of the American national anthem. Pearson made valuable contributions to the United Nations Relief and Rehabilitation Administration and was asked to chair the interim commission charged with writing the United Nations constitution. He skilfully organized preliminary work and then the Quebec City conference that consolidated it all.

In April 1945, Pearson arrived in San Francisco for the United Nations inaugural conference. Canada played a minor role in the proceedings, but the respect Pearson had earned in creating the organization led to widespread support for his becoming its first secretary-general. As John Kennedy watched the public proceedings from the press gallery, Pearson was involved in a behind-the-scenes battle that saw him win majority support but lose when his nomination was blocked by the Soviet Union over concern that he was from the West and that Canada was too closely tied to the United States.[15] Among the twenty-two Canadian delegates and parliamentary observers who consoled him afterwards was the man who would become his chief political rival: John Diefenbaker.

If John Kennedy grew up comfortable in the presence of power, Lester Pearson learned that same ease while on the job. Both men's primary passion was not domestic but global affairs. One was a teacher of history and the other a lifelong student. They shared a confident poise, love of sports, laconic wit, sense of irony, and self-deprecating humour. They could not have been more different than John Diefenbaker.

Diefenbaker was born into poverty in 1895 in the village of Neustadt, about 100 miles northwest of Toronto. In 1903 the family moved to the rugged, windswept territory that two years later would become Saskatchewan. For the next two years they moved from town to town and from one drafty cabin to the next as his father, William, sought itinerant teaching jobs. Finally settling on a homestead secured with a ten-dollar registration fee, William taught and farmed while his wife, Mary, sold eggs and butter. John and his younger brother, Elmer, brought meat to the supper table from their traplines.

Amid the golden, undulating prairie of summer and merciless winters that always seemed longer than the last, Diefenbaker grew up unaware of his poverty. Blind to the limits imposed by his region, class, and non-British roots, the six-year-old looked up from his homework one afternoon and announced that someday he would be prime minister. His mother, of course, replied that if he worked hard, anything was possible. The boy was serious. His Uncle Ed helped find books and watched him devour them with an insatiable appetite for knowledge.

When he was fifteen, the pioneer life ended. William became a customs office inspector and settled the family in Saskatoon. Young John always had one or more part-time jobs and often sold newspapers. One morning he was at a train station picking up his daily supply when he happened upon Prime Minister Sir Wilfrid Laurier, in town to dedicate a new building. They chatted amiably until Diefenbaker said, "Sorry prime minister, I can't waste any more time on you. I've got work to do."[16] Laurier's well-appointed private rail car whisked him home shortly after the brief encounter with the cheeky newsboy—back to English/French central Canada, the Laurentian bastion of Canadian economic and political power, far from the ethnically diverse prairie folks who worked hard but enjoyed comparatively little wealth or influence. Laurier represented both Diefenbaker's dream and the forces against which he would struggle to realize it.

Because most politicians were lawyers, and because the law promised to level the marble of Montreal and Toronto mansions with Saskatoon clapboard, Diefenbaker sought a law degree. In March 1916, though, he responded to the wartime call for volunteers. Lieutenant Diefenbaker celebrated his twenty-first birthday on a troop train winding its way to Halifax through the endless rocks and trees of northern Ontario's Precambrian Shield.

In Britain, Diefenbaker's 196th Western Universities battalion undertook preparation for service at the front. As the young man was training in a mock trench, a heavy pickaxe was accidently dropped on his back. He was hospitalized and then deemed unfit for further service. In February 1917, he was sent home. Saskatchewan doctors confirmed that the accident had led to anxiety and a heart ailment that resulted in a chronic shortness of breath. The injury plagued him for the rest of his life. He endured back pain, a weak heart, and even occasional bouts of internal bleeding. As Kennedy would, Diefenbaker suffered in private and without complaint.[17]

With time granted for military service, he quickly completed his master of arts and law degrees. In June 1919, he opened a practice in Wakaw, a small community fifty-five miles northeast of Saskatoon. He developed a reputation as an effective criminal defence lawyer, eager to take cases involving those without a lot of money, power, or a British name. In 1924 he established a second office forty miles south in Prince Albert.

Diefenbaker's political career began in 1920 with his election to a three-year term on Wakaw's village council. His growing facility with words and use of broad gestures and fierce glares rendered him as effective in council chambers as he was before judges and juries. He offered himself as a Conservative Party candidate in the 1925 federal election. He explained that the Liberal's 1911 advocacy of free trade with the United States had inspired him to become a Conservative—a Tory. While free trade was popular in Saskatchewan because it would help farmers, he believed its integration of the Canadian and American economies would eventually lead to political union and therefore must be opposed.[18]

Saskatchewan was a Liberal stronghold, so Diefenbaker paid a price for his Tory nationalist principles. Tommy Douglas, who served as the province's premier for seventeen years in the 1940s and 1950s, once quipped that "the only protection the Tories had in the [1920s and 1930s] were the game laws."[19] Diefenbaker campaigned enthusiastically and endured hecklers calling him a Hun. He ultimately earned fewer than half the votes of his opponent. The loss began a string of defeats that shook neither his Ottawa dreams nor good spirits. A perhaps apocryphal tale he loved to tell had him at an outdoor event with a list of speakers so long and uninspiring that when he finally made it to the podium the audience had dwindled to only one man. Diefenbaker thanked the gentleman, who replied, "Don't thank me, sir, I'm the next speaker!"[20]

Early in his life, John Kennedy learned that his success depended on his family's money and connections as well as surrounding himself with a strong group of loyalists. In Pearson's postings and work in international organizations, the Canadian diplomat learned the value of teamwork along with the art of negotiation. Diefenbaker reacted differently to his losses. He became a lone wolf. Success in the courtroom depended upon prosecutorial interrogation and jury-swaying theatrical speeches. Tough and dirty Saskatchewan politics pitted his vision and ambition against those who had no respect for a working-class Conservative with a German name. Like many other self-made men, he developed an inflated sense of importance and trusted no one.

A spate of bad health traced to his war injury forced Diefenbaker to sit out the 1930 federal election. He thereby missed the remarkable Bennett sweep that created a Conservative majority government. He and R.B. Bennett were kindred spirits. Both were born into poverty and held childhood dreams of becoming prime minister. Diefenbaker was from Ontario and Bennett from New Brunswick but both became successful prairie lawyers. They shared a love and talent for campaigning and for mesmerizing oratory. Most importantly, both espoused a populist desire to help middle- and working-class people struggling for a good chance at a good life.[21] Diefenbaker and Bennett came to know and respect each other through the five years of Bennett's administration and never disagreed on policy decisions. They were Red Tories before the term was coined, and members of the progressive wing of the Conservative Party before the word was added to its name.

Diefenbaker closely followed American politics and was especially enamoured with the Depression era's most famous populist, the mercurial Louisiana senator Huey Long. Long used the radio to rail against the unfairness of cloistered money and power. After a particularly moving address, Diefenbaker wrote to him, "As a Canadian admirer of yours and of the great fight you are putting up for the underdog, I take the advantage of every opportunity offered to hear you over the air. . . . Today public opinion is demanding the carrying out of your ideas regarding wealth, and this applies not only in the United States but also in Canada."[22]

Shortly after being returned to the Opposition benches in 1935, Bennett sought to assist the political career of the talented young man by personally donating $2,500 to Diefenbaker's trust account.[23] Much later, to make it more financially attractive for Pearson to leave the diplomatic corps for the insecurity of political life, powerful Liberals led by Walter Gordon established a secret $100,000 fund.[24] Like Kennedy and Pearson, Diefenbaker would suffer political embarrassments but never a rumour regarding untoward financial dealings. Kennedy did not have to care about money, and neither Pearson nor Diefenbaker ever did.

A scandal might have destroyed Diefenbaker's career just as it was beginning. He had no children with his first wife, Edna, who died in 1951, nor his second, Olive, whom he married two years later. However, in 2011, Toronto businessman John George Dryden claimed to have DNA proof that he was Diefenbaker's illegitimate son.[25] In 2013, retired

Saskatoon police officer Stan Goertzen claimed he was Diefenbaker's grandson and arranged a DNA test that showed a familial link to Dryden.[26] Accusations were made of Diefenbaker having an illicit affair with his Saskatoon housekeeper and, later, a woman in Ottawa.

Diefenbaker never mentioned children, nor are there any archival hints about them. However, the insistence of Goertzen and Dryden, accompanied by their demands for nothing but the truth, certainly raises interesting questions about a possible secret life that, while no match for Kennedy's apparently insatiable libido, stands in contrast to Diefenbaker's stodgy image.

Like Kennedy and Pearson, Diefenbaker was a voracious reader who assumed a student's passionate interest in history, biography, and global affairs. In July 1936, Diefenbaker and his wife visited London, witnessed the unveiling of the Vimy Ridge memorial in France, and were then emotionally moved by visits to French and Belgian First World War battle sites and cemeteries. They watched Hitler open the Berlin Olympics. As Diefenbaker learned more about the world and Canada's role in it, he became an even more virulent anti-communist and anti-fascist. However, his populism and nationalist desire to stop the long march toward continentalism through protecting and enhancing Canadian autonomy never turned into anti-Americanism.[27]

In 1940 Diefenbaker was acclaimed as Lake Centre's Conservative Party candidate for the March 26 federal election. Robert Manion had been the Conservative leader for two years and despite his best efforts, the party remained inadequately funded and organized. Given the lack of support, Diefenbaker ran again as if he were an independent. He tirelessly visited towns, farms, and hamlets. Over the course of five weeks, he spoke at fifty-seven meetings and wrote and delivered five radio addresses. To crowds big and small he extolled his populist vision of Canadians enjoying equal opportunity regardless of class, race, or ethnicity. From his modest Prince Albert home, and with a spring blizzard raging, he heard the radio announce that the Liberals had won a majority. After losing five elections in a row, however, he had won his seat. He was elected by only 280 votes, but it was a sweet victory at long last. He would never lose again.

The forty-five-year-old man with the six-year-old's dream was finally on his way to Ottawa. He knew there was a lot he didn't know and so for a while he remained quiet in the House and caucus.[28] Establishing a habit that would earn him the respect of many but for which he would also pay a price, he remained aloof from the camaraderie among fellow MPs. He was a teetotaller who enjoyed evenings with a book and was often in bed by nine. His Spartan routine kept him from the dinners, bars, and parties where gossip was traded, alliances forged, and knives sharpened.

While Diefenbaker learned, the Conservative Party floundered through a succession of leaders and policy shifts. In the midst of the prolonged drift and confusion, Diefenbaker played a minor role in organizing a September 1942 party policy conference in Port Hope, Ontario. He helped adopt a number of left-leaning, progressive policies that were consistent with his Red Tory, populist inclinations. The party met again in December to address the leadership vacuum and, although an MP for only two years, he joined four other westerners offering themselves as candidates. He didn't stand a chance. His quixotic leadership campaign and reputation as a fierce competitor who always prepared himself well for debate earned him a spot on the Opposition's front benches.

His growing importance in the party resulted in his being chosen as one of its representatives on the parliamentary delegation to observe the formation of the United Nations in San Francisco. Neither he nor Pearson met Kennedy. The young journalist did not mention Canada in any of the seventeen articles he submitted for publication. Most reflected Kennedy's hope for the UN and worry that the Cold War divide would mitigate the new organization's potential as the world tumbled into a new era of peril.[29] Pearson felt the same as Diefenbaker, who wrote, "I saw the United Nations as man's last chance for peace."[30]

Joe Kennedy had been grooming his oldest son, Joe Jr., for political office. However, late in the war he had volunteered for an outrageously dangerous mission. He was to fly a PB4Y-1 Liberator packed with an unusually large payload of explosives across the English Channel to Europe and parachute out, allowing the bomber to crash into a Nazi V-1 rocket site. He was killed when his plane exploded over England.

His father transferred his dreams to his second son, John. In a June 1946 *Look* magazine article, John said, "I am only doing the job that Joe would have done."[31] The job involved entering public service by vying for the Democratic Party's nomination in Boston's largely working-class Eleventh Congressional District—part of which had once been held by his maternal grandfather, John Fitzgerald, whom everyone called Honey Fitz. Kennedy would later name the presidential yacht the *Honey Fitz*.

Despite his pedigree, Kennedy was not a natural politician. He spoke haltingly from a lectern with a thin and reedy voice. He was uncomfortable with glad-handing and small talk. He was, however, an indefatigable campaigner. He was also respected as an author and war hero—and his status as a Fitzgerald and Kennedy opened doors. His father made calls and ensured that money was plentiful. The skinny twenty-nine-year-old, who looked even younger, won the hard-fought battle and then the 1946 election to Congress. He would never lose an election.

Kennedy arrived in Washington just as America was deciding whether to retreat into a cocoon of isolationism, as it had done after the First World War. Several factors kept America in the game. First was a decision by a twenty-six-year-old Russian cipher clerk working in Ottawa's Soviet embassy. Late in the evening of September 5, 1945, just weeks after atomic bombs obliterated Hiroshima and Nagasaki and ended the Second World War, Igor Gouzenko stuffed 109 secret documents under his coat. He endured a frightening night and frantic morning, failing to persuade anyone at the *Ottawa Journal*, Department of Justice, or Supreme Court to believe in his desire to defect and the explosive power of his stolen papers. A Royal Canadian Mounted Police (RCMP) intelligence division sergeant, alerted of the young Russian scurrying about the city, finally listened.

Prime Minister Mackenzie King was soon informed that Gouzenko's documents offered proof of a Soviet spy infiltration in several government departments, including atomic weapon studies at the National Research Council. Mackenzie King met with President Truman at the White House and then British prime minister Clement Attlee in London. If the Soviets were spying in Canada, the leaders concluded, then they were spying everywhere. To avoid jeopardizing ongoing negotiations with the Soviets, it was agreed to keep the shocking revelation a secret.[32] It held until FBI director Hoover and Canadian spy William Stephenson leaked word to a Washington-based reporter named Drew Pearson. His syndicated column in over 350 American newspapers spilled the beans. While remaining silent about all of their other activities, on February 20, 1946, the Soviets admitted to spying in Canada.

Shortly afterwards, the American State Department received an eight-thousand-word telegram from George Kennan, the highly respected chargé d'affaires in Moscow. The missive was widely read and enormously influential when first received, and then even more so when published in the journal *Foreign Affairs* under the pseudonym Mr. X. He argued that the Soviet goal was world domination and the destruction of the United States and its allies. Under American leadership, he wrote, Western, democratic states must unite to stop communism's spread.[33]

Two weeks later, Winston Churchill travelled to Missouri's Fulton College. He knew his speech would be important, and he'd asked Canada's ambassador to the United States, Lester Pearson, to help him craft it.[34] With President Truman on the stage beside him, Churchill declared that an "iron curtain" had descended across Europe. He urged Americans to recognize the Soviet Union as the primary threat to world peace and American interests. He asked the United States to lead an opposition to the communist state that "does not desire war . . . but does desire the fruits of war and the indefinite expansion of its power and policies."[35]

The Gouzenko revelations and arguments made by Kennan and Churchill staggered American isolationists. In March 1947, Truman stepped into roiling unrest in Greece and Turkey with the assertion that the United States would assist any country that was threatened from within or without by communist aggression. His pledge became known as the Truman Doctrine, and would evolve into the policy known as containment. The theory behind it was simple: if one country fell to communism then others would soon topple like dominoes in a row. In order to keep those dominoes erect, the Soviet empire needed to be surrounded by Western-allied states. The expressed need to fight and contain communism informed Cold War decisions for the next half-century.

Another increasingly important tenet of American foreign policy had actually been announced more than a century earlier, in 1823. President James Monroe declared that the United States considered the western hemisphere to be within its sphere of influence, and as such, European powers should stay on their side of the Atlantic. Theodore Roosevelt added a more belligerent corollary in 1904, stating that the United States would intervene if any western hemisphere country failed to pay its debts or acted in a way that threatened harm to its neighbours or America. For four decades, the Monroe Doctrine and Roosevelt Corollary had had little effect on Canada. That changed with the Cold War. The change was outlined on February 8, 1950, in a secret State Department memo to Truman that, had it been released, would have both alleviated the fears of many Canadians and rattled Canadian nationalists.

The memo observed: "Our commitments and risks are so extensive and important that Canada in a military sense must be considered as if it were an integral part of the United States. It is as important to our security to protect Canada, as it is to protect California. Canada is the most logical avenue for a large-scale attack on the United States. Even if it were not for the commitments in the Atlantic Pact [NATO] and the extension of the Monroe Doctrine to Canada, it would be necessary to protect Canada instantly from any threat."[36] The threat from a dangerous new enemy was being complicated by the existential threat from a benevolent old friend.

In 1949, Kennedy decided to contest for a seat in the more powerful and prestigious Senate.[37] He based his campaign on the premise that America's Cold War fight was the most important issue of the day and that it touched every government concern. On April 20, 1950, for instance, reiterating the thesis of *Why England Slept*, he said in a House floor debate that the deficit needed to be trimmed because, "Does not the gentleman think that a very important item in the cold war is the economic stability of our country so that we will have resources in case of war."[38]

Kennedy campaigned furiously with daily schedules that imperilled his tenuous health. His father used various means to funnel several million dollars to the effort. He saved the *Boston Post* from bankruptcy with a $500,000 loan and then, two weeks before the election, saw the influential paper flip from supporting the Republicans to endorsing his son.[39] Kennedy defeated the far more experienced Henry Cabot Lodge by a narrow 51.5 percent to 48.5 percent margin. Aides Kenneth O'Donnell and Dave Powers contended that the campaign's key factor was not Kennedy's anti-communist message, famous name, war hero status, or even the money, but his charming personality. "There's something about Jack—and I don't know quite what it is—that makes people want to believe him. . . . They want to identify their views with him."[40]

In late 1953, the newly minted Senator Kennedy was forced to consider Canada for the first time. In 1931, Prime Minister R.B. Bennett had initiated negotiations with President Herbert Hoover that led to the signing of the Great Lakes–St. Lawrence Deep Waterway Treaty. It involved sharing the enormous cost to build a channel from Lake Superior to the St. Lawrence River, and then canals, locks, and dams to the Atlantic. It would link the world to Canadian and American Midwest farms and to the manufacturers ringing the Great Lakes. Hydroelectric power plants along the waterway would feed growing cities. As a treaty, it needed Senate approval, and senators from the Deep South and the Atlantic coast feared its effects on their states. The Senate said no in 1934, and said it again on each of the six occasions it resurfaced. Both Massachusetts senators voted against the project. In 1953, the seaway was again a topic before the Senate, but this time with the knowledge that in December 1951, the Canadian Parliament had voted to forget the Americans and build it alone.

The Canadian decision put the thirty-six-year-old Kennedy in a tricky spot. During his Senate campaign he had listened to Boston longshoremen, businessmen, and lobbyists, and opposed the seaway based on the old worry that it would divert significant traffic from New England ports to the St. Lawrence. With the Canadian go-it-alone decision now looking like more than a bluff, however, Kennedy ordered respected counsel and speechwriter Ted Sorensen to lead a detailed analysis.

With controversy and pressure building, Kennedy accepted an invitation to speak at the Université de Montréal. It was his first trip to Canada. The junior senator and his wife of three months, the twenty-four-year-old Jacqueline, arrived on a cold December 4, 1953, at Montreal's Windsor train station. Only two men met them: an American consulate representative and a Canadian Pacific Railway photographer who quickly snapped two pictures and went home. The glamorous young couple were guests of honour that evening at the annual St. Mary's Ball, where the city's who's who mingled, dined, and raised money for the local hospital.

Before donning his tuxedo, Kennedy addressed the students and faculty of the university's Literary Society. Always quick to reference Cold War fears, he said, "Today, the charged atmosphere of suspicion and fear which has resulted in my country from the external and internal threat of communist imperialism has caused a number of incidents which have caused alarm and resentment among Canadians and Americans alike."[41] He added that Canada and the United States were fighting communism together, and that the struggle was more than a military battle as it involved winning the trust and support of the world's people.[42] Detailing further links between the two countries, he explained that 20 percent of American exports went to Canada and that America was Canada's best customer.

Kennedy then explained the difficulty the American Congress was having in coming to a decision regarding the seaway. He detailed the American system of checks and balances and quoted Sir John A. Macdonald, albeit somewhat out of context, who once called the American system a "skilful work." He quoted eighteenth-century Irish nationalist and conservative political philosopher Edmund Burke. Burke had said in his famous 1774 "Speech to the Electors of Bristol" that political representatives should be free to vote their conscience.[43] Kennedy's reference to Burke was a strong hint that he was preparing to do just that.

A few weeks later, on January 14, 1954, Kennedy rose in the Senate chamber and delivered a courageous speech. He began by noting his state's current and long history of opposition to the seaway. His vote, he said, would rest on the answers to two fundamental questions. The first was whether the seaway would be built regardless of American partnership. "I have studied the Act passed by the Canadian parliament authorizing the construction of the St. Lawrence Seaway by Canada . . . and the official statements of the Canadian government make it clear that Canada will build the Seaway alone and cooperate on the power project with New York, although the door is left open for American participation if we should so decide at this session of Congress."[44] A solely Canadian project,

Kennedy continued, would inflict enormous costs on America, as Canada could dictate tolls, traffic, and admission of foreign shipping. He balanced these arguments with "sectional interests" and noted that the seaway would have negligible economic impacts on the port of Boston.[45]

The second determining question, he argued, was whether the seaway would make America safer. For over twenty years, he said, every president and secretary of defence, as well as the National Security Council and National Security Resources Board, had contended that partnership would do just that. Kennedy explained the degree to which American participation in the seaway project would be part of the continued development of an integrated North American defence strategy.[46] He concluded: "Both nations now need the St. Lawrence Seaway for security as well as for economic reasons. I urge the Congress promptly to approve our participation in its construction."[47]

Finally, after decades of opposition the Senate approved the daring measure. A number of Boston and Massachusetts papers attacked the young senator.[48] Two months later he was warned by a member of Boston's city council not to march in the city's large and boisterous annual St. Patrick's Day parade lest he be abused by dockworkers angry that the seaway would kill their jobs. Kennedy ignored the advice and marched without incident.

Kennedy ensured that his Senate speech was copied and widely distributed. On February 14, he appeared on NBC's nationally televised and enormously popular *Meet the Press*. It was the show's first episode broadcast in colour, although few Americans had colour sets. A poised Kennedy reiterated points made in Canada and in the Senate. The host remarked that the senator's "sensational victory [had] created international interest. He is in the news again because of his position on the St. Lawrence Seaway."[49]

Just as Kennedy's stature was going up, however, another health calamity knocked him down. In 1947 he had been diagnosed with Addison's disease, a potentially life-threatening malfunction of the adrenal glands that causes weight loss, muscle weakness, fatigue, and nausea. He ingested daily doses of cortisone to manage the symptoms, along with various other medications for periodic respiratory and urinary tract ailments and recurring bouts of colitis—later called irritable bowel syndrome. The long-term cortisone treatment caused a slow degeneration of his vertebrae. In the fall of 1954 the senator was on crutches, taking steps one at a time and sideways. In October, he underwent a three-and-a-half-hour operation that affixed a metal plate to vertebrae in his lower back. A post-operative infection brought a priest to administer last rites. Four months later he underwent a second operation to remove the plate and replace destroyed cartridge and bone.[50]

While recuperating in Palm Beach and still reflecting on his St. Lawrence Seaway fight, he asked Sorensen and others to gather information on senators who had taken similarly principled stands. The exercise began as an article but ended up a book. It celebrated eight senators who acted with a greater concern for national interest than popularity or political expediency.[51]

Kennedy's idea of courage did not reflect the liberal, Enlightenment philosophy that had informed America's founding ideas—the Lockean notion that government exists to protect people's liberty, equality, and property. Kennedy's book, like his speech in Montreal, channelled not John Locke but the more conservative Edmund Burke whose ideas were at the heart of Canada's foundation. An historian and statesman, Burke was more practical and pragmatic than the ideologue Locke. Burke did not believe that people were born with natural rights, and he advocated a strong government able to control citizens and situations. It was Burke, not Locke, who argued that elected representatives were better educated and informed than most of their constituents and so needed the freedom to vote according to their knowledge and conscience.[52] Elected politicians, Burke suggested, were decision makers and not mindless pollsters or their constituent's megaphones.

In his 1790 *Reflections on the Revolution in France,* Burke argued that governments and the people who led them should not be chained to political ideologies. Such ties, he contended, served only to restrict freedom of thought and action, render leaders dependent on mob mentality, and invite leaders and the led to become "entangled in the mazes of metaphysic sophistry."[53] A person judging all issues according to predetermined ideas may be principled, he argued, but also dangerously adverse to compromise, new thoughts, and changing circumstances.

Kennedy's *Profiles in Courage,* and indeed his entire public life, was testament to both tenets of Burke's conservative philosophy. Like Burke—in fact, like Diefenbaker and Pearson—Kennedy was always uncomfortable with and suspicious of narrow ideological identification. He ignored labels in determining whether to accept or reject people and ideas.[54] Shortly after being elected to the Senate, Kennedy had an interesting exchange with a reporter, who told the senator that his readers were wondering if he was actually a liberal. He replied, "I'd be very happy to tell them that I am not a liberal at all. I'm a realist."[55] When another reporter asked if he wished to be known as a liberal or conservative, he replied that he hoped to be known as responsible.[56] Upon assuming the presidency, he appointed a number of Republicans to positions of power. Burke would have applauded his responses, and the fact that party identification and ideological orthodoxy played no part in Kennedy's dealings with Canadian issues or leaders.

*Profiles in Courage* was published in January 1956 and became a national bestseller. Speculation of how much Sorensen and other Kennedy aides had helped write the book was largely dismissed as political mudslinging. Its important message, commercial success, and 1957 Pulitzer Prize for Biography or Autobiography amplified Kennedy's name recognition and boosted his reputation as a man of substance.

It certainly helped bring him to the attention of Democratic Party leaders seeking to create a presidential ticket able to defeat President

Dwight Eisenhower and Vice President Richard Nixon in 1956. Kennedy was coy about his desire to win the vice-presidential nomination but when the Democrat's presumptive presidential nominee, Adlai Stevenson, allowed delegates at the party's convention in Chicago to choose his running mate, Kennedy went for it. He faced withering criticism about his youth, limited experience, Catholicism, and for missing the vote to censure witch-hunting Republican blowhard Senator Joseph McCarthy. Kennedy fell only thirty-eight votes short of winning the nomination on the second ballot. Southern delegates then swung to Tennessee senator Estes Kefauver on the third ballot and the contest was over.

The failure disappointed but did not crush Kennedy. He had introduced himself to delegates and party leaders, won more national exposure, and impressed everyone with the gracious manner in which he accepted defeat. He and his brother Robert, who had managed the nomination fight along with his other campaigns, learned a great deal about the people, methods, and determination needed to win a national effort. Kennedy worked hard for the Stevenson campaign that fall. He delivered speeches in twenty-four states while making contacts that "Bobby" dutifully recorded.

In 1957, Kennedy and Jacqueline celebrated their fourth anniversary. Jacqueline was intelligent, well read, well travelled, bilingual, and from a wealthy family. She mesmerized Kennedy as few women had ever done.[57] The marriage was rocky from the start, however, as Kennedy continued to work tirelessly and travel endlessly while recklessly pursuing sexual conquests. When on an August 1956 Mediterranean cruise, during which he and friends entertained a parade of women, he received word that Jacqueline had miscarried their first child. The holiday and antics continued for a couple of days until a friend, Florida senator George Smathers, argued that if he wanted to someday be president, Kennedy should fly home to his wife.[58]

The public ignored the lingering questions about his book's authorship and knew nothing of the marital infidelities. Jacqueline's charm and the

Pulitzer's prestige offered tremendous cachet as Kennedy worked through 1957 on his way to the Democratic nomination for the presidency.

While Kennedy was striving for greater recognition, Lester Pearson became the most famous Canadian in the world.[59] It had not been his goal, but then neither was public office. In December 1957, Pearson appeared in Oslo to accept the Nobel Peace Prize. It was granted for his role in urging the world's major powers back from the precipice of a third world war through the establishment of a United Nations peacekeeping force to stand between Israeli and Arab armies. Pearson's speech was characteristically humble and articulate. He put his finger on the issue that would be the primary focus of Kennedy's thousand days in the White House and of Canada's relationship with him and his government. "Of all our dreams today there is none more important—or so hard to realise than that of peace in the world. May we never lose our faith in it or our resolve to do everything that can be done to convert it one day into reality."[60] Pearson then acknowledged that the Cold War was at the core of many of the world's tensions. He presented an argument that Diefenbaker would make throughout his time in office, and that Kennedy would champion in his last one hundred days; he linked peace and disarmament. "So far as abolishing arms are concerned, those of Nobel's day are now out of date but I know, as you do, that if the arms which man's genius has created today to replace them are ever used they will destroy us all. So they must be themselves destroyed."[61]

Pearson's Nobel Prize was the culmination of a career dedicated to international diplomacy. In the fall of 1946, Prime Minister Mackenzie King had passed the external affairs portfolio to the highly respected Montreal corporate lawyer and Member of Parliament Louis St. Laurent. The prime minister asked Pearson to leave his diplomatic post and serve as St. Laurent's undersecretary of state for external affairs. The creation of the St. Laurent-Pearson partnership marked the beginning of what some call Canada's golden age of diplomacy, 1946 to 1957.[62]

The golden age was a period of idealism and pragmatism in which, due to a confluence of three factors, Canada asserted its national interest on the world stage with confidence and effectiveness. First, beyond St. Laurent and Pearson, Canada was blessed with a remarkable group of talented diplomats and bureaucrats. The men were nearly all Oxbridge educated, Protestant, upper-middle-class scholars and academics. Among the august group were Escott Reid (who coined the phrase "Golden Age" but said it applied from 1941 to 1951), Hume Wrong, Norman Robertson, Charles Ritchie, Arnold Heeney, and George Ignatieff. Second, unlike Europe and Asia, Canada had emerged physically untouched from the war, was experiencing an unprecedented economic boom, and, for a while, had the world's fourth-largest military. Finally, the diplomatic corps was afforded tacit support by the trust most Canadians felt for government. The men and moment allowed Canada to remain cautious, and concerned first with domestic considerations, but still "punch above its weight" in the pursuit of its functionalist and internationalist agenda.[63]

The first major accomplishment of the golden age was Canada's important role in the creation of the North Atlantic Treaty Organization. Escott Reid and Pearson wrote a speech that Reid delivered in which he called for a new collective security group that could be called upon to deal with an emergency that the United Nations would or could not. Joseph Stalin inadvertently gave credence to the idea when, in February 1948, he ordered the invasion of Czechoslovakia and then blocked UN efforts to respond. More Soviet threats and then its blockade of Berlin in June further demonstrated the need for Reid and Pearson's vision to become a reality. Tentatively at first, but then with growing enthusiasm, the United States was in.

With the assurance that the aging Mackenzie King would soon retire and that St. Laurent would succeed him, Pearson left the security of the civil service for politics. A few weeks later, in August 1948, a Liberal Party convention ratified Mackenzie King's decision and selected St. Laurent as its leader and the country's new prime minister. In September, Pearson was appointed Canada's secretary of state for external affairs. To get him into the House of Commons, the MP for the safe Liberal seat of Algoma East was moved to the Senate and a by-election announced. Pearson knew so little of the large riding on Lake Huron's rugged east shore that he needed a map to find it. He quickly learned the tricks of retail politics, worked hard, and on October 25 won the rural Ontario seat that he would never lose.

NATO remained Pearson's primary goal, and he pushed to have it embrace social and economic as well as military goals. American undersecretary of state and Pearson's old friend Dean Acheson—another preacher's son—dismissed this broadening of NATO's mandate as typical Canadian moralizing.[64] The hard work of Pearson, Wrong, Reid, and others, however, led to the acceptance of article 2 specifying an economic mandate. In April 1949, ten Western European nations, along with Canada and the United States, proclaimed the North Atlantic Treaty Organization. Pearson was a little concerned when, at the Washington signing ceremony, the Marine band played Gershwin's "I Got Plenty o' Nuttin'." Pearson was asked but declined the honour of being NATO's first secretary general. He later called NATO's creation his crowning foreign affairs achievement.[65]

Just over a year later, a late-June Sunday sun was finally warming the lake at Pearson's Gatineau Hills cottage. The afternoon's dignity and repose was shattered when Escott Reid, who had a place nearby, roared up the lane with the news that communist North Korea had just invaded non-communist South Korea. Pearson drove to the nearest phone—at the general store in town—and called St. Laurent. The Cold War had turned hot. The battling twins of the Korean Peninsula offered a test of containment policy, Canada's influence in world affairs, and its relationship with America.

As Pearson had hoped he would, Truman asked for a Security Council resolution to dispatch a UN force to re-establish the border. The Soviet Union was involved in a boycott due to an unrelated matter and so the motion passed in its absence. Canada joined the effort and, while preparing more men and weaponry, contributed three destroyers to the allied effort. Acheson belittled Canada's commitment as one token ship. Pearson corrected him, but the American scoffed and said that it was therefore three tokens.[66] Canada eventually sent the Twenty-fifth Infantry Brigade, consisting of about 2,500 troops and two thousand reservists, and an air force transport squadron. By 1952, eight thousand Canadians were in Korea.

Throughout the Korean War, Pearson tried to employ a diplomacy of constraint. He encouraged India and Asian countries to play a greater role in regional issues while reminding American decision makers that this was a multinational operation in which the contributions of Canada and others should be respected. Pearson did not want the United States to become so engulfed in Asian entanglements that it lost sight of European interests and goals.[67]

Despite regular American-led meetings with allies, however, Canada's opinion was often ignored. In one such meeting, Acheson went around the table soliciting opinion on a particular issue but failed to call on Canada. When the British representative noted the slip, Acheson snorted, "Oh well, we always count on Canada being with us." When finally recognized, Pearson began, "Now speaking on behalf of the United States and Canada . . ."[68] It was a cute joke but his point was serious. Somewhat uncharacteristically, Pearson publicly revealed his frustration with American hubris when, in a speech at Toronto's Empire Club, he said Canada had no interest in being "the echo of somebody else's voice."[69]

The speech was not enough for Canadian nationalists, including respected Canadian historian Arthur Lower. In a public letter, he scolded Pearson for his "blatant pro-American policies." Pearson responded that pragmatism was necessary to advance Canadian interests and fight for

its principles while supporting one's friends, even if those friends sometimes demonstrate what he called "immaturity, roughness, and a lack of
comprehension of the problems of other people . . . [Canada is] con-
stantly faced with the problem of trying to influence United States
policy which will protect both our interests and our conception of what
is good for the world."[70] The widely read letters reflected the golden
age's fundamental dilemma and foreshadowed Pearson's struggles with
Diefenbaker and Kennedy.

By the time the Korean armistice was signed in July 1953, 22,000
Canadians had served and 516 were killed. Only eight years after the
Second World War, Canada had beaten its ploughshares back into swords.
Before the war there were 47,000 Canadians in uniform. By 1953 there
were 104,000.[71] New armaments were rolling off assembly lines. The
Truman Doctrine and the strategy of containment had triumphed. On
the other hand, 516 Canadian mothers may have wished that Pearson's
diplomacy had stayed at his cottage.

The United States could ignore Canada's interests and diplomatic
efforts and disparage its military but it could not deny geography. Dwight
D. Eisenhower was sworn in as president of the United States in January
1953. He inherited an increasingly integrated continental defence
system that had grown from the Second World War's Permanent Joint
Board on Defence to the reality of radar stations strung across Canada.
Eisenhower approved the Mid-Canada Line, which was built by Canada
using McGill University technology, and hence came to be known to some
as the "McGill Fence." The Pinetree Line, closer to the border, was a joint
venture, with Canadians constructing two of the stations. The Far North's
Distant Early Warning (DEW) Line was entirely American-built.
Beyond the listening posts, American bombers, fighter planes, and submarines continued to operate from bases constructed in Newfoundland
and Labrador during the Second World War, despite the fact that in
1949 it had become a Canadian province.

The integration made America safer, but it necessitated Canada trading sovereignty for security. On a visit to Canada in November 1953, President Eisenhower made the point as clear as could be. "Defensively as well as geographically we are joined beyond any possibility of separation."[72]

While Canada's autonomy withered, Lester Pearson's international stature grew. He was NATO's council chair in 1951 and then a year later the president of the UN General Assembly. In 1955 he was invited to become the first Western foreign minister to visit the Soviet Union. Following Stalin's death in 1953, Nikita Khrushchev emerged from the scorched earth of a prolonged power struggle as his successor. The short, fat war hero had a quick smile and a hearty laugh, and his gruff peasant manner hid the sharp intelligence of a master politician. Pearson toured Moscow and was moved by the devastation still evident outside Leningrad a decade after Hitler's troops had retreated. At an opulent Crimean palace, Khrushchev charmed, flattered, and then lambasted Pearson for Canada's NATO membership. He said the Soviet Union had no reason to fear the West, as it would soon out-produce and outpace every Western country. He threatened war if the alliance between the West and Germany continued. While Canada had escaped physical harm in the century's first world wars, he warned, it would not be so lucky in the third.[73]

Pearson later endured eighteen vodka toasts with Khrushchev who, unlike his wobbly guest, weathered the evening nonplussed. Pearson later called it "conviviality beyond the line of duty."[74] Upon his return to Ottawa, Pearson told the House of Commons that his conversations with the Soviet leader left him convinced that the West needed to be even more vigilant and to engage the Soviet Union, as Khrushchev clearly intended to expand the communist ideology through territorial conquest and secretly funded insurrections.[75]

While on his trip, Pearson had met with Egyptian president Gamal Abdel Nasser. A number of crosscutting issues, including the need for tolls to finance the massive Aswan Dam project after America withdrew promised support, led Nasser to nationalize the Suez Canal in July 1956. By the end of October, Israel had invaded Egypt, and British and French bombs were falling on the Canal Zone. The Soviet Union declared its opposition to the attacks, and the United States supported the Soviet position. It was a dangerous mess that threatened to escalate into a broader and perhaps nuclear war.

Pearson flew to the United Nations headquarters in New York. After American efforts led to a ceasefire agreement, Pearson proposed the creation of a UN peacekeeping force to stand between the belligerents. The peacekeeping idea had been floated for some time by American secretary of state John Foster Dulles and others. As far back as 1943, Diefenbaker had advocated the idea and he had repeated it in response to Middle East tensions in the early 1950s.[76] With the Suez Crisis, the idea's time had come. American UN ambassador Henry Cabot Lodge wrote the motion advocating the creation of the UN force and Pearson presented it. He then moved from delegation to delegation, gathering support and keeping everyone talking. The motion finally passed 51–0 with the nineteen-member Soviet bloc abstaining. On November 5, the United Nation's first peacekeeping mission, led by Canadian general E.L.M. Burns, arrived at the canal.

Pearson was widely celebrated. An American bubble gum company even included him in a Great Men of History series of collectible cards for children to ponder while they chewed. Other cards included Washington, Napoleon, and Caesar.[77] Many Canadians were proud of their local boy made good, but others were upset that this was the first time Canada had sided with the United States over Britain.[78] British Columbia MP and Diefenbaker's future external affairs minister Howard Green spoke for the disappointed when he stated in the House that Pearson's actions represented "a disgraceful period in Canada's history." Green claimed that Pearson was once again "a choir boy to the Americans."[79]

Prime Minister Louis St. Laurent had the governor general call an election for June 10, 1957. In power since 1935, Liberals had begun to consider themselves the country's natural ruling party. However, in the spring of 1956 the government had seriously misplayed its offer of an $80 million loan to an American-owned company called TransCanada Pipelines that hoped to build a natural gas line from Alberta to southern Ontario. Before even introducing the bill to allow the loan, the government cut off House debate. People sniffed at the perceived arrogance and lack of respect for Parliament. The government's majority assured the bill's passage, but in winning it lost the country.

The pipeline debate and soon-to-follow Suez crisis made the Liberals appear too anxious to sidle up to the Americans. More accurately, the Liberal stances reflected the slow post-war drift toward continentalism that many Canadians of all political stripes justified as an economic and security necessity. It was this trend that Diefenbaker hoped to arrest. He would present himself as Canada's saviour, while those convinced that the country needed even closer ties to the United States perceived him as King Canute ordering the sea's relentless waves to stop crashing.

After losing the ill-fated 1948 leadership campaign, Diefenbaker became even more cantankerously independent of the party. One night in the middle of the 1949 election, he and a friend bundled up some party advertising material that had arrived from Ottawa, rowed a small boat onto the moonlit waters of a nearby lake, and dumped it.[80] He also shunned the power of the Ku Klux Klan, which remained powerful in Saskatchewan Conservative politics. However, on his own initiative and with his own money, he embraced the equally shadowy Gladstone Murray. Murray was secretly employed by a cabal of Toronto-based businessmen nervous about the growing popularity of democratic socialism.[81] Diefenbaker used Murray's slanderous anti-socialist, anti-Co-operative Commonwealth Federation (CCF) propaganda pamphlets to help battle the left-leaning voters whom the Liberals had gerrymandered into his riding to defeat him. He could play dirty too. Diefenbaker won with a larger plurality than before. He was the only Tory elected in Saskatchewan. The party, meanwhile, fell from sixty-seven to forty-one seats.

Before the August 1953 federal election, the Liberals redrew Diefenbaker's constituency right out of existence. He easily secured the nomination in the newly created riding of Prince Albert. He was an indefatigable campaigner. He also flew to other provinces to support Tory candidates. Diefenbaker won the new riding by over three thousand votes and was again Saskatchewan's only successful Progressive Conservative. However, the Liberals won yet another majority.

When party leader George Drew's health forced him to resign, it appeared to finally be Diefenbaker's time. Eighty percent of the caucus backed him, and every Progressive Conservative provincial government offered volunteers and organizational support.[82] He ran a disciplined campaign and entered the Ottawa Coliseum in December 1956 with 55 percent of the pledged delegates.[83] Most of the Toronto-based Tory old guard remained suspicious of the prairie populist, said vicious things behind his back, and quietly supported a "Stop Diefenbaker" movement. But it didn't matter. Canada's first televised convention saw delegates drawn to Diefenbaker's magnetism and momentum. Typical was the experience of university student and future prime minister Brian Mulroney. He arrived ready to work for another candidate but within a day was vice chairman of youth for Diefenbaker.[84] Diefenbaker's nomination speech offered emotional poetry: "I have one love . . . Canada; one purpose . . . Canada's greatness; one aim . . . Canadian unity from the Atlantic to the Pacific."[85] The contest wasn't even close. Earning 711 votes to his competitors' combined 510, he won on the first ballot.

During the Conservative's December convention, Prime Minister St. Laurent had been golfing with President Eisenhower at Georgia's storied Augusta National club. The Liberal leader was seventy-five years old when he announced the June 1957 election. Critics joked that, in a pinch, the party would run him stuffed.[86] They might well have done so, for St. Laurent and his Liberals had no idea what was about to hit them.

Within four months of being elected Opposition leader, Diefenbaker had re-organized and galvanized the party. He had done it all while ignoring its old bosses. Advertising man Allister Grosart was hired to introduce new campaigning techniques involving television and image-making.[87] Three years before a telegenic Kennedy taught Americans about television's political power, Grosart trained Diefenbaker to exploit it. Diefenbaker synthesized all that he believed and had been talking about throughout his career into a single, nationalist vision based on the principles of Canada's founding fathers.

Sir John A. Macdonald was Canada's first prime minister and the man who had led the country's creation. His confidence in Canada was matched by his concerns about the United States. The 1864 negotiations that led to Confederation happened when and how they did partly due to fears of American invasion in retribution for Canadian and British actions taken during the Civil War. To counter America's Manifest Destiny, the belief that the United States was bound to someday control all of North America, Sir John's National Policy turned Canada's orientation from north–south to east–west, and allowed the country to grow behind tariff walls and on steel rails.

Blue campaign posters paired photographs of Macdonald and Diefenbaker and called them the two Johns—nation builders. Diefenbaker argued that Liberal continentalist policies were threatening Canada's future by refuting the economic nationalism through which the country flourished. Diefenbaker lashed out at what he characterized as the Liberal's slow-motion surrender of sovereignty.[88]

On April 25, a crowd packed Toronto's Massey Hall for Diefenbaker's first major speech of the campaign. He said that to save Canada, Canadians needed to renew their pride, restore their faith, and recapture control of their national identity. Canada would then be able to exert greater autonomy. Diefenbaker hearkened back to Macdonald's National Policy with his proposed National Development Policy. More Canadian power plants should be built, he said, and more ownership of mining and petroleum companies should be encouraged. The manufacturing sector should grow not by rejecting American customers but by finding new ones around the world.[89]

Rather than building Canada by moving west, as Macdonald had done, Diefenbaker spoke of saving it by turning north. He envisioned what he called "highways to resources" that would result in the building of northern power plants, mines, and towns. "My purpose and my aim with my colleagues on this platform," he said, "will be to bring to Canada and to Canadians a faith in their fellow Canadians, faith in the future and the destiny of this country."[90] Three years before John Kennedy's 1960 presidential campaign would abscond with the tag line, Diefenbaker called his vision the New Frontier.

An important element in Diefenbaker's nationalism, encapsulated in the phrase "One Canada," channelled Macdonald's Quebec partner George-Étienne Cartier. In the 1865 Confederation debates, Cartier spoke of creating a new state that would allow a new nationality to flourish. "If union were attained we would form a political nationality with which neither the national origin, nor the religion of any individual would interfere."[91] It would be a new and Canadian nationality, one that celebrated the richness of its ethnic complexity. Cartier would have been proud to hear Diefenbaker say, as early as 1946, "Canada must develop, now that we achieved this citizenship, unity out of diversity—a diversity based on the non-homogenous peoples of many religions, peoples of clashing economic differences based on distance, and jurisdictional differences as between federal and provincial authorities. The great challenge to our generation is to fuse these differences."[92]

Diefenbaker did not believe in ethnic nationalism. It locates identity in the blood and encourages nativism and racism while excluding or attacking those deemed "outside" or "different." It feeds fear and builds walls. Rather, Diefenbaker's One Canada was informed by his belief in civic nationalism, which promotes ethnic and racial complexity within a state that offers identity based on natural and acquired citizenship. It encourages community and builds bridges between groups and individuals. Diefenbaker's nationalist passion led to his demanding greater autonomy to promote a more secure unity and deeper identity. Canadians were being asked to recall, renew, or perhaps invent a nationalist pride. This was not a negative, reactive anti-Americanism but a positive, active pro-Canadian nationalism meant to reflect confidence and the country's founding ideals. It was an inspirational and aspirational message delivered by a compelling messenger.

Diefenbaker's speeches resembled performance art. Pace and volume rose and fell as the right index finger jabbed the air and the eyes flashed.[93] The crescendo of every speech came with his ringing exhortation that Canadians were being presented with the decision of their lives. The future, indeed, the survival of their country, he insisted, was at stake. He linked his party to a love of Canada, and the Liberals to those would who would sell it out.[94] Diefenbaker sought not to deny America's importance but, for the good of Canada, to better manage the bilateral relationship with it. After all, Canadians understood, as Social Credit leader Robert Thompson would later say, "The Americans are our best friend whether we like it or not."[95]

Those breathing the rarefied air of Toronto and Montreal boardrooms, newsrooms, faculty lounges, private clubs, or Parliament Hill cloakrooms didn't like Diefenbaker's message; they didn't like it one bit.[96] He was challenging their power by challenging the eastern, elite, liberal, consensus they had established and assumed to be an indisputable given. He was threatening to replace their narrative with something more western and inclusive.[97] Perhaps worst of all, he wasn't even speaking to them. They gnashed their teeth as Diefenbaker's vision, and the stark choices in which he framed it, resonated among those made nervous by 1957's shifting sands and Khrushchev's beeping satellites. Diefenbaker and his nationalist vision soared when measured against the increasingly technocratic policies St. Laurent proposed and the sincere but uninspiring manner in which he proposed them.

Beyond all that, Diefenbaker continued to be a force of nature on the campaign trail. He shook every hand, remembered every name, retold every tale, and laughed at every joke. He never met a voter with whom he did not agree. As he overwhelmed the tired Liberals, the number one song on the billboard charts for eight straight weeks was Elvis Presley's "All Shook Up." Elvis was popular for much more than his lyrics, and those baffled by the Diefenbaker phenomenon, then and later, could not fathom that Diefenbaker, too, resonated beyond the sometimes-disjointed words of his speeches.[98] Charisma cannot be taught or learned, but when in its presence, neither can it be denied.

On June 10, Election Day, Diefenbaker and his wife, Olive, were resting at their modest Prince Albert home when the radio announced that his Progressive Conservatives would win. They took 112 seats, the Liberals 105, the CCF 25, Social Credit 19, and independents 4. It would be a minority government, and the Conservatives had earned only 39 percent of the popular vote, but it was still an upset victory. Diefenbaker flew to Regina, the nearest television studio, and in an address to the nation said, "When I accepted the leadership of this party I said to the party and to the people, I would be guided by these words from the scriptures: 'He who would be chiefest among you shall be the servant of all.'"[99] A nickname already coined by a few advisors was born: he was "Dief the Chief."

Three months later St. Laurent announced his retirement. In December, the same month he picked up his Nobel Prize, Lester Pearson declared his candidacy for Liberal leadership. In mid-January, Liberal

Party delegates stuffed themselves into the old Coliseum at Ottawa's exhibition grounds. Serious folks manipulating policy planks and leadership votes worked alongside those in funny hats chasing the next free drink and seductive wink. Pearson became the leader of the Liberal Party of Canada and of Her Majesty's Loyal Opposition.

As Canada headed toward a crossroads, Pearson soon demonstrated how radically different the world of partisan politics was from that of international diplomacy. When measured against the prairie populist of remarkable skill, Pearson's years of service seemed to count for little. For a while, he appeared to be a lost, weary, and wary traveller. Meanwhile, Diefenbaker's nationalist vision, reborn on the prairies and based on Canada's founding principles, was about to run headlong into a hurricane neither he nor Pearson saw coming.

# T W O

---

# THE COLLISION

THE DAY AFTER THE 1957 ELECTION, Diefenbaker got his hair cut, then went fishing with friends and a few reporters. When teased about not having caught much, Diefenbaker said, "No, I caught the big one yesterday."[1] He had decades of experience as a campaigner and Opposition member but not a day in government or in an executive leadership position.

The first daunting task was the creation of a Cabinet. Many of those best qualified were also those who had fought against his becoming party leader. He demonstrated confidence and political acumen in making allies of adversaries with men like Howard Green, Douglas Harkness, Davie Fulton, and Donald Fleming. Ellen Fairclough, who had also opposed his leadership aspirations, became the first woman, and Michael Starr the first person of Ukrainian descent appointed to a federal Cabinet. He later appointed James Gladstone of the Blackfoot First Nation to the Senate, making him Canada's first Aboriginal senator. Until appointing Sidney Smith in September, Diefenbaker acted as his own external affairs minister. He asked the experienced and wise Robert Bryce to continue as clerk of the Privy Council and secretary to the Cabinet.

The Cabinet was sworn in at 11 a.m. on June 21. Four hours later, just eleven days after the election, its first meeting was called to order.

Most ministers had not yet met their staffs, and some had not even found their new offices.[2] They walked through the beautifully hand-carved wooden doorway into the East Block's Privy Council chamber and settled into large, red-leather-bound dark oak chairs surrounding a big, oblong, red-leather-topped table. The intimidating gazes of twelve previous prime ministers stared down from portraits on the walls. It was the same room used for Cabinet meetings by every prime minister since Macdonald and so was both rich in daunting historical significance and, due to the growth in the size of Cabinet over the years, somewhat cramped. Diefenbaker entered last and took his seat in the large, ornately carved chair at the table's head.

The hour-long meeting addressed several issues left over from St. Laurent's government. A $12 million northern road project was quickly approved and former Ontario premier and federal Progressive Conservative leader George Drew was appointed high commissioner to the United Kingdom. The next morning, ministers met to address more leftover decisions. Diefenbaker was then off to a Commonwealth conference in London.

He was thrilled to meet Churchill, who flattered him, and the Queen, who awed him.[3] He was intent upon rebuilding the relationship between Britain and Canada that had been harmed a year earlier by the 1956 Suez Crisis. He hoped that restoring trust and goodwill would enable Canada to enhance its economic ties to Commonwealth countries in general and Britain in particular and thereby bolster Canada's economic independence by decreasing its reliance on American markets and investment.[4]

To advance the cause, he advocated a Commonwealth conference in Ottawa. British prime minister Harold Macmillan was rather cool to the idea because it would complicate current discussions regarding Britain's joining the European Economic Community, more commonly called the European Common Market. It had been formed in March 1957 when France, West Germany, Italy, the Netherlands, Belgium, and Luxembourg signed a treaty designed to tear down trade barriers between members and eventually create a European economic and political union. It would come into effect in January 1958. Diefenbaker ignored Macmillan's unease and conference delegates eventually agreed to meet in Canada.

At a July 6 press conference upon his return to Ottawa, Diefenbaker acknowledged the importance of continued American investment and trade but repeated his belief that Canada needed to broaden its perspective and opportunities. He then stated an intention to pursue a 15 percent diversion of Canada's trade from the US to Britain.[5] It was the kind of remark he could toss off in opposition or in a campaign, but he had yet to learn, if indeed he ever truly did, that he could not simply say things as prime minister without inviting consequences. The announcement surprised everyone, including his ministers and finance department bureaucrats, none of whom had been consulted. Such a diversion would have necessitated enormous changes and violated international trade rules. It was an obvious political and economic gaffe.

While the unachievable 15 percent trade diversion was soon forgotten, Diefenbaker's trade diversification goals were not. In a speech delivered on September 7 at Dartmouth College in Hanover, New Hampshire, he spoke glowingly of Canadian-American friendship and of being united in the fight against communism. He then explained that American investors owned majority control in Canada's mining, manufacturing, and oil-producing sectors and that American transactions made up 60 percent of Canada's exports and 73 percent of its imports. "This has inherent dangers for Canada. It makes the Canadian economy altogether too vulnerable to sudden changes in trading policy in Washington. . . . There is an intangible sense of disquiet in Canada over the political implications of large-scale and continuing external ownership and control of Canadian industries."[6]

The trade conference Diefenbaker had promoted in London was convened later that month at the pretty resort town of Mont-Tremblant,

eighty miles northwest of Montreal. UK trade officials called Diefenbaker's
15 percent diversion bluff by offering to create a British-Canadian free-
trade zone. The proposal surprised finance minister Donald Fleming.
After a couple of days of investigation, the idea, like the 15 percent
notion itself, was allowed to die. The 160 delegates from fifteen countries created a new Commonwealth council to promote trade, and agreed
to remove some tariffs and regulatory trade barriers, and to improve
transcontinental telephone communications. Britain and Canada also
pledged to reduce bilateral trade barriers involving some food and agricultural products.[7]

While marred by some stumbling out of the gate and bereft of substantive achievement, the Ottawa news conference, Dartmouth speech,
and the London and Mont-Tremblant Commonwealth meetings served
notice that Diefenbaker's nationalist campaign message had been a genuine statement of intent and not just salesmanship. The new prime minister
would continue Canada's Cold War fight in partnership with the
Americans, but there could be no doubt among anyone paying attention
that the protection and promotion of Canadian sovereignty would guide
his administration's strategic goals. Among those paying attention were
Senator Kennedy's advisors.

As part of his still undeclared race for the White House, Kennedy
accepted an invitation to address the convocation at Fredericton's
University of New Brunswick on October 8, 1957. The university's
chancellor, Lord Beaverbrook, perhaps got a little ahead of himself in
introducing Kennedy as "the next president of the United States."[8]
Kennedy was awarded an honorary doctorate of laws, as Diefenbaker
had been at Dartmouth, and then addressed the audience with a speech
laced with bromides and barbs."Unquestionably the new Canadian government under Prime Minister Diefenbaker has received a mandate to
explore means by which Canada may renew a closer trade connection
with Great Britain . . . but in reading the statements by your Prime

Minister on several occasions, both in this country and in the United States, it is quite apparent that the main outlines of Canadian policy are but little altered. Both of our peoples delude themselves if they believe that there is some new and previously unexplored line of policy which Canada can now explore."⁹

After pronouncing that Canada had little freedom of action, he praised Canadian independence. He then immediately questioned it and those seeking to protect it:

> Canada has achieved a national strength and prestige which simply does not allow any portrayal of the country as an appendage of either Great Britain or the United States. . . . The United States and Canada are more than ever continental partners . . . our natural resources should not be neatly compartmentalized nationally. . . . The deep penetration of American venture capital and business management into Canadian enterprises in such sectors as mining and fuels has aroused natural fears among Canadians. And there are more than a few Canadians who are appalled that the hopes for a distinctively national cultural tradition are being suffocated by a loud cacophony south of the border.¹⁰

Kennedy advocated bilateral meetings and processes for "joint consultation and management." He spoke of establishing "permanent consultative channels" to avoid dealing with each new problem on an ad hoc basis. While Eisenhower and Congress had said nothing of economic reprisals in response to Diefenbaker's nationalist trade goals, Kennedy offered an oblique warning: "If the Canadian government is in fact able, as intimated at the recent Commonwealth Conference at London and Mt. Tremblant, to divert a larger portion of its trade to Britain, this should not be occasion for the United States to launch a new program of economic retaliation and harassment. . . . It would be a pity to rigidify the

Canadian economy merely for the sake of breaking lances with a phantom American colonialism."[11] Kennedy was asking Canadians to sink the founding ideas from their past and inspiring ideas about their future into a pool of faith in America's good graces.

At this point Kennedy was a pest who could be ignored. Diefenbaker needed to deal with President Eisenhower. Due to his heroic efforts as supreme commander of the Allied Forces in the Second World War, Eisenhower, or "Ike" as most called him, was famous and deeply respected before he became president. Eisenhower was a military man who hated war. He was a hard worker whose calm public persona and frequent golf games made it all look easy. He was a non-political man who became a political genius.[12]

Eisenhower's long-term strategic response to possible Soviet attacks on the United States and Western Europe was dubbed the New Look. Announced in January 1954, the New Look sought to protect the United States and its allies not through large and expensive land-based armies but through promising to employ weapons so horrible that no sane person would ever want to see them used. His policy established a nuclear balance of power with the communist world—some called it a balance of terror—designed to maintain peace through teeth-baring, chest-puffing coexistence.[13] The New Look's implementation saw cuts to the army and navy and the allocation of 40 percent of the defence budget to the air force.[14] It would act as the nuclear weapons delivery team and the first line of defence in stopping Soviet bombers. There were obvious ramifications for Canada. If Soviet bombers were to be stopped before they reached the American border, they would in all likelihood be blasted out of the sky somewhere between the Arctic Circle and the Great Lakes. Eisenhower had made Canadian air space central to America's defence with little understanding or consideration of his northern neighbour. At a White House meeting early in the Eisenhower administration, external affairs minister Lester Pearson had been shocked at the president's flimsy understanding of a particular bilateral issue and of Canada in general and muttered dismissively, "You'd think his caddie would have mentioned it to him."[15]

In December 1953, Eisenhower visited Canada. The joint statement released after meeting with St. Laurent repeated the pledge made a decade before at the creation of the Permanent Joint Board on Defence: "The full respect of each country for the sovereignty of the other is inherent in these principles [but] the defense of North America must be considered as a whole."[16] Pearson knew that continental defence and sovereignty were at odds. He had repeatedly badgered Truman's secretary of state Dean Acheson for more consultation. Once, after having pushed a difficult NATO deal through the American executive and legislative branches only to find Pearson on him again, Acheson had had enough: "If you think, after the agonies of consultation we have gone through here to get agreement on this matter, that we are going to start all over again with our NATO allies, especially with you moralistic, interfering Canadians, then you're crazy."[17]

Eisenhower's powerful secretary of state, John Foster Dulles, knew Canada better than his boss. Like FDR, Dulles vacationed in Canada. He owned the isolated and ruggedly beautiful thousand-acre Duck Island, eleven miles off scenic Prince Edward County, which reaches into Lake Ontario near Belleville. His Canadian connection, however, did not mean that he understood or respected Canada's desire to be involved in decisions affecting joint defence. On a plane ride with Pearson, Dulles complained about Canadians always wanting to be consulted. He said that if he were putting on the eighteenth green, Pearson would interrupt to insist on being consulted on club selection. Pearson joked that he would probably suggest a nine-iron.[18] Pearson feared that if Soviet bombers were ever on their way, the Canadian prime minister would have little or no input regarding a response.[19] Diefenbaker came to office suspecting what Pearson already knew—the New Look was no new partnership.

On the morning of the Diefenbaker government's second day, among the issues Cabinet had discussed were Defence and External Affairs reports regarding two decisions pending from St. Laurent's final days. The first involved a one-year extension of the Canada-United States Agreement on Overflights. It allowed the American air force to continue to fly planes carrying atomic bombs over Canada. They could also use Canadian bases if it was established that enemy aircraft had entered North American air space.[20] The agreement reflected joint defence principles established by Roosevelt and Mackenzie King that St. Laurent had already pledged to extend. External Affairs and Defence both recommended the extension. A decision such as this would normally have gone through the Cabinet Defence Committee, but the new government had yet to establish it. Those who would later comprise the committee all approved, and Cabinet, advised that this was merely an extension that could be revisited in a year, followed suit.[21]

Diefenbaker and national defence minister Major-General George Pearkes discussed the second and more portentous leftover decision on the flight back from the London Commonwealth Conference. In 1954, in order to make the North American elements of Eisenhower's New Look work, the United States created the continental air defence strategy and began negotiating Canadian co-operation and coordination. By December 1956, Canadian and American military leaders had agreed upon the broad principles of an arrangement called the North American Air Defense Command (NORAD). Four months later, Eisenhower signed off.

Chair of Canada's Chiefs of Staff Committee General Charles Foulkes was a strong advocate of NORAD. He argued that the American and Canadian forces would remain separate but that an integrated command and control structure would be established to allow quick responses to emergencies. As with the Overflights Agreement, St. Laurent's Cabinet had discussed and agreed to NORAD in principle.[22] On July 23, at the insistence of General Foulkes, new defence minister Pearkes brought the old recommendation to Cabinet. The agreement began: "Until substantial measures are taken to implement a comprehensive disarmament plan we must continue to provide a reasonable air defence for this country."[23] The Cabinet approved the Foulkes report as an informal understanding.

A week later, Cabinet appointed Air Marshal C. Roy Slemon to work with his American counterpart as Canada's first North American air defence deputy commander in chief. Slemon was dispatched to NORAD headquarters in Colorado.[24] The integrated operational control headquarters became active in September, although everything was on an interim basis until a final agreement was signed.[25] There was a great deal left to be decided—most importantly, how to protect Canadians and Americans while respecting Canadian sovereignty and ensuring joint civilian control.

Diefenbaker was surprised when the Americans immediately began pressuring him to allow the stockpiling of tactical nuclear weapons at their air force and submarine bases at Goose Bay, Harmon, and Argentia, Newfoundland.[26] He quickly realized that the NORAD decision had implications he had not fully considered; it had been too rushed.[27] Experienced diplomat and close Pearson friend George Ignatieff, whom Diefenbaker later appointed as a special foreign affairs advisor, believed that the agreement came about as it did because General Foulkes and other Canadian military leaders had become "too cozy" with their American counterparts.[28] Foulkes often bragged of having spoken with Brad and Rad—Admiral Arthur Radford and General Omar Bradley. Foulkes later confessed that in wanting to impress them and the new prime minister, he had "stampeded the incoming government."[29] In a

1965 letter to Diefenbaker, Defence Minister Pearkes apologized for his complicity in the stampede.[30] Diefenbaker would never again rush a decision, sometimes to the point of appearing unable to make one. He would never act without full Cabinet consultation and approval, sometimes wasting valuable time trying to capture an evasive consensus. Further, he would never again completely trust his generals. Sometimes he went too far, as during a 1961 meeting when the defence minister had to stop Diefenbaker's ruthless berating of Air Marshal Hugh Campbell.[31]

A mutual lack of trust also coloured the relationship between Diefenbaker and the bureaucrats that served his government. Pearson had been one of their own and they trusted and admired him. Many in the bureaucracy grew to at least respect the new prime minister. Undersecretary of state for external affairs and Pearson friend and colleague John Holmes, for instance, noted in 1958 that "[Diefenbaker] could hardly have been more friendly [and] very willing to accept advice provided the advice is clearly and succinctly stated."[32] However, few in the bureaucracy grew to trust Diefenbaker any more than he trusted them.

In August, Diefenbaker plucked the experienced and well-respected Henry Basil Robinson from External Affairs to be his foreign affairs advisor. Robinson (his friends called him Basil), was a charming man with great administrative skill and personal integrity who had served with distinction in the Second World War. Regardless of what they are called in any state's organizational chart, departments of defence and external affairs are very different animals. While Defence tends to see conflict and opportunities through a military perspective, External Affairs peers through a broader diplomatic prism. The two are often, and to a strong leader, helpfully, in conflict. Robinson's primary role was to act as a liaison between the two and bring the prime minister the advice he needed. Diefenbaker joked that Robinson's real job was to handle the External Affairs "Pearsonalities."[33]

Defence was only one of myriad issues Diefenbaker found himself juggling as he prepared for the fall resumption of Parliament. Meanwhile, as Opposition leader, Pearson had begun raising concerns in the House of Commons about whether NORAD would operate independently of NATO. Diefenbaker re-emphasized that negotiations were ongoing and that external affairs and not defence or military leaders were conducting them.[34] Behind the scenes, Diefenbaker repeated his demand to negotiators that a final NORAD agreement reflect a partnership of allies. Canada would obviously be the junior partner in the two-nation agreement, but his directives and questions made it clear that it would be a partnership nonetheless. Diefenbaker also sought to mitigate American domination by ordering that NATO allies be kept informed of all NORAD arrangements and activities.[35]

While Diefenbaker was working to balance Canada's defence policies with Ike's New Look and his own desire for increased sovereignty, Senator Kennedy continued his presidential campaign. On December 3, 1957, he spoke in Chicago at the National Conference of Christians and Jews. His words were jarring. He meant them to be. "We are in peril today—and by that I do not mean simply the danger to our lives and our fortunes, to our unscarred shores and our unsurrendered flag. For we could lose more than a war, more than our lives—we are in peril of losing our whole way of life, not only our nation's peace and freedom but our own peace of mind and freedom to think, our cherished concepts of democratic government and individual liberty."[36] Kennedy was testing a campaign theme that sought to scare Americans with the idea that Eisenhower and the Republicans were allowing the United States to fall behind the Soviet Union in military might, science, education, and other important areas of endeavour.

To his stunned audience, and making points directly involving Canada, Kennedy continued, "Our much-vaunted DEW line network of guidance and detection installations for continental defence, only recently completed at great expense and stretching up into the Arctic, may now be completely outmoded. Designed for aircraft and not missiles, it cannot even see the present Russian satellites. Not only are the European bases of our Strategic

Air Command vulnerable to Soviet Intermediate Range Missiles, but so also are the cities and bases on our own shores, now within range of missiles launched by a submarine 500 miles out to sea. . . . Clearly we are in midpassage—between a dying and a world not yet born."[37] Whether it liked it or not, Canada would be present at the birth he had in mind.

Shortly after Kennedy's encouragement to be afraid, most Canadians and Americans tried to put fear aside to celebrate Christmas. For Diefenbaker, Christmas came a little late but with a joy he found impossible to hide. On January 20, 1958, just days after becoming Liberal Party leader, Lester Pearson took his seat in the House of Commons. His first action as leader of Canada's Loyal Opposition was to move an amendment to an interim supply bill that asked for the government's resignation. It was an old parliamentary rabbit that opposition parties occasionally pull from their hats. It never worked, and everyone expected the trick to be easily dismissed with the amendment defeated, but Pearson went further. He added that because the country was in recession and Diefenbaker's government was bungling economic matters, it should resign. Then, without an election, the governor general should ask the Liberals to form a government to save the country.[38]

Diefenbaker threw his head back and laughed. Then, in a brilliant two-hour attack, he ripped into Pearson's proposal as a new example of Liberal arrogance. He produced a report prepared for the recently deposed St. Laurent government that warned of an economic downturn. He slammed the Liberals for not releasing it, or discussing it during the summer campaign, or doing anything to address the problems it detailed.[39] As Diefenbaker raged on, Pearson sank deeper and deeper behind his desk. Word spread of Diefenbaker's speech and the public galleries filled. Liberal frontbencher Paul Martin called Diefenbaker's performance "one of the greatest devastating speeches in Canadian history."[40] Pearson later admitted, "He tore me to shreds."[41]

Pearson's blunder allowed Diefenbaker to do what he had been itching to do for weeks: he had the governor general call an election. Canadians had been surprised and impressed with Diefenbaker as a campaigner the year before, but through the late winter and on to the March 31 voting day, he was like nothing the country had seen before. Hearkening back to Macdonald at his peak and Laurier and Bennett at their best, Diefenbaker undertook something more akin to a crusade.

Beginning at a Winnipeg rally that drew more than five thousand people on a frigid February evening, the campaign became a juggernaut. He spoke of prosperity and opportunity. He spoke of his vision for a new and more independent Canada and of moving from a reliance on the neighbour to the south to the opening of the undeveloped north. He asked people to envision a nation bereft of ethnic division and racial prejudice. He spoke with passion and eloquence and an unbridled enthusiasm that sometimes overwhelmed his audiences, and sometimes even himself. His speeches were like those of old-time tent revivals. On paper they jumped from one non sequitur to the next but when heard, or perhaps it is more accurate to say when experienced, they were different. Diefenbaker put politics into poetry and appealed to people's hearts.

Crowds grew in size and enthusiasm as the campaign developed an unmistakable and inexplicable momentum. People met him with cheers and tears. Women fainted and men reached to touch him as he passed. "Follow John," the slogan said, and there was no doubt that Canadians were about to do just that. Banners and ads spoke of Canada's need not for a Progressive Conservative government but for a Diefenbaker government.

Pearson the diplomat worked hard at being a politician, but he came across as a nice, well-meaning professor who often bored his small audiences. A campaign begins to lose the moment it begins to react, and from the outset Pearson tried vainly to react to Diefenbaker. To a half-filled hall in Regina, for instance, he read his text and promised to present Liberal policies "without any quavering clichés or evangelical exhortations."[42]

He insulted the people of the North by criticizing Diefenbaker's idea as building roads from "igloo to igloo."[43] More than once, he refused to stop and shake hands with people, saying that he did not want to bother them.

Diefenbaker's victory surprised no one, but its magnitude startled everyone. The Progressive Conservatives won 208 seats, an unprecedented percentage of the House. The party held a majority of seats in every province but Newfoundland. The Liberals were reduced to only forty-eight MPs and the Co-operative Commonwealth Federation to eight. Social Credit was wiped out. On election night, Pearson's wife, Maryon, quipped to her exhausted husband, slouched in a chair with hair askew and a wilted carnation sagging from his lapel, "We've lost everything, Mike. We've even won our own seat."[44]

Diefenbaker received a host of congratulatory messages. Among them was a polite note from Eisenhower and an effusive message from Vice President Richard Nixon, who wrote, "I, personally, could not have been more pleased that you have now earned a majority from the Canadian people. . . . There is no question but that history will record that you are one of the great political campaigners of our time. The fact that within the space of just a few months you were able to do what you did against what appeared to be insurmountable odds is an achievement which has seldom been equalled in history."[45] Diefenbaker heard nothing from Senator Kennedy.

# THREE

## IKE, THE CHIEF, AND THE CANDIDATE

TWO WEEKS AFTER DIEFENBAKER won his majority, a group of concerned congressmen asked American ambassador to Canada Livingston Merchant to appear before the Senate Foreign Relations Committee. Merchant understood Diefenbaker's message and that it had resonated with Canadians. As he told the group, "There is in this rapidly developing nation a growing consciousness of national destiny and nationalism."[1] Asked if Diefenbaker represented a growth in anti-Americanism, Merchant acknowledged the trend but said it was really "a very powerful Canadianism" that was at play.[2] He assured the anxious senators—anxious about the prime minister's nationalist message—that Diefenbaker appeared ready to co-operate in matters of mutual defence. However, he warned them, Americans needed to be more sensitive than ever to perceptions of infringement on Canadian sovereignty.

Diefenbaker read a transcript of Merchant's testimony. He was impressed by the accuracy of the analysis but resented that his words, actions, and policies were being perceived in prominent circles as anti-American.[3] He was content that Merchant, Eisenhower, and, to a lesser degree, Dulles grudgingly accepted that his interactions with the United States were not simply political ploys or reckless obstinacy.[4]

With Sputnik's October launch fresh in everyone's mind, Diefenbaker and Eisenhower attended the December 1957 NATO conference in Paris, where it was agreed that the United States would store tactical nuclear weapons at European NATO bases while maintaining ownership and control. In the event of a Soviet attack, weapons would be made available to NATO troops, including the six thousand Canadians in Germany and France.[5] The agreement allowed Diefenbaker to slyly claim that Canada's NATO troops did not have nuclear weapons. He could maintain his nuclear virginity while sleeping with the neighbour.

The question was whether he could finagle the same purity-with-perks arrangement with NORAD.[6] To do so, Diefenbaker needed to balance pressure from the Americans, his defence department, and his generals to acquire nuclear weapons against External Affairs' advice to reject them. He also needed to meet—and be seen to be meeting—NATO and NORAD commitments while honouring Canada's UN pledge to support disarmament and oppose nuclear proliferation. If all of that wasn't enough, he had to appease Canadians opposed to nuclear weapons and those who yearned for their security.

A number of Cabinet debates centred upon these conflicting considerations as well as the weapons' price, cost sharing, and how to match the military's need to act quickly in an emergency with the prime minister's insistence on respect for Canadian sovereignty.[7] On January 13, 1958, a week before the Pearson blunder that would throw the country into an election, Diefenbaker and his Cabinet agreed to begin negotiations with the Americans to acquire nuclear weapons in Canada and Europe.[8] Diefenbaker emphasized secrecy to avoid stirring Canada's nascent anti-nuclear movement, as was already happening in Britain. Further, to be consistent with American law, he conceded that no matter where the weapons ended up, they would be owned by the United States. He insisted, however, that the absence of joint and civilian control of their use was a deal breaker; he didn't want the generals or the Americans to launch the things without his consent.[9]

Diefenbaker introduced the NORAD agreement to Parliament on June 10. It contained all the safeguards upon which he had insisted. There would be joint and civilian control over continental defence strategies and any actions taken in an emergency. NORAD's commander-in-chief would be responsible to the Canadian Chiefs of Staff Committee and the American Joint Chiefs of Staff and, through them, the two governments. The agreement stated: "The integration of forces increases the importance of the fullest possible consultation between the two governments on all matters affecting the joint defence of North America, and that defence co-operation between them can be worked out on a mutually satisfactory basis only if such consultation is regularly and consistently undertaken."[10] The civilian control and consultation pledge offered the protection of Canadian sovereignty upon which he had insisted. Pearson raised a few points of clarification and criticized the process through which the agreement had been reached but, as he had supported the idea with the same safeguards while minister of external affairs, he did not oppose it.[11]

A month later, President Eisenhower arrived for a three-day Canadian visit. He and Diefenbaker discussed a number of issues. With respect to NORAD, the prime minister reported that despite the assurances in the agreement, there remained widespread fear among Canadians that the country was sacrificing sovereignty by turning their defence over to American generals.[12] Eisenhower noted that commanders would need to react quickly in an emergency but repeated the NORAD pledge to respect Canadian sovereignty through the implementation of the joint command structure that would ensure civilian control and Canadian Cabinet involvement in important decisions.[13]

The NORAD agreement and Eisenhower's personal promise to respect Canadian sovereignty through consultation afforded additional impetus to the nuclear weapons negotiations. On September 23, Diefenbaker rose in the House and said that, as part of Canada's commitment to NORAD and continental defence, it would purchase American-made Bomarc surface-to-air anti-aircraft guided missiles and construct bases for them in North Bay, Ontario, and La Macaza, Quebec. Bomarc missiles could soar four hundred miles at two thousand miles per hour and explode a nuclear warhead within a thousand yards of an incoming Soviet bomber. The simultaneous detonation of its warhead and those aboard the plane would wreak destruction on the ground below and spread murderous fallout for miles—but a plane would be stopped and a city saved. Diefenbaker, of course, did not go into that level of detail. The Bomarc purchase was big news. But the House and media shunted it to one side because of what Diefenbaker said next. He was killing the Arrow.[14]

The Arrow project began when the St. Laurent government asked the Canadian subsidiary of a British-based multinational, A.V. Roe and Company, to research, develop, and build a fleet of six hundred supersonic all-weather interceptor jets capable of defending Canada against Soviet bombers. The new CF-105's design and capabilities were stunningly innovative but expensive. In 1953 each plane was expected to cost $1.5 million to $2 million. By 1957, the price tag had rocketed to $8 million each.[15] Worse was that, despite the best efforts of External Affairs and the company, the Americans and Europeans didn't want it. The Americans were aggressively pushing their CF-104 Starfighter jet as a cheaper alternative. With the Arrow's production run cut and economies of scale gone, costs threatened to soar higher and faster than the jet. The defence department warned St. Laurent that the Arrow was syphoning money from other parts of its budget that could not afford to be cut. It recommended scrapping the cutting-edge fighter.[16] St. Laurent refrained from making the announcement before the June 1957 election.

Diefenbaker was presented with even worse numbers but the same arguments. In addition, the late-1957 Sputnik launches suggested that a Soviet attack might not be delivered solely by the bombers that the Arrow was being designed to bring down. Defence Minister Pearkes reported that Bomarc missiles, along with American-made Starfighter jets, would provide Canada with an effective and cheaper defence. He argued that while the Starfighters were not as good as the Arrow—at that point, it looked as if no plane in the world would be in the Arrow's league—they would be good enough. The Cabinet Defence Committee recommended killing the Arrow.[17] Cabinet secretary Robert Bryce independently studied the issue and agreed.[18]

Diefenbaker concurred, but he announced that the Arrow project would continue for the time being, with a review in six months. He explained his thinking to his Cabinet. The announcement of a future announcement would create a bargaining chip with the Americans; if sticking with the Arrow remained an option, they might cut the price of the Bomarcs and Starfighters.[19] It worked. The Americans blinked and prices went down. Cabinet approved the purchases, the review was done, and on Friday, February 20, 1959, the Arrow program was cancelled.[20]

In killing the Arrow, Diefenbaker decided that fiscal prudence and defence needs outweighed the loss of nearly fourteen thousand jobs and government support for a company that promised Canadian-based technological innovation. He had chosen to ignore the intense lobbying efforts of A.V. Roe and Company and the patriotic fervour of the Arrow's many supporters.[21] Two years before President Eisenhower warned of the military-industrial complex, Diefenbaker proved that he would not be its handmaiden: the Arrow was dead; the Bomarc and larger nuclear question was its phoenix.

By this point, Diefenbaker was no longer a rookie prime minister. He had made important domestic decisions and acquitted himself well on the world stage. Beginning in October 1958, he had undertaken a seven-week world tour. He began by visiting UN secretary-general Dag Hammarskjöld in New York. The gruelling trip then took him to Britain, France, Italy, Germany, Australia, New Zealand, Pakistan, India, Ceylon, Malaya, and Singapore. While in Paris he sat with NATO secretary general Paul-Henri Spaak and then the alliance's supreme commander, the mercurial

American general Lauris Norstad. Norstad also led the American troops in Europe. They discussed NATO's strategic plans and the weaponry that Norstad believed was necessary to implement them. Diefenbaker then did something he would do only once throughout his long trip. He asked the general for a written summary of their discussion.[22] Perhaps Diefenbaker suspected that, like his own generals, Norstad could not be trusted. His instincts would prove sound.

The prime minister returned to Canada having established personal relationships with many important world leaders. He had developed a richer appreciation of their problems and perspectives, and a deeper understanding of Canada's role in the world. With what was waiting upon his return, he would need it.

The decision to station American tactical nuclear weapons on Canadian soil would prove to be the most consequential of his administration. The proposed acquisition would involve five Canadian weapons systems. The Bomarc missiles in Canada and Lacrosse missiles in Europe were ground-based, anti-aircraft weapons. The Lacrosse missiles were later replaced by Honest Johns—the name had nothing to do with the president or prime minister. The sixty-four Canadian-based CF-101B Voodoo interceptor jets could carry two nuclear-tipped missiles each, as would the eight squadrons of European-based CF-104 Starfighter jets. The Royal Canadian Navy had seven platforms that could host nuclear weapons, including its planes, helicopters, torpedoes, and depth charges.[23] Beyond all of that, the Americans wanted to store air-to-air missiles and nuclear warheads at their Newfoundland and Labrador bases and at their submarine base in Argentia, Newfoundland.

News of the bilateral negotiations and internal disagreements finally leaked. On February 20, 1959, Diefenbaker rose in the House to offer clarity. His statement laid waste to critics who claimed then and later that he did not understand what he was bargaining for. "The full potential of these defensive weapons is achieved only when they are armed with nuclear warheads. The government is, therefore, examining with the United States government questions connected with the acquisition of nuclear warheads for Bomarc and other defensive weapons for use by Canadian forces in Canada, and the storage of warheads in Canada. Problems connected with the arming of the Canadian brigade in Europe with short-range nuclear weapons for NATO's defence tasks are also being studied."[24]

No one disputed his misuse of the word *defensive*. Labelling weapons as defensive or offensive is militarily inaccurate but politically useful. Diefenbaker was correct in identifying the land-based Bomarcs as defensive; they could only be aimed at incoming Soviet planes already in Canadian airspace. However, it was hardly accurate to lump them with nuclear-armed jets, ships, or subs that could take the fight to the enemy. Use of the political marketing ploy sullied the nuclear debate on both sides of the border.

The February announcement and the subsequent reinvigoration of nuclear negotiations offered a moment of tranquility in Canadian-American relations. But two events warned again that the collision was drawing nigh. First, less than a month later, a heart attack killed secretary of state for external affairs Sidney Smith. On June 4, Diefenbaker appointed Vancouver's Howard Green as his successor. Green was a First World War veteran and had been in Parliament since 1935 and in Cabinet since the 1957 election. He and Diefenbaker had shared a desk in the House.

Green supported the NORAD and Bomarc decisions. Upon taking up his new post, though, he enjoyed long discussions with undersecretary Norman Robertson, who had become an increasingly strong voice in expressing support for disarmament and worries about whether winning the missiles was worth the potential loss of Canadian sovereignty.[25] Defence officials had been fighting back against what they considered Robertson's naïveté and arguing that Diefenbaker's insistence on civilian control and Canadian consent for their use in an emergency might not be technically possible.[26] Green was soon converted to Robertson's views. They agreed that there was a glaring contradiction in Canada's accepting nuclear weapons while simultaneously supporting disarmament and demanding an end to nuclear proliferation. They were less concerned with meeting Canada's commitments to the United States, NATO, and NORAD than with being entrapped by them. They distrusted the United States for having already dragged Canada into Korea and feared new and perilous entanglements that belied its national interests or stole its autonomy.[27] Green's bringing these views to Cabinet widened the natural split between External Affairs and Defence just as Diefenbaker was publicly promising to narrow it.

The second event involved the American air force's planned test of NORAD's ability to respond to a Soviet attack. Code-named Sky Shield, the September 10 operation would see 250 planes simulating an attack met by a thousand interceptors. Diefenbaker and Green worried about the ramifications of shutting Canadian air space for six hours, that so many aircraft could mistakenly provoke a Soviet response, and about the optics of such a provocative test when Khrushchev would soon be visiting the United States. Cabinet also complained that military and not political leaders had initiated and were planning the test with little civilian involvement. This oversight did not augur well for a nuclear weapons agreement that Diefenbaker had repeatedly insisted must ensure civilian control of military action. Diefenbaker had raised these concerns during his visit to Washington. On August 27, he approved a note to Eisenhower restating Canadian objections.[28]

Canadian ambassador to the United States Arnold Heeney was called to the State Department twice the next day. Both times he was inelegantly dressed down regarding Canadian temerity. Eisenhower dashed off a personal letter to Diefenbaker. Like all of their correspondence, it reflected the friendship the two had developed, as it was addressed *Dear John* and signed *Ike*.[29] In this instance, however, friendship didn't matter—the president was irked. Diefenbaker responded by repeating his objections to Sky Shield. On September 15, the Americans called the whole thing off.

The Sky Shield episode embarrassed Ambassador Heeney. He risked a memo to Diefenbaker urging him to repair his government's internal lines of communication. In a subsequent conversation, Heeney told Diefenbaker that a number of influential Americans were increasingly worried that anti-Americanism was rampant in Ottawa. Diefenbaker denied the concern but said he understood it.[30] Sky Shield taught the Americans that Diefenbaker was capable of changing his mind and pulling the rug from beneath them and his own generals should they make plans without fully consulting him. Diefenbaker learned something himself: if pushed, the Americans could be made to back down.

In January 1960, Diefenbaker delivered a major defence address to the House in which he clearly outlined his government's two-track nuclear weapons policy. He would continue to negotiate for the weapons while simultaneously advocating disarmament. He noted that Khrushchev's recent remarks about moving from bombers to missiles validated Canada's scrapping the Arrow and developing its missile defence strategy. He advised that talks with the Americans to acquire nuclear weapons were proceeding. He spoke of having appointed General E.L.M. Burns, respected leader of the Suez peacekeeping mission, as the government's advisor on disarmament.[31]

The fifteenth regular session of the United Nations convened that September. In his address to the General Assembly, President Eisenhower focused on his desire to ease Cold War tensions. He offered his support for the UN and Secretary-General Hammarskjöld, both of whom had been under fire from Khrushchev for working to end European colonialism in Africa.[32] The next day, Khrushchev specifically blasted Hammarskjöld, citing UN actions in the Congo as an example of bias against socialist governments. Amid demands for Hammarskjöld's resignation, delegates heard Khrushchev shouting as translators spoke in dulcet tones through their headsets: "shameful," "colonialists and their stooges," and "abuse of his position."[33]

The speaking order rendered Diefenbaker the first Western leader to respond to Khrushchev's tirade. The speech reflected his Red Tory, populist support for the downtrodden and powerless, distaste for bullies, and respect for Eisenhower and America. "We do not always agree with the United States, but our very existence—with one-tenth of the population of the United States and possessing the resources we do—is an effective answer to the propaganda that the United States has aggressive designs."[34] He said that if Khrushchev loved independence as he claimed then he should free Eastern Europe's Soviet "colonies." With the stick swung, he offered the carrot. He called for better relations between West and East that would earn benefits for people on both sides of the Iron Curtain. He extended Canada's support for negotiations to end nuclear testing as a pathway to full disarmament and a safer world. He ended with a rhetorical flourish: "My hope is that we shall not leave this place without having done something for mankind, so that we shall be able to say to the peoples of the world that death's pale flag shall not again be raised in war, that fear shall be lifted from the hearts and souls of men."[35]

The Soviet delegation had left halfway through his remarks. When he finished, every delegate except those from communist bloc countries rose in a boisterous standing ovation. Diefenbaker received warm notes from a number of world leaders, including Eisenhower and Macmillan. A number of American ambassadors around the world told their Canadian counterparts how much they respected Diefenbaker's principled stand and political courage.[36] Eisenhower had not been present for the speech, but a couple of days later he and Macmillan sat with Diefenbaker in a private UN lounge and both praised it again.[37]

The private meetings with Eisenhower and others, the resumption of negotiations to bring nuclear weapons to Canada, and then his triumph at the United Nations all seemed to indicate that Diefenbaker was gathering confidence and earning respect. Even Canadian civil servants, who still missed working with Pearson, acknowledged that their old friend and boss was not the only Canadian who could skilfully balance and advance Canadian national interests.[38] It also appeared that, despite bumps like the Sky Shield test, Canadian-American relations were good and getting better. It would not last.

Arnold Heeney had enjoyed a late summer holiday at his cottage. On the second last day of August, the ambassador was preparing to return to Washington when he stopped by Diefenbaker's office for what he thought would be a brief goodbye. The drop-in evolved into two long and disturbing conversations.

The prime minister was concerned about a number of issues, but mostly that his mail was indicating a troubling growth in anti-Americanism among Canadians. Diefenbaker believed that the bitterness in some and anger in others sprang from the perception that Canada was being pushed around, a distrust of the American military, economic aggressiveness in pursuit of American interests, and Americans robbing Canadians of foreign markets. He also noted with considerable frustration that the only time the American press seemed to notice Canada was to be critical. This biased blind spot tarnished America for Canadians and Canada for Americans.

With much left to discuss, Heeney postponed his departure and met with the prime minister again the next day. Diefenbaker returned to his point and supported it by reading parts of letter after letter. Heeney was aghast at the bile expressed by so many Canadians from every region and walk of life. He offered that the anti-American trend was particularly difficult to fathom because in the twenty-two years in which he had dealt with the United States in one capacity or another, there had never been an administration that tried harder to meet Canadian wishes. Diefenbaker agreed.

Both were baffled. Neither knew what could be done, but they were equally worried that the trend could negatively impact the future of Canadian-American relations. Diefenbaker asked Heeney to warn American officials about the trend and assure them that he would do all he could to stem it.[39]

They also discussed the American election that was only ten weeks away and growing more intense. Ever the diplomat, Heeney did not betray an opinion. Diefenbaker was not so coy. As he had told Eisenhower, he liked Nixon and believed him to be the best choice for America, Canada, and the world. He admitted distaste for Kennedy, believing him to be a rich upstart who was not ready to be president.[40]

Kennedy had been waging a brilliant campaign. He battled accusations of being too young, too inexperienced, and too beholden to his father's connections and money. He bravely and directly addressed the belief of some that a Roman Catholic could not be president and the conviction of others that a Roman Catholic should never be president. He struggled every day with the chronic pain in his back and other ailments that would have kept a lesser man in bed. Richard Nixon enjoyed the advantage of eight years as vice president for the perennially popular Eisenhower. Nixon did not, however, enjoy Eisenhower's full support. In fact, when asked at a press conference to name a single idea that Nixon had contributed to the administration, the president mumbled, "If you give me a week, I might think of one."[41]

Nixon was also up against something his considerable intelligence and experience could not overcome. Kennedy had become a celebrity. He was smart, handsome, witty, and amiable. He always seemed to be enjoying himself. He was a war hero and Pulitzer Prize–winning author who was loved by a beguilingly beautiful wife. Respected journalist Eric Sevareid wrote that Kennedy's candidacy was a test of "the charm-school theory of high politics."[42] Beginning in 1957, he was on the cover of nearly every major magazine in America. Kennedy's father told reporters, "I'll tell you how to sell more copies of a magazine. Put his picture on the cover. . . . He can draw more people to a fund-raising than Cary Grant or Jimmy Stewart. Why is that? He has more universal appeal."[43]

The campaign addressed a number of issues, including the stubborn recession, civil rights, and education, but it focused on national security. Kennedy had captured the issue with a Senate speech on August 14, 1958, in which he said, "[We] are about to lose the power foundation that has long stood behind our basic military and diplomatic strategy. . . . We have possessed a capacity for retaliation so great as to deter any potential aggressor from launching a direct attack upon us. . . . The hard facts of the matter are that this premise will soon no longer be correct. We are rapidly approaching that dangerous period which [American Army] General Gavin and others have called the 'gap' or the 'missile-lag period'—a period, in the words of General Gavin, 'in which our own offensive and defensive missile capabilities will lag so far behind those of the Soviets as to place us in a position of great peril.'"[44] When the campaign began in earnest, Kennedy moved beyond Gavin's warning and proclaimed that the gap was not a future fear but present fact.

The "missile gap" was a powerful sound bite. It resonated among Canadians and Americans who had been taught to fear communists under their beds and over their heads and to prefer being dead than red. The missile gap invited them to be even more frightened. Canadians heard themselves referenced when Kennedy laid out six keys to deterring a Soviet attack. The second: "The adequacy of American defenses to reduce the success of that Soviet striking power . . . will include our distant early warning system, anti-missile missiles when available and other interceptor and defense devices."[45] He concluded with a list of military steps that needed to be taken, including, "Our continental defense system, as already mentioned, must be redesigned for the detection and interception of missile attacks as well as planes."[46]

Throughout the campaign, Kennedy returned again and again to the missile gap. He argued that America was in trouble and millions of lives were in jeopardy because the Soviets had so many more missiles than the United States. Money must be found, he said, to close the missile gap while bolstering the military if America was to continue as a world leader, or indeed to survive. He returned so often to the missile gap that friends worried about him overplaying his hand. Canadian John Kenneth Galbraith, for instance, was a Harvard University economist who had published the popular and influential 1958 book *The Affluent Society* and become a trusted Kennedy confidant. He wrote to Kennedy's pollster and political advisor Lou Harris, "J.F.K. has made the point that he isn't soft. Henceforth he can only frighten."[47]

The problem with the missile gap was that there was no missile gap. Eisenhower had U-2 spy plane evidence demonstrating that it did not exist. Despite Khrushchev's brazen threats and spectacular rocket launches, the American president knew the Soviet Union had fewer warheads and missiles than the United States. However, he could say nothing about this knowledge without exposing how he had acquired it and so he remained silent, sacrificing partisan advantage to national security.[48] Khrushchev knew what Eisenhower knew. He admitted to his son Sergei that part of the reason he could never allow Americans to inspect Soviet sites—or, later, to accept Kennedy's September 1963 offer to co-operate in space exploration—was that it would shatter the illusion of Soviet strength. Sergei later remarked, "We have nothing to hide. We have nothing. And we must hide it."[49]

As happens with all presidential candidates, Kennedy received regular briefings from national security staff. He was told that there was no missile gap. Despite knowing the truth, he continued to sell the illusion.[50] Later, in a December 1962 Oval Office meeting, Kennedy's secretary of defence spoke of the budget problems inherent in rectifying the missile gap that had been created by "emotionally guided but nonetheless patriotic" individuals. Kennedy grinned and sheepishly admitted that he had been one of them.[51]

Diefenbaker carefully monitored the race for the White House. He remained unmoved by Kennedy's charm and celebrity. He had met Nixon several times and respected his wisdom and experience. He maintained his belief that the young senator was brash and dangerous and his hope that Nixon would beat him.[52] Diefenbaker's September meeting with Eisenhower and Macmillan at the UN occurred the day after the first televised presidential debate, where a cool, tanned, well-briefed Kennedy had outperformed an ill and ill-prepared Nixon. Diefenbaker expressed disappointment in the result. He said that Nixon should not have agreed to debate Kennedy in the first place, as he had everything to lose and nothing to gain.[53]

Diefenbaker also watched the subsequent debates and observed to an aide that Kennedy had stumbled when discussing two islands near China that the Chinese claimed as their own but America was pledged to defend. He believed the manner in which Kennedy had spoken revealed him to be untrustworthy. Diefenbaker wondered if Kennedy had the character needed to follow Eisenhower.[54]

The election was razor close. Of the 68.8 million votes cast on November 8, 1960, Kennedy won only 118,574 more than Nixon. It was the closest presidential election since Grover Cleveland's even narrower popular-vote victory in 1884. Although nearly tied in terms of cast ballots, Kennedy won 303 electoral college votes to Nixon's 219. Nixon was told of voter fraud in a number of states, most blatantly in Illinois, but seeking to do the honourable thing, he ignored his advisors and did not contest the results.[55]

On the day after the election, a troubled Diefenbaker told an aide that with Kennedy in the White House the world would be closer to war than it had been in years.[56] He nonetheless sent a congratulatory letter to the president-elect. Two weeks passed without a reply. Only after Ambassador Heeney inquired as to a possible problem did Kennedy send not a letter but a brief and impersonal telegram.[57] Diefenbaker never forgot the perceived insult.

Just days before Eisenhower was to leave office, he met Diefenbaker for the last time. They affixed their signatures to the Columbia River

Treaty, which, like the St. Lawrence Seaway agreement before it, was the culmination of years of successful bilateral negotiations and co-operation on an infrastructure project that promised benefits for both nations. They escaped their aides to enjoy a brief walk during which they chatted about family and other non-political matters, as would two old friends.

Before leaving office, Eisenhower sent personal letters to only five national leaders, one of whom was Diefenbaker. "As the moment approaches for me to relinquish the duties of my present office, my thoughts turn to the friendly association I have been privileged to have with you over these many months," he wrote. "I shall look forward to any future opportunity to renew our personal contacts."[58]

Eisenhower left for a well-earned retirement on his idyllic Gettysburg farm. The old soldier was able to sip his coffee each morning and reflect on the wars he had fought and avoided while gazing over the fields on which a spectacular Civil War battle had been waged almost a hundred years before. He could also be satisfied that communications and relations with America's northern neighbour were on a solid foundation. However, while Ike looked out over the old battlefield, a new and potentially more deadly one was being prepared.

# F O U R

---

# THREE HOURS IN WASHINGTON

## FEBRUARY 20, 1961

JOHN G. DIEFENBAKER AND JOHN F. KENNEDY had met once before. The prime minister and senator had shaken hands and exchanged a few words at a Washington reception. That brief encounter and Kennedy's presidential campaign were all it took. Diefenbaker didn't care for him. His animosity was unsurprising, really. Diefenbaker had devoted his life to backing folks with little money or power against those with plenty of both. He had no time for people born on second base who acted like they'd hit a double, and Kennedy was born on third. He was a brave, smart, and tremendously hard-working man whose great station and poor health offered easy excuses to do nothing for anyone. Instead, he dedicated himself to public service. He donated his public office paycheques to charity. But his privileged upbringing and family's ostentatious affluence and influence nonetheless represented everything that Diefenbaker disdained.

Kennedy often joked about his family's wealth and power. One evening in 1958, for instance, he interrupted a speech to produce a fake telegram from his father and pretended to read: "Jack. Don't buy a single vote more than necessary. I'll be damned if I'm going to pay for a landslide."[1] Diefenbaker was as unamused by such jokes as former president Harry

Truman. When asked about Kennedy's Catholicism, Truman replied, "It's not the Pope I'm afraid of, it's the Pop."[2]

Diefenbaker's opinion of Kennedy was hardened by the president-elect's delayed response to his post-election congratulatory note. Then, after having endured a lifetime of nativist slurs regarding his Germanic name, he was insulted when, at the February 8 White House press conference announcing his upcoming visit, Kennedy had called him "Deefunbawker."

More than his visceral distaste for the man, Diefenbaker was concerned about Kennedy's view of Canada. Two weeks before the January 20, 1961, inauguration, Kennedy's incoming secretary of state Dean Rusk met for forty-five minutes with Canadian ambassador Arnold Heeney. In his professorial tone and Georgian drawl, the Rhodes Scholar, war veteran, and long-time State Department official said he knew Canada well because of a few fishing trips he'd enjoyed with his son. Rusk said he and the president-elect believed Canada's special relationship with the United States was causing problems with other allies. He challenged Heeney to justify it.[3] Heeney was stunned. He patiently explained the nature and complexity of the two country's long and friendly interactions that, of course, Rusk must have already understood. Heeney warned Diefenbaker of Rusk's gamesmanship or Kennedy's veiled threat (he could not decide which was at play).[4] When told of Rusk's fishing reference, the prime minister snapped, "Is that all he thinks we are good for?"[5]

While Diefenbaker worried about the man he didn't like, Kennedy was warned about the man he didn't know. In preparation for the prime minister's White House visit, planned for a month after the inauguration, Rusk prepared a seventeen-page memorandum and attached a short biography of Diefenbaker. The documents contained great detail, such as the prime minister's slight deafness in his left ear and the fact that he was a teetotaller.

Rusk urged Kennedy to understand two points. First, Canada mattered to American security: "Loss [of] the contributions of the Canadian military . . . would be intolerable in [a] time of crisis."[6] Second, the recent surge in Canadian nationalism needed to be carefully understood in case it affected joint continental defence. Rusk wrote, "The primary problem the United States faces in its bilateral relations with Canada lies in an evolving attitude of introspection and nationalism . . . a Canadian inferiority complex which is reflected in a sensitivity to any real or fancied slight to Canadian sovereignty. Thus the essential element in problems involving Canada tends to be psychological."[7]

Because Canadian nationalism could pose a threat to American security, Rusk explored it in some depth. Ignoring that Canadians were linked by a complex and unique identity and had known the rush of national pride before, he argued that their nationalism was not boosted but born with Canada's contributions in the Second World War and post-war prosperity.[8] That conclusion led Rusk to Diefenbaker.

Kennedy read that Diefenbaker was Canadian nationalism's greatest advocate. However, Rusk wrote, the prime minister's speeches and policy initiatives were just reactions to domestic political problems. Diefenbaker was not "really interested" in promoting Canada's self-interest. Rusk argued, "The Conservative Party is motivated now by a desire to bolster its waning popularity."[9] This alleged political desperation was leading Diefenbaker to become more "self-assertive" and "insistent" about Canada's interests, and more "anti-American."[10]

With his groundwork laid, Rusk detailed a number of bilateral issues that needed to be addressed. Most crucial among them was Canada's accepting American nuclear weapons for its European- and Canadian-based weapons systems. Rusk believed that Diefenbaker would eventually take the weapons but that he was procrastinating partly because external affairs minister Howard Green was such a strong and internationally known advocate for nuclear disarmament. He conceded that Green's disarmament goals were similar to America's but concluded that Green was a problem because, like his prime minister, he was a "strong nationalist and a hyper-sensitive guardian of sovereignty."[11]

Rusk advised that the delay in accepting American nuclear weapons was confusing the Canadian public and encouraging the growth of anti-nuclear groups. Diefenbaker and Green were creating problems for Kennedy and endangering Americans, Rusk argued, by encouraging Canadians to consider what was best for them, or, as he put it, "promoting an undesirable introspection regarding the country's present and future defence role, particularly with reference to the United States."[12]

The document concluded, "Diefenbaker is vigorous, self-confident, and a shrewd politician and he brought his party back into power on a dynamic platform of Canadian nationalism. He is not believed to have any basic prejudice against the United States."[13] Rusk advised that the best way to approach Diefenbaker was to offer consultation on all nuclear matters. He concluded, with no hint that he appreciated or cared about his condescending tone, that the prime minister, like all Canadians, would respond favourably if offered respectful, friendly, and intimate contact with American officials.[14]

Diefenbaker's visit would occur just as Kennedy was reorienting America's Cold War strategy. Eisenhower had sought to avoid direct confrontation with the Soviet Union by overseeing covert operations and initiating his New Look nuclear deterrent. He wanted a secure and stable coexistence. Kennedy, on the other hand, seemed to mean what he'd said on the campaign trail and in the soaring prose of his inaugural address. He saw America as lagging behind in a race for supremacy and survival; it needed to quickly catch up, and be willing to pay any price or bear any burden to do so. Kennedy wanted a new world order in which America would be safer because, as he had argued so long ago in *Why England Slept*, none would question its awesome power or willingness to use it. The status quo would not do. Soviet imperialism and communism were to be engaged, rolled back, and defeated.[15]

Eisenhower's nature, experience, and Cold War vision had allowed him to respect Canadian sovereignty and the country's natural desire to determine its national self-interest as an important middle power. Kennedy was a younger man in a greater hurry. His belief in an immediate crisis, manifest in his invention and advocacy of the missile gap, and desire to push back Soviet advances meant he needed Canada to move quickly and step smartly into line. Diefenbaker's well-grounded, historically based civic nationalism and desire to enhance Canadian sovereignty were about to be hit by a freight train in a Brooks Brothers suit.

On the cool February morning that Diefenbaker boarded his Washington-bound plane, Kennedy had been president for four weeks. Diefenbaker, on the other hand, was a battle-hardened veteran of three and a half years. He had been elected in an upset then re-elected in a landslide. He could boast a number of domestic political achievements despite the obdurate recession that had begun before he took office and, although technically over, continued to inflict pain upon too many Canadians.

Diefenbaker's Roads to Resources initiative had seen highways built to the North from British Columbia and Saskatchewan, with more planned. The South Saskatchewan River Project was creating new hydro-electric power for a vast region while helping with irrigation and tourism. The Agricultural Rehabilitation and Development Act was increasing the amount and stability of farm wages while assisting with rural development, land use, and water conservation. Old-age pensions had been increased and provinces had been awarded more tax points that led to improvements in hospital insurance programs. Taxes had been lowered, with the middle class enjoying the greatest benefit. Winter job creation programs helped many people find employment. And while a great deal of work remained to be done before tragically overdue dignity and justice could be realized by Native peoples, an important step had been taken when Diefenbaker extended the franchise to Aboriginal adults.

His proudest achievement was the creation of the Canadian Bill of

Rights. Passed by the House of Commons in a unanimous vote in August 1960, it fulfilled his lifelong ambition to honour Canadian citizenship and move toward a greater guarantee of equality for all. Linked to the bill, and reflecting his determination to create an unhyphenated Canadian identity, he had the census changed so that in 1961, for the first time, rather than having to indicate their racial or ethnic background, citizens could check a box proclaiming to be Canadian.

Diefenbaker had also worked through the administrative learning curve common to many new governments. He had reacted to troubles by, among other things, adjusting his Cabinet. Since becoming external affairs minister in March 1959, Howard Green had proven himself quite adept at forwarding the disarmament side of the two-track nuclear policy. Defence Minister Pearkes, on the other hand, appeared less persuasive in promoting its pro-nuclear side. In October 1960, Diefenbaker replaced Pearkes with Douglas Harkness. Harkness had served with distinction as a lieutenant colonel in the Second World War's Sicily campaign. First elected to a Calgary riding in 1945, he demonstrated impressive political skills in the House and then as Diefenbaker's minister of agriculture. Harkness believed that all Canadian weapons systems should be equipped with American nuclear weapons as fervently as Green believed they should not. Smart, hard-working, and each convinced that his approach was correct, the two men were scorpions in a bottle. Having them serve together while promoting competing agendas was an initially artful but ultimately grievous decision. Only one of them could win, but Diefenbaker could lose.

On the plane to Washington, Green updated Diefenbaker on the current state of global disarmament talks and said he was hopeful that progress would soon be made. Cabinet secretary Robert Bryce briefed on a number of bilateral economic issues. Newly installed defence minister Harkness was not along for the trip.

The Canadians arrived at the White House North Portico a little after noon. Bright sunshine bathed the Oval Office in light. Kennedy and Diefenbaker, both thin and six feet tall, smiled and shook hands. After grouping them and their aides around the president's large desk for photographs, the press was ushered out and Diefenbaker sat alone on a white couch with Green, Bryce, and Heeney on another facing Rusk and Ambassador Merchant, who sat on a third. Kennedy gingerly took up the padded, red-oak rocking chair that somewhat eased the pain from his perennially problematic back.

Diefenbaker was invited to begin. He noted the long friendship enjoyed by the two countries. Guessing the president had been warned of Canada's anti-American sentiment, he broached the issue. He spoke of growing concern regarding American investment and corporate ownership, particularly in Canadian resource industries. That concern, however, should not be construed as anti-American. Kennedy nodded.[16]

They then embarked on a quick tour of the world's troubled spots and tested for areas of agreement. Diefenbaker's sincere anti-communist beliefs were made clear. Recent violence in the Congo's struggle for post-colonial independence, South Africa's racial conflicts, and tensions in Laos and Vietnam were discussed and dispatched relatively quickly. The first snag came when Diefenbaker raised China.

Following the Second World War, the United States had supported Chiang Kai-shek's Nationalists in the Chinese Civil War. In 1949, Nationalist forces withdrew to the island of Taiwan, and America recognized the government there as China's legitimate rulers. Mao Zedong's communist government in Beijing was deemed a temporary aberration. America's position made less sense with every year that Mao remained in power. As Diefenbaker had argued with Eisenhower and many other world leaders, he said the Beijing government should be recognized. He explained that Canadian-Chinese trade preceded Mao's revolution and that even if recognition did not happen, Canada's trade in non-strategic goods would continue.[17]

Kennedy agreed that Communist China would eventually be recognized. However, he would not be altering the long-standing policy of containing and isolating "Red" China while offering unbending support for Taiwan.[18] Diefenbaker moved to his real reason for mentioning China in the first place. He said that America's China policy was hurting Canada. He explained that tons of Canadian wheat that had been sold to China were at that moment rotting in British Columbia warehouses. The wheat sales were important economically to Canada, but they were essential to China, which was in the midst of a food shortage. (Over the next few years, fifteen million to thirty million Chinese people starved to death.[19]) Further, America's Trading with the Enemy Act and Foreign Assets Control (FAC) regulations prevented New Jersey's Standard Oil from participating in Chinese trade. Therefore, its Canadian subsidiary, Imperial Oil, was unable to provide bunker oil to the ships waiting to transport the wheat.

As part of their preparation for the trip, Ambassador Heeney and others had met with State Department officials and deputy national security assistant Walter Rostow. Among the things they discussed was the wheat and oil question.[20] Consequently, when Kennedy asked for a copy of the pertinent regulations, staff had one handy.

Kennedy began reading aloud, but Diefenbaker was in no mood to play student to the president's tutorial. He interrupted, saying that he already knew and understood the law and regulations. He needed Kennedy to understand that American legislation should not restrict Canada's freedom of action. Diefenbaker explained that a similar situation had arisen in 1958, when FAC regulations stopped the Ford Motor Company of Canada from quoting on a Chinese contract. His working with Dulles and Eisenhower had led to the establishment of appropriate exemptions that allowed Canadian subsidiaries of American companies to sell non-strategic goods to China. The agreement was based, Diefenbaker explained, on Eisenhower's recognition of Canadian sovereignty. One country should not be able to pass laws that restricted the economic activity and autonomy of another.[21] Kennedy sat with the regulations on his lap and said nothing.

Diefenbaker continued to press. All Kennedy had to do to solve the current wheat problem and ensure that similar difficulties would not arise again, he said, was to implement policies that matched the ideas he had raised in his University of New Brunswick speech back in October 1957. Kennedy was reminded of having said: "Canada has achieved a national strength and prestige which simply does not allow any portrayal of the country as an appendage of either Great Britain or the United States. To be sure, Canada has some special links with each of these two English-speaking nations, but it possesses most certainly a national destiny of its own to which it is well and timely to give foremost recognition."[22]

Quoting a man to himself is always tricky. Kennedy did not take the bait that Diefenbaker, the old fisherman, had laid before him. He suggested that to resolve the Imperial Oil case, Canada should apply for an exemption to the FAC regulation. Diefenbaker said no. He would not be satisfied with an exemption for just this case. Canada should not, he said, accept a situation where it would have to return, cap in hand, to argue future case-by-case exemptions. Doing so would imply that the United States retained a right to interfere with Canadian business transactions. Caught off-guard by Diefenbaker's forcefulness, Kennedy promised to study the Imperial Oil situation.[23]

Diefenbaker then pivoted to a related point. He explained the decade of pain that America was inflicting on Canadian farmers. In the 1950s, a dramatic increase in American trade and agricultural subsidies had led to a 10 percent rise in the amount of cheap American wheat being sold in European markets. Canada suffered a 7 percent decline in wheat sales to the region. Canada's share of global wheat sales had fallen from 27.4 percent to 20.6 percent while the American share had risen from 10 percent to 41.9 percent.[24] The St. Laurent government had complained to Eisenhower but nothing had been done.

Shortly after the 1957 election, and in keeping with his trade diversification goals, Diefenbaker had sent officials to China, India, and elsewhere to secure new markets to replace the European sales being swiped by the United States. The initiative led to the signing of a number of new deals, including one with China. However, American FAC regulations had complicated some deals and blocked others. Diefenbaker brought the problem to Eisenhower and Canadian wheat was soon on its way to China.[25] Now, Diefenbaker explained, it was frustrating to have to fight an old battle with a new president.

Kennedy remained cool. Returning again to the specific case at hand, he promised do what he could to bend FAC regulations so Imperial Oil could sell fuel to the waiting British and Norwegian ships. But, he repeated, he would only do so if Diefenbaker made a specific, formal, and public request to the State Department. Even then, his support for the exception would be granted only if Canada could prove that it had no domestically available bunker fuel. It was Diefenbaker's turn to maintain his cool as he heard the American president detailing what he would allow a Canadian company and the Canadian government to do. Once again, Diefenbaker said no.[26]

When later told of the Oval Office standoff, finance minister Donald Fleming observed that "Kennedy seemed very slow to grasp the Canadian point of view."[27] Fleming was wrong. Kennedy understood perfectly. He was simply more concerned about his Cold War instincts and American policy regarding Communist China than about Canada making its own trade decisions. He was no doubt also abiding Rusk's warnings about Canadian nationalism.

The president moved the subject sideways and stated that he opposed Canada's trade with Cuba. Diefenbaker was taken aback but replied that, as with China, Canadian companies had been interacting with Cuba for decades and would continue to trade in non-strategic goods. Besides, he added with a little dig, despite Eisenhower's 1959 embargo, Canadian trade with Cuba was still less than America's. Kennedy let the Cuba discussion drop, perhaps because at that moment the Central Intelligence Agency (CIA) and Cuban refugees in a Guatemalan jungle were planning a bold move that he hoped would change the game.[28]

With mounting tension filling the sunny room, Kennedy turned from trade to terror. He asked Diefenbaker to explain his government's policy regarding American nuclear weapons. The prime minister outlined his two-track policy and said Canada would meet its NORAD and NATO responsibilities. Employing a metaphor recently coined by Pearson, he said Canada would not limit itself to a "bird-watching position." "We will not," he assured Kennedy, "accept a policy which will lay upon the United States a responsibility which we should carry ourselves."[29] Canadian negotiators had been told, he said, to insist upon joint custody and the Canadian government's right to decide when Canadian-based weapons would be fired.[30] There would be no annihilation without representation.

Kennedy replied that he would encourage his negotiators to establish a double or two-key system, like that employed by Britain, in which an American and British general ostensibly had to co-operate to initiate a launch. The two-key system sounded good. However, it is not evident whether Kennedy or Diefenbaker understood or would say out loud that double-key was doublespeak. In fact, the two-key system was designed to safeguard against accidental launches and malfunctions and not to guarantee that two governments would have to agree before firing.[31]

Further, they must have understood, although again neither said, that American nuclear weapons would not come to Canada by themselves. Accepting the weapons meant accepting more American soldiers on Canadian soil. American detachments had been in Newfoundland and Labrador, not yet part of Canada, since the 1941 Roosevelt-Churchill land lease deal that swapped bases for fifty old destroyers. On the day that Diefenbaker and Kennedy sat talking in the White House, the bases remained strategically important to the Americans and a welcome source of employment to many Newfoundlanders. The proposed nukes would thereby test sovereignty while boosting solvency. With so much left unsaid, Kennedy agreed to advance the negotiations along the lines that Diefenbaker outlined.[32]

They broke for a working lunch in the West Wing's elegant Family Dining Room. Howard Green later said that, while in the cloakroom, Kennedy quietly approached him with an assurance that he supported his efforts toward disarmament.[33] Kennedy also spoke with one of his aides— a conversation that enabled him to tell Diefenbaker after lunch that changes would be made to ensure that American laws would not stop the transport of Canadian wheat to China.

The break allowed Kennedy and Diefenbaker to become better acquainted. Kennedy teased, "Would I be right in thinking that the United States is not unhelpful to you for political purposes in Canada."[34] Diefenbaker smiled and said that it would not be an inaccurate conclusion. They admired a large, mounted sailfish that Kennedy boasted of having caught during his Acapulco honeymoon. He asked if Diefenbaker, who he had been told was an avid fisherman, had ever caught one as large. Diefenbaker bragged that just a few weeks before he had landed a 140-pound blue marlin off the coast of Jamaica. Kennedy laughed and taunted, "You didn't catch it!"[35]

Diefenbaker noticed how the Oval Office had changed since Eisenhower's time. It had reflected the old general's Spartan lifestyle with everything in its place and paintings portraying pastoral scenes. Kennedy's Oval Office was still beautiful, with the same green-grey carpet and curtains, but it now reflected a man more comfortable with clutter; paintings of vessels in rough waters spoke of his love for the sea. The large and ornately carved desk had been a gift from Queen Victoria to President Hayes in 1879. It was made from timbers from the British Arctic exploration ship *Resolute*. On the desk was an etching of PT-109 and beside it, encased in plastic, rested the coconut Kennedy had carved to seek rescue from the South Pacific island. There was also a small brass plaque inscribed with the fisherman's prayer: "O, God, Thy sea is so great, and my boat is so small."

Diefenbaker said nothing about the changes but remarked on a couple of paintings that depicted American ships triumphing over British vessels in the War of 1812. The war had been a source of argument for decades, with American textbooks claiming an American victory while generations of Canadians were taught that Britain and Canada had won. Canadian kids loved the stories about a brave Laura Secord warning of invading Americans and of British troops burning the White House. Diefenbaker told Kennedy of a British naval triumph in the war but Kennedy, the history buff, said he'd never heard of it. He promised that if a painting depicting that battle could be located he would hang it with the others.[36]

During the working lunch, the group traded salacious gossip while sipping soup. Then, obviously unsatisfied by the progress made, Kennedy again raised the nuclear weapons question. Diefenbaker repeated what he had said. The American record of his response is important in light of all that came later: "The Canadian Government will not decide at the present time whether or not Canadian forces should be equipped with nuclear weapons. Efforts in the disarmament field are still in progress. If and when the Canadian Government reaches this decision, there must be provision for joint control and joint custody. . . . The president expressed his pleasure at this willingness to move ahead in this field . . ."[37] There could have been no misunderstanding of Diefenbaker's position.

With cordial goodbyes, the encounter ended at 2:45 p.m. As Diefenbaker and Heeney walked from the White House to their waiting car, they agreed that things "could not have gone better."[38] In the House of Commons later that afternoon, the prime minister characterized the visit as "a revealing and exhilarating experience. The President . . . has the kind of personality that leaves upon one the impression of a person dedicated to peace, to the raising of economic standards not only in his own country but in all countries, and to the achievement in his day of disarmament among all the nations of the world."[39] The meeting, he said, left him quite pleased with the state of Canadian-American relations. He outlined some of the issues covered and concluded that his underlying goal was met because he and Kennedy had agreed upon "the distinctive quality of the Canada-US partnership, with each nation discharging its responsibility towards the attainment of the common purpose and without the sacrifice of sovereignty by either country."[40] He also announced that President Kennedy and his wife, Jacqueline, had accepted his invitation to visit Ottawa.

While Diefenbaker had revised his opinion of Kennedy, the visit merely cemented Kennedy's thoughts on Diefenbaker. He had been unable to charm or cajole the stubborn Canadian into doing anything he had wanted him to do. He told aide Arthur Schlesinger that he found Diefenbaker insincere and untrustworthy. Those around Kennedy knew the worst crime one could perpetrate was to bore him. Diefenbaker had committed that offence. Kennedy told his brother, Robert, "I don't want to see that boring son of a bitch again."[41]

Diefenbaker's triumphant day ended in sadness. His mother had died while he was away in Washington. He was told after his late-afternoon address to the House. After lingering in a Saskatoon hospital for nearly a year and suffering a number of ailments and then dementia, Mary had finally succumbed. It was to his mother that Diefenbaker had first expressed his dream of someday occupying the prime minister's office. And it was there he learned that the long, painful goodbye to the woman he cherished was over.

# F I V E

---

# THE TRIUMPHANT AND TERRIBLE SPRING

IN MARCH 1960, Diefenbaker was horrified to read that South African police had fired from armoured vehicles into a non-violent protest outside the Sharpeville municipal office.[1] Sixty-nine people, many of them children, were killed. Scores more were wounded. The massacre sparked international condemnation of South Africa's segregationist political system of apartheid. As an accepted social practice, apartheid had grown more virulent by degrees after the end of the Boer War in 1902. In 1948, South Africa's all-white government enshrined apartheid into law. Black South Africans could not vote or hold elected office, were restricted in where they could live, work, play, associate, travel, and much more.

American response to the Sharpeville massacre was muddied. Henry Cabot Lodge moved a motion at the UN's Security Council to "deplore" the killings, but the State Department immediately issued a press release insisting that he had acted without instruction. It clarified that the United States "regrets the tragic loss of life" and, ironically, given what was happening in Southeast Asia and Central America at the time, that it did not make a practice of interfering in the internal matters of other countries. Eisenhower remained silent. He was worried that any statement would invite comparisons with American racial laws, Jim Crow practices, and race-based violence.[2]

Canada's response was different. Diefenbaker had spoken against racial and ethnic discrimination his whole life. He rose in the House of Commons and condemned the Sharpeville massacre as a tragedy that should never have happened. He said it sprang from apartheid, a system that was wrong in South Africa because racial discrimination is wrong everywhere. He urged the South African government to end apartheid not only because it was morally right to do so but also before it led to either a tyranny to maintain it or a revolution to end it.[3] He soon had a chance to put his words and convictions into action.

After a whites-only referendum in October 1960, the South African government had announced its desire to become a republic but remain in the Commonwealth. According to Commonwealth rules, it had to first withdraw from the organization and then apply for re-entry. Its application would be considered at London's March 1961 Commonwealth Conference, just two months after Kennedy's inauguration. British prime minister Harold Macmillan was the conference chair. He had already announced his support for South Africa's return. Diefenbaker warned him that Canada would oppose re-entry unless accompanied by a pledge to purge apartheid.[4] Macmillan wrote and then phoned Diefenbaker in an attempt to swing him to the British position. Diefenbaker refused to budge.

The conference began with palpable tension among the delegates and within the Canadian delegation. Diefenbaker wanted apartheid ended, a split between white and black Commonwealth member states avoided, and Canada's small but important South African trade, including military equipment, protected.[5] His broad consultations included a meeting with African National Congress leader Oliver Tambo. He urged Diefenbaker to join the fight that he and Nelson Mandela were waging against monumental odds.[6]

When Diefenbaker's time came to address the conference, he said that apartheid stood against Canadian values and those for which the Commonwealth should stand. He argued that welcoming South Africa back would be interpreted as Commonwealth members supporting the country's harsh enforcement of abhorrent racial policies. Not only would the Commonwealth be hurt, but communists could also win adherents in Africa and elsewhere by speaking of white colonizers oppressing black majorities. While he stopped short of declaring that South Africa should not be readmitted, his stark analysis left little doubt as to his opinion.[7] He had put Canada on the side of India and African countries and left Britain, New Zealand, and Australia on their own.

Speaking as he did took considerable political courage: he had canvassed his Cabinet and opinions being expressed in Canadian newspapers and found them as split as his advisors and the Commonwealth delegates in London.[8] He stuck to his guns. When Macmillan proposed a weak communiqué that avoided criticizing South African racial policies, Diefenbaker demanded a clearer reflection of points made. On the conference's third day, with momentum moving toward the positions championed by Diefenbaker and India's Jawaharlal Nehru, South Africa withdrew its application. Apartheid suffered its first blow.

Diefenbaker's opposition to Macmillan was the first but not the last time that he would confound critics and those accusing him of wanting to move Canada backward by re-lacing old British ties. His actions were as noteworthy and politically courageous as any Kennedy had celebrated in his prize-winning book. The prime minister had put Canada on the right side of history. Among the crowd of those who understood the moment's importance and met him at Ottawa's airport to offer congratulations were two young Progressive Conservatives in their twenties who would one day succeed him: Joe Clark and Brian Mulroney.[9]

While Diefenbaker was concerning himself with the dusty, bloody roads of Sharpeville, Kennedy was being humiliated on a hot beach in Cuba. His Cuban misadventure began two years earlier, on January 2, 1959, when

Fidel Castro and Che Guevara led their tired, triumphant revolutionaries past cheering crowds lining Havana's wide boulevards. Castro's revolution overthrew the ruthless and corrupt Fulgencio Batista, who had stolen power in 1952 and then kept it largely due to America's muscle, money, and mob.

The revolution enraged a great number of powerful Americans. American investors had controlled Cuba's economy through their ownership or domination of mining, oil, telephone and electric facilities, and sugar production. Seventy-four percent of all Cuban exports were sold in the United States. Havana was a playground for gamblers and others wanting a filthy, forgotten weekend. There were too many dollars at stake to trust a gang of bearded young men who were not known or owned, and who owed nothing.

Eisenhower, nonetheless, quickly recognized the new Cuban government and sent an ambassador. He approved $800 million in aid.[10] However, Castro soon consolidated his power by punishing enemies with arrests, assassinations, and an absurd show trial. The White House took notice but did not react. It had to do something, though, when Castro began nationalizing foreign-owned businesses and expropriating foreign-owned land and giving it to peasants. Eisenhower revealed his growing fears in a July 6 diary entry in which he called Castro "a little Hitler."[11]

Eisenhower placed embargoes on Cuban-American trade in guns, sugar, and oil. Months of diplomatic ping-pong followed as tougher embargoes led to more nationalized property and businesses and then more embargoes. Castro eventually seized about a billion dollars in American-owned assets, including the mob-owned casinos.[12] In October 1960, Eisenhower announced further embargoes and shuttered the American embassy.

Eisenhower's actions in Cuba were consistent with the Roosevelt Corollary to the Monroe Doctrine. Castro's audacity could encourage other Latin American nationalists and his increasingly close relationship with the Soviet Union was unacceptable.[13] Eisenhower privately approved CIA plans for removing Castro through the same covert tactics that had overthrown governments in Iran in 1953 and in Guatemala the year after.[14] Presidential candidates Nixon and Kennedy were briefed.

Two days after assuming office, Kennedy met with CIA director Allen Dulles. Dulles and national security advisors approved the final plan. CIA trained, Guatemalan-based Cuban exiles would storm the south coast Bay of Pigs beach just before dawn. They would establish a provisional government. Cubans would greet them as liberators and Castro would be doomed. Dulles said they needed to move quickly before the exiles lost their nerve and the region lost its weather.[15] With his goal of pushing communism back everywhere so recently and boldly proclaimed in his inaugural address, the new president could hardly refuse a chance to give it a shove just ninety miles from Florida's coast.[16] He signed off.

Eight American B-26 bombers, repainted to look like Cuban aircraft, left Nicaragua and thundered through the Cuban sky on April 15, 1961. They attacked three airfields but destroyed only five of Castro's thirty-six planes. Two days later, the exiles hit the beach. It was supposed to be a surprise and it was supposed to be dark—it was neither. They were torn apart. With men dying on the sand, Kennedy was told to save the mission by approving American air strikes. He refused. The invasion quickly tumbled into a deadly debacle. After two days of smoke, blood, and confusion it was over. One hundred and fourteen exiles were killed and 1,189 were marched down crowded streets past jeers and cheers to dirty jails.

The Bay of Pigs handed Kennedy a failure and Diefenbaker a problem. Canadian-Cuban connections date back to 1601, when Samuel de Champlain spent four months on the island. Trade in fish, wood, rum, and sugar began in the nineteenth century. Economic relations developed steadily. Canada left Britain's Cuban legation for its own in 1945. By the 1950s, Canada's banks held 28 percent of Cuban deposits, and its life insurance companies issued 75 percent of its policies.[17] Diefenbaker approved the recognition of Castro's government a day after the British and Americans. Canada's commercial secretary wrote from Havana,

"Canadians are warmly regarded by the new revolutionary government and by the Cuban people, at a time when both the United States and Britain are under a cloud here due to support given the previous regime."[18]

Three months after taking power, Castro had been well received on an American tour, though Eisenhower played golf to avoid him. On April 26, 1959, Castro arrived in Montreal. He asked RCMP officials to help train his police and security forces and was cheered that evening when he spontaneously dropped in at a number of events around the city. He was to meet with Diefenbaker, but problems at home forced him to leave the next day.

When Castro nationalized all remaining foreign assets in October 1960, he exempted Canadian firms. When Royal Bank and Bank of Nova Scotia shareholders got jittery and decided to leave Cuba, Castro arranged for the protection of their people and assets and ensured they were paid market value for buildings and properties. Meanwhile, Canadian trade in newsprint and food products increased to meet the vacuum created by the American withdrawal.

Every country in the western hemisphere followed Eisenhower's lead in cutting Cuban ties—except Mexico and Canada. Diefenbaker's independent stand drew biting American criticism. The Canadian embassy in Washington and consulate in New York were picketed.[19] Diefenbaker was warned that because of the anti-Canadian sentiment among Florida's Cuban exiles, he should cancel his winter vacation to the state. He brushed off concerns and headed south.[20]

During Diefenbaker's White House visit, Kennedy spoke of his concerns regarding Canadian trade with Cuba. The next month, Secretary of State Rusk blasted Ambassador Heeney for Canada's ongoing relations with Castro. Rusk said the United States would not allow a communist government to stay on the island and that Kennedy would do anything, including military intervention, to crush it. Heeney explained the history of Canadian-Cuban interaction and his belief in influencing communist governments through active engagement. Rusk insisted, "U.S. policy was not going to be altered because Canada didn't like it."[21] Heeney had not asked for an alteration. Days later, the doomed men hit the Cuban beach. As a good leader must, Kennedy publicly, personally, and gracefully shouldered the blame. But he was shattered. He wondered aloud to aides how he had been so stupid.[22]

Diefenbaker's reaction to the fiasco was measured. In a speech to the House he spoke of his regret for the loss of life and acknowledged that Castro was a communist. He did not overtly criticize Kennedy but said, "Like many other small and defenceless countries [Cuba is] part of a global ideological contest in which the interests of the Cuban people have been subordinated to the interplay of outside forces beyond their control."[23]

External Affairs Minister Green was less discreet. He was informed of the Bay of Pigs operation while attending a NATO meeting in Oslo. He told reporters that the invasion was a mistake and offered Canada as a mediator between Cuba and the United States. Kennedy was angered by Green's remarks and ordered Rusk to teach the Canadians about the complexities of the Cuban situation from the American point of view. Heeney was summoned to the State Department for yet another scolding.[24]

Four months after the Bay of Pigs fiasco, Castro's lieutenant Che Guevara sent a box of Kennedy's favourite Cuban cigars to presidential aide Richard Goodwin. The gesture led to a meeting where the young rebel told the shocked Goodwin that Castro wanted to re-establish relations with the United States and end contact with the Soviet Union. Goodwin rushed to Washington. While puffing one of the cigars, Kennedy reclined in his rocker and declined the offer. The Bay of Pigs was too recent. Plus, an agreement to live with Castro might be interpreted by other Latin American countries as US acceptance of Marxist-leaning governments in the hemisphere.[25] And the bottom line was this: Kennedy didn't want co-existence with the Cuban communist; he wanted him gone.

The primary lesson Kennedy learned from his Cuban disaster was the same one that Diefenbaker had gleaned from his rushed NORAD decision: he would never again fully trust his generals or accept military advice without tough and thorough questioning.[26] He told his close friend and influential journalist Benjamin Bradlee, "The first advice I'm going to give my successor is to watch the generals and to avoid feeling that just because they were military men their opinions on military matters are worth a damn."[27] Heads rolled, including that of CIA director Allen Dulles. Kennedy also approved a new covert program called Operation Mongoose to disrupt the Cuban economy, weaken the government, and depose or even assassinate Castro. A few weeks later, battle-scarred but wiser and more determined than ever to bring the stubborn Diefenbaker on side, Kennedy headed to Ottawa.

After his humiliating loss in the 1958 election, Lester Pearson considered quitting politics.[28] Who could blame him? He was sixty-one years old with a distinguished diplomatic career that included a Nobel Prize. But after long conversations with his wife and a number of trusted friends, most importantly confidant and advisor Walter Gordon, he decided that rather than retire he would rebuild.

His first step was the creation of the Study Conference on National Problems. In September 1960, two hundred relatively young academics, journalists, bureaucrats, and a few Liberal MPs gathered at Queen's University in Kingston, Ontario. Liberals hoped that the group understood the new television age, was more attuned to Elvis than Ike, and could change the party from the old-guard beast their grandparents had known to an effective machine for the future.[29] Many of them would later play major roles, including John Turner, Judy LaMarsh, Jean Marchand, Keith Davey, Maurice Sauvé, and Pauline Jewett. The conference was a valiant attempt to marry policy and politics.

The conference's pivotal moment was a speech by journalist Tom Kent, who argued that Canadians were moving left. He spoke of the growing

numbers being attracted to the CCF in Canada and the Democrats in the
United States.[30] The party, he argued, had to grab a liberal, progressive
flag, run left to meet the people, and then jump out in front to lead them.
Pearson was persuaded.[31] Five months later, at a national Liberal rally
convened in Ottawa, the party adopted a new platform that reflected the
Kingston ideas and called for universal health care, a new Canadian pension plan, urban renewal, a more widely available and generous unemployment insurance scheme, and a guaranteed income supplement.

While Pearson's Liberals were taking notice of Kennedy and his
Democratic constituency, two years earlier, Kennedy had noticed Pearson.
In October 1958, Pearson had delivered a series of lectures at the Fletcher
School of Law and Diplomacy at Boston's Tufts University. Harvard
University Press subsequently published the lectures as a small book entitled *Diplomacy in the Nuclear Age*. Pearson wrote of avenues to peace and
celebrated the roles of professional diplomats and international organizations such as NATO. Senator Kennedy enjoyed it so much that, with Ted
Sorensen's help, he penned a glowing review for the August edition of the
popular magazine *Saturday Review*. It began with a blushingly positive
assessment of Pearson:

> Still in full vigour as leader of the Opposition in Canada,
> Mr. Pearson's stature cannot be assessed for another decade. Yet
> already 'Mike' Pearson has been the chief architect of the Canadian
> foreign service, probably unequalled in any nation; he has been a
> brilliant ambassador and foreign secretary; he has been a central
> figure in the growth of the Atlantic Community and NATO,
> even taking a leading role in the shaping of the United Nations.
> In diplomacy he has always been the guardian of good sense and
> has enjoyed the confidence of very many nations. He has also
> been a superb interlocutor between the realm of statesmanship
> and scholarship.[32]

Kennedy's review expressed support for the book's contention that it was dangerous to base military policy solely upon nuclear deterrence. Kennedy agreed with Pearson's observation that the Cold War contest was being played out not just between the US and the Soviet Union but as "a competition of alliances." Further to the point, Kennedy praised Pearson's criticism of the "silent subservience of Soviet allies" and his celebration of the Western model where allies are encouraged to be independent, outspoken, and critical.[33] His review no doubt helped the sales of Pearson's book. He would soon be helping Pearson even more.

# S I X

---

# THREE DAYS IN OTTAWA

## MAY 16 TO 18, 1961

AIR FORCE ONE TOUCHED DOWN at Ottawa's Uplands airport on a cool and overcast Tuesday afternoon. Two thousand guests rose from their bleacher seats inside the massive Royal Canadian Air Force (RCAF) Hangar 11 as five hundred children screamed and waved little American and Canadian flags. A roar of applause erupted as the plane's big white door yawned open to reveal the president and Mrs. Kennedy. Tanned from a recent Florida vacation, they paused, smiled, and waved before descending the stairs. They moved slowly, shook hands with Governor General Georges Vanier, Diefenbaker, and their wives and then strolled along the red carpet into the hangar. Coronation trumpets blared a royal welcome. The Honour Guard was inspected, an RCMP band played the American national anthem, and outside, a twenty-one-gun salute pierced the breeze.

Troubles began when the dignitaries assembled on the large stage. Diefenbaker gazed at the crowd, television cameras, the RCMP's hundred-man Colour Guard, and glowered at the American security agents, conspicuous in their steely attentiveness. In preparing for the visit, a disgruntled Diefenbaker had told aides that surely Canadians could protect the president and, as such, there was no need for the massive American security detail that had arrived beforehand and insisted on stationing armed men everywhere, even inside the Parliament Buildings. Diefenbaker took the president's secret service intrusion as an insult.[1] That was strike one.

The press had been given copies of the welcoming speeches. Vanier stuck to his but the president and prime minister wandered a little. Diefenbaker said all the right things but offered a rather clunky greeting to Jacqueline Kennedy: "The welcome extended to you Mr. President, is not lessened by the fact that Mrs. Kennedy, whose charm and beauty has enchanted Canadians, springs from a racial stock representative of one of the two basic races of Canada."[2] As was his habit, he self-deprecatingly apologized before offering a few words of what he called "fractured French." He then earnestly read a few lines that were largely indecipherable to those who actually knew the language.

The crowd roared when Kennedy stood to speak. He said he was happy to be in Canada and pleased to see the prime minister again. He reminded everyone that he and Diefenbaker had met at the White House and that he had appreciated the prime minister's wise counsel in the early days of his administration. He said of Canadian-American relations: "Together we have worked in peace, together we have worked in war and now in this long twilight era that is neither peace nor war we must stand together even more firmly than before."[3] Everything he said was fine, but as he had at the White House press conference in February, and though reminded of his error, Kennedy mispronounced the prime minister's name—"Deefunbawker." This time, though, he had done it with the ever-sensitive Diefenbaker not eight feet away. That was strike two.

Jacqueline Kennedy was fluently bilingual. President Kennedy struggled with languages. On the plane to Ottawa she had helped him memorize a few lines in passable French. Rather than simply recite what he had practised, however, Kennedy extemporized a little. He admitted to the crowd that he did not speak the language, and then added, "I am somewhat encouraged to say a few words in French, having heard your Prime

Minister."[4] The crowd laughed. Diefenbaker managed only a wan smile. It was strike three, and they hadn't even left the airport.

As the Kennedys walked toward the waiting motorcade, the clouds parted as if on cue and bathed them in sunshine. They rode the ten miles to Government House—the governor general's residence, often called Rideau Hall—in the 1953 Cadillac limousine that had been used two years before by the Queen. Groups of smiling, cheering people waved from the roadside as Kennedy approached the city. The motorcade was forced to slow several times as admirers surged forward for a closer look, with many holding children on their shoulders. Fifty thousand normally staid and steady people of Ottawa welcomed Kennedy to their city in the same manner as teenage girls might have greeted Elvis.

The reception was not unexpected. Kennedy's popularity was soaring in Canada, as it was in the United States. Gallup polls indicated that at the time of the Ottawa trip over 80 percent of Americans approved of him and his presidency. Kennedy knew policy and actions mattered but believed that the key to his popularity was televised news conferences. Every week he entered the State Department auditorium and viewers watched a riveting display of prodigious memory, impressive intelligence, keen understanding of complex issues, and razor sharp wit. He was serious but also smiled, joked, and poked fun at himself. These were not Franklin Roosevelt's scripted fire-side chats or even the carefully edited films of Eisenhower responding to press questions, but live and lively exchanges of ideas that informed and entertained. Kennedy called them the "Six O'Clock Comedy Hour" and understood that they enhanced his power by boosting his celebrity.[5] He told Ted Sorensen, "We couldn't survive without TV."[6]

Kennedy and his advisors were well aware of the power of his popularity and unafraid to use it to their advantage. In preparation for the visit, American ambassador Merchant's telegram to Rusk could not have been blunter: "President Kennedy has fired the imagination of many Canadians, and there is almost no criticism at moment of US or administration. This affords us superb opportunity advance our objectives with Canadian public and government, because even those who resist American influence in Canada are now well impressed by new administration and their criticism is muted. . . . Impact on public opinion will consolidate US position here and useful opportunity is also provided by visit to win stronger adherence to our global policies on part PM and his Cabinet colleagues."[7] Like Joe Kennedy had suggested, his son was a star. Kennedy was too wise a politician to leave sheathed such a powerful weapon.

Since 1906, visiting foreign dignitaries had planted ceremonial trees at Government House. A twelve-year-old red oak had been prepared for Kennedy. With the press at a polite distance, the president, prime minister, governor general, and their wives walked onto the expansive lawn. Kennedy was offered a short-handled silver spade and invited to toss a few shovelfuls of well-mixed soil into the pre-dug hole. The ceremony was not originally on the president's schedule, but he graciously smiled, bent low, and gamely shovelled eight small scoops.[8] He suddenly stopped. He raised a hand ever so briefly to his forehead and slowly straightened up. His tender back that had been injured in youth, reinjured in war, and pieced together through many dangerous and one life-threatening surgery had gone out.

Kennedy adeptly concealed what had happened. He gingerly handed the shovel to Diefenbaker and suggested that he take a turn.[9] Diefenbaker offered it to Jacqueline, who threw three small shovelfuls for the happy photographers and film crew. The group walked slowly back to the mansion but Kennedy left his smile with the oak. His hands were driven deep into his suit jacket pockets. Once in his Rideau Hall rooms, he soaked in a steaming hot tub, trying in vain to ease the pain.

Men in tuxedos always look good. Kennedy and Diefenbaker were not exceptions to the rule that evening when they gathered for the 8 p.m. black-tie Government House dinner and reception. Ottawa's elite was there. One hundred and twelve guests enjoyed roast spring lamb and three varieties of wine and liqueurs. It was a time for Diefenbaker to forget the insults, for Kennedy to forget his pain, and for the two men on whom so much was riding to relax a little and enjoy themselves, but only Kennedy seemed to do so. A photograph in the *Globe and Mail* the next morning showed a smiling Vanier flanked by a beaming president and radiant Jacqueline. Beside her was Diefenbaker, hunched over and gazing sternly or perhaps sadly into the middle distance.[10] The picture captured his mood.

While Kennedy all but ignored Diefenbaker, he and Opposition leader Lester Pearson hit it off like old friends. They spoke of global events and people they knew in common. At the reception after dinner, Kennedy again sought out Pearson and asked his opinion on a range of issues. The inordinate amount of time and attention lavished on Pearson left Diefenbaker infuriated and publicly insulted.[11] Even though he was prime minister, he had again been shunned; he was again an outsider. It may have been an impossibility in baseball, but at Rideau Hall that night, Kennedy racked up strike four.

In bright sunshine and a forty-two-degree-Fahrenheit chill, crowds gathered at 9:30 a.m. the next morning around the Canadian War Memorial. The brief ceremony began with the American national anthem. Kennedy inspected a one-hundred-man Honour Guard, laid a wreath at the stately and sombre memorial, and then stood for "O Canada" and "God Save the Queen." With the large crowd waving and cheering, he and Diefenbaker walked slowly across Wellington Street toward the Peace Tower that soared like a sentry above the Parliament Buildings' Gothic splendour. What Kennedy's hosts didn't know, and the crowd couldn't tell, was that he was enduring searing pain with each step.

Olive Diefenbaker shepherded Jacqueline Kennedy around the city. Jacqueline had arranged for seven Oleg Cassini gowns to be designed and flown to Washington from Paris. For her meeting with the RCMP commissioner, whom she knew would be resplendent in his bright-red serge dress uniform, she wore a red Pierre Cardin suit. A photograph of the

First Lady and the Mountie made the cover of *Life* magazine.[12] Olive was cropped from the picture.

Mrs. Diefenbaker did not like Mrs. Kennedy. She believed that this woman of a different class and generation was callow and that the whispery voice was an affectation.[13] She was nonetheless polite and accompanied her through various stops, including the National Gallery. Three thousand people had gathered outside to see Jacqueline. Nude statues inside had been draped to avoid causing offence. Upon her return to Washington, Jacqueline wrote to Cassini explaining how well the gowns had gone over in Ottawa and challenging him to top them for her upcoming trip to Paris.[14]

Kennedy and Diefenbaker had been carefully briefed in preparation for their meeting. Even the American press, which had turned ignoring or insulting Canada into an art form, seemed to understand that a great deal was at stake. On the day before Kennedy arrived in Ottawa, a particularly insightful *New York Herald* article had noted, "Canada and the United States are entering a change in their relationship and understanding and forbearance will be required on both sides if the change is to take place without rancour or recrimination. The Americans are up against the exploding expansion of the Canadian economy and the purposeful demand for recognition of Canadian nationality that goes with it . . . the relatively new Canadian ambition to separate Canada from the United States as it has already separated itself from Britain on the stage of world affairs."[15] The *Herald* was one of many newspapers that the speed-reading Kennedy saw each morning, so he no doubt contemplated the argument. The editorial was reprinted in the *Ottawa Citizen*, so Diefenbaker would have seen it too.

On their way from the War Memorial, the strolling Kennedy and Diefenbaker waved at the large crowd gathered on the expansive Parliament Hill lawn. They nodded at the smiling staffers and ramrod-erect soldiers in fine dress uniforms as they entered the East Block. Demonstrating either that he wished to begin lightheartedly or perhaps showing a petty side of his nature, Diefenbaker led Kennedy to his spacious second-floor office and straight to the huge blue marlin that he'd had taxidermists prepare and mount specially for the visit. He then showed the president a recently hung painting depicting a War of 1812 British naval victory. Kennedy smiled at both and uttered a few kind words, no doubt understanding the game afoot.

Sir John A. Macdonald loomed large in the room. On an oak side table stood a two-foot-tall bronze statue of Canada's first prime minister. Behind the desk, and above an ornate marble fireplace, hung a large portrait in oil. Kennedy was thus exposed to Canada's Jefferson, Madison, and Washington, all rolled into one man. While others sat on green leather couches and chairs, and cameras snapped like mad mosquitoes, Diefenbaker took his place behind the dark oak desk. Kennedy smiled beside him, on a padded rocking chair brought in for the occasion. An aide shuffled photographers away and business finally began.

Kennedy immediately acknowledged the elephant in the room. He confessed that the Bay of Pigs operation had been an unfortunate mistake but insisted that he still wanted to be rid of Castro. He asked if Diefenbaker would assist in that effort by aligning Canada's Cuban trade policies with those of the United States and other countries in the hemisphere. Diefenbaker said no.[16]

He explained that trade with Cuba was in Canada's best interests and would therefore continue. He admitted that external affairs minister Howard Green had not spoken for him or his government when offering to mediate between Cuba and the United States, and made it clear he understood that no such help had been requested or was necessary. Kennedy pledged that the United States had no immediate plans to invade Cuba but reserved the right to do so if provoked by Castro or if the Soviets took action in Berlin or elsewhere. If a crisis involving Cuba should arise, Kennedy promised, Diefenbaker would be consulted before any American action was taken.[17]

Getting nowhere on Cuba, Kennedy moved on to explain his Alliance for Progress initiative, an idea mentioned in his inaugural address. In March he had announced the program to great fanfare, surrounded by two hundred Latin American diplomats. It involved loaning $20 billion to Latin American countries to help them stand against communism by developing their economies and making important social reforms in areas such as land ownership. It represented an attempt to turn away from decades of heavy-handed American incursions in the region and toward something more resembling a partnership. Kennedy asked if Canada would participate by increasing its foreign aid to one percent of gross domestic product with more financial assistance directed to Latin America.[18] Diefenbaker said no.

He explained that Canada was already helping in a number of areas around the world, including Latin America. Further, Canadian companies had many long-established connections and contracts in Latin America and this trade, rather than aid, was having positive effects in the region. He also explained that his government was currently cutting and reallocating its expenditures so the one percent target was out of the question as it would entail bumping foreign aid spending by a factor of five.[19] Kennedy's project would have to proceed without Canada.

Because it was related to the Cuban and broader Latin American discussion, Diefenbaker anticipated Kennedy's next point by raising the issue of Canada and the Organization of American States (OAS). The OAS began with a Washington conference in 1889. It was hoped that regular meetings could arbitrate disputes and allow more structured economic development. The Cold War added an anti-communist element to the multilateral relationships and led to the formal creation of the OAS in 1948. By 1961, with its headquarters in an imposing building on Washington's Constitution Avenue, just blocks from the White House, the OAS boasted twenty-one members. Canada, conspicuously, was not among them.

Kennedy wanted that changed. He urged Diefenbaker to have Canada join the OAS. He argued that membership would invite economic benefits while allowing Canada to exert more influence in South and Central America.[20] It was understood that Canada's membership would also strengthen America's hand by placing a stable, liberal-democratic, anti-communist state at the OAS table. Diefenbaker said no.

Before the Second World War, Canada had no legations in South or Central America; by the time Diefenbaker took office there were eleven. Canadian trade, although still quite small in many of the countries, was increasing in nearly all of them. In 1957, Canada's ambassador to Colombia had written to Ottawa arguing against OAS membership. Like many other Canadian diplomats, he was suspicious of organizations that could splinter the world into competing regions. He was also convinced that OAS membership would do little to bolster Canada's influence or promote its interests as the organization was so obviously dominated by the United States. Since Canada already had a respected UN presence, and Canadian diplomats and business leaders were enjoying success in promoting Canada in Latin America, he saw no advantage in joining the OAS.[21] These points were reiterated by Diefenbaker's first external affairs minister, Sidney Smith, who, after a tour of Latin American, reported that the region was developing quickly and offered tremendous potential for growing Canadian trade but that potential would be more quickly and easily realized if Canada remained independent of the United States and OAS. Howard Green came to a similar conclusion during a subsequent trip.[22]

Only four years later, the same logic held true, and Diefenbaker explained it all to Kennedy. He added that he did not want to see a situation where some issue or another would leave Canada stuck between having to either support the United States or most (or even all) other OAS members.[23] Kennedy joked that if there were a situation in which Canada and the United States disagreed, the United States would probably be wrong.[24] Diefenbaker did not laugh. He agreed only to consider Kennedy's request to have Canada send an observer to the next OAS Economic and Social Council meeting.

Having hit yet another brick wall, Kennedy shifted the discussion to Vietnam. The Vietnam War was in fact many wars rolled into one complicated and tumbling tragedy. It was among the last of the colonial-era conflicts, reignited when France was freed from Hitler and then attempted to reclaim its Indochina colony, consisting of Cambodia, Laos, and Vietnam. It was a nationalist war, with the leaders and the led fighting to get rid of the French, and then Japanese, the French again, and now the Americans.

Canada's involvement began when it took part in the 1954 Geneva Convention that negotiated the end of Korean hostilities. When the ceasefire and related issues were resolved, Canadian representative John Holmes flew home. The conference continued in order to address France's decision to finally end their imperialist misadventure in Southeast Asia. The remaining delegates hammered out a number of agreements, including that Western powers would leave the region and Vietnam would be temporarily split at the seventeenth parallel. Three International Commissions for Supervision and Control were created to oversee Laos, Cambodia, and Vietnam. They were to supervise the ceasefire, refugee relocation, and the withdrawal of French troops and the communist forces of Ho Chi Minh's Vietnam Revolutionary League—the Vietminh. They would also monitor an election in 1956 intended to reunite Vietnam. Appointed to run the commissions—quickly renamed the International Control Commissions (ICCs)—were neutral India, communist Poland, and, representing the West, Canada. Prime Minister St. Laurent reluctantly accepted the unsolicited assignment and put Pearson in charge.[25] Fourteen ICC teams of uniformed military men and civilians were soon stationed across the region, with a number of mobile teams moving to trouble spots to observe, inspect, mediate, and report.

Meanwhile, Ho Chi Minh consolidated his power in the northern portion of Vietnam while the quasi-democratic Ngo Dinh Diem did the same in the South. When it became evident that Ho Chi Minh would win the 1956 election, the world watched irony in action as the communists insisted the democratic election take place while the Americans, who, like the South Vietnamese government, had not signed the Geneva agreement, refused to let it happen. Canada and the Vietnam ICC said nothing about the cancelled elections. By 1957 Canada had 127 officials in the region and was spending about $4 million a year for their work.[26]

In his transition meetings with Kennedy, President Eisenhower warned that if a third world war began, its spark would not be Berlin, but Southeast Asia.[27] Shortly after taking office, Kennedy approved the withdrawal of American military advisors from Laos and new covert activities in Vietnam. He boosted financial and military aid to allow Diem to better equip and enlarge his army, and appealed to the ICC to allow a larger American Military Assistance Advisory Group (MAAG). Diefenbaker directed Canada's ICC representatives to approve the MAAG increase despite the fact that it obviously violated articles 16 to 20 of the Geneva Accords that Canada had pledged to defend.

Kennedy's pre-Ottawa trip briefing papers stated, "The Canadian Government shares our view that the situation in Viet-nam is serious and we can count on their continued efforts to serve Free World interests in the ICC."[28] There was also an appreciation of the fact that while Kennedy was in Ottawa, a new conference in Geneva would be attempting to bring sanity to a region bereft of reason. A Walter Rostow memo to the State Department had warned Kennedy, "If the conference fails and if the situation in Viet-Nam worsens, we shall be up against the question of putting American troops in Viet-Nam."[29] Rostow recommended that if that should happen, the United States could use Canada to help justify the further Americanization of the war.

With the warnings of Eisenhower and Rostow in his mind, Kennedy asked Diefenbaker to step up Canada's ICC efforts and activity. He wanted Canada to do more to secure the Vietnam-Laos border. He wanted the

ICC to find and more publicly report instances of Vietminh subversion in South Vietnam. He also asked for more Canadian foreign aid to South Vietnam.[30] Diefenbaker said no.

He explained that Canada would continue to do what it could on the border and with the rest of its mandate but no more. He said that Canada needed to retain at least a semblance of neutrality for the ICC to wield what little power it had and for Canada to retain credibility within it. Canada's offering direct aid to South Vietnam would compromise its neutrality in the region while directly violating the ICC's mandate and the terms of the Geneva Accords.[31] Diefenbaker reminded the president that Howard Green was unable to be with them in Ottawa because he was currently in Geneva addressing the Laos-Vietnam situation. He had been sent with instructions that Canada had neither plans nor a desire to increase its involvement in either country beyond its current ICC role.

Kennedy urged Diefenbaker to change his mind. Diefenbaker reiterated his belief that acting in Vietnam along the lines that the president proposed was neither in the region's nor Canada's best interest. Kennedy was forced to drop the subject. He later complained to Pearson that Canada's actions in Vietnam made it appear as if the ICCs comprised "two neutrals and a Pole."[32]

Having failed to move Diefenbaker on any of the issues he had brought forward, Kennedy raised the question of Britain's desire to enter the European Common Market. Prime Minister Macmillan understood that Britain was no longer the powerhouse it had been. Common Market membership, he believed, would improve the country's prospects by rendering it part of the group of nations that pledged to eliminate tariffs and other trade barriers between its members.[33] Macmillan also believed that membership would bolster Britain's fading prestige and influence on the continent.

Kennedy had expressed support for Britain's membership. Besides obviously helping Britain, it would reinforce Western Europe's economic strength and stability, better enabling it to defy communism and the Soviets.[34] In their April meeting in Washington, Kennedy and Macmillan acknowledged that French president Charles de Gaulle opposed Britain's Common Market membership because it would increase British and, because of their close relationship, American influence in Europe. De Gaulle also worried about splintering the Commonwealth that he believed had been an important factor in chasing Hitler from France in the last war and could be equally effective in keeping Khrushchev out in this one.[35] It was with these concerns, hopes, and goals in mind that Kennedy asked Diefenbaker to support Britain's Common Market application.[36] Diefenbaker said no.

He had already told Macmillan of Canada's opposition. Britain's membership, he said, would threaten the many trade preferences that Canada enjoyed with Britain and possibly other Commonwealth countries. Most significantly, it would jeopardize the sale of Canadian wheat and other agricultural products. He agreed with de Gaulle that British membership could kill the Commonwealth, and that death could have serious repercussions for Canada and the West. Kennedy tried to persuade Diefenbaker to reconsider but was told to expect no shift in the Canadian position.[37]

At that point the dead-eyed marlin had overseen nearly fifty minutes of tense conversation. Kennedy said nothing about his back but was no doubt showing the signs of pain and impatience his colleagues knew well—slow rocking and teeth tapping. They had saved the most contentious issue for last. Kennedy asked Diefenbaker to accept American nuclear weapons.

Shortly before leaving for Ottawa, Kennedy had read a report by former secretary of defence and tough old hawk Dean Acheson. "A Review of North Atlantic Problems for the Future" supported Kennedy's desire to move away from Eisenhower's reliance on a massive nuclear deterrent and toward a more flexible response with increased emphasis on conventional forces.[38] Acheson's report also argued that America should ask its

NATO allies to mobilize more troops. Of note was its assessment of current allied contributions, which observed, "With the exception of the United States and Canadian forces, all these units have a reduced combat effectiveness because of personnel manning levels, equipment problems, and austere combat and logistics support forces."[39] Canada was doing its bit. Dean Rusk had seen Acheson's report, and yet his pre-Ottawa memo stated that Canada had to improve its defence capability, and suggested that it could start to do so by acquiring nuclear weapons. Rusk's memo also reminded Kennedy that until the weapons were in Canada, a hole would remain in the continent's defence and America's security.[40]

Kennedy broached the subject by speaking of their mutual desire to keep their people safe. Of course Diefenbaker agreed. Kennedy reminded the prime minister that they had discussed Canada's taking nuclear weapons during their talks in Washington and said that his position had not changed. He wanted Canada to arm its Bomarc missiles and other weapons systems with nuclear warheads, to store nuclear weapons at a number of Canadian bases and the American bases in Newfoundland and Labrador, and to provide nuclear weapons to Canada's NATO troops.[41] Diefenbaker said no.

He promised that Canada would continue to do its part in European and continental defence. He explained that he remained committed to ongoing negotiations and hoped that they would end with Canada accepting American nuclear weapons.[42] However, he reiterated his two-track policy and his belief that, while the global movement toward disarmament seemed to be stumbling, progress toward a nuclear-free world was still possible. He briefly repeated the conditions he had discussed in Washington and from which he had not budged since negotiations began: there must be guarantees of civilian control over launches and of full consultation between the two governments in times of emergency.

Diefenbaker then outlined a political complication that he had not mentioned before but that Rusk had warned Kennedy about back in February. He spoke of the women's and university-based groups that were rallying growing numbers of Canadians to support disarmament and oppose the presence of American nuclear weapons in Canada. He spoke of receiving more mail every week asking that he not accept the weapons under any circumstances. Making the situation even more delicate, he said, was that Pearson and the Liberals were vocally opposed to the acquisition of nuclear weapons. So was the Co-operative Commonwealth Federation. The CCF had achieved limited electoral success at the federal level, but was nevertheless a party to be taken seriously, given its ties to agrarian movements in the west, intellectuals in the east, and organized labour throughout the country. Diefenbaker explained his fear that more converts to the anti-nuclear cause meant fewer votes for his Progressive Conservatives—an important consideration with an election less than a year away.

Popular support for the anti-nuclear movement had been debated in Diefenbaker's Cabinet before Kennedy's arrival. An increasingly frustrated Douglas Harkness had shown Cabinet a *Toronto Star* public opinion poll indicating that 45 percent of Canadians agreed with him and Canadian military leaders that the weapons should be acquired. Only 21 percent were opposed; 34 percent were undecided.[43] The defence minister argued that the anti-nuclear, pro-disarmament groups were to be ignored as they were a minority and nothing but troublesome pacifists.[44] Diefenbaker was not ready to dismiss the anti-nuclear groups or believe the polls. He once said that only dogs knew what to do with polls. He put less stock in them than in his instincts and mailbag.[45]

Diefenbaker understood that the volatility and direction of Canadian opinion was being reflected and affected by women. The *Toronto Star*'s Lotta Dempsey was a driving force behind the creation of Voice of Women for Peace (VOW), the most important of several women's groups. Josephine Davis became one of its most influential spokespeople and organizers. She and others had met with Pearson and earned his public support. Maryon Pearson became an honorary sponsor. She signed a widely released letter advocating disarmament and told a journalist, "Men get casual and used to talking about piles of bombs here and piles of bombs there." Women, on the other hand, are more inclined to peace because, "they produce life and want to see their children live."[46]

Davis and others had met with Diefenbaker in June 1960. The prime minister was polite but offered no support; his wife, when approached, refused to become associated with VOW. He understood, though, that public protest can inform public opinion and that he needed to carefully monitor the shifting tides. After the meeting he began paying even more attention to mail addressing the nuclear issue and listened with new interest to Howard Green's views on disarmament.[47]

Kennedy had been warned about Diefenbaker's growing concern for the political ramifications of the nuclear decision, which is why he framed the issue in terms of public safety and a global response to communism.[48] When that approach failed, he tried to minimize the political risks of accepting the weapons by teasing Diefenbaker: "I could get a parade in Boston at any time on nuclear weapons, but it would not be serious."[49] Diefenbaker ignored the remark.

Kennedy was, in fact, quite worried about Canada's growing anti-nuclear advocates. A similar anti-nuclear movement was growing in France and gathering substantial momentum in Britain. He could not allow civil society protests to shake allied commitment to an American-led, nuclear-backed effort to push back communism.[50] Diefenbaker repeated that he wanted the weapons but needed to be sure he shared control over their use and that he had to consider the rifts their acquisition would create among Canadians. He promised to do all he could to shift public opinion.

As Kennedy began to respond, Diefenbaker interrupted to say he was ready to approve the swap deal that for over two years had been working its way through the American and Canadian military and bureaucracy. The United States would give Canada sixty-six McDonnell F-101 Voodoo supersonic jet aircraft valued at $105 million along with $50 million in supporting equipment. Canada would pay only $25 million. In addition, the United States would buy thirty to thirty-five Canadian-made transport planes, until the total price tag reached $150 million. Canada would contribute $50 million toward the purchase. Finally, Canada would take over the staffing and maintenance of the Pinetree Line radar stations for which it was not already responsible.[51]

It was a sweet deal for Canada. It boosted Canadian defence capacity, created jobs, and augmented Canadian sovereignty by replacing American soldiers at the Canadian-based radar stations with Canadians. Kennedy had already been briefed on the deal and agreed to sign on. Finally, after nearly an hour, Kennedy and Diefenbaker had agreed on something. But the flickering candle of consensus was quickly snuffed.

Ambassador Merchant warned the prime minister that the American Voodoo jets had to come equipped with nuclear weapons. Diefenbaker was taken aback. At a January 23 Cabinet Defence Committee meeting, he had been told that the Voodoos could be armed with either conventional or nuclear-tipped air-to-air missiles. The Canadian and American military wanted nuclear warheads on the planes, but Diefenbaker was quite rightly recalling that conventional weapons were an option.[52] He told Merchant that he was mistaken and refused the nukes on the planes.

It was Kennedy's turn to say no. He insisted that without the nuclear weapons on the jets, he would encounter perhaps insurmountable political problems in persuading Congress to complete the swap deal. Diefenbaker was undeterred. He replied that if an emergency arose, he would allow the nuclear warheads to be quickly shipped north to arm the jets. Kennedy dismissed the idea as impractical. The only way the deal could go forward, Kennedy insisted, was if the jets were delivered with nuclear weapons. Further, if the nuclear weapons were not accepted he would consider Canada a neutral state in the Cold War.[53]

Rusk had flung the same rhetoric at Green in Geneva. Both men intended it to sting. Before Diefenbaker gathered himself, Kennedy repeated his pledge to sign an agreement with Canada similar to the British double-key arrangement. He promised it would ensure Canadian consent before nuclear weapons stationed in Canada could be used.[54] He emphatically insisted that Canada simply must take the weapons. Again, Diefenbaker said no. Given the volatility of Canadian public opinion, and in the absence of a signed shared-use deal, he could accept no nukes on the Voodoo jets or for any other Canadian weapons system, at least for the moment.

Kennedy became more forceful. He asked about Lester Pearson's thoughts on accepting nuclear weapons in Canada. Diefenbaker had heard his unimpeachable Cold War credentials mocked and now Kennedy was insinuating that he might go around the prime minister and interfere in Canada's domestic politics to obtain his goals. Diefenbaker refused to lose his temper. Having already mentioned Liberal support for anti-nuclear movements, he calmly explained that at the National Liberal Rally in Ottawa just four months earlier, Pearson had spoken of his party's willingness to consider nuclear weapons for Europe but never on Canadian soil.[55]

Kennedy could not have been surprised; his preparatory briefing had told him as much. Plus, he had read Pearson's *Diplomacy in the Nuclear Age*. The book criticized American reliance upon nuclear deterrence and expressed Pearson's belief that, while necessary in light of Soviet power and aggression, the weapons were immoral and their proliferation unconscionable. Stepping back from his ruthless tactics, Kennedy finally consented to the swap deal, but only after Diefenbaker agreed to relegate the question of nuclear warheads for the Voodoos to lower-level bilateral negotiations.[56] The stubborn man from Saskatchewan had again stymied him.

The two-and-one-half-hour meeting ended with handshakes and tense smiles. Kennedy and his team left the room frustrated by their inability to win even a single concession. They broke for lunch at the prime minister's residence. Both men spoke privately with aides about other issues competing for their attention. Kennedy communicated with the White

House through a secure telephone line that had been installed for the occasion in the prime minister's personal library.[57]

At 3 p.m., amid cheers from another huge Parliament Hill crowd, President Kennedy was escorted into Centre Block. The House of Commons galleries were packed and senators crowded in among their House colleagues. Drawing admiring glances, Jacqueline sat in the public gallery with Olive.

Kennedy was warmly introduced to sustained applause from the parliamentarians around him and the public above. From a lectern atop the clerk's long table before the Speaker of the House, Kennedy offered remarks in his characteristically clipped cadence. "The Prime Minister was the first of the leaders from other lands who was invited to call upon me shortly after I entered the White House; and this is my first trip . . . it is fitting, and appropriate and traditional, that I should come here to Canada—across a border that knows neither guns nor guerrillas." A round of applause met his aphorism: "Geography has made us neighbors. History has made us friends. Economics has made us partners. And necessity has made us allies. Those whom nature hath so joined together, let no man put asunder."[58] He paused and looked directly at Diefenbaker.

The poetry of what followed was similarly "Kennedyesque." So too, was the prose—the iron fist within the velvet glove. He acknowledged that, although the two countries were as one on most issues, a number of irritants remained. Contradicting what FDR had said back in 1938, and reflecting the suggestion Secretary of State Rusk had made on how to get along with Canadians, he said, "We are allies. This is a partnership, not an empire. We are bound to have differences and disappointments— and we are equally bound to bring them out into the open, to settle them where they can be settled, and to respect each other's views when they cannot be settled."[59]

Kennedy's next point was pleasantly phrased, and those who were not in the private meeting earlier could be excused for missing the subtle jabs at Diefenbaker regarding nuclear weapons, the Alliance for Progress, and Cuba. "It is equally clear that no Western nation on its own can help those less-developed lands to fulfill their hope for steady progress. And, finally, it is clear that in an age where new forces are asserting their strength around the globe—when the political shape of the hemispheres are changing rapidly—nothing is more vital than the unity of the United States and Canada."[60]

Kennedy then crossed the line:

The Hemisphere is a family into which we were born—and we cannot turn our backs on it in time of trouble. Nor can we stand aside from its great adventure of development. I believe that all of the free members of the Organization of American States would be heartened and strengthened by any increase in your Hemispheric role. Your skills, your resources, your judicious perception at the council table—even when it differs from our own view—are all needed throughout the inter-American Community. Your country and mine are partners in North American affairs—can we not now become partners in inter-American affairs?[61]

Just hours before, Diefenbaker had told Kennedy that Canada would not join the Organization of American States, yet here was the president, breaking diplomatic protocol and the dictates of common courtesy by demanding in public that which had been refused in private. Diefenbaker sat and steamed.

Kennedy's advisors had shared a draft of the speech with Ambassador Heeney, who had seen nothing wrong with the OAS passage. His approval indicated the degree to which Heeney misunderstood not just Diefenbaker's opposition to OAS membership but the nationalist basis of that opposition.[62] Howard Green understood. He later came as close as any member of Diefenbaker's Cabinet to publicly criticizing Kennedy's brazen assertions when, shortly afterwards, he said in a House debate, "One of the least effective ways of persuading Canada to adopt a policy is for the president to come here and tell us what we should do."[63] Kennedy's ongoing determination to change Diefenbaker's mind was evident seven months later when he met Canadian chargé d'affaires Andrew Ross in Caracas and demanded to know when Canada would join the OAS.[64]

Meanwhile, Diefenbaker and Kennedy met the next morning for a working breakfast. Diefenbaker did not mention Kennedy's OAS comments in the House, and remained silent about the slights at the airport and reception. The small talk ended, however, when Kennedy tried again to change Diefenbaker's mind on the nuclear issue. Diefenbaker was in no mood to bargain. No new points were made. No concessions were offered.

The joint communiqué issued at the conclusion of the visit emphasized agreement on the need for disarmament but said nothing about nuclear weapons in Canada. It noted discussions about hemispheric relations but nothing about Cuba or Canada joining the OAS. It mentioned issues involving Laos but not Vietnam. It talked of expanding world trade but ignored Britain and the Common Market.[65] In fact, it said not much at all and, in so doing, revealed a great deal about all that had been left unresolved.

A smaller but still substantial crowd waved as Kennedy's motorcade left Ottawa for the Uplands airport. Air Force One soon had Kennedy back in Washington but he had mistakenly left something behind. Shortly after the president had left the prime minister's office, one of Diefenbaker's assistants found a one-page briefing memo written by deputy national security assistant Walter Rostow. The "Memorandum for the President" was subtitled "What We Want from the Ottawa Trip."[66]

While Kennedy was en route to Washington, the assistant gave it to foreign affairs advisor Basil Robinson. He handed it to Diefenbaker with the advice that it be immediately returned to the president. Diefenbaker read it and was outraged. It listed four areas where Kennedy was to "push" the Canadians: toward a commitment to the Alliance for Progress, joining the OAS, contributing more to foreign aid, and more effectively monitoring the Laos-Vietnam border. It summarized many of the points Kennedy had made in their meetings but glaringly absent was anything regarding nuclear weapons. The talking-points memo was harmless on the surface, and not unlike a document anyone might carry into an important meeting.

However, Diefenbaker bristled at the word *push* that began each point. He believed it revealed a desire to bully Canada and treat it as a supplicant or satellite.[67] Except perhaps in light of Kennedy's stinging and personal remarks, his indignation is a little hard to understand. Not only is the word *push* in this context somewhat innocuous, in a pre-visit briefing memo prepared for the prime minister, Heeney had written, "As to Canada-USA bilateral questions, I should expect that our current and planned defense arrangements might profitably be discussed. Here the so-called 'swap' deal might usefully be given a push."[68]

Diefenbaker was nonetheless upset and there was no placating him. He read the memo over and over and firmly underlined the word *push* twice in blue ink each of the four times it appeared. He ignored Robinson's advice to return it and had the memo placed in the private, locked cabinet in his office that he called the vault. It would not gather dust for long. When it was retrieved, it would be as political dynamite.

Kennedy once sent two advisors to Vietnam and upon hearing their independent reports asked, "Did you two gentleman visit the same country?"[69] A similar question could be asked regarding Canadian and American reactions to the Ottawa visit. Despite the Rostow memo and Kennedy's numerous slights, Diefenbaker considered the visit a roaring success. He had been beside the popular president as thousands of Canadians were cheering. He had stood up to the president when being pushed. Diefenbaker later observed that Kennedy must have returned to

Washington believing himself to have failed because Canada had refused to submit to the American leader's wishes.[70] He sent 16-mm newsreel accounts of the visit to Cabinet ministers.[71] In a private letter to his brother, Diefenbaker declared that he and Kennedy had got along well and that the president had a "brilliant intellect and a wide knowledge of world events."[72]

On the other hand, Ambassador Merchant wrote to Kennedy with praise for being forthright with Diefenbaker. The Canadians, he argued, had been given plenty to think about. In words that would have enraged the prime minister, he wrote that Canadians "have had some of their complacency and smugness salubriously shaken, and will be examining their consciences as well as their pocketbooks. . . . At least we should see a greater Canadian restraint in offering gratuitous advice unaccompanied by acceptance of responsibility."[73]

Kennedy's opinion of Diefenbaker had not changed. When Diefenbaker was told that Kennedy had injured his back planting the tree, he immediately sent a kind note wishing him a speedy recovery.[74] Kennedy responded with a brief telegram: "Many thanks for your gracious message. The tree will be there long after the discomfort is gone. The visit with the Canadian people is a shining memory for both of us."[75] He was more honest with an aide: "That bastard insisted that I get a shovel and dig. It was one of the most painful episodes I've ever had."[76] It would be well over a year before the full consequence of the injury would unfold.

# SEVEN

## TRIPPING INTO WAR

### VIENNA AND BERLIN

WITH THE KENNEDY VISIT OVER, Diefenbaker turned his attention to domestic issues. The most vexing among them remained the economy. Despite a number of tax incentives to business, farm programs, trade initiatives, and jobs programs, unemployment was still high and growth low. Linked to the economic troubles was a political problem.

It began in 1959 when Bank of Canada governor James Coyne, who by traditional and legal mandate was to be apolitical, made a number of speeches that criticized the government's economic policies. Diefenbaker grew increasingly unhappy with the speeches and Coyne's high-interest-rate monetary strategy. Tensions grew when the bank's board approved an exorbitant pension that the fifty-year-old Coyne arranged for himself. In June 1961, Diefenbaker fired Coyne. When denied an open hearing to defend himself, Coyne sparked a media firestorm by releasing documents supporting his criticism of the government's fiscal policies and following them with spurious remarks. Pearson skilfully used the clumsily handled mess to hammer Diefenbaker on his management of the Coyne affair, the economy, and the government in general. As one newspaper after another turned against Diefenbaker, Canadians who had agreed in 1958 to "Follow John" began rethinking their allegiance.

Kennedy had his own problems and among them was the growing calamity in Vietnam. Days after leaving Ottawa, Kennedy received a request from Frederick Nolting, his ambassador in Saigon, for sixteen thousand more American advisors. The American military personnel in the region were fast becoming more than advisors as they directly engaged in confrontations to prop up Diem's faltering South Vietnamese army and corrupt regime. At least fifteen hundred were needed right away. The numbers would clearly violate Geneva Accord restrictions. However, Nolting also reported that he had a good relationship with the Canadians on the Vietnam ICC and trusted them to pressure the Polish and Indian commissioners to approve.[1] North Vietnamese general Võ Nguyên Giáp heard about the impending American buildup and launched a formal ICC protest. A special commission hearing was convened. The Canadian ICC ambassador worked to have Giáp's charge effectively dismissed by forcing a vote to have it sent to Saigon for comment.[2] As expected, Giáp's protest vanished in a bureaucratic fog.

By December, the Canadians had persuaded the ICC to approve the fifteen hundred advisors, along with shipments of more American planes, helicopters, trucks, and assorted weapons and ammunition. The external affairs office in Ottawa got word to Kennedy that the Vietnam ICC wanted American troops to arrive in small numbers rather than in one conspicuous group.[3] Over the course of several days, the men and equipment were unloaded at a harbour within view of the hotel that was home to the Canadian ICC delegation.

The same Canadian delegates were silent about Agent Orange. The chemical defoliant robbed enemy fighters of their jungle cover by burning the leaves off trees. It also poisoned food and water and would later inflict soldiers and civilians with horrible cancers and their children with debilitating birth defects. From 1961 to 1972, American aircraft dumped nineteen million gallons of the dioxin-based liquid over 4.5 million acres of jungle, crops, and water sources. Much of the Agent Orange was manufactured in Canada and tested near the Canadian Forces base at Gagetown, New Brunswick. As with the American soldiers and hardware pouring into the country, there was no mystery about the catastrophic effects of Agent Orange pouring over it—only wilful blindness.[4]

Hugh Campbell served as a Canadian representative on the Vietnam ICC from 1961 to 1963. He later confessed, "I was bloody ashamed of the things I was required to do. . . . I don't recall any occasion when I saw anything in print that we should cover for the Americans, but at the same time, if you did not, you would be in a very difficult position."[5] Diefenbaker was never ashamed. In their Ottawa meeting he had refused to do everything Kennedy wanted, but he had not said he would do nothing. Canadian actions in Vietnam were consistent with his anti-communist beliefs, support for America's Cold War leadership, and with expectations as the West's ICC representative. Through sanctioning ICC actions in Vietnam, Diefenbaker helped grease the slide down which Kennedy was slipping into war.

While overlapping foreign crises screamed for attention, Kennedy also needed to focus on a host of domestic issues. By the spring of 1961 the American economy had eased out of a painful ten-month recession, but growth remained low and the unemployment rate hovered at 7 percent. Kennedy tried to employ the same social assistance/tax cut/job creation strategy as Diefenbaker but saw little of his proposed Program for Economic Recovery and Growth passed into law. Congressional Republicans and many conservative southern Democrats opposed his desire to intervene in the economy. Vice President Lyndon B. Johnson had been a powerful and persuasive Senate majority leader. Kennedy worried that legislators would disrespect him if he relied too heavily on his vice president and so refused to employ Johnson's vote-swaying skills to advance his legislative agenda.[6]

Kennedy also faced the escalating violence meeting the non-violent civil rights movement. On May 4, 1961, thirteen members of the Congress of Racial Equality, both black and white, left Washington on two buses bound for the segregated South. They were determined to bring attention to the racist practices that remained in place despite the *Boynton v. Virginia* Supreme Court decision five months earlier that rendered segregation on interstate travel unconstitutional. On May 15, the day before Kennedy had departed for Ottawa, 100 Ku Klux Klansmen stopped one of the buses outside Anniston, Alabama. They slashed its tires, set it on fire, and blocked the doors to watch the young people inside burn. An undercover police officer inside brandished a pistol and allowed his fellow passengers to escape. When the other bus reached the Anniston terminal, police watched as riders were savagely clubbed.

President Kennedy had originally wanted the rides stopped, but his brother, Attorney General Robert Kennedy, persuaded him to intervene. The Freedom Rides inspired Robert the moralist and John the realist to take greater risks—risks they knew could shatter their already splintering party and jeopardize hopes for re-election in 1964. The rides cemented in their minds that the full force of the federal government needed to be brought to bear if America was to ever marry morality, legality, and common practice.[7]

Just days after returning from Ottawa, on May 25, Kennedy summoned a special joint session of Congress. Oddly, given the bloody events that were still capturing headlines and turning stomachs, he did not mention the Freedom Rides. Instead, he announced the audacious goal of sending a man to the moon. The speech's main purpose was even bigger than that. He issued a valiant call to arms. Although he did not directly mention Canada, there was little doubt among the Canadians who tuned in or read about his message the next day that, like it or not, they and their country were in jeopardy.

Kennedy began with a stirring portrayal of America as the world's primary defender of freedom. To stand against those who despised and threatened peoples' liberty, he contended, the United States needed economic and social progress at home and abroad, stronger strategic alliances, a more robust military, and a renewed commitment to nuclear disarmament. He requested of Congress a whopping $1.6 billion increase for military aid for allies and a complete restructuring of the American army, with an additional $100 million to equip it. He called for $60 million to strengthen the marines and enable them and other special forces to move more quickly and nimbly to areas of crisis. He called for a tripling of civil defence spending to help Americans build bomb shelters. Americans had to be prepared for nuclear war, he said, because they should not assume that the next war would be fought far from home or waged by rational enemies in rational ways.[8] Just as he had in his campaign, Kennedy was promoting patriotic sacrifice, propagating lofty goals, pursuing a reversal of communist advances, and, at the same time, stirring crazy-eyed panic.

Canadian governments had been similarly scaring and preparing people for years. At regular intervals, test sirens blared from schools and city halls, children practised hiding under their desks, and TV programs were interrupted to test the emergency response networks. Toronto, Montreal, or anybody's hometown could be the next Hiroshima.

In 1959, Diefenbaker doubled to $10 million the budget allocated to building bomb shelter facilities and improving early-warning systems. That year, Canada spent $2.05 per citizen on civil defence while the United States spent only thirty-three cents.[9] Among other preparations was the building of a 100,000-square-foot bunker on a hilltop west of Ottawa. St. Laurent had approved its construction in January 1957. By 1961, the secret underground complex was nearly finished. It contained stores of food and water and rooms for senior government officials to work and live deep underground. It had a communication network through which they could direct whatever civil authority was left aloft and whatever Canadians were left alive. It was dubbed the Diefenbunker.

Kennedy's May 25 speech sparked a renewed wave of bomb shelter construction. *Popular Science* magazine tastelessly noted, "The shelter business is booming like a 25-megaton blast . . ."[10] An article outlining the difference between bomb and fall-out shelters and how to build them recommended that families should remain underground for at least two weeks after a nuclear attack, and concluded with the guardedly optimistic prediction, "Things would be tough, but probably not impossible. . . . Civilization could be rebuilt."[11]

Bomb shelters, tests, and the animated Bert the Turtle, who taught kids how to duck and cover, offered people the illusion of control over a situation in which they had none. Soviets felt the fear and folly too. A popular Soviet joke asked what one should do in case of a nuclear attack. The answer was to cover oneself in a sheet and crawl slowly to the nearest cemetery. Why slowly? To avoid panic.[12] Khrushchev did not joke. He said, "In the case of a nuclear war, the living will envy the dead."[13]

Diefenbaker was moved by the awesome responsibility shouldered by all world leaders, and the thought of his own country serving as a nuclear battlefield was a particularly heavy weight to bear. He scribbled in the margin of a speech he was drafting, "The thought of a third world war, especially one in which nuclear weapons would be used is a constant companion of one who has the responsibility and trust which rests on me."[14]

With citizens prepped and Congress debating his funding and program requests, Kennedy devoted the last week of May to preparing for his Vienna meeting with Soviet chairman Nikita Khrushchev. Khrushchev was a brilliant tactician who embraced and advanced communism's strategic goals as a true believer. A coal miner's son, Khrushchev fought in the Russian Revolution's civil war and then worked his way through party ranks. As secretary of the Ukrainian Communist Party, he finished the merciless work of the 1937–38 Great Purge, in which tens of thousands of Ukrainians deemed dangerous to the state were executed and bulldozed into mass graves.[15] As a lieutenant general, Khrushchev organized the Ukraine's guerrilla campaign against the Nazis. Stalin rewarded his bravery and ruthless efficiency with an appointment to the Politburo—Moscow's supreme policy-making body. Stalin died in 1953. After manoeuvring his way through a long power struggle to replace the fallen leader, Khrushchev had political opponents purged or killed. Hungary's

1956 attempt to liberalize its society was met with Soviet tanks. Nikita Khrushchev was not to be toyed with.

Khrushchev did not have to worry about polls or public opinion. However, the next Communist Party Congress was scheduled for October 1961. The chairman knew that hardliners were upset with his leadership and especially with his inability to solve nagging problems in Berlin. The growing flood of East Berliners moving west was embarrassing and expensive. Rumours flew that Khrushchev would be unseated. He needed a victory. The new American president who talked tough but whose Cuban failure suggested weakness offered a chance to snatch one.[16]

Khrushchev was twenty-three years older than Kennedy but much healthier. Only Kennedy's family, friends, and staff knew that the episode with the Ottawa oak had put him on crutches. He hobbled to meetings and passed the crutches to an aide before entering the room. Refusing to succumb to the constant agony, he was fitted with a new and uncomfortable back brace that secured him from his armpits to his hips. It held him erect and mitigated pain when he needed to sit for any length of time or ride in a motorcade. The back pain added to a host of other physical ailments that continued to torment him. High fevers, bouts of diarrhea, colitis, urinary infections, stomach, colon, and prostate problems, insomnia, high cholesterol, and the continuing difficulty with regulating his Addison's disease all plagued the first months of his presidency. He regularly swallowed or had injected corticosteroids, procaine, Lomotil, Metamucil, paregoric, phenobarbital, testosterone, trasentine, penicillin, Tuinal, amphetamines, and a cocktail of antibiotics.[17] During the 1960 campaign, Kennedy began to see Dr. Max Jacobson. Celebrity clients called him "Doctor Feelgood." After the Ottawa episode, Jacobson regularly appeared at the White House to inject Kennedy with a mixture of pain medication and amphetamines. Jacobson chartered a separate flight to Paris for the first leg of the Vienna trip. The White House doctors were carefully balancing and administering their prescriptions for the president, unaware that Dr. Feelgood was also injecting his.[18] The public and nearly all those with whom Kennedy interacted each day, meanwhile, still believed the televised vision of youthful vigour and knew nothing of his precarious health or the degree to which he was medicated.

While Kennedy could not move forward with Diefenbaker, he moved backwards with Khrushchev. At their first Vienna meeting, on June 3, 1961, seated on a pink couch in the American embassy, Kennedy mentioned that they had briefly met three years before when Khrushchev attended a meeting of the Senate Foreign Relations Committee. The sixty-seven-year-old Khrushchev dismissively allowed that he remembered him as a "promising young man."[19] The chairman's dig set the tone.

The meeting was less a conversation than a hectoring. Kennedy was dazed by Khrushchev's arguments, manner, and belligerence. Even when they took a lunch break stroll through a garden, Khrushchev repeatedly circled the president and badgered him with shouts and gestures.[20] At the end of the first long and frustrating day, Kennedy collapsed into a hot tub and then painfully paced the floor muttering, "He treated me like a little boy, like a little boy."[21] It didn't get better.

The next day they addressed the world's trouble spots and a host of other issues, but talk kept returning to Berlin. In the wake of the Second World War, the demolished city was split into four zones of occupation that were later melded into two, like Germany itself. West Berlin became the West's protectorate, despite its location 110 miles inside the Soviet's East German sector. An enormous infusion of American aid in the form of Marshall Plan money helped Western Europe and West Berliners recover from the war's destruction and deprivations, but a generation later their family members and former neighbours stuck in the East still suffered. With every decision Kennedy made he considered possible repercussions in Berlin. Berlin was the new Alamo that could be neither forgotten nor lost. Khrushchev understood. He told an aide, "Berlin is the testicles of the West. Every time I want to make the West scream, I squeeze on Berlin."[22]

Khrushchev told Kennedy that the Soviet Union had lost twenty million people in the Second World War and so was determined to see Germany permanently divided and weak. To this end, he was preparing to sign a peace treaty with East Germany that would render Germany's division permanent. If the United States accepted the treaty and its consequences, he would guarantee continued access to West Berlin. If not, it would be cut off and amalgamated into the new German state. Kennedy insisted that Germany's division was temporary, and that he would never negotiate away the people of West Berlin. Khrushchev agreed only to postpone his treaty signing until December.

Khrushchev's treaty would instigate war. That horror was rendered even more ominous by his refusal to seriously entertain nuclear disarmament. Kennedy was visibly shaken when the Soviet leader dismissed with a shrug the millions of people who would die in a nuclear exchange. At the end of their final meeting, Kennedy again failed to back Khrushchev away from a Berlin confrontation. He was told, "It is up to the US to decide whether there will be war or peace." Kennedy replied, "Then Mr. Chairman, there will be war. It will be a cold winter."[23]

Khrushchev knew he had bested the president. He told members of the Soviet Presidium, the ten-member council that since 1952 wielded supreme legislative power, that Kennedy was young enough to be his son, that he was intelligent but weak, and that he actually felt sorry for him.[24] Kennedy left Vienna angry and dismayed. He knew the Bay of Pigs blunder and now his Vienna performance had rendered an unthinkable war more likely.[25] He confided to *New York Times* journalist James Reston: "Roughest thing in my life. He just beat the hell out of me."[26] He had arrived ready to negotiate but then failed to adjust when it became clear that Khrushchev had come to bully. Kennedy flew to London and expressed fear and regret to Prime Minister Macmillan, who later observed, "For the first time in his life

Kennedy met a man who was impervious to his charm."[27] Macmillan might have more accurately counted Khrushchev as the second.

On Tuesday, June 6, home from work and with dinner dishes done, Canadians watched their televisions with growing dread as a tired-looking Kennedy characterized his discussions with Khrushchev as "blunt," "sober," and "frank." "We have wholly different views of right and wrong, of what is an internal affair and what is aggression, and, above all, wholly different concepts of where the world is and where it is going."[28] He touched on a number of topics but said that he'd left Vienna with no hope that progress would be made in talks currently underway to ban nuclear testing. Kennedy said the most "sombre" talks involved Berlin. He spoke of Khrushchev's threatened East German peace treaty. Laying down the gauntlet he said, "We and our allies cannot abandon the people of West Berlin."[29]

Over the next weeks, Kennedy continued to put into action the thesis he had argued so many years before in *Why England Slept* and reiterated in his May 25 speech to the joint session of Congress: to avoid war, he needed to prepare for it—and convince his enemy of a willingness to wage it. A letter to Canadian-born economist, trusted confidant, and newly appointed American ambassador to India John Kenneth Galbraith revealed that he was also motivated by a need to save his presidency: "There are limits to the number of defeats I can defend in one twelve-month period. I've had the Bay of Pigs, and pulling out of Laos and I can't accept a third."[30]

While Kennedy worried about another defeat, Khrushchev planned for victory. He publicly announced that he was increasing his defence budget by a third. He cancelled plans to reduce his number of men in uniform. The moves were designed to erase doubts that, as he had said at a recent ceremony commemorating the Soviet repulsion of the Nazi army, "The clock is ticking."[31]

Diefenbaker followed the Kennedy-Khrushchev manoeuvering with grave concern. Shortly after Kennedy had left Ottawa in May, Diefenbaker ensured that swap-deal negotiations regarding plane sales and the Pinetree Line management progressed quickly. The Americans bowed to Diefenbaker's insistence and the Voodoo fighter jets were retrofitted and delivered without nuclear weapons.[32] Further, despite agreement that Canada would pay half the cost of all the parts and associated equipment for the jets, it ended up paying only a third.

Just six days after Kennedy's jarring televised report of his Vienna encounter, Diefenbaker announced the swap deal in the House. He was careful not to gloat. "I would stress that the approach of both Governments has not been based on narrow self-interest, but reflects a genuine effort to find a way for each to co-operate with the other to the benefit not only of both but of mutual allies as well."[33]

On July 22, Diefenbaker and Kennedy spoke briefly on the telephone. It was a staged and stilted affair. Both men read from notes about the opening of a new mutual defence communication system in the Far North. Diefenbaker was in Whitehorse with the American consul general, the commander of the Alaska force overseeing the project, and a number of Canadian military officials. Kennedy said, "I want to congratulate the people of Canada upon adding a great new link to the communication system that binds this continent together, and I know that the Governor of Alaska and all the people in our 49th State welcome this great addition to their contact with Canada and the rest of the United States."[34] Both agreed that the day marked another important step in joint continental defence.

Two days later, on July 24, Diefenbaker brought the long-debated question of deploying American nuclear weapons in Canada back to his Cabinet. The Green-Harkness split remained an open wound. Diefenbaker sought to heal it by emphasizing the new threats that had emerged from Vienna. He expressed determination that Canada must prepare to contribute to a conflict that could start in Berlin but quickly move to Canadian skies.[35]

Green rehashed old arguments. He pleaded for his colleagues to consider the horror of Canadian cities being obliterated in a nuclear exchange. With the present circumstances, he contended, Khrushchev could interpret Kennedy's moving of nuclear weapons to Canada as a belligerent act; in that case, war could become more likely.[36] Not surprisingly, Harkness argued the opposite position. He focused on getting nukes for the Bomarcs. He contended that Khrushchev would surely understand that the short-range Bomarcs were defensive weapons, even when equipped with nuclear warheads. They were essential to Canadian and North American defence, he said, but effective only if properly armed.[37]

Cigarette butts cascaded from the heavy, dark-glass ashtrays atop the big oblong Cabinet table as the room filled with smoke and old arguments. Diefenbaker listened patiently and allowed airtime for all. When everyone had spoken, he reminded the group that Vienna had changed everything. Then, in a rare move, Diefenbaker sided with Harkness. Cabinet supported the prime minister's insistence on expediting the negotiations to deploy American nuclear weapons in Canada, and agreed to begin by accepting them at the Newfoundland and Labrador bases.[38]

Before External Affairs could implement Diefenbaker's decision, Kennedy was back on television. On the evening of July 25, using a map and charts to illustrate his point, he explained that Berlin had become the spot where American courage and resolve was being tested. "We cannot and will not permit the Communists to drive us out of Berlin, either gradually or by force."[39] He then announced a series of actions that, even more than his May 25 speech, represented an undeniable mobilization for war.

Kennedy asked Congress to approve an additional $3.25 billion for defence. He called for 875,000 additional men for the army, 29,000 more for the navy, and an increase of 63,000 for the air force. He called for draft quotas to be tripled, reserve units to be activated, and tours of duty to be extended. He reactivated ships and planes that had been slated for retirement. He warned that the deficit would rise and that tax increases could be necessary to pay for it all. [40]

He reiterated his May 25 assertion that Americans needed to prepare for nuclear war. "To recognize the possibilities of nuclear war in the missile age, without our citizens knowing what they should do and where they should go if bombs begin to fall, would be a failure of responsibility."[41] Civil defence initiatives had been shifted to the purview of the defence secretary and folded into plans for continental security. Kennedy now pledged an additional $200 million for new structures to be built, others renovated, and more food and water to be stockpiled. He warned, "In the event of an attack, the lives of those families which are not hit in a nuclear blast and fire can still be saved—if they can be warned to take shelter and if that shelter is available."[42] Rather than watching Ben Cartwright and Marshall Dillon shooting bad guys on TV, Canadians watched again as the American president spoke of real bad guys preparing to shoot them.


It was time for Diefenbaker to take a stand in public as he had with Cabinet. He did so where he thought he could win the widest press coverage—at the Halifax meeting of the Canadian Weekly Newspapers Association. His speech was detailed, emotional, and persuasive. "Faced by the overwhelming power of Soviet might in East Germany close to West Berlin with large divisions fully armed, would you place in the hands of those who guard against the portals of freedom nothing but bows and arrows?"[43] He advocated supplying nuclear warheads to all Canadian weapons systems at home and in Europe. The speech was a clear attempt to influence public opinion, as Diefenbaker had promised Kennedy. It was carefully written and well delivered; it was also ignored. Outside of Halifax, no newspaper afforded it prominence or editorial comment.[44]

Upon his return to Ottawa, he pushed External Affairs to accelerate renewed negotiations with the Americans. A message then arrived from

Kennedy. The August 3 letter began by noting that he was "pre-occupied with the Soviet challenge to our position in West Berlin." It argued that the situation necessitated strength and unity in the NATO alliance and in the defence of North America. Kennedy reminded Diefenbaker that, in February and May, he had agreed to resume negotiations to accept American weapons on Canadian soil and asked that those talks begin immediately and "with vigor."[45] Diefenbaker replied that he appreciated Kennedy's concerns, was moving quickly to address them, and hoped they would resume soon. He asked that nothing be said publicly about the negotiations.[46] It was a private correspondence, but through leaks in either Washington or Ottawa, it was soon public.

Only ten days after Kennedy's missive, on August 13, 1961, East Germany began building the Berlin Wall. What started as strings of barbed wire was soon a ninety-six-mile ring of concrete nearly twelve feet tall and three feet wide encircling the eastern portion of the city. From the wall's 302 towers, machine-gun-toting guards observed anti-vehicle trenches and metal fencing and had clear shots at anyone attempting to cross. East German authorities claimed the wall was erected to keep dangerous, fascist elements out. But everyone knew of the 3.5 million Germans who had already fled the hardships of the East for the American-subsidized West. The Berlin Wall was there to keep liberty out and people in. It was the concrete epitome of Churchill's Iron Curtain.

With Berlin pouring cement and Kennedy marching to war, many Canadians continued to scorn the idea of accepting American nuclear weapons. Anti-nuclear and pro-disarmament organizations led by women's groups, clergy, and university professors grew in number and size. The Co-operative Commonwealth Federation and the Liberals continued to offer support. Pearson rose in the House of Commons and, expressing points he had been making for years, called nuclear weapons morally and politically wrong and insisted they had no place in Canada.[47]

Diefenbaker prepared for war. As Kennedy had, he swept aside concerns of a fiscal deficit and approved changes needed to add muscle and steel to the military. Eleven hundred more troops were dispatched to augment Canada's NATO forces in Europe. Canada's overall troop ceiling was raised from 120,000 to 135,000. Plans were made to train 100,000 new recruits to assist with civil defence. The defence budget was increased by $250 million.[48] Three months earlier the Acheson report, upon which Kennedy had based his European flexible response strategy, had said that Canada was the only NATO ally pulling its weight. Diefenbaker saw to it that Canada would be pulling even more.

It was still not enough for the Americans. Escott Reid, the Canadian ambassador to Germany since 1958, flew to Ottawa and briefed Diefenbaker on the morning of August 17 about Canada's role in the ongoing tension in Berlin. Reid and Ambassador Heeney then consulted with State Department officials and prominent senators in Washington. Reid returned with news of an American consensus that Canada was failing the United States and NATO and needed to immediately acquire nuclear weapons.[49] Diefenbaker asked External Affairs to develop options regarding Canadian policies related to current tensions and the roles the UN could play in relieving them. Diefenbaker's request, like his decision to increase military capacity and his stubbornness with Kennedy, reflected the ideas of functionalism and internationalism that had begun in the Second World War and informed Canadian foreign policy throughout its so-called golden age. They also demonstrated Diefenbaker's desire, as he had expressed several times, to keep Canada from becoming "a mere tail on the America kite."[50]

By the end of August, Howard Green presented a draft proposal to Cabinet that outlined the rules and procedures for the transportation, storage, and use of American nuclear weapons in Canada. Many were untenable. Hours of discussion and debate ensued. Diefenbaker ordered the work redone so a clear and practical Canadian position could be put on the table. He demanded strict confidence but offered to meet with Kennedy if that would move the talks forward.[51]

While important progress was being made in Ottawa, Ambassador Heeney faced mounting frustration in Washington. He attempted to smooth the waters with a dinner party at the Canadian embassy. He invited some senior State Department staff along with secretary of state Dean Rusk and McGeorge Bundy, a foreign- and defence-policy expert and one of Kennedy's most trusted national security advisors. The food and wine were good but the results were not. Bundy was especially harsh. He expressed the president's disappointment in NATO allies that were not sufficiently effusive in their support for American actions in Berlin. Then, twisting his argument, he claimed that he, Rusk, and others didn't care what allies did or said, or one whit about their public opinion problems. Characterizations of Canada's inadequate support for Kennedy became so unfair and rude that a few days later Bundy penned an apology. He assured Heeney that, despite the fact that he and Rusk had said otherwise, no one in Kennedy's administration considered Canadians appeasers.[52] The note was a nice gesture, but once insults are cast they are tough to reel back in.

On the first of September, Diefenbaker spoke to the Canadian Bar Association in Winnipeg. He delivered what the *Globe and Mail* called "the best and clearest statement a Canadian government spokesman has ever delivered on an issue of foreign policy."[53] West Berliners' freedom was non-negotiable, he said, and he advocated addressing the current crisis and related issues through NATO and the UN. However, should peaceful and diplomatic efforts fail or should the Soviet Union take other provocative actions, then Western allies should meet force with force.[54] A week later, the fall session of Parliament began and Diefenbaker formally announced the troop and weapon enhancements he had ordered over the summer.

His September pronouncements established a balance of support for hopeful diplomacy and military preparedness, a position from which Diefenbaker could advance Canadian interests while respecting American strategic goals, their mutual allies, and international organizations.

Despite American insults and clumsy diplomacy, negotiations to bring nuclear missiles to Canada began anew, but with Diefenbaker more convinced than ever of the need for rock solid guarantees of bilateral control and consultation.[55]

By mid-September, Kennedy was reading that a Canadian-American nuclear agreement was on its way. Private State Department memos praised Diefenbaker for moving the file forward despite domestic political pressure.[56] Then, just as it looked like the long-delayed deal would finally come together, it crumbled. Problems began with a *Montreal Gazette* headline: "JFK Presses Canada on Nuclear Warheads."[57] The story quoted from a *Newsweek* article that was due out in a couple of days. It cited White House sources who claimed that Kennedy was pushing a reluctant Diefenbaker to accept American nuclear weapons.[58]

Diefenbaker could not believe it. First, he had made it clear to all involved that due to the delicacy of Canadian public opinion, the talks had to be secret. Second, it had been only four months since he'd been infuriated by Kennedy's private memo that presumed to "push" Canada. Here was more talk of Canada being pushed, but this time in a popular magazine. Washington quickly realized that damage had been done. Messages whipped between the White House, State Department, and the embassy in Ottawa. Rusk, Bundy, Undersecretary of State George Ball, and others debated blame and then groped for ways to fix it.[59]

Publicly, Diefenbaker swallowed his ire. He attempted to salvage the negotiations by speaking first in the House and then on the popular CBC television program *The Nation's Business*. He ignored the *Newsweek* leak and did not directly address the nuclear talks, offering instead that if any agreement were made with the Americans affecting Canadian defence and security, he would involve and inform the Canadian people. He deftly danced away from a question about Kennedy's August 3 letter by stating that national security precluded him from discussing his communications with world leaders.[60]

The source of the *Newsweek* leak was never revealed. Everyone knew, however, that the magazine's Washington bureau chief, Benjamin Bradlee, was among Kennedy's closest friends. A fellow Bostonian and Harvard alum, Bradlee had the looks and lifestyle of a movie star. By the 1950s, the Bradlees and Kennedys were Georgetown neighbours. They enjoyed many dinners and weekends at Palm Beach, Camp David, and the White House. Over drinks and cigars, Kennedy often brought Bradlee into his confidence and at least twice discussed Diefenbaker.[61]

Diefenbaker's statesmanlike reaction to Kennedy's ill-timed letter, insults from his administration officials, and the *Newsweek* leak put the nuclear negotiations back on the tracks until the president derailed them again. In a speech to the United Nations on September 25 Kennedy said, "Every man, woman and child lives under a nuclear sword of Damocles, hanging by the slenderest of threads, capable of being cut at any moment by accident or miscalculation or by madness. The weapons of war must be abolished before they abolish us."[62] He continued with a bold call for nuclear disarmament. He spoke of a new American agency that he had created the day before to negotiate a "general and complete" disarmament under "international control." Kennedy argued that the place to begin was a nuclear test ban agreement. He said the United States was ready to begin a global disarmament program based on six proposals. The third was: "prohibiting the transfer of control over nuclear weapons to states that do not own them."[63]

Kennedy had not directly mentioned Canada. It is unlikely that he even considered the impact of his speech on Canadians. But no one involved in the negotiations to bring American-owned nuclear weapons to Canada under joint Canadian-American control could have missed the speech's significance. Basil Robinson and Diefenbaker agreed that it represented a "pronounced change" from the position American officials had been advancing for years, and that Kennedy had discussed in February and May. Robinson later wrote that Diefenbaker believed "the public position now taken by the President had killed nuclear weapons in Canada."[64] They agreed that more and more it was becoming clear that we would not be having nuclear weapons in Canada unless there was a war. Similarly, Kennedy's parsing of the words *control* and *own* meant that it was unlikely Canadian forces in Europe could ever take possession of American nuclear weapons, as that too would contradict the president's new policy.

Canadian doves and anti-nuclear activists were ecstatic. They cheered Kennedy's new support for disarmament and determination to end proliferation. They redoubled their efforts to win Diefenbaker's support for their position, which suddenly appeared to be Kennedy's as well. Representatives from the Voice of Women met with Diefenbaker and pressed him to see what he had already seen: Kennedy's speech had rendered the deployment of American nuclear weapons in Canada impossible.[65] Politely expressing worries that communists had infiltrated their group, he dismissed their presentation.[66]

Shortly afterwards, booming through Diefenbaker's large East Block office windows came chanting and singing that was not as easy to ignore. About eight hundred protestors organized by the Canadian Campaign for Nuclear Disarmament carried signs and relentlessly shouted anti-nuclear slogans from Parliament Hill's vast lawn. Diefenbaker accepted a petition from the Canadian Committee for the Control of Radiation Hazards (CCCRH) containing 150,000 names gathered from across the country.[67] Among the signatories were photographer Yousuf Karsh, author Hugh MacLennan, diplomat and influential civil servant Hugh Keenleyside, and a Montreal university professor and gadfly journalist for the widely read Quebec journal *Cité Libre* named Pierre Trudeau.[68] Diefenbaker met with CCCRH leaders and confessed to being moved by their arguments.[69]

If all of that were not enough, Diefenbaker received a report from the Boeing Company, maker of the Bomarc missile. Its claims were staggering. In cold, technical language, it contradicted the Americans, Harkness, and his generals. If armed with conventional rather than nuclear warheads, the Bomarc-A and Bomarc-B missiles would not be as effective in bringing down enemy bombers but would still be fully functional and a potent weapon in a country's defensive arsenal.[70] Diefenbaker had been lied to. Boeing released its report, and it was picked up by a number of Canadian and American newspapers.[71] Arriving so soon after Kennedy's UN speech, and coming as it did amidst the anti-nuclear weapons protests and pressure, the Boeing report was the final straw.

Diefenbaker suspended nuclear negotiations. They would wait until after the federal election, to be called in the spring. Meanwhile, he said, in the event of a war, American nuclear weapons could be quickly transferred to Canada.[72] Willis Armstrong, head of the State Department's Canada desk, understood what had happened. He composed a memo to Rusk explaining that "recent events" had put Diefenbaker in the untenable position of being unable to negotiate the acceptance of American nuclear weapons without looking like a Kennedy lackey. Armstrong took comfort in the fact that Diefenbaker had merely suspended the talks, and not cancelled them completely.[73]

Kennedy ordered Ambassador Merchant to change Diefenbaker's mind. He got nowhere. Merchant never liked Diefenbaker. In a 1959 message to Eisenhower he had denounced Diefenbaker's "truculent nationalism."[74] Through the summer and fall of 1961, more personal insults found their way into his political analysis. A November 27 report began: "Please inform the President that during the course of a long rambling talk with Prime Minister Diefenbaker. . . ."[75] A few weeks later he wrote that Diefenbaker and his Conservative Party were losing public support and becoming more anti-American. He added, ominously given what was to follow, that only Pearson and the Liberals could be trusted to be friendly to the United States.[76]

Canada remained the only NATO country that could easily make or acquire nuclear weapons but did not. A decision delayed is sometimes not indecision but a decision in itself, and the year ended with Kennedy and his men gnashing their teeth over a Canadian prime minister who simply would not do as he was told. The next months would tell whether the Canadian people were perhaps more pliant than their leader.

# EIGHT

---

# OVERSTEPPING BOUNDS IN THE 1962 ELECTION

AS NEW YEAR'S EVE REVELLERS KISSED and hoped for the redemptive power of a new beginning, Kennedy had been president for nearly a year. His eyes were a little darker and grey flecks had found their way into his thick brown hair. Kennedy was always concerned about his appearance and weight, and although his waistline remained at thirty-two, stress and regularly injected cortisone shots were introducing a noticeable puffiness to his face.[1] The Ottawa tree incident was continuing to take its toll.

Diefenbaker was tired. At the beginning of 1962, he was sixty-six years old and had been prime minister for four and a half years. His curly hair was now completely silver and his bright but sunken eyes sported permanent dark circles. Some added weight, along with the ruthless partnership of years and gravity, had given him jowls. He smiled less and growled more. Diefenbaker was also developing a slight tremor that grew worse when he was fatigued or agitated. Colleagues worried and critics shamelessly guessed that the prime minister was suffering from palsy or even early-onset Parkinson's disease.[2] While Kennedy would not face re-election until 1964, Diefenbaker needed to rally himself to go to the people in the next few months. He was party leader as well as prime minister, and so electoral politics began to colour his decisions even more than usual.

Meanwhile, Lester Pearson's primary job was still to take Diefenbaker's. Over the previous two years he had reinvigorated and reconstructed a shattered and demoralized Liberal Party. Policy had been reimagined. Keith Davey was restructuring the party's communications apparatus, modernizing its fundraising processes, and attracting new, exciting candidates. A unique conscript was Toronto Maple Leafs hockey star Red Kelly. Although Kelly had no political experience whatsoever, he easily won his party's nomination in Toronto's York West riding. In the next election Kelly defeated the lawyer who would later help and then hurt hockey players, the infamous Alan Eagleson. His success was testament to the exploding power of television and celebrity in politics.

While Kennedy and Diefenbaker had carefully plotted their way to the pinnacle of political success and then tackled their jobs with obvious relish, Pearson's image remained that of a reluctant leader and unenthusiastic politician. Private letters to his son, Geoffrey, now the first secretary of Canada's embassy in Mexico, revealed that he found politics a burden. He missed the more "instructive and interesting" world of diplomacy.[3] In the House and on the hustings he was still no match for Diefenbaker's fiery oratory and masterfully quick retorts, but he was improving.

Parliament had been recessed since September and would resume on January 18, 1962. Diefenbaker juggled a number of contentious files, including Britain's continuing efforts to join the Common Market. He had been badgering Prime Minister Macmillan for over a year with negative impacts the move would have on Canada, and with the point that since all Commonwealth countries would be affected by Britain's decision, they should be involved in making it or, at the very least, be fully consulted. Macmillan had grown increasingly frustrated with Diefenbaker's stubborn opposition to Britain's wishes. Macmillan later dismissed him as "a very crooked man . . . so self-centred as to be a sort of caricature of Mr. Gladstone."[4] Diefenbaker knew that President Kennedy was exerting pressure on the Common Market's original six—especially de Gaulle—to support Britain's membership. For a host of reasons, trade mattered to Kennedy. Like Diefenbaker, he was bedevilled by an economy in recovery but unable to regain its post-war momentum. Part of America's economic sluggishness was tied to a significant and growing trade imbalance: more American dollars were going out than coming in, and gold reserves were shrinking.

Kennedy also understood the connection between economic growth and stability at home and American influence abroad. He knew that the prolonged period of post-war prosperity and its enormous trade surplus had allowed the unprecedented largesse of the Marshall Plan and the costly posting of American troops around the world. He warned his National Security Council that unless the current trade imbalance was addressed, sustainable prosperity would not return—but many of those soldiers would.[5]

In his January 11 State of the Union address, Kennedy offered the usual shopping list of policy priorities. Highlighted among them was the Trade Expansion Act. He couched it in Cold War terms, observing, "At year's end the economy which Mr. Khrushchev once called a 'stumbling horse' was racing to new records in consumer spending, labor income, and industrial production. . . . We are gratified but not satisfied."[6] The new bill would try to deal with the trade deficit by targeting Europe with a flood of American exports. Kennedy's plan would only work if Europe was stable and prosperous, and that was more likely if Britain joined the Common Market. The State of the Union address and the new trade bill were public declarations of points Kennedy had repeatedly made with Macmillan, and showcased some of the reasons why he was so irritated with Diefenbaker and de Gaulle.[7] Once again, in standing up for Canada, Diefenbaker was frustrating Kennedy's ambitions for America.

Kennedy renewed his efforts to encourage Commonwealth support for Britain's inclusion in the Common Market by trying again to bring

Diefenbaker on side. On January 12 and 13, the Joint Canada–United States Ministerial Cabinet Committee, made up of Cabinet members from both governments, devoted most of its time to discussing Kennedy's new trade initiatives and the Common Market question. Secretary of State Rusk reported to the president that the Canadians refused to budge. The group agreed to keep their disagreement from their bland communiqué.[8]

Diefenbaker prepared to deliver a trade speech of his own. He did not have assigned speechwriters. His standard practice was to gather ideas, statistics, and drafts from a number of sources and then shuffle them together with his own ideas while leaving room to make things up on the fly.[9] He used that haphazard method to prepare for his January 25 address to the Montreal Real Estate Board. To the group of carefully coiffed and dark-suited Quebec businessmen, he boasted that prairie farmers were happy to be shipping more wheat to China than ever before. He did not mention that Kennedy was still chagrined about Canadian-Chinese trade. Similarly, he explained Canada's opposition to Britain's Common Market membership but avoided Kennedy's contrary position. He predicted that, despite his efforts, Britain would eventually join. Therefore, the government needed to work diligently to protect Canadian interests in upcoming Commonwealth meetings but be ready to adjust its trade priorities. He spoke of Kennedy's new promotion of American exports while taking care not to criticize the president or the plan.[10] Despite the enormous pressure from Kennedy and Macmillan, the speech was diplomatic and restrained.

Four days later, Kennedy's special advisor Arthur Schlesinger stopped in Vancouver on his way to meetings in Tokyo. In a conversation with reporters Schlesinger blasted Diefenbaker's refusal to join the OAS and his trade policies involving Cuba and China that rendered Canada an unreliable ally. Anything that helped Castro, he said, hurt the Western alliance.[11] It was a blunt frontal attack made doubly shocking by the fact that Schlesinger delivered it on Canadian soil. It is hard to imagine that he acted without Kennedy's knowledge or approval.

Diefenbaker responded in the House. He was calm and measured, but he sent a message that the president was sure to hear: He would continue to act not in America's but Canada's best interest. That would include maintaining trade with Cuba and China, remaining outside the Organization of American States, and continuing to oppose Britain's entry into the Common Market.[12] Shortly afterwards, Diefenbaker met with representatives from the Farmers Union. They expressed concern that Kennedy's new trade policies, specifically the goal of increasing America wheat sales in Europe, would hurt Canadian exports. Thinking he was among friends, Diefenbaker tried to reassure the group by letting it slip that Kennedy's trade bill would probably not get through Congress. He was then embarrassed to read what he'd thought was a private comment in the next morning's *Globe and Mail*.[13] Diefenbaker said nothing in response.

A week later, another American came north to launch another attack on Diefenbaker. Powerful New York Republican senator Kenneth Keating spoke on the CBC program *Newsmagazine*. "I have always regarded Canada as one of our most dependable allies . . . but I cannot understand, therefore, the apparent unwillingness of the Canadian authorities to co-operate fully in imposing economic sanctions against Cuba—and for that matter also against Red China . . . every sale which bolsters the Cuban economy strengthens Castro's hold on the Cuban people and supports his dictatorship."[14] Diefenbaker swallowed in silence the exasperation caused by yet another prominent American criticizing his government for refusing to do Kennedy's bidding.

Arnold Heeney had been doing terrific work with the increasingly difficult task of representing Canada in America, but due to health issues he asked to be replaced. In February 1962, Diefenbaker appointed Halifax-born and Harvard-educated Charles Ritchie. Ritchie was an experienced diplomat, civil servant, and former ambassador to West Germany and the UN. He was among the "Pearsonalities" who had worked with the future Liberal leader in London, Washington, and Bonn, where they became close friends. He was witty, a skilled writer, and a keen observer of people in power. In 1959 Diefenbaker had appointed Ritchie's Oxford-educated brother Roland to the Supreme Court.

Upon his arrival in Washington, Ritchie was shocked at the depth of anti-Canadian, anti-Diefenbaker sentiment. At a private party, Secretary of State Rusk cornered and lambasted him about Canadian actions and attitudes. Respected and influential American journalist Walter Lippmann confessed to Ritchie afterwards that he had never seen or even heard of any foreign ambassador being addressed in such rude terms.[15]

As Pearson had decades before, Ritchie found most American government officials either ignorant or dismissive of Canada. Others seemed to lack an understanding of Canada's right to promote its national interests, or of its usefulness in promoting America's. He confided to his diary, "Do the Americans realize that our differences of outlook from them in international affairs make us more valuable to them than if we were mere satellites? I sometimes doubt it."[16]

Kennedy had the new ambassador wait an unusual and insulting length of time before agreeing to accept his Letters of Credence. When the day finally arrived, Ritchie sat in the Oval Office feeling uncomfortable through a stilted conversation punctuated with pauses that too often slid into long silences. Ritchie was astonished when the president suddenly half rose from his rocking chair, waved his arm, and said, "Shoo, shoo!" Ritchie could not believe he was being dismissed in such a crude manner. He quickly realized that Kennedy was looking past him and at his daughter, Caroline, who was attempting to lead her pet, Macaroni the pony, in from the portico.[17]

Among Ritchie's first tasks was helping Diefenbaker respond to a message from Moscow in which Khrushchev invited Diefenbaker to attend a disarmament summit in Geneva. The invitation was discussed in Cabinet and with Ritchie in light of the fact that Macmillan and Kennedy had both stated that they wanted disarmament talks to resume, but first at a lower-level meeting of foreign ministers. Diefenbaker and Green were quite keen on the resumption of talks but wary of Khrushchev's motives. They held the British-American line. In a letter to Khrushchev and in a follow-up speech in the House, Diefenbaker praised the Soviet disarmament initiative and expressed hope that the Geneva meeting would be fruitful, but said Green would attend for Canada.[18]

In his January 1962 State of the Union address, Kennedy had spoken of a "global civil war."[19] He listed five "basic strengths" that would allow the West to stand against communist aggression. Among them were the "united strength of the Atlantic community" and the "regional strength of our Hemispheric relations."[20] It was unspoken but clear that Canada was in a unique position as the only country other than the United States that was part of both groups. Kennedy needed Canada to be strong and, as he had stated over and over again, Canada could only attain maximum strength by accepting nuclear weapons.

Ambassador Merchant understood Kennedy's point and his job. A February 26 wire to Rusk stated, "As you know greatest single outstanding problem between US and Canada is Canadian failure to face up to question [of] nuclear warheads."[21] He spread the blame for Canada's not having nuclear weapons with a wide brush. He reminded Rusk that the leak of Kennedy's August letter to Diefenbaker just as the prime minister was preparing to resume negotiations had been a setback. He stated with obvious annoyance, and in contradiction of the Boeing report, that the Canadian Armed Forces had taken delivery of "expensive military hardware which were next to useless without nuclear tips."[22] Merchant always placed the lion's share of blame on Diefenbaker. After having observed a particularly raucous House debate, he wrote, "Prime Minister Diefenbaker's remarks on nuclear weapons . . . are nothing short of dismaying since they represent irresponsible treatment of subject of vital importance to Canada and US. They probably stem from compound of ignorance of complex subject and profound reluctance [to] face up to disagreeable subject, an unfortunate propensity [to] point to US as immovable stumbling block, and the heat of moment in lively parliamentary exchange with Pearson for whom he feels positive personal dislike."[23]

The pique came to a point a few days later. Diefenbaker was responding to more of Pearson's questions. He was tossing typical Question Period answers back across the aisle, stuffed with more partisan blarney than facts—it is called Question Period, after all, and not Answer Period. As the questioning turned to interrogation, however, Diefenbaker began digging a hole with a number of clumsily worded non-answer-answers and then slipped headfirst into it. He said that in the case of an emergency, nuclear weapons could be quickly shipped to Canada. In response to follow-up questions, he admitted that there was, in fact, no signed agreement for such a contingency.[24] There was instant pandemonium. His candid admission contradicted what he had been saying for years.

Liberal Paul Martin then stood and listed a number of subjects discussed during Kennedy's Ottawa visit. He insisted that a secret nuclear weapons deal had been agreed upon and asked for details. Diefenbaker swatted the question away by repeating, quite truthfully, that there was no deal, secret or otherwise. He was not worried about his slip and the inevitable Liberal piling on. He was baffled, though, by the quite accurate details that Martin seemed to have at his disposal regarding in-camera meetings with the president.[25]

Diefenbaker had External Affairs ask the American embassy if it could shed light on how Martin had come to know what he obviously knew so well. Merchant was quickly on the phone to the prime minister swearing that Martin had not received information from him or any other American. However, in a subsequent meeting with Diefenbaker and in a report to the State Department, Merchant sheepishly admitted that Washington was shocked to learn that Americans had indeed been

Martin's source. An American officer had spoken with someone in Detroit and an American general had talked with someone else in Bermuda. Somehow, the content of the conversations had ended up in the hands of senior Liberal Members of Parliament.[26]

While American officers had indeed been indiscreet, it was later discovered that former external affairs employee Doug LePan was Martin's source.[27] LePan had been among those targeted in a process that had begun in 1948, in which gay men were investigated and swept from public service ostensibly due to a fear that communist spies could blackmail them into surrendering state secrets to keep their homosexuality under wraps. One Canadian diplomat had been driven to suicide. Diefenbaker had been appalled by the witch hunts and had ordered the practice reviewed, but he allowed it to continue.[28] LePan had written to Pearson, who had passed the information to Martin.

Many people were, at that time, accusing Diefenbaker of being paranoid. The Martin incident, coupled with the scathing Merchant reports and public insults from high-ranking American government officials and Kennedy himself, proved the old adage that just because you may be paranoid doesn't mean they are not out to get you.

Amid the ratcheting tensions, Kennedy turned to Diefenbaker for help. A group of Americans in Cuba had been accused of spying and were arrested. The United States had no diplomatic corps on the island nation, so when the trial began, Kennedy asked if the Canadian embassy in Havana could intervene. Diefenbaker quickly sent word to embassy officials and the Americans were soon sent home. On April 1, Kennedy wrote a personal letter of thanks to the prime minister and Merchant added a note expressing "admiration" for Diefenbaker's quick and successful handling of the situation.[29] It was a ray of light that served only to emphasize the gathering darkness.

Two weeks later, the light shone a little brighter. Kennedy signed a three-page letter to Diefenbaker expressing regret that relations between Canada and the United States were becoming "increasingly disparate." He said that he understood and shared Canada's desire for nuclear disarmament but needed Diefenbaker's help again. In what Kennedy saw as a continuing effort to split the Western alliance, Khrushchev had proposed a nuclear test ban treaty that would allow no independent verification of compliance. Kennedy asked Diefenbaker to join him and Macmillan in opposing the obviously duplicitous treaty proposal. He ended, "I hope you will agree with me that Canada and the United States should stand together on this issue of vital importance to our common safety."[30]

The next day, a reporter happened to ask Diefenbaker whether the Soviet Union could be trusted to live up to the terms of the proposed test ban treaty. Diefenbaker said no. He explained that the many instances since the Second World War in which the Soviet Union had broken its promises proved that a test ban treaty would need to include a robust process for inspection by neutral parties. The comment was ignored in the House and Canadian press but not by the White House. Kennedy wrote to express his gratitude: "I want to let you know right away of my great appreciation of this authoritative and timely recording of the Voice of Canada."[31]

The proposed treaty became moot a couple of weeks later when Khrushchev resumed nuclear testing. Kennedy announced on March 2 that the United States would need to do the same. The dream of disarmament faded as each blast filled the air with carcinogenic radiation. A week later, Howard Green left for the eighteen-power disarmament talks in Geneva that now promised scant likelihood of progress.

Diefenbaker consulted with Pearson on Tuesday, April 17, and the next day visited the governor general. Parliament was dissolved and the election set for June 18. On the day the writ dropped, most Canadians had more on their minds than politics. With each newscast or headline detailing Khrushchev's or Kennedy's boasts and threats, they were reminded of the constant risk of a nuclear holocaust.

As perhaps an inoculation against the harshness and horror of the times, popular culture offered salve without satire and tranquility oblivious to irony. The number-one song that week was the saccharine "Johnny Angel" by the strikingly sweet Shelley Fabares. The top movie was the even sweeter *State Fair*, in which the perennially wholesome Pat Boone and safely sexy Ann-Margret insisted on frequently and inexplicably breaking into song. More Canadians than ever owned television sets, and the most popular programs that month offered equally non-threatening, popular piffle: Lucille Ball, Andy Griffith, Dick Van Dyke, and even a talking horse named Mister Ed.

While popular culture clung to a nostalgic past that had never really existed, Canada's political culture charged forward. Diefenbaker's barn-burning 1958 campaign was only four years past, but it somehow already seemed an anachronism. The Co-operative Commonwealth Federation had morphed into the New Democratic Party in July 1961 and was offering a social democratic alternative to the two mainstream parties. Its newly elected leader was former Saskatchewan premier Tommy Douglas. He had kept taxes low and the budget balanced while introducing a number of earth-breaking reforms that included Canada's first public health care system. The Social Credit Party was born in Alberta as a conservative-populist response to the Depression. It had formed governments in Alberta and British Columbia and won federal seats before losing them all in the 1958 Diefenbaker sweep. In 1962, however, the Socreds were back in fighting form and especially strong in Quebec due to the party's charismatic deputy leader Réal Caouette.

Then, of course, there was the resurgent Liberal Party. Every poll since November 1960 indicated that Canadians liked Diefenbaker more than Pearson but the Liberals more than the Progressive Conservatives.[32]

The seemingly contradictory polls had to have worried Diefenbaker, since Canadian federal elections are really just hundreds of local elections held on the same day. With no one directly choosing the prime minister, the Canadian voter is less a public relations person involved in a hiring than an architect designing a House.

Of perhaps greater significance than parties and popular pastimes was a shift in perceptions of political leadership. Maybe the change reflected the growing emphasis on youth that was born of the baby boom. Its first wave was finishing high school and exerting enormous cultural and economic influence. Perhaps the change was helped along by the fact that by 1962, many people had been enjoying televisions in their home for nearly ten years. In sending beautiful people directly into everyone's living room every day, TV was creating a more effortless, immediate, and overwhelming fascination with celebrity than radio, newspapers, magazines, or movies could.

John Kennedy represented the perfect meeting of a man and moment. His age, looks, grace, and vigour symbolized the untapped potency of youth and celebrity. Nothing better illustrated how the game had changed than his first televised debate with Richard Nixon. Those who listened on radio said Nixon had won. Those watching the tanned and telegenic Kennedy knew otherwise. From the thousands who cheered his arrival in Ottawa to the fawning media coverage that followed, it was apparent that Canadians had fallen under his spell. Decades after watching the Kennedy motorcade move slowly through Ottawa, Canadian poet Carolyn Smart remains awed that as a little girl she saw Jacqueline and glimpsed the president's waving hand.[33] Irish author Brian Gallagher was only ten years old when he saw Kennedy speak in Ireland. More than fifty years later, Gallagher recalls not the president's words but the whiteness of his smile, the sharp cut of his perfectly tailored blue suit, and deep tan. "He didn't look like the old, ugly, rumpled politicians we knew. He looked like a movie star."[34]

The TV images of the effervescent American John invited Canadians to look at their own John a little differently. Diefenbaker looked, acted, and spoke the same as he did only four years earlier, when he'd wooed voters with his nationalist vision and populist charisma. He had not changed, but Canada and Canadians had. In 1962 he appeared to be exactly what he was—the product of an older generation attempting to carry on in a new era, closer to the yesterdays embodied by Eisenhower than Kennedy's rush to tomorrow.

These ephemeral changes represent only Kennedy's oblique influence on the 1962 Canadian election. His frustration with Diefenbaker's nationalist obstinacy and refusal to make a definitive decision on nuclear weapons led to a much more direct role. That spring, with election signs being hammered into still partially frozen front lawns, Kennedy remained primarily concerned with Nikita Khrushchev. Always anxious to learn more about his enigmatic opponent, he read everything he could and asked to speak with anyone who had met him. Kennedy's advisors recommended a meeting with Lester Pearson.

Kennedy telephoned the Liberal leader and invited him to a White House dinner celebrating Nobel Prize winners. He asked Pearson to arrive early to discuss Khrushchev. Pearson replied that he was happy to do so but worried that Diefenbaker would protest a visit to the White House from the leader of the Opposition. Kennedy asked if Pearson had an honorary degree from Harvard. He did, so Kennedy asked if he had one from MIT. Again he was told yes. What about Boston College? When Pearson said no, Kennedy promised to arrange the degree on the necessary date to create another reason to visit America.[35]

On April 4, Diefenbaker's office received a courtesy call from the American embassy explaining that Pearson would be invited to the president's reception on April 29. Diefenbaker was incensed.[36] Kennedy was clearly meddling in the election. Canadians would see Pearson basking in the reflected glow of the president they admired while surrounded by respected intellectuals and heroes. After long and often heated debates,

Diefenbaker decided that objecting would look petty and cause more damage than the event itself.[37] He seethed in silence.

Pearson received his degree and made his way to the White House. For twenty minutes he and Kennedy sat alone in the president's private study discussing Vietnam, the Columbia River Treaty, the Common Market, nuclear testing and disarmament, current tensions and trouble spots and, of course, Khrushchev. Pearson was told of things going on behind the scenes and Kennedy probed for advice. They were interrupted only when Kennedy's daughter, Caroline, ran in twice. On the third time she stopped, stamped her foot, and said, as only a petulant four-and-a-half-year-old could, "C'mon Daddy, stop working!"[38]

The 175 guests, who included Mrs. Kennedy, Vice President Johnson, and the attorney general, stood as the president and Pearson made their entrance together. They were introduced together and stood side by side as they mingled. In his toast, Kennedy mentioned only one of the august group by name. "Ladies and gentleman, Mr. Lester Pearson informed me that a Canadian newspaper said yesterday that this is the president's Easter egghead roll on the White House lawn. I want to deny it . . . I think this is the most extraordinary collection of talent, of human knowledge, that has ever been gathered together at the White House—with the possible exception of when Thomas Jefferson dined here alone."[39]

The White House reception and Kennedy's respect for Pearson—some called it friendship—was widely reported across Canada in the second of the election campaign's eight weeks. An Associated Press (AP) photograph of a smiling Pearson standing with a smiling Kennedy and chatting with respected novelist Pearl Buck accompanied a glowing article in papers across the country.[40]

McGeorge Bundy later told Kennedy that Diefenbaker was upset with the invitation, the private meeting (which the Canadian press mistakenly reported as not twenty but forty minutes long), and about his gushing over Pearson at the dinner. The president asked that word be sent to Pearson that the Liberals should not make political capital of the dinner and their private talk. Revealing perhaps more than intended, he said it would make things "so obvious."[41] But Kennedy was not finished with his "so obvious" tactics.

Diefenbaker had been once again criss-crossing the country shaking hands, putting his extraordinary memory of names and faces to work, and delivering barn-burning speeches. The crowds still showed up but they were smaller. They still applauded but a little quieter. They left more quickly. Somehow, the magic was gone.

With the campaign in trouble and Diefenbaker both tired after a bumpy flight from Newfoundland and fighting a cold, Ambassador Merchant arrived at the prime minister's home on May 4. He had come to announce his decision to retire. Instead of allowing the ceremonial visit to end pleasantly, he asked, again, whether Diefenbaker had changed his mind about American nuclear weapons. Whether it was the flight or the cold, or maybe just exasperation at being asked a question he had answered so many times, Diefenbaker hit the roof. His eyes blazed, his face reddened, and both fists pounded his desk. He shouted about the many ways in which the president had shown disrespect for him and Canada and how the Nobel dinner and private talk with Pearson had been an unacceptable interference in the election.

Merchant cowered. Diefenbaker raged. He shouted that Walter Gordon, the Liberal national campaign chairman and Toronto riding candidate, had said in a speech the night before that Pearson's White House meeting proved that Liberals were more respected by Kennedy because they were better able to handle foreign affairs. It was an argument, Diefenbaker said, that Pearson was sure to use throughout the campaign.[42] Merchant tried to interrupt several times to defend the president, but Diefenbaker just yelled louder.

From his pool of wrath and resentment, he withdrew the Rostow talking-points memo that the president had accidently dropped during his

Ottawa visit. It was insulting, he shouted, that Kennedy would presume to "push" him to adopt positions that were contrary to his government's stated policies and Canada's interests. He threatened to make the memo public. If Canadians saw the memo, he said, they would understand how Kennedy really felt about Canada. Its release would enable him to campaign as the only leader capable of standing up to a bully.[43]

Merchant was aghast. Forgetting diplomatic decorum, his voice raised to meet his ire. He shouted that it was inappropriate to have kept the memo in the first place and to be now threatening to release it. Diefenbaker would not stand down. What Merchant had expected to be a fifteen-minute courtesy call turned into two-hour yelling match.[44]

An obviously upset Merchant withdrew to the embassy and sent an uncharacteristically long, hand-delivered letter to Undersecretary of State George Ball. He outlined what had happened and suggested that Kennedy be immediately informed. To smooth things over, he suggested, the president should meet with or at least call Diefenbaker. Ball spoke with McGeorge Bundy who, with Dean Rusk, walked to the Oval Office.

Using language he'd perfected in the navy, Kennedy hollered that Diefenbaker was "a prick," "a shit," "a fucker," and more. He presented the option of "cutting his balls off."[45] When the yelling stopped, Rusk asked what should be done if Diefenbaker released the memo. The president menacingly whispered, "Just let him try it."[46] The meeting ended with Kennedy shouting, "That son of a bitch," and telling the retreating men that he would never again see or speak with Diefenbaker.[47]

In a phone call in which Bundy reported the president's heated reaction, he and Ball took turns insulting the Canadian prime minister and marvelling at his impertinence. Ball spoke of Canada and the Conservative Party benefiting from Soviet wheat sales and even more from the Chinese deal. "Diefenbaker will probably be re-elected by Mao."[48] Bundy concurred and asked if America should offer wheat to China in order to, as he put it, "pull Diefenbaker down."[49]

Merchant returned to Diefenbaker's home on May 12. He found a much calmer prime minister. He carefully responded to each of the points Diefenbaker had raised in their stormy previous encounter. He ended by saying that releasing the Rostow memo would represent a grievous breach of diplomatic protocol and wreak terrible damage on Canadian-American relations. It would end, he said, any relationship with the president. He did not mention Bundy's threat. Merchant concluded with the forthright assertion that Diefenbaker should immediately return the memo. Diefenbaker said he would neither return nor release it but warned that if circumstances changed, he would give the embassy forty-eight hours' notice before sending it to the press.[50] He refused to define the circumstances he had in mind.

Merchant flew to the White House. Still amazed that Diefenbaker had kept the memo in the first place, Kennedy was now hearing that the prime minister was threatening to blackmail him with it. Again his anger spilled into profanity: "That son of a bitch!" Ignoring the many times Diefenbaker had supported his administration, Kennedy railed about nuclear weapons and the recently announced Canadian wheat sale to the Soviet Union, which, he complained, had been arranged without even a courtesy call to Washington. Finally calming himself, Kennedy said there was nothing that could be done about Diefenbaker—for the moment. He again refused to call Ottawa.[51]

Had Diefenbaker known the true extent of Kennedy's interference in the campaign, he might not have stopped at threatening to release the memo. With the Kingston conference and Ottawa rally, the Liberal Party had reimagined its policies in an attempt to capture Canada's growing ideological left and large middle. National campaign director Keith Davey, appointments secretary and political advisor Jim Coutts, Walter Gordon, and others met with Pearson and reminded him that ideas are good but wasted without victory.[52] Movements seek the acceptance of an idea. Parties exist only to win and retain power. They decided that the best way to win in 1962 was to copy Kennedy's campaign of 1960.

Pearson's team had all read Theodore White's brilliant *The Making of the President 1960*.[53] It outlined factors that had determined Kennedy's success, including the use of frequent and targeted polling. Kennedy had hired former marketing executive Lou Harris to undertake polling that would be exclusive to the campaign. While other campaigns contracted pollsters who played no role in turning raw numbers into action, Harris became part of Kennedy's strategy team.[54] For the first time in electoral politics, random sampling was employed to correlate and analyze massive amounts of data and then use it to help shape the candidate and message according to mathematically demonstrable facts rather than backroom intuition.

Walter Gordon approached Harris about helping Pearson defeat Diefenbaker. Harris had previously been asked to assist British Labour Party leader Harold Wilson and had gone to Kennedy for advice. The president admired and saw eye to eye with Prime Minister Macmillan, against whom Wilson was running, and so asked Harris to decline the job. After meeting with Gordon, Harris went again to the White House. He was soon on a plane to Ottawa.[55]

To disguise the fact that Kennedy's pollster and political advisor was helping the Liberals, Harris assumed his wife's maiden name—Smith—and the State Department created a phony passport.[56] He avoided Parliament Hill, where he might be recognized, and instead attended weekly meetings at Pearson's home. Harris hired five hundred women to make daily calls across the country and quiz a random sample of Canadians about a variety of issues. The results were intriguing—and illuminating. Their polling determined, for example, that Canadians preferred Pearson in a straight tie, and so the old bow ties were thrown away. It also determined which cities Pearson would visit, the policies he would emphasize, and that Davey and Coutts would sell not the leader but the Liberal team of nationally known candidates such as Gordon.[57]

Kennedy drew on Harris and a number of other sources to closely follow the election. Harris later said, "He was all but shouting from the sidelines. He hated Diefenbaker. . . . He obviously couldn't say anything publicly. But every day or two he would want to know how the election was going."[58] American radio stations close to the Canadian border began airing editorials that slammed Diefenbaker and praised Pearson.[59]

While Canadian voters were unaware of the American involvement in the election, they certainly knew of an unfolding monetary emergency. Canada's Louis Rasminsky had played a crucial role in negotiating the creation of the 1944 Bretton Woods agreement and then the International Monetary Fund (IMF), both of which were designed to stabilize global currencies. Canada was a part of Bretton Woods until September 1950 when, in order to allow the Canadian dollar to float on the open market, it became the only signatory to withdraw from the agreement.

In 1961, Diefenbaker appointed Rasminsky to the governorship of the Bank of Canada. The Canadian dollar had been hovering above the American greenback for some time but, reacting to the effects of the recession and investor worries about the fiscal deficit, Rasminsky let it sink. He hoped to stimulate growth by making Canadian products cheaper in foreign markets. For a while it worked. In the spring of 1962, however, the dollar's measured decline became a runaway sled plummeting downward. On April 29, in the middle of the campaign, Diefenbaker decided to halt the slide and peg the dollar at 92.5 cents against the American dollar. To make it happen, large quantities of Canadian dollars and bonds needed to be purchased quickly. He asked the IMF for help.

The IMF requested the support of the American Federal Reserve, and that brought the White House into the negotiations. Undersecretary of State Ball and Treasury Secretary C. Douglas Dillon led the Kennedy administration's response to the sudden and serious Canadian monetary crisis. They knew Kennedy's thoughts about Diefenbaker and that he had the power to influence the IMF's actions. However, they never discussed punishing Diefenbaker by hurting Canada. Diefenbaker's finance minister, Donald Fleming, flew to Washington and explained that in return for the cash infusion, he would reduce his government's deficit and hopefully avoid another run on the dollar by cutting program spending and instituting a temporary 15 percent surcharge on some imported items. Long-term changes in trade laws and regulations would come later.[60]

Dillon and Ball discussed the mess with Kennedy and congressional leaders. It was a matter of time before Canada's sudden monetary crisis would negatively affect American business, so it was in America's interest to stop the slide. Consequently, while Kennedy was unhappy that Canada would be imposing surcharges on some American exports, he supported the IMF's and Federal Reserve's actions.[61] Diefenbaker had written to Macmillan. Despite economic challenges of its own, Britain matched America's $100 million. The two contributions comprised two-thirds of the fund created to buttress the Canadian dollar.[62] The collapse was averted. Canada then acted as the prodigal son and was accepted back into the Bretton Woods family, where it stayed for another eight years.[63]

While Kennedy remained statesmanlike throughout the brief monetary crisis, Pearson was far less sanguine. His campaign created the Diefenbuck. Reprinted in newspapers across Canada and handed out at campaign stops, a cartoon dollar bill showed a cruel caricature of the prime minister in place of the Queen. The bill's right side displayed "92½¢" where the one-dollar notation would normally be. The Diefenbuck was effective negative campaigning; it played on the established perception that the government was mishandling the economy. However, negative attacks from both the Liberals and Conservatives soon made it difficult for either party to sell constructive messages.

At various stops, rambunctious crowds shouted insults and interruptions that roughed up both leaders. Some protesters expressed rage while others used fun tactics to raise important issues. In May, a group of Doukhobor women in Trail, British Columbia, stopped Diefenbaker's speech cold when they lined up before the stage, stripped naked, and sang "Do as the Doukhobors Do." The rousing song urged Diefenbaker to keep nuclear weapons out of Canada and support global disarmament while claiming that the only way "big shots" would listen to women was if they disrobed. Its last verse:

> Of course, down in Cannes on the coast of France,
> You'd get no attention minus bras and pants,
> If you'd hit the beach in a grin or less,
> They'd think you had on last year's bathing dress.
> But up there in Canada at twenty below
> People keep covered from head to toe.
> Kennedy would send a cup of coffee or two
> If we did as the Doukhobors do.[64]

On the long slog's final day, Diefenbaker presided over a large and boisterous rally in Hamilton. He and Olive then flew to Prince Albert to await results in a specially outfitted railway car. Pearson and Maryon lounged in the party's Château Laurier suite. Numbers crept in according to the time zones' deliberate pace, though Diefenbaker's bad news came quickly. Progressive Conservative candidates had lost the Maritimes. Pearson shook his head when Quebec voters abandoned the Conservatives for the Social Credit. Ontario split, with the NDP and Liberals doing well in cities and the Conservatives in rural areas. The prairies were the same, with farmers demonstrating their pleasure with Diefenbaker's farm-friendly policies. British Columbia divided like Ontario.

By the wee hours, all but the military votes had been counted, and Pearson and Diefenbaker were both disappointed. It would be a Progressive Conservative minority government. The Conservatives fell significantly from 208 to 116 seats. The Liberals won 100 seats, more than doubling their previous 48. The NDP grew from 8 to 19 and the Social Credit exploded from 0 to 30. Five of Diefenbaker's Cabinet ministers lost their seats, as did NDP leader Tommy Douglas. The Conservatives' popular vote had collapsed from 53 percent in 1958 to 37 percent. Despite everything that had worked in the Liberal Party's favour, their share of the popular vote had risen only a little, from 33 percent to 38 percent.[65]

Harris conducted a large post-election poll and reported optimistic news. Despite the tepid rise in the Liberal's popular vote, taking the "Kennedy approach" had paid dividends. The party was attracting the same people as Kennedy and the Democrats: urban, educated, young, middle and upper class, and ethnic minorities.[66] These groups, Harris told his Liberal friends, represented Canada's future. Conservative support rested with each of the groups' mirror opposites and, like Diefenbaker himself, hearkened back to a quickly receding past. With a new government and ethnic-nationalist awakening in Quebec, Diefenbaker was losing that important province—a province he seemed to neither understand nor afford adequate attention. The Liberals were on the right road, Kennedy's advisor concluded, and only needed to take a few more steps in the same direction. A minority government suggested that the road would be relatively short, as another campaign could not be far away.

Pearson tried to recover his strength while also mourning the death of his mother, who died the day after the election. A new run on the dollar gave Diefenbaker little time to rest. Three weeks after voting day, his dear friend Bill Brunt died in a car accident. A week later, Diefenbaker stepped off his Harrington Lake porch and into a gopher hole. His ankle snapped. Doctors declared it a bad break and consigned him to bed. When blood vessels burst, they discussed amputation, but slowly and painfully it healed. For five weeks, the grumpy and emotionally erratic patient ran the country from beneath the sheets or from a chair in his garden.

Kennedy took the news of Diefenbaker's victory with typical stoicism. The president would play an even bigger role in the next Canadian election and the whirlwind that would lead to its call. First though, came a calamity that altered careers and history's trajectory while threatening nothing less than life on earth.

# N I N E

---

# CUBAN MISSILES AND CANADIAN COUP D'ÉTAT

The president of the United States sat in his pyjamas. He was propped up in bed with the *New York Times* when interrupted by his national security advisor, McGeorge Bundy. Kennedy greeted him with a jaunty good morning and began to gripe about the article he was reading. He stopped at the sight of Bundy's grim expression. Moments later, now on a couch and hunched over a small table, Kennedy examined fuzzy, black-and-white photographs recently obtained from American U-2 spy planes—photos that provided indisputable proof that Soviet missile bases were being built in Cuba.

Kennedy's first reaction was personal. "He can't do that to me."[1] He collected himself, paced the room in silence for a moment, and then listed men he wanted to attend an emergency meeting. Those who gathered came to be called the Executive Committee, or the Ex Comm.

Later that morning, Tuesday, October 16, fifteen men huddled around the long table in the White House Cabinet Room. The president sat at the centre with his brother across from him; that is, when Bobby was not nervously pacing with his arms wrapped tightly around his chest or his right hand rubbing his chin. Only the Kennedys knew that hidden microphones were recording committee conversations. The Ex Comm began with an examination of the photographs. A CIA expert was helping to decipher the grainy images when little Caroline burst in yelling, "Daddy, Daddy, they won't let my friend in." With a broad smile, the president led his daughter to the door, asking gently if she had been eating candy again. He probed a little more when she sheepishly looked down and whispered no. In a minute he was back but the smile was gone.[2]

A free-ranging meeting ensued, without an agenda or observance of ranks or titles. Kennedy spoke least. Once it was established that the missile bases were indeed in Cuba, debate centred not on whether but how to get them out. A quickly established consensus supported a massive and immediate air strike. But would all the missiles be destroyed? Would a follow-up invasion be needed to get them all? Could some missiles already be operational, putting American cities at risk of incineration even as bombs were falling over Cuba? Would Khrushchev retaliate against Berlin and instigate a nuclear war in Europe? Would bombing Cuba lead to a Soviet attack on America?

Secretary of State Rusk dominated the meeting with his plodding, professorial manner. Among the many points he raised was the importance of informing America's allies. Further, since Washington had no direct contact with the Cuban government, he suggested the OAS or Canadian ambassador in Havana could be used to communicate directly with Castro and maybe divide him from Moscow.[3] Later, Treasury Secretary Dillon wondered whether European NATO allies would support an attack on Cuba based on America's fear of the missiles' proximity when for years they had been living in the shadow of Soviet missiles.[4] Near the end of the meeting, when Vice President Johnson returned to the question of allied response and involvement, he argued that America should act alone. He felt OAS and NATO leaders could not be trusted to keep quiet or offer substantive help. Kennedy finally weighed in. He summed up the options discussed and ended by ordering that no one, including allies, should be told about the missiles.[5]

The group met again at 6:30 p.m. The generals wanted to attack, but with so much unknown and unpredictable, every scenario ended with a rapid escalation leaving millions dead. Rusk returned to the question of America's allies, though only to say that NATO countries would probably oppose a Cuban invasion. Such an action, he said, could precipitate the overthrow of several OAS governments. Further, he argued, "If we go with the quick strike, then . . . you've exposed all of your allies . . . to all these great dangers . . . without the slightest consultation or warning."[6] Kennedy's quick retort echoed Johnson's absence of trust: "But, of course, warning them, it seems to me, is warning everybody."[7] The options continued to be sussed out and the secret kept.

At the end of the first day—despite the fact that Canada could be within the missiles' range, and that Canada was not just a neighbour and NATO member but also a NORAD partner with a shared responsibility for continental defence—no one suggested consulting or warning Diefenbaker. The oversight was fascinating, especially given that Kennedy observed during the evening meeting that the Cuban crisis was more political than military.[8] That is, Soviet intercontinental ballistic missiles had been pointed at American cities for some time, and its bombers and submarines represented a constant threat. The missiles in Cuba had not significantly altered the global nuclear balance of power. They were, however, reducing North Americans' response time in the event of an attack to nearly nothing, meaning that all those backyard bunkers would be just holes in the ground, as useless as the plywood desktops above the heads of cowering first graders.

Kennedy and his advisors should have anticipated Soviet action in Cuba. In November 1961, seven months after the Bay of Pigs debacle, Kennedy had formed the secret Special Group (Augmented) to destabilize Cuba and kill Castro. Led by General Edward Lansdale and overseen by

Attorney General Robert Kennedy, the group conducted Operation Mongoose. Using CIA and Cuban operatives, it collected intelligence, organized anti-Castro radio programs, and undertook schemes such as poisoning wells and crops, derailing trains, and blowing up ports and bridges. Its station in Miami employed about twelve thousand people and boasted the western hemisphere's third-largest navy.[9] Despite the money, men, and Robert Kennedy's pressure, however, Mongoose accomplished little, except to afford Castro another reason to distrust America. It also handed Khrushchev incentive to continue the slow and steady incursion into Latin American that he'd begun in earnest after the CIA's 1954 overthrow of Guatemala's democratically elected government.[10]

While Operation Mongoose was, among other things, trying to get Castro to smoke LSD-laced cigars, the American OAS delegate initiated and helped carry the vote to impose an arms embargo on Cuba.[11] In January 1962, Cuba was kicked out of the organization. The Cuban expulsion made Diefenbaker's refusal to join the OAS seem prescient, for the move would have surely pitted Canada against the United States and other members. The next month, after arranging to purchase a large quantity of his favourite Cuban cigars, Kennedy signed a sweeping new trade embargo that cut all remaining American-Cuban trade except for medical supplies.

Meanwhile, the Pentagon planned another invasion of Cuba. This time, unlike the CIA's Bay of Pigs disaster, the operation would be larger and conducted by the American military. Operations Plans 314 and 316 called for a massive air strike followed by a multi-pronged amphibious assault.[12] In March and April, the United States carried out Lantphibex 1-62 and Quick Kick, the largest military exercises in the country's history. The forty thousand personnel included ten thousand who demonstrated America's ability to put troops in Cuba by practising an amphibious landing on Vieques, a small Caribbean island just east of Puerto Rico.[13]

The month after Kennedy's enormous Caribbean military exhibition, Khrushchev began conversations with Soviet first deputy premier Anastas

Mikoyan about placing nuclear weapons in Cuba to stave off what appeared to be an imminent American attack.[14] A Soviet delegation disguised as agricultural scientists met with Castro on May 27. Castro accepted the offer of Soviet nuclear missiles.[15]

Of course, if Khrushchev had only wanted to dissuade the Americans from invading Cuba, then a contingent of soldiers would have sufficed. It is unlikely that Kennedy would have risked a direct engagement with Soviet troops. Khrushchev must have also considered that his action would address the missile gap that, despite Kennedy's campaign rhetoric, was actually in America's favour by a wide margin. The ability of Cuban-based medium-range ballistic missiles (MRBMs) to hit American targets would compensate for the relatively tiny number of Soviet intercontinental ballistic missiles. Further, deploying Soviet MRBMs in Cuba would only be fair play given that the United States had placed similar weapons in Turkey and Italy. The Turkish missiles were just five minutes' flying time from Khrushchev's summer residence in Sochi. The Cuban missiles would also serve as a bargaining chip that would allow Khrushchev to exert pressure elsewhere, including the much-coveted Berlin. Finally, by embarrassing Kennedy and impressing the Chinese and other communist governments, Khrushchev could win support from the hardliners around him who were still questioning his leadership.[16]

In late July 1962, about fifty thousand Soviet troops and eighty-five ships began the covert and complex operation of transporting the missiles, ammunition, and supplies to Cuba. Khrushchev planned to have everything in place by November so that after the American mid-term elections he could travel to the UN and announce their combat readiness.[17] But the operation did not stay secret for long. By the end of August, CIA director John McCone reported to Kennedy that between four thousand and six thousand Soviet personnel had arrived in Cuba and that the ports were busy unloading large crates from Soviet ships.[18] From sixty thousand feet in the air, American U-2 planes collected photographic evidence of the construction of new military bases while Operation Mongoose spies reported a sharp increase in the number of Soviet ships arriving at the island's ports.[19]

Kennedy called up fifteen thousand reservists. He also made an announcement to the press designed to calm fears while offering a shot across Khrushchev's bow. "If at any time the Communist build-up in Cuba were to endanger or interfere with our security in any way or become an offensive military base of significant capacity for the Soviet Union, the United States would do whatever must be done to protect its security and that of its allies."[20] Khrushchev responded to Kennedy's statement by having foreign minister Andrei Gromyko declare at the UN on September 21 that any attack on Cuba would constitute a declaration of war on the Soviet Union and invite a full retaliatory attack.[21]

Like their American counterparts, Canadian military personnel knew something was about to break and that Cuba would be the focus of it all. That month, Flying Officer Robert Ough was one of three young Canadian airmen sent to train with the new American-made P-3 Orion four-engine anti-submarine and maritime surveillance aircraft at the Boca Chica Naval Air Station in the Florida Keys. Until the appearance of the Orions, the Canadian-made CP-107 Argus was the best marine reconnaissance aircraft around. For years, the fifteen-man Argus crews had been spotting, tracking, and reporting Soviet submarines whose crews must have thought they were well hidden among their fishing fleets off the Canadian and American coasts. From their rooms in the Blue Marlin Hotel in Key West, Ough and his mates watched waves of American jets screaming out over the ocean. They sipped beer with American airmen who spoke of nothing but Cuba.[22]

On October 2, two weeks before Bundy brought the U-2 pictures into the president's bedroom, Kennedy ordered his secretary of defence, Robert McNamara, to prepare for air strikes on Cuba to take place as early as October 20. Throughout this tense period, with the two superpowers stepping toward each other like gunfighters in an old western movie, Kennedy made no direct contact with Diefenbaker.

Kennedy had told Diefenbaker during his Ottawa visit the year before that he believed Canada's policy toward Cuba was hurting America's efforts to isolate and remove the tiny communist state. Subsequent to that tense exchange, Rusk had repeated the point to Green, and American ambassador Merchant told a number of Canadian Cabinet ministers that part of Kennedy's problem with Diefenbaker, and the reason that Canada's influence in Washington was waning, was that Canadians seemed unable to share America's fears and support its goals with respect to Cuba.[23] Kennedy and his men had no effect on Diefenbaker's views or Canadian policy.

Diefenbaker's special aide Basil Robinson had travelled with him to London in late August. He was reassigned to serve with Ambassador Ritchie in Washington as the deputy head of mission. In September, he reported being shocked to find that all of the city's cocktail-circuit chatter was about Cuba. He reported on October 3 that everyone in Washington seemed to know about a spike in the delivery of Soviet military material. He noted that George Ball had told the House Select Committee on Export Control that the isolation of Cuba to combat the spread of communism in the hemisphere was being continued and that a military incursion was on the table.[24] Later that day, Green received word about a significant increase in the number of Soviet aircraft flying over Canada toward Cuba and stopping, mostly at Gander, Newfoundland, to refuel—presumably transporting military goods.[25] Everyone seemed to know something was happening. The only people left in the dark were the people themselves.

For six tense days Kennedy's Ex Comm secretly debated options. To maintain the ruse of normalcy, Kennedy kept to his schedule and even travelled to make congressional mid-term election campaign speeches while the Ex Comm met in different rooms to keep reporters from wondering why the Cabinet Room lights were on so late every night. Kennedy feigned a cold to return to the White House. While obviously distracted, he somehow dealt with other business, including finally sending a message to Diefenbaker. But rather than inform, his note chastised—and it had nothing to do with Cuba.

Dated October 20, 1962, the dense and detailed three-page letter expressed disappointment with Canada. The UN General Assembly was advocating the creation of an eighteen-nation disarmament conference along with a moratorium on nuclear testing. Canada was planning to support the idea. Back in April, Kennedy had written to Diefenbaker about his opposition to an unverified test ban, and in response to a reporter's question the next day the prime minister had supported the president's concerns. Kennedy now repeated his argument. "I am convinced that there is no safety in such a proposal and it leads away from the only honest and workable road to arms limitation. . . . Should Canada cast its vote in favor of a moratorium this year, it . . . will be seen by the Soviet Union as a successful breach of the Western position. . . . Mr. Prime Minister, I cannot overemphasize my concern in this matter."[26]

In fact, Canada had worked behind the scenes to have the motion amended to include a verification process. Diefenbaker's reply explained that Canada would support a final resolution only if it contained adequate safeguards.[27] The disdain with which Canada and Diefenbaker were held was revealed in a handwritten note a White House staffer stapled to Diefenbaker's letter. "I recommend against the reply," it said. "Why thank him for nothing?"[28] Kennedy responded anyway. His terse note said only that he had found their frank exchange of views "useful."[29]

Meanwhile, Canadian external affairs officials met with American intelligence officers in Ottawa. The Americans said nothing about the number or offensive capacity of the missiles in Cuba, or of the Ex Comm deliberations. However, they revealed that media reports regarding the Soviet military buildup in Cuba were indeed true. Howard Green's deputy minister, Norman Robertson, and Privy Council secretary Robert Bryce were informed. They ran to the East Block to tell Diefenbaker.[30]

Diefenbaker considered the scraps of information and determined that while no one could be sure what Khrushchev was doing in Cuba, he was certainly up to something. He ordered a message sent to Moscow announcing that Soviet aircraft of any description were immediately banned from Canadian air space. Soviet allies Poland and Czechoslovakia were alerted that if any of their aircraft landed in Canada they would be searched for weapons.[31]

By Sunday, October 21, five days after first meeting, the Ex Comm decided to establish a naval blockade to stop the importation of more military hardware. Because a blockade was an act of war, they opted instead to call it a "quarantine." Khrushchev would be told to dismantle and remove the missiles and bases already on Cuban soil. Plans were made for a Cuban air strike and invasion in case he refused, moved on Berlin, or sent his bombers over Europe or the North Pole.

Kennedy met that evening with an old family friend, British ambassador to the United States David Ormsby-Gore. Because Pentagon leaks were rampant, he had already informed his prime minister that something big was about to happen involving Cuba. In a wide-ranging conversation, the ambassador offered support for the quarantine. Kennedy prepared a letter to Macmillan explaining the situation so that he would "have as much time as possible to consider the dangers we will now have to face together."[32] Kennedy was on the telephone with Macmillan several times throughout the crisis.

The next day, Kennedy dispatched envoys to Britain, Germany, France, and Canada, and personal messages to other allied leaders. Former secretary of state Dean Acheson flew to Paris and met with President de Gaulle. The wise old general's first question was, "In order to get our roles clear . . . have [you] come . . . to inform me of some decision taken by your President—or have you come to consult me about a decision which he should take[?]" Acheson replied, "I have come to inform you."[33] De Gaulle leaned back and smiled. When Acheson offered to show him photographs of the Cuban missile sites, de Gaulle waved them off. He was being asked for nothing and so he asked for nothing.

Despite the harsh words and hard feelings that had poisoned their relationship, former ambassador Livingston Merchant was brought out of retirement to carry Kennedy's message to Diefenbaker. Word was received that he wished to see the prime minister at 5 p.m. that afternoon. External affairs officials hurriedly composed a briefing memo. Merchant's impending visit allowed them to contextualize the rumours they had been hearing from NORAD commanders and Pentagon sources and had already reported to Diefenbaker.[34] Even given these warnings and rumblings, their memo was surprisingly cogent given they had only a couple of hours to swallow their personal terror, digest and weigh scraps of conflicting information, and then consider options and construct recommendations.

The memo began by stating that the crisis threatened Canadian as well as American cities. "We are aware through intelligence channels that as of October 16 the U.S.A. had satisfied itself through photographic and other intelligence media that offensive ballistic missiles with a range of between 1100 and 2200 miles were being installed in Cuba in sufficient number (an estimated 40) to directly threaten the security of the U.S.A."[35] It then accurately guessed each of the options that the Ex Comm had bandied about. It warned that any of them could quickly lead to a nuclear holocaust capable of reducing Canadian cities to radioactive wastelands. The memo concluded with a recommendation that Canada should support the United States but also help to defuse the situation by advocating the creation of a UN group of eight neutral nations to conduct on-site investigations of the missile bases. If the idea was vetoed in the Security Council, it could be taken to the General Assembly, where debate would tar the Soviet Union and Cuba as aggressors. Although the memo was rushed to the prime minister's office, Diefenbaker did not get a chance to see it before meeting Merchant.

Merchant arrived at the Cabinet Room at 5:15 p.m. American chargé
d'affaires Ivan White and three intelligence officers accompanied him.
Diefenbaker, Green, and Harkness greeted the men with solemn handshakes. Merchant handed Diefenbaker a letter from the president. It
summarized what was known about the missiles, outlined plans for the
quarantine, and stated that he would be requesting an emergency
Security Council meeting in which the United States would ask for UN
observers to oversee the missiles' removal. Kennedy's letter asked only
one thing of Diefenbaker: "I hope that you will instruct your representative in New York to work actively with us and speak forthrightly in
support of the above program in the United Nations."[36] Kennedy's letter
said nothing of NORAD, Canada's military role, or emergency military
alert levels. Ignoring the fact that Diefenbaker was only now being told
of the crisis, the letter concluded with unintentional irony. "It is most
important that we should all keep in close touch with each other, and
that I will do all I can to keep you informed of developments as I get
them."[37] Diefenbaker looked up at Merchant. For a moment he said
nothing, but his jaw set and his cold blue eyes narrowed.

In his 1961 memo preparing Kennedy for Diefenbaker's Washington
visit, Secretary of State Rusk had written, "Our defence arrangements
have to be conducted with meticulous regard for Canadian sensitivities.
In general, they require that consultation in joint defence matters be
guaranteed and details of operations specified in advance."[38] The
NORAD agreement and a series of diplomatic notes exchanged between
the two countries guaranteed consultation. After the botched Bay of Pigs
invasion, Diefenbaker had asserted that Canada be promptly informed
and fully consulted regarding potential Cuban problems because of the
hemispheric "hornet's nest" that troubles there would cause.[39] Diefenbaker
had reiterated the point again at their Ottawa meetings. Throughout the
nuclear missile negotiations, Diefenbaker had steadfastly and repeatedly
insisted on consultation. He was not speaking from emotional sensitivity,

as Rusk had insultingly suggested, but the realities of an allied partnership between sovereign states.

Like de Gaulle in Paris, Diefenbaker quickly realized why Kennedy's messenger was there. He snarled that the presidential campaign season must have just begun, then asked why Kennedy had not followed Canada's requests and NORAD protocols and come to him earlier. Merchant sidestepped the question and laid out the photographic evidence of the missiles. He said that the president would be appearing on television in about an hour and a half to tell the world. He read them the speech.[40]

Harkness interrupted with a couple of technical questions about the level of alert at which American forces had or would be placed. Merchant equivocated. Diefenbaker noted a sentence in which Soviet foreign minister Gromyko was called "dishonest and dishonourable." He suggested that since the president would need to negotiate with the Soviets, it might be better to avoid insulting them. Anticipating the external affairs memo he had not yet seen, Diefenbaker asked why the president had not taken news of the missiles in Cuba immediately to the UN. The tactic, he said, would have won international support for the United States and a condemnation of the Soviet Union while seeking a diplomatic solution rather than this treacherous military confrontation that could quickly escalate into a global nuclear war. Merchant said there had been no time.[41]

Despite the bad blood between Merchant and Diefenbaker, the jarring nature of the news, and the breaking of promises and protocol, the meeting remained a calm affair. It ended with Diefenbaker promising that Canada would live up to its NATO and NORAD responsibilities.[42] Merchant returned to the American embassy and telegrammed Washington. He reported that Diefenbaker was upset about the absence of consultation but that Canada would nonetheless support Kennedy's position. He also noted Diefenbaker's suggested amendment to the president's speech, and the line was dropped.[43] Diefenbaker was told that Canadian ambassador Charles Ritchie was summoned to the State Department where George Ball told him what the president was about to tell the world. In Europe, Dean Acheson spoke with all NATO ambassadors, including George Ignatieff, who had been appointed by Diefenbaker to the position in January 1961. Ball and Acheson both stressed the need for allied solidarity with the president's decisions and whatever actions became necessary.[44] Meanwhile, Diefenbaker went home for dinner and to watch the speech.

On Monday, October 22, at 7 p.m.—two in the morning in Moscow—President Kennedy began a seventeen-minute speech with a curt, "Good evening, my fellow citizens." To avoid being distracted by pain, Kennedy had carefully re-laced his back brace and sat atop two pillows. He looked tired but determined. He was blunt in reporting the evidence and noted ominously that the medium-range missiles could travel one thousand nautical miles and so were capable of striking Washington, the Panama Canal, Cape Canaveral, Mexico City, and any southeastern American city. He explained that yet-to-be-completed sites would soon allow targets to be hit as far north as Hudson Bay, Canada.[45]

Like a prosecutor before a jury, Kennedy laid out international laws and treaties and American statutes that rendered the creation of the Soviet sites in Cuba illegal. He detailed the number of times he had warned the Soviets against taking such action, and instances where Soviet leaders had misrepresented themselves. Ignoring the clandestine Canadian-American nuclear weapons transfer negotiations, but at least for the moment being truthful, he said, "Our own strategic missiles have never been transferred to territory of any other nation under a cloak of secrecy."[46]

He listed seven initial steps that would be taken to try to avert disaster, beginning with the quarantine. Without being specific, he said that the American military was also preparing for other options should they become necessary. He said that any missile launched from Cuba on any nation in the western hemisphere would be considered an attack by the Soviet Union on the United States, and that such an attack would invite a full retaliatory response. He called for action from the OAS and for an emergency meeting of the UN Security Council, which he hoped would vote to order the dispatching of impartial UN observers to oversee the dismantling and withdrawal of all offensive nuclear weapons from Cuba. Kennedy ended with a call to Khrushchev to remove the missiles and end his quest for world domination.[47]

The escalation Kennedy had feared began minutes after he stopped speaking. Khrushchev sent Kennedy a private note pledging that Soviet ships would not respect the quarantine. He ordered *Aleksandrovsk*, the Soviet ship closest to Cuba (and laden with missiles and nuclear warheads), to increase its speed and make for the island's nearest port.[48] If Americans tried to stop or board *Aleksandrovsk*, the captain was under orders to open fire and, if necessary, scuttle the ship, plunging its nuclear weapons to the ocean's floor.[49] Soviet engineers and Cuban soldiers worked through the cool night and beneath hot, bright lights to meet suddenly jumped-up deadlines.

Diefenbaker watched the speech with Olive and then repaired to his study to finally read the external affairs memo. He drew lines of emphasis beside the recommendation to call for UN on-site inspectors. Lester Pearson telephoned to discuss the situation. Diefenbaker had told Merchant that he would say nothing publicly until the next day, but Pearson suggested that the Canadian people were owed something now from their government. They agreed that with such short notice, the House floor was the best place for a statement. Diefenbaker scribbled a few disjointed phrases on a couple of small pieces of paper, tucked the external affairs memo under his arm, and was driven the five minutes down Sussex and up Wellington to Parliament Hill.

The prime minister strode into a House that was deep into an evening debate. The Speaker recognized him at once. Diefenbaker glanced only briefly at the papers scattered on the desk before him, and then laid out Canada's official response to the most dangerous moment in its history. He began with firm and unequivocal support for Kennedy. He had seen the photographic evidence, he said, and was convinced the bases were there and offensive in nature. He chided Khrushchev for instigating the crisis and for his dishonesty in having pledged to provide Cuba with nothing but defensive weaponry. Consistent with the external affairs memo he had just read and Canada's post-war diplomatic strategy of defusing situations by involving international organizations, he expressed agreement with the president that the United Nations must play a role in resolving the crisis. The UN action he proposed, however, went beyond what Kennedy had suggested.

Diefenbaker said the Soviet Union would probably react to Kennedy's speech by denying the existence of offensive bases in Cuba. "But I suggest that if there is a desire on the part of the U.S.S.R. to have the facts, a group of nations, perhaps the eight nations comprising the unaligned members of the eighteen nation disarmament committee, be given the opportunity of making an on-site inspection in Cuba to ascertain what the facts are, a major step forward would be taken. . . . As to the presence of these offensive weapons, the only sure way that the world can secure the facts would be through an independent inspection."[50] Pearson understood the points Diefenbaker made and the support he was offering the United States. He commended Kennedy's staunch firmness and Diefenbaker's "measured response."[51]

The Americans were angry. Merchant interpreted the request for UN observers not as a way to prove Khrushchev was lying, as Diefenbaker had intended, but as a suggestion that Kennedy was.[52] He wired a scathing report to Washington. The prime minister's clumsily worded stab at Khrushchev and endorsement for UN involvement were perceived as negating his strong support for the president. It was the beginning of a series of avoidable misunderstandings.[53]

Kennedy's speech ignited worldwide shock and dismay. Thousands of Canadians and Americans rushed to their places of worship; others rushed to their pubs. Thousands more purchased food, water, and additional supplies. Parents preparing their children for bed that night wondered if there would be a tomorrow. Twenty-five hundred family members and non-essential personnel were evacuated from the American military base at

Guantánamo Bay, Cuba. White House staff members were told to get their families out of Washington. Kennedy asked Jacqueline to leave with the children but she refused. The president's Virginia bunker was prepared. Outside of Ottawa, the Diefenbunker was cleaned and stocked with fresh supplies and its communications system tested. No one, including the leaders, knew what would happen next. Hoping for the best seemed naive.

Kennedy had recently read *The Guns of August*, the sorry tale of miscalculations that tripped Europe into the First World War. He feared that the superpowers would do it again, but this time with weapons that would render the consequences immeasurably more catastrophic.[54] All it would take was a commander adhering to some obsolete standard operating procedure, an overzealous officer, or even a crazy gunner or pilot to start something that neither he nor Khrushchev intended or, once begun, could stop.

In the navy, Kennedy had learned the oxymoron of military efficiency, and he knew just how war's fog can affect judgment. The Bay of Pigs had taught him how easily military planning could go awry and how expert guarantees were often just hopes, and facts mere guesses. In a private conversation with his brother, Kennedy observed, "These brass hats have one great advantage in their favour. If we listen to them and do what they want us to do, none of us will be alive later to tell them that they were wrong."[55]

Diefenbaker shared Kennedy's trepidation about his own brass hats. Maintaining civilian control over military decisions, after all, had been a crucial concern in the establishment of NORAD and the acceptance of nuclear weapons in Canada. Now, and without his knowledge, those fears were being justified.

America's Defense Condition (DEFCON) system has five levels. Only the commander in chief—the president—can move various branches of the military, or all of them together, from one level to the next. Each level brings the armed forces to predetermined states of alertness.

DEFCON 5 represents normal. DEFCON 1 is active war. At 4:49 p.m. on Monday, October 22, just over two hours before Kennedy's televised speech and twenty-five minutes before Merchant sat down with Diefenbaker, NORAD's commander, American general John Gerhart, was ordered to move his American forces to DEFCON 3. It is the maximum peacetime alert. It assumes imminent action.

Gerhart's actions were coordinated with America's Strategic Air Command, which had B-52 bomber fleets fuelled and armed, with personnel suited up and standing by. One of eight squadrons circled in the air waiting for the order to deliver their deadly payloads. B-47 bombers were loaded with nuclear weapons and scrambled to locations around the country. Missiles equipped with 1.5-kiloton warheads were installed on F-106 fighter jets.

Because of NORAD's military integration, Canadian forces needed to come to the same alert level as their American counterparts. However, General Gerhart's request to do so did not arrive at Air Chief Marshal Frank Miller's office until after the president's 7 p.m. speech.[56] As chairman of the Chiefs of Staff Committee, Miller, like Gerhart, had latitude in implementing military actions, but only at the behest of his civilian masters—in Canada's case, the defence minister acting on the wishes of the Cabinet and prime minister.

When Defence Minister Harkness returned to his office after watching Kennedy on television, an anxious but stoic Miller was waiting. Harkness agreed that the order to raise Canada's alert level to the equivalent of the American's DEFCON 3 should be issued at once. When told that Diefenbaker was on his way to the House, he rushed to hear the speech. The moment the prime minister took his seat, Harkness approached and whispered that they needed to talk. In the prime minister's small office behind the Speaker's chair, Harkness explained that issuing the elevated alert order was a formality and must be done immediately. Diefenbaker said no.[57]

Harkness could not believe it. To his dismay and amazement, Diefenbaker argued that the situation was too delicate. The fate of millions of Canadians hung in the balance. Such action on the Canadian government's part, he said, could increase the likelihood that Khrushchev, a notorious hothead, would escalate hostilities further. Diefenbaker also explained that just minutes before, he had announced that Canada wanted both sides to step back from the brink to afford UN inspectors time to do their work. He could not immediately devalue that stance by elevating Canada's alert level. Plus, Kennedy had known about the missiles for seven days before acting. He had known definitively for only a few hours, and Parliament for mere minutes. Something of this magnitude deserved careful deliberation. Cabinet needed to be consulted. Finally, he explained that Canada's decision to raise its alert level was Canada's to make and that he would not do it just because Kennedy or the Pentagon wanted it done. Canada, he thundered, was an American ally, not a satellite, and had options beyond snapping a salute and obeying when issued an order from Washington.[58]

Howard Green had entered the tiny, ornately carved room halfway through Diefenbaker's explanation. For the first time in a long time, Green sided with Harkness. Diefenbaker shook his head. Harkness was aghast. With increasing volume he argued that according to NORAD commitments, Canada had no choice.[59] Diefenbaker wouldn't budge. Cabinet would be consulted in the morning. Diefenbaker had become convinced that Harkness was "a puppet of the military men," the same military men he'd learned to distrust after the rushed NORAD decision years earlier. He would not be "stampeded" again before taking time to properly consider and consult.[60]

While Harkness was appalled at what he concluded was Diefenbaker's inability to take a stand, a similar decision was being made in London. After Kennedy's speech, American general and NATO's supreme allied commander Lauris Norstad visited Prime Minister Macmillan. He asked that British forces match the alert level of the Americans. Macmillan said no. To the surprised general who, like his president, was not used to hearing the word, the prime minister cited the same arguments that Diefenbaker was presenting in Ottawa. He believed that an elevation would be unnecessarily provocative in an already perilous situation. Perhaps, like Kennedy, he nursed thoughts of the First World War, the tragic blunder that had slain a generation of British youth, when he told Norstad that mobilization can sometimes not avert but cause a war.[61] Royal Air Force pilots and crews gathered at bases, but their gleaming white V-bombers remained on the ground.

Macmillan sent a message to Diefenbaker advising how he had reacted to Kennedy's request for an elevated alert and suggested that they both refrain from taking aggressive action that could disturb the Cuban situation's delicate balance. In the midst of such enormous stress, Diefenbaker must have felt relief that Canada's oldest ally had come to the same decision as he had. He did not know that other NATO allies were similarly upset about Kennedy's lack of consultation and nuclear brinksmanship. Dutch foreign minister Joseph Luns was the only one to say so publicly; many others, like Diefenbaker and de Gaulle, fumed in private.[62]

Harkness left the fiery meeting and marched back to his office to find an impatient Miller. According to the current war book that dictated policy and procedures in times of military emergency, only the prime minister could order an elevated alert. The book had been cancelled while it was being rewritten, but it still provided the only available guidelines for what the two men could and could not do in such an emergency. They decided to ignore the book, the spirit of the law dictating such actions, Cabinet's constitutional authority, and the prime minister's directive. Instead, they obeyed President Kennedy.

Harkness ordered Canada's NORAD and regular forces to take all actions necessary to bring them to the equivalent of DEFCON 3.[63] Military personnel sprang into action. Soldiers were called to duty. Jets were scrambled. Ships were armed, fuelled, and sent to sea. Canadian air marshal Roy Slemon, deputy commander at NORAD headquarters at Colorado Springs, issued the necessary orders to coordinate Canadian forces with their American counterparts.

That night, Canadian Flying Officer Ough was back in Summerside, PEI, and had been with his wife and another couple at the movies enjoying Alec Guinness in *Tunes of Glory*. They heard Kennedy's speech on the radio and knew the Canadian forces would be involved. He packed a bag. Later that evening, Ough was called to report to base. He kissed his wife goodbye with no clue as to when or whether they would see each other again. Crews from Summerside joined those from other bases flying loop patrols over the Canadian and American Atlantic coast, with stops to rest and refuel at American bases in Norfolk, Virginia, and Jacksonville, Florida. The patrols also took them south to Puerto Rico, east to Gibraltar, the Azores, and the UK, and north to Iceland. When finished his first patrol, Ough sat with a beer and a buddy. "You know," he said, "when this is done, we may not have homes to go home to."[64]

Some days seem longer than others. As that extraordinarily long Monday ended, Kennedy did not know what Khrushchev would do. And neither really knew what any of the thousands of young men armed with sophisticated weaponry but all-too-human fears and foibles would do. Few Americans knew that during the most perilous moment in their nation's history, Canadian planes and ships were guarding Washington, Boston, and other coastal cities. What Prime Minister Diefenbaker did not know was perhaps most shocking of all. After his House speech and several meetings, he had gone home to bed. He fell asleep either unaware or intentionally blind to the fact that with life-and-death decisions taken contrary to his wishes, Canada had just experienced a coup d'état.

# T E N

## THE DEEPENING CRISIS

AS DAWN BROKE OVER CUBA ON TUESDAY, October 23, six American RF-8 Crusader jets thundered through the cloudless sky. They skimmed the treetops while cameras in their bellies clicked four photographs per second. Hours later the pictures were in Washington. They showed that, with all pretence gone, the construction on the missile sites was moving ahead with increased speed.

While the pictures were far clearer than the earlier ones taken from higher altitudes, they did not reveal that there were now 42,822 Soviet soldiers in Cuba. Nor did they show that the ships *Aleksandrovsk* and *Almetyevsk* had arrived along with twenty-four nuclear warheads to add to the ninety already on the island.[1] Most shockingly, and something Kennedy would never know, was that eight of the missiles were already operational and ready to be launched at a moment's notice.[2] Further, in anticipation of an American invasion, short-range tactical nuclear weapons were prepared for firing. Khrushchev had authorized the Soviet commander in Cuba to use them at his discretion.[3]

Defence Minister Harkness began his day with the Chiefs of Staff in his spacious office. They looked at new intelligence reports and reviewed the unusual and unconstitutional action they had taken the night before.

Discussions led to Harkness issuing additional orders to better coordinate army, navy, and air force activities with each other and the Americans.[4]

Cabinet convened at nine o'clock. Harkness reviewed the new intelligence and took questions. With no mention of what he had done or what Canadian forces were at that moment doing, he concluded with another request that the prime minister elevate the alert level to match America's DEFCON 3. Diefenbaker patiently listed the points he had made the previous evening. With the United States and the Soviet Union wobbling on the precipice of a global nuclear war, and Canada stuck between the protagonists, Canada should avoid doing anything provocative, he said.[5] He spoke of his message from Macmillan, noting that Britain was also not doing everything Kennedy asked.

Green had supported Harkness the night before, but now, before the full Cabinet, he reversed himself and spoke in favour of waiting. This situation, he explained, verified the fears he had been bringing to Cabinet for some time—namely, the country's entangling defence arrangements with the United States, and now America's unilateral actions, were "stampeding" Canada into doing things that it would never do on its own. If Canada's forces simply obeyed the orders of America's president, he said, the country would be reduced to nothing but an "American vassal."[6]

Emotions flew quickly out of control. With voices raised and faces reddened, Harkness and Diefenbaker tore into each other. Other Cabinet members sat in stunned silence. Finally, trembling with rage and in a menacing tone, Diefenbaker softly hissed, "Canadian mothers do not want their sons to be killed in any foreign war and the Cuban business is no affair of Canada's."[7] The Cabinet split but the majority backed Diefenbaker. Canada's military alert level would not be raised.[8]

With the stormy meeting over, Harkness raced back to his office and the Chiefs of Staff who were waiting impatiently for Cabinet's decision. For the third time, Harkness ignored the prime minister, and this time Cabinet as well. He told the chiefs to carry on. The only hint that he realized his orders were potentially treasonous came with his instruction to carry on as quietly as possible. The chiefs were to direct all communications regarding operations to him.[9]

Far from the picture of the irrational or confused leader later painted by critics, Diefenbaker continued to consult broadly. He called Prime Minister Macmillan and said that, despite American pressure, Canada was maintaining its current military alert level. Macmillan confirmed that Britain was doing the same and agreed that if Canada and Britain went to the higher state of alert it could make a bad situation dangerously worse.[10]

Diefenbaker also took an unprecedented walk to Pearson's office to seek advice. Their long conversation ended with Pearson supporting Diefenbaker's handling of the crisis. Diefenbaker invited Pearson to attend a defence committee intelligence briefing. Agreeing that the Canadian people needed to be reassured and that the government's position should be explained again, they determined a question that Pearson would ask in the House that would allow Diefenbaker to make a statement.[11]

None of Diefenbaker's consultations and briefings changed his mind. He became even more convinced that it was not in Canada's or the world's interest to escalate the Cuban standoff by involving Canada's forces through an increased alert level. Further, he believed that the man who had botched the Bay of Pigs and been bested in Vienna could not be trusted to handle the situation. He later wrote, "[Kennedy] still thought he had something to prove in his personal dealings with Khrushchev [and was] perfectly capable of taking the world to the brink of thermonuclear destruction to prove himself the man for our times, a courageous champion of Western democracy."[12]

Pearson was miffed later that afternoon when Diefenbaker kept the spotlight they had agreed to share squarely on himself. He rose in the House before the Opposition leader could pose his planted question and even pirated some of the phrases Pearson had used in their conversation.[13] The prime minister announced that he was continuing to meet with military leaders, Cabinet, Pearson, officials from External Affairs and Defence, and consulting with Canadian embassy officials in Washington. Canada, he said, condemned the Soviet action and fully supported the American reaction. He reiterated that the Canadian government did not question the veracity of anything the president had said in his speech or the wisdom of the quarantine. However, he emphasized that there was merit in immediately sending UN on-site inspectors to Cuba. He explained, and later sent private assurances to the State Department to this effect, that Canada's support for the dispatch of inspectors was not intended to question but to verify the president's evidence and thereby strengthen the American position.[14]

Diefenbaker's second public announcement and private letter did not change American minds about what they still considered tepid, conditional support. Robert Kennedy, who was at his brother's side throughout the crisis, said amidst the tension, "Canada offers all aid short of help."[15] Diefenbaker did not hear the misinformed barb, but he could have retorted that America offered consultation short of actually consulting.

With Soviet ships rushing toward the quarantine line, Kennedy was paying little attention to Diefenbaker. Not wanting the missiles of October to turn into his own "guns of August," he deftly micromanaged the crisis, asked question after question, and double-checked everything and everyone. He ordered a review of standard operating procedures for all American forces and for the nuclear missiles stationed in Italy and Turkey so that only he, and not some soldier, sailor, or pilot, could start the world's third and possibly final world war. He was pleased when the OAS met in an emergency morning session and voted twenty to zero, with three abstentions, to support the quarantine.

That afternoon, the Security Council convened. US ambassador Adlai Stevenson lectured Soviet ambassador Valerian Zorin on his government's placing of nuclear weapons in Cuba. With no instructions from the Kremlin, the desperate Zorin was like an actor without a script; he played for time. He categorically denied the existence of Soviet offensive weapons in Cuba.[16] Stevenson produced pictures and in a humiliating few minutes proved him wrong.

When informed of Diefenbaker's refusal to raise Canadian alert levels, Kennedy picked up the phone. A year and a half before, he had read the memorandum prepared for Diefenbaker's Washington visit. It stated, "A loss or diminution of U.S. use of Canadian air space and real estate and the contributions of the Canadian military, particularly the RCAF and the Royal Canadian Navy, would be intolerable in time of crisis."[17] This was a time of crisis and he needed Canada to play its part fully, immediately, and without qualms. The call did not go well.

Kennedy was tired and angry. He admonished Diefenbaker for refusing to trust the evidence he and Stevenson had presented to the world. Kennedy ordered Diefenbaker to immediately demonstrate support for his actions by publicly issuing the alert order. Diefenbaker began to explain the reasons for not doing so but Kennedy cut him off. He demanded that Canada unequivocally support the United States at the UN. Diefenbaker accused Kennedy of not wanting a genuine UN debate but a rubber-stamping of his already implemented decisions. Diefenbaker then made a point that Rusk and others had raised in Ex Comm meetings the week before. He argued that the Cuban missiles did not actually change the threat to the United States because American cities had been within range of Soviet ICBMs for some time; the new Soviet deployment did not alter the nuclear balance of power. Kennedy interrupted again to repeat his demand for the elevated Canadian alert. Diefenbaker cut him off and snapped, "When were we consulted?" "You weren't!" shouted the president and slammed down the receiver.[18]

Soviet ships drew closer to Kennedy's line in the sea. At an 11 a.m. Ex Comm meeting on Monday, October 22, Kennedy had raised the idea of asking OAS members to contribute ships to help with the quarantine and related measures. Ignoring the purpose of NORAD and the fact that Canadians were already working with Americans in the current crisis, Rusk advised against the idea, not because the help wasn't needed but because "our armed forces think only Americans can fight."[19]

The American officer responsible for finding and tracking Soviet submarines was Admiral E.B. "Whitey" Taylor. On October 16, the day Kennedy was told about the missiles, Taylor went to Halifax. He met with Rear-Admiral Kenneth Dyer, commander of Canada's Atlantic fleet. Taylor knew he did not have enough ships to increase his patrols in Cuban waters and at the same time maintain vigilance along the east coast and North Atlantic. Dyer agreed to help.[20]

At that point, Canada had twenty-nine warships and forty long-range aircraft ready for active service.[21] With NATO agreements already in place and, coincidentally, a joint Canadian-American naval training exercise already in progress, the two navies were able to quickly mobilize and efficiently operate as a coordinated unit. Believing that Halifax could be a potential enemy target, Dyer moved his headquarters and, from an undisclosed location, coordinated Canada's most complex naval operation since the Second World War.[22] The Canadian navy's involvement meant that Taylor was able to move more American ships and planes to the Cuban quarantine line.[23]

The Canadian and American ships and planes moved from a training exercise to an actual emergency with command and control processes adjusted or even made up as they went along—and it all worked.[24] Canadians moved closer to Soviet fishing fleets. On the first day, a Canadian aircraft spotted, tracked, and reported a Soviet submarine. Three days later another was found. Meanwhile, after the Harkness order that raised their alert level, the Royal Canadian Air Force began assisting in patrols far off the coast of Newfoundland. The Canadian Argus aircraft had a greater range than the American's Lockheed P2V Neptunes, so the RCAF squadron led the operation. Soon, six Soviet submarines were confirmed and were being tracked, with a seventh suspected.[25]

The Canadian-American rules for tracking enemy submarines, which had been discussed for years, were finalized on August 31, 1961. If a sub was hailed and did not respond and identify itself, it would be deemed hostile. Five depth charges would be dropped as a signal to surface. Moscow was told of the new protocol in October. It refused to accept the new rules of engagement and so did not pass the information along to its submarine commanders. This failure to communicate meant that if a Canadian followed the existing procedure and dropped depth charges near a Soviet submarine, its commander would consider his ship under attack and follow his own standard operating procedure for response. It nearly happened. A Soviet submarine captain believed himself under attack and ordered the preparation of his nuclear-tipped missiles. Only the insistence of his political officer kept him from issuing the order to fire that would have destroyed an American city and quite possibly sparked a global nuclear war.[26]

The Canadian report of Soviet submarines shocked the Americans. American admiral Robert L. Dennison told Kennedy that the Canadians had for years been tracking Soviet subs along the coast and confirmed that at least four were plying through and under the choppy waves.[27] No one could tell with any certainty how many were carrying nuclear weapons or how many were within nearly instantaneous striking distance of major cities.[28]

A few hours after his shouting match with Diefenbaker, President Kennedy signed the proclamation making the quarantine official. It would begin at 10 a.m. the next morning, shortly before Soviet ships were predicted to reach the line. At 9:30 p.m. that night, Robert Kennedy surprised the Soviet ambassador by showing up alone outside the 16th Street NW embassy gate. Anatoly Dobrynin walked Kennedy to his nearby residence. In a dimly lit living room, they sipped coffee and spoke of what would happen the next day. Dobrynin assured Kennedy that the Soviet ships would not stop. Kennedy promised that the American ships would stop them. Then, the ambassador said, there will be war.[29]

Castro had moved to an underground command post across the river from the Havana zoo. Khrushchev was in an underground bunker facility outside of Moscow. Diefenbaker stayed at home, but the Diefenbunker was supplied and ready. Kennedy remained in the White House. A young folk singer named Bob Dylan was among those who believed the end was near. He quickly wrote a new song that he believed could be his last: "A Hard Rain's A-Gonna Fall."[30]

Kennedy's Ex Comm met at ten the next morning—Wednesday, October 24. The ships were ready and American bomber crews had been given their Soviet target coordinates. In addition to the back-channel communications in which Robert Kennedy had been involved, the president and Soviet chairman had been exchanging letters. Each oozed a harsh tone. Each indicated a refusal to retreat from the precipice at which they stood.

Kennedy's military and civilian advisors crowded around the long Cabinet table that was littered with papers, coffee cups, and scraps of largely ignored food. Aides rushed in and out of the room with files and notes. The anxiety that seemed to hover in the air was rendered even more intense by the simmering hostility and distrust that had developed between the president and his generals. Kennedy had redrawn the quarantine line closer to Cuba to allow more time. He permitted an oil tanker and then an East German passenger ship to pass through. He was then told that six Soviet ships and a submarine were approaching the line. Then, suddenly, they stopped. It was either the end of the crisis or a pause before Armageddon.

Diefenbaker had called together his tired and stressed Cabinet. Many of the ministers had placed food and liquor orders for the Diefenbunker. A new debate swirled regarding the alert-level question. While Diefenbaker and Green had not budged in their opinions, the developing drama that was being meticulously reported in the media had swung three-quarters of the Cabinet to Harkness.[31] Another Harkness-Diefenbaker shouting match ensued. Harkness insisted that Canada was failing in its continental defence commitments. Diefenbaker repeated that nothing had changed since they made their previous decision and that he would not be pushed by Kennedy. He defied the growing consensus.[32]

An exasperated Harkness returned to his office. There, he was told that the American Strategic Air Command had been raised to DEFCON 2. It was the last stage before war. He rushed to Diefenbaker's office with the news. Diefenbaker listened and was silent for a moment. He already had Cabinet's support to approve the elevated alert level. It was up to him. Gazing down at his desk he muttered, "All right, go ahead." Harkness ordered Canadian forces to the equivalent of DEFCON 2.[33]

Diefenbaker publicly announced the alert-level shift in the House the next day. He called the Soviet weapons a "direct and immediate menace to Canada."[34] Pearson stood in support of the decision. He also backed Diefenbaker's refusal to simply rubber-stamp Kennedy's requests without proper due process and an assessment of Canadian national interests. "Backing the United States," Pearson said, "does not necessarily mean that all the details of that action are to be approved without qualification. . . . [We] can be grateful that the United Nations has been called into action at this time . . . with all its weaknesses . . . the world organization is in existence today, and stands between humanity and destruction."[35]

Ambassador Ritchie and Basil Robinson met with Secretary of State Rusk. They reviewed all that Diefenbaker had said and that Canada was doing. Rusk expressed gratitude for the Canadian support and said that he and the president were looking forward to quickly getting UN inspectors into Cuba.[36]

Canadians and Americans remained terrified. American stores reported an uptick in gun sales. People claimed that they were not arming themselves to shoot Cubans or Russians but their neighbours who, once the bombs started to fall, might try to break into their shelter or home to steal food. Many young women were propositioned by earnest young men: "We're all going to die soon anyway," various iterations of the line went, "and surely you would not want to go a virgin?"[37] Howard Green and his wife drove to their cottage just north of Ottawa to enjoy a night away and what remained of the Gatineau Hills' fall colours. An exploding electrical transformer awakened them. Green said, "I thought that was it. I thought it was a bomb."[38]

On October 25, Khrushchev sent a note to Kennedy calling the quarantine piracy and promising again that Soviet ships would pierce it. He pledged that the missiles would never be removed from Cuba.[39] Soviet engineers in Cuba used American radio time signals to precisely target the R-12 missiles at a number of cities. However, deep in his bunker, Khrushchev met with advisors and explored ways that he could claim victory in order to walk the crisis back.[40] Secretary-General U Thant became an important player in the debates taking place at the UN.[41] He supported Brazil's proposal that the United States and Soviet Union agree to remove all nuclear weapons from Latin America with the promise that neither would ever station them in a country that was not at that point a nuclear power. The plan would have ended discussions of Canada ever acquiring nuclear weapons. Before it could gain traction, however, Kennedy killed it, and thereby halted a significant step toward stopping nuclear proliferation.[42]

The multi-level, overlapping official and back-channel negotiations invited misunderstanding. The situation was made worse by time zones and problems with timely and accurate translations. In the middle of the muddle, an American U-2 spy plane wandered into Soviet airspace and Soviet aircraft scrambled to intercept it. Then a U-2 was shot down over Cuba by a Soviet anti-aircraft missile. It all seemed to be spinning out of control.

After receiving a conciliatory letter from Khrushchev offering to remove the missiles in exchange for an American pledge to never invade

Cuba, Kennedy received a more harshly worded letter that also demanded the immediate removal of American Jupiter missiles from Turkey. Kennedy took his brother's advice to ignore the second letter and accept the terms of the first. He wrote to Khrushchev agreeing that if UN officials could observe and confirm that work on the missile bases had stopped and that all weapons were removed, then he would work with the UN to promptly end the quarantine. He promised to never invade Cuba.[43]

Robert Kennedy met again with Soviet ambassador Dobrynin. Kennedy offered a copy of the president's letter and then added a secret sweetener. In six months, America's Jupiter missiles would be removed from Turkey.[44] They had been installed during Kennedy's presidency and, although he had questioned their value, he had never ordered their removal. If this deal was not accepted, an unusually subdued Robert Kennedy said, then there would be a nuclear confrontation that neither Dobrynin's boss nor his own brother could control. The Kennedy brothers kept the side deal secret even from most members of Ex Comm.

Sunday, October 28 brought a flood of news to Khrushchev. He received confirmation of the downing of the American U-2 in Cuba, and Kennedy's official letter and secret message. He also received a letter from Castro arguing that the Americans should never be trusted and that the time to act had arrived. Castro urged an immediate pre-emptive nuclear strike on the United States. Khrushchev was also told that Cuban forces were now firing at every American plane they saw and that it was only a matter of time before another one was either shot down or returned fire.[45]

Khrushchev dictated a letter to Kennedy agreeing to his terms. To quickly defuse the situation, he read it over Radio Moscow. Even before the broadcast ended, Soviet engineers began disassembling the missiles. It was over. Not everyone was happy. American general Curtis LeMay, the man who had organized the firebombing of Tokyo and once said the best thing to do with Cuba was to "fry it," was infuriated with a president he thought was weak and had blown a golden opportunity.[46] Castro was angry because Khrushchev was removing the weapons that he had hoped would ensure Cuban security.[47]

Castro refused to allow United Nations observers into Cuba, but Khrushchev saw that his soldiers and engineers worked as quickly as possible. At a November 20 press conference, Kennedy announced that U-2 flights and other intelligence had confirmed that the launch sites and missiles were gone and that the Soviet IL-28 aircraft would soon be gone too. In April 1963, the Jupiter missiles in Turkey were quietly and without fanfare dismantled and scrapped. Their nuclear warheads were returned to the United States.

Kennedy emerged from the thirteen days of turmoil and terror a hero. A November poll reported that 80 percent of Americans approved of Kennedy's presidency and his handling of the crisis.[48] The November mid-term elections sent three more Democrats to the Senate, the first gain for a president's party since Roosevelt in 1934. The United States Information Agency conducted polls in Western Europe and Latin America and reported in January that people were overwhelmingly happy with Kennedy.[49] A similar Canadian poll indicated 79.3 percent of those asked supported the president.[50] A CTV poll released on Christmas Eve revealed that 49 percent of Canadians chose Kennedy as the world leader they admired most. Macmillan was second with 16 percent.[51] A Privy Council memo to Diefenbaker concluded, "The main lesson to be drawn from all this is that when the U.S. President chooses to psychologically mobilize the American people on the occasion of a serious threat to them, the Canadian people will be drawn up in the process also."[52]

Since before Confederation, links to the British motherland had been a defining element of Canada's identity. The choice to ignore Britain to follow Kennedy suggested that the old ties were mere nostalgia. Just as Canadians appeared willing to surrender their cultural sovereignty for

American movies, books, and television, their reaction in a crisis indicated their benign willingness to offer up their political sovereignty as well. Polls, media coverage, and letters to the editor showed that the president's bold and decisive stand had added gravitas to his glamour and substance to his celebrity, further mesmerizing the already besotted Canadians. When the crunch came, they were less interested in the prowess of their prime minister to promote their sovereignty than the power of the president to protect their security.

Diefenbaker understood the moment's inherent danger. After an extensive debriefing process, External Affairs submitted a long memo to Diefenbaker that questioned Canada's alliance with the United States and the foundation of the NORAD agreement. The memo noted that the agreement contained a consultation pledge and that diplomatic notes exchanged between the United States and Canada detailed how the consultation would occur. However, neither the agreement nor anyone involved in its implementation anticipated a situation in which the United States would take unilateral action after a period of secret planning. "The Agreement did not foresee the circumstance in which one country would be aware of the impending need for an increased degree of air defence readiness but would not inform the other country of this need before the time for taking action had arrived, or would not consult with the other country about the implications of the developing situation and the kind of air defence measures that should be taken to meet it."[53] In other words, despite the Canadian public's love of Kennedy and all things American, the department did not like the idea of Canada being treated throughout the crisis like it was an American state, with the prime minister consulted no more than a governor, or like a satellite deserving no consultation whatsoever.

Other important Canadians agreed. Canada's NATO ambassador, George Ignatieff, observed, "Though the world heaved a collective sigh of relief, the Cuban confrontation had in a sense reinforced some of the worst fears of many NATO countries, including Canada. When the chips were down and decisions were being made that might plunge the world into a nuclear holocaust, all NATO could do was hold its breath while Washington took whatever steps the president and his military advisors deemed appropriate."[54] Dean Rusk later admitted, "We did not want multilateral management of the Cuba crisis."[55]

In a frank and wide-ranging interview with ABC and CBS news divisions on December 17, Kennedy explained that when he'd briefed congressional leaders just before his televised speech to the nation, they were understandably critical of decisions made; they had not had the six days he had taken to carefully weigh options. He admitted, "If we had to act on the Wednesday, in the first twenty-four hours, I don't think we would have acted as prudently as we did."[56] Given these reasoned thoughts, it is surprising that Kennedy could not fathom Diefenbaker's wish to do as he had done and take time to seek proper advice before setting policy. Of course, by the time he contacted Diefenbaker, time was no longer available. Later in the same interview, Kennedy referenced the American-allied response to the crisis but mentioned only OAS members. He said nothing of the Canadian military involvement.

Kennedy's staff prepared a nine-page report outlining international press reaction to the crisis. It included comments on newspaper coverage from every continent and more than twenty countries. Neither Canada nor a single Canadian newspaper was mentioned.[57]

An October 27 *Washington Post* editorial praised Diefenbaker's unhesitating support for Kennedy. "Whatever the differences on Cuba policy between Canada and the United States of America in the past, they have been swept aside by the Soviets' provocation. . . . The Prime Minister, whose record testifies to his independence from the United States pressure, is speaking for the great majority of Canadians . . . it is deeply reassuring that no cool air is blowing from Canada."[58] The paper was an outlier as an American consensus grew that Canada had let Kennedy down. On November 2, Diefenbaker received a note from the embassy in

Washington saying that the Cuban crisis had turned the tenor of talk in the city about Canada from frustration to anger. Irritation about Diefenbaker's refusal to immediately and publicly announce a higher alert status when asked to do so was added to the already harsh feelings regarding the long-delayed nuclear weapons decision.[59]

Three days later, Diefenbaker tried to turn Canadians from cheerleaders back into Canadians. He delivered a speech in which he reminded them and Kennedy that treaty arrangements must be based on the premise that signatories are equal, sovereign states. "Canada and the United States are members of NORAD under which we are joined in the air defence of North America. As I look back on the Cuban crisis, I believe that it emphasized more than ever before the necessity of there being full consultation before any action is taken or policies executed that might lead to war. . . . In light of this experience, it should be made clear that consultation is a prerequisite to joint and contemporaneous action . . . for it could never have been intended that either of the nations would automatically follow whatever stand the other might take."[60]

The Cuban Missile Crisis also offered lessons for Kennedy about Canada. Rusk had warned him that Canada was essential to America's security and that Diefenbaker's nationalism threatened that security. Before the crisis, Kennedy's advisors had dismissed Diefenbaker as a dithering old man and Canada's foreign policy as "neurotic."[61] Diefenbaker had been dodgy, but now he had proven that Rusk was right; he was dangerous. Kennedy would soon be tempted to do with Diefenbaker what he was doing with other recalcitrant leaders and governments that threatened his goals and American interests.

# ELEVEN

---

# TOPPLING A GOVERNMENT

JOHN KENNEDY WAS BEGINNING to sound and act a lot like Dwight Eisenhower. In a December 17, 1962, radio and television interview, Kennedy said that the United States and the Soviet Union must develop ways to better understand each other and to peacefully coexist.[1] Following the Cuban Missile Crisis, a system allowing teletype messaging between the White House and the Kremlin was installed to improve communications. It became known as the hotline, giving rise to the popular image of a red telephone on the president's desk, despite the fact that it was really a process of communication and no such phone existed, red or otherwise. Kennedy combed through the defence budget and began questioning the return on the investment in weapons systems that were enormously expensive but did not appreciably improve American security. One of those systems was the Skybolt air-to-surface missile. Under his fresh scrutiny it was deemed not just costly but obsolete. He announced its cancellation.

Kennedy's decision precipitated an immediate British backlash. While scrapping the Skybolt made good fiscal and military sense in Washington, it hurt Prime Minister Macmillan. He had contracted with the Eisenhower government to have the missiles placed in Britain, where they would play a key part in national defence. Despite being warned about Britain's reaction,

Kennedy again paid the price of acting without consulting an ally.[2] Kennedy and Macmillan had already scheduled a December 18 meeting in the Bahamas. They would escape their cold capitals and try to end the sudden chilliness in their relationship in Nassau's welcoming warmth. For the first few conversations, the temperature didn't temper British rancour.

Diefenbaker had done what he always did when Macmillan planned to visit America, and invited him to Ottawa either before or afterwards. Wanting to fly home from the Bahamas, Macmillan instead invited Diefenbaker to join him there after Kennedy left. On December 20, the day before he was scheduled to fly south, Diefenbaker received a phone call from the *Toronto Telegram*'s Burt Richardson. He had gone to Nassau as part of the large international press pool. Richardson said that the British-American talks had broken down. He told Diefenbaker that 125 reporters would greet him at the airport and demand comments about how he would help to defuse the spat. "Regardless of what the doctrinal professors of the State Department and External Affairs say," Richardson reported, "Kennedy is anxious to improve relations with you."[3]

On the plane to Nassau, Diefenbaker pored over an external affairs briefing package. It offered a view of Kennedy that was indeed quite different from the *Telegram* reporter's sunny optimism. Assistant undersecretary of state H.H. Carter's memo warned that Kennedy was more dangerous to Canadian interests than he had ever been. "I am sure that the feeling now uppermost in the consciousness of Kennedy and his advisers is that they handled the Cuba crisis without any assistance from their Allies; and that they handled it successfully. . . . A year ago, therefore, they were looking for diplomatic aid and comfort from their more experienced friends and, in particular, the British. The situation prevailing today is altogether different."[4] Carter suggested questions that could arise from the press and the two leaders and Diefenbaker scribbled more of his own. Diefenbaker prepared to discuss a host of issues, including his continued opposition to expanding the nuclear club. If asked about Canada's delay in raising the alert level during the Cuban crisis, he would remind Kennedy that he had not been properly consulted.[5]

The Nassau talks had been tough. However, before Diefenbaker arrived, Kennedy and Macmillan had worked out a deal. Instead of the now discredited Skybolts, the United States and Britain would share costs and production facilities to create a British fleet of nuclear-armed Polaris submarines. The subs would be part of Britain's contribution to NATO, but in times of trouble they could be withdrawn to defend Britain. Kennedy and Macmillan worried about de Gaulle's reaction to the new weapons arrangement and so agreed that France should be offered a similar deal. They also agreed that a new multilateral NATO nuclear-force arrangement should be established and they sketched out some guiding principles.[6]

Because the meetings ran long, Kennedy's departure was delayed. Macmillan asked him to stay a little longer to share lunch with Diefenbaker. Richardson had obviously misread Kennedy's desire to patch things up with Diefenbaker; the president flatly refused. Macmillan coaxed him with the promise of great lobsters but Kennedy snapped that he could get better lobsters back home at Hyannis Port. Finally, grumbling his agreement to stay, Kennedy told Canadian economist and American ambassador to India John Kenneth Galbraith, part of the American delegation, "Your prime minister is coming down. You have to stay with me. I don't want to be alone with him."[7]

Diefenbaker arrived still thinking he would be playing a mediator's role but found there was nothing left to mediate. The three leaders met at the palatial home of Canadian industrialist and financier Robert Holt. Diefenbaker and Kennedy had not seen each other since May 1961, and their last phone conversation had ended in recriminating shouts. Kennedy arrived late. As they shook hands, Diefenbaker's first words were, "Well, Mr. President, what are we going to do about the North American unemployment problem?" Kennedy said, "Well we solved ours by reducing taxes."[8] He turned and walked away.

While seated outside and cracking lobster tails, Macmillan and Kennedy told Diefenbaker about the new British-American weapons agreement. They discussed a range of issues including Canadian trade with China and Cuba. Kennedy expressed surprise that Canadian wheat sales to China were increasing. He asked if Canadian connections could help negotiate the release of Americans being held in China and Diefenbaker promised to do his best. Kennedy expressed thanks for the helpful role the Canadian embassy in Havana had played during the Cuban crisis and praised Canadian ambassador Ritchie, whom he had first met with his father in London. Kennedy spoke of his hope to have a man on the moon by 1967.[9] The lunch was light and affable. Later, however, Kennedy remarked to Pearson, "There we sat like three whores at a christening."[10]

Air Force One whisked Kennedy away shortly after lunch. In a meeting with Diefenbaker that afternoon, Macmillan boasted that the new submarine-based nuclear missiles would enable the mobile launch pads to hurtle a nuclear warhead one thousand miles and so end Moscow's ability to threaten or blackmail Britain. He also admitted to Diefenbaker that Britain's chances of gaining membership to the European Common Market were probably fifty-fifty.[11] It was the last time they would discuss it; a few weeks later, Charles de Gaulle vetoed Britain's membership. For the time being, the idea Diefenbaker had tried to kill was dead.

Diefenbaker conducted a long press conference and sat for several interviews with journalists. He stretched the truth in suggesting that he had been part of the discussions regarding NATO leadership and the European nuclear deterrent.[12] He and Olive then treated themselves to a brief Bahamian vacation. They lounged on the white sand and he fished the crystal-blue water. He read, napped, and swam twice a day. As Diefenbaker enjoyed a brief reprieve from the pressures of his office, Kennedy was about to try to remove him from it.

Two months before, on October 30, with Khrushchev just beginning to remove his missiles from Cuba, Diefenbaker's Cabinet had returned to their hand-wringing over the question of nuclear weapons. Defence Minister Harkness said recent events proved they were more necessary than ever. Despite the Americans dismissing the idea over a year before, External Affairs Minister Green reiterated his notion of storing warheads near the border, earmarking them for bases in Canada, and then shipping them north in an emergency. Eventually, Diefenbaker approved the creation of a Cabinet subcommittee with Veterans Affairs Minister Gordon Churchill acting as the mediator between Harkness and Green. Diefenbaker directed that they were not to debate whether to acquire the weapons. They were to draft a plan to get them.[13]

Harkness believed that a Cabinet majority now wanted nuclear weapons. He understood that the Cuban crisis and Kennedy's handling of it had brought more of the country to his position. He remained resolute in his belief that Canada's national defence and NATO and NORAD commitments demanded that the military have nuclear weapons in all Canada's weapons systems.[14] Consequently, he grew increasingly frustrated when the subcommittee made little progress. Green expressed worries about anti-nuclear groups and the ability of Canada to control its own defence and spoke yet again of delay to allow the continuation of disarmament talks. Harkness appealed for Diefenbaker's intervention but was rebuffed. As Christmas approached, Harkness became convinced that the prime minister had moved from being unwilling to incapable of making a decision.[15]

Shortly after Diefenbaker returned from Nassau, and with no decision on nuclear weapons in sight, everything changed. NATO's supreme allied commander was due to retire. General Norstad ended his career with a tour of NATO capitals and, on January 3, 1963, he arrived in Ottawa. He was welcomed to the Uplands airport by Canadian Air Chief Marshal Frank Miller, associate defence minister Pierre Sévigny, and a group of television and print reporters. Norstad visited the governor general, lunched with Harkness and members of Canada's Armed Forces Chiefs of Staff, and then convened a press conference. Due to the position he was leaving and because many American newspapers were touting him as a possible presidential candidate, what he had to say was afforded particular attention on both sides of the border.

With Miller at his side, both men impressive in their stiff dress uniforms bedecked with rows of colourful medals, Norstad made a brief statement in which he said there were "none finer" than Canada's NATO soldiers.[16] At that point he could have left, but he opted instead to take questions. He began with gentle diplomacy, stating that he was happy with the way Canada was fulfilling its NATO commitment. Scrappy Southam News reporter Charles Lynch then pressed him on Diefenbaker having taken three years to decide whether Canada's NATO troops would have nuclear weapons. Norstad stickhandled but Lynch persisted. "Does it mean, sir," he asked, "that if Canada does not accept nuclear weapons for these aeroplanes she is not actually fulfilling her NATO commitments?" Norstad's answer inspired gasps. "I believe that's right. She would be meeting it in force but not under the terms of the requirements that have been established by NATO. . . . We are depending upon Canada to produce some of the tactical atomic strike forces."[17]

Norstad had made a career of being diplomatically delicate with NATO's governments. But here he was stating publicly what he had been arguing privately for years, in Canada, and with Canada's top general at his side. An exasperated Sévigny ended the press conference after thirty-five minutes of watching Norstad hammer his government and, in contradicting much of what Diefenbaker had been saying for two years, calling the Canadian prime minister a liar.

Many newspapers, especially those in the Southam chain, had already turned on Diefenbaker. The day before Norstad's arrival, for example, the *Ottawa Citizen*'s editorial page printed one column arguing that the general's visit offered Diefenbaker a good opportunity to finally announce a nuclear weapons deal with the United States. On the same page, Charles Lynch ignored the fact that Diefenbaker had been invited to Nassau and accused him of demeaning his office by horning in on the Kennedy-Macmillan talks.[18]

With the table set by such attacks on Diefenbaker throughout the Christmas holidays, Norstad's comments became the media's main course. Editorials across the country praised Norstad and took swings at Diefenbaker for failing to do as Kennedy had wanted and what the general had just said was essential. The *Montreal Gazette*, for example, applauded Norstad's "bold statement" and called him "the highest and most reliable authority."[19] In Halifax, the *Chronicle-Herald*'s front page reported the press conference in glowing terms, with a picture of a stern-looking Norstad. Its editorial called Diefenbaker's delay of the nuclear decision "muddled," and suggested that, as a result, Canada had "failed to live up to our word."[20] The *Toronto Telegram* editorial argued, "The Government of Canada must now face up to its responsibilities in this field or be prepared to accept the judgement of Canadians generally that it is incapable of decision in the most important single area of Canada's role in international affairs."[21] The American embassy sent copies of these and other newspaper reports to the State Department along with equally critical comments made by House Opposition members.

In the days following the press conference, many newspapers that had stuck with the prime minister turned on him. Most important among them was Canada's only national newspaper, the *Globe and Mail*. For years it had been against the acquisition of nuclear weapons, but two days after Norstad's bombshell press conference it changed its mind. Its January 5 editorial argued that Canada should either accept them in Canada and Europe or withdraw from NATO and NORAD. "We cannot have it both ways," the piece read. "We cannot be in NATO and not of it." The broadside hurt Diefenbaker even while its final sentence made the point he had been making for years: "Canada's right to be consulted before the United States takes action endangering North America should be firmly established on the political level before we can be expected to accept our full responsibility for joint defence under NORAD."[22] The prime minister was running out of friends.

After igniting the firestorm, General Norstad left for Washington. Apologies followed from neither him nor any other American official. In fact, five days later Norstad told a Canadian reporter, "The alliance would suffer a great loss if Canada did not fulfil its nuclear commitment to NATO."[23] The next day, on January 9, President Kennedy called Norstad to the White House. The summons was not to reprimand him for directly interfering in Canadian domestic affairs but to proceed with a decision made long before the Canadian kerfuffle and pin on his already bedecked uniform a Distinguished Service Medal. In the East Room ceremony, Kennedy praised him for displaying "great skill" and "sensitivity" in acting simultaneously as the ranking American general in Europe and NATO commander. Perhaps without spite, but certainly with full knowledge of what had just happened in Ottawa, Kennedy lauded Norstad for having, "in a unique way held the confidence of our allies in Europe and, of course, our partner to the north, Canada."[24]

Diefenbaker was incensed. That the White House ceremony happened despite Norstad's Ottawa press conference and its fallout led Diefenbaker to believe that either Kennedy did not care what the general had done or that he had spoken either at the president's behest or with his approval.[25] Canadian ambassador Charles Ritchie agreed, later writing, "I found it impossible to take seriously the American official explanation that he [Norstad] was speaking not as a U.S. representative but in his former NATO capacity. This was another American turn of the screw to bring down the Conservative government."[26] While Diefenbaker and Ritchie were angry, Pearson was inspired.

Throughout his diplomatic and political career, Pearson had been staunchly opposed to nuclear proliferation and to nuclear weapons being placed in Canada. He had repeatedly called his opposition a moral issue. He and his wife, Maryon, supported Canadian anti-nuclear groups and international efforts to promote nuclear disarmament.[27] However, in the fall of 1962, with Diefenbaker taking flak for the perception that he had failed to support Kennedy in the Cuban crisis, Pearson was undergoing a period of existential angst.

Two months before Norstad's Ottawa press conference, Liberal defence critic Paul Hellyer had attended a NATO conference in Paris. Hellyer met with Norstad and then with Canadian officers and servicemen. He was told over and over that the Canadians needed American nukes. Then he sat with Canada's NATO ambassador, George Ignatieff. Ignatieff argued that while the absence of nuclear weapons kept Canadian troops in Europe from meeting their full potential, it did not render them ineffective. Plus, Ignatieff advised, equipping Canadian troops with nuclear weapons would be a strategic error as it was based on the faulty assumption that a Soviet attack on the West would come through Germany.[28] The contradictory advice reflected the fight that had been going on for years in Ottawa between Defence and External Affairs. Diplomats considered the whole picture and generals wanted more weapons. Hellyer sided with the military.

Hellyer reported to Pearson and spoke with Ivan White, chargé d'affaires at the American embassy in Ottawa. He expressed shock at having heard that Canada's reputation was suffering because it refused to supply its forces with nuclear weapons.[29] Pearson was noncommittal in his response. White was excited. He sent a report to the State Department, sharing Hellyer's intention to bring his concerns to the Liberal Party leadership and added that the Liberals presented an opportunity to turn Canada toward "some realism" in its defence policies. He suggested actions be taken to secretly support Hellyer's view, perhaps with the publication of material or "any information which [the]

Department believes we might be justified giving Hellyer on unattributed basis."[30] A dirty seed was planted.

Hellyer cranked up the pressure on Pearson by making a speech in Walkerton, Ontario. Contradicting Liberal Party policy, he advocated bringing American nuclear weapons to Canada and stationing them with Canadian troops in Europe. He said it was not a moral decision, as Pearson had so often called it, but a practical, military, and economic matter. He mailed Pearson a copy of the speech only after he had delivered it. He later said that he needed to speak out of turn because Pearson always wanted to postpone decisions—interestingly, the same accusation Harkness was whispering about Diefenbaker.[31] Hellyer also wrote a long letter to Pearson recommending that Canada's most celebrated diplomat ignore his former peers and heed the generals. Hellyer urged caucus members to change the party's nuclear policy to improve national security and allow Canada to meet its NATO and NORAD commitments. He claimed to have heard that if Canada did not soon accept the weapons, America would end its procurement of Canadian military products and production-sharing agreements. Hellyer saw the rare opportunity to marry good policy and good politics: Canada should have the weapons, and the post–Cuban Missile Crisis mood meant that more Canadians than ever agreed.[32]

Hellyer was ignoring, and hoping others would forget, that in October 1960 he had said, "The Bomarc missile is about the most useless expense of money you can devise. The Government might as well collect taxes and dump the money into the Northumberland Strait."[33] That was then. Now he was winning the backing of powerful Liberal caucus members and trusted advisors who joined him in attempting to persuade Pearson to perform a similar policy pirouette.

Respected former deputy minister of trade and commerce and Pearson advisor Mitchell Sharp had written to his leader in November explaining that Toronto's "elite" supported the acquisition of nuclear weapons.[34] Liberal Party stalwart Jack Pickersgill composed a particularly long and thoughtful memo in which he repeated Hellyer's points about meeting NATO commitments. He linked Canada's relationship with the United States with domestic political considerations: "Canada is not and will not ever become a nuclear power on its own; that our commitment relates exclusively to our position in an alliance for the defence of the continent and of the free world and that our position in the alliance, which we had a large part in forming, depends upon the confidence of the allies, particularly the U.S., in our *loyalty* and *reliability*. I am almost equally concerned *as a practical politician* about retaining the support of the armed forces without which we cannot win an election."[35]

Pearson was in a bind. In February 1961 he said, "Canadian possession of atomic weapons for the defence of Canada is not necessary . . . [weapons] obtained from the USA and whose use could only be authorized by Washington, would not give us any defence whatever against the main threat, which is missile attack . . . by including Canada in the nuclear powers it would make our voice less effective in support of the abolition of all nuclear weapons."[36] He had maintained that stance in the 1962 election. "It is possible for Canada to play her full part in continental defence without becoming a nuclear power."[37] A few weeks later, in May 1962, he told a Victoria audience, "We won't take nuclear weapons, acquire them or use them, either under our own control or under the control of the United States."[38] Then came Kennedy and Cuba and General Norstad.

Coming just weeks after he'd made such an impression on Paul Hellyer in Europe, the general's press conference delivered a one-two punch on Canadian defence policy. Pearson was given a copy of Norstad's comments. The notes he scribbled in the margins as he read indicate that Norstad's argument about Canada's NATO commitments resonated. After all, Pearson had been among the organization's chief architects.[39]

Pearson packed the Norstad transcript and letters from Hellyer and others, flew to Manhattan, and checked into the Sheraton-East Hotel. He was scheduled to attend the Council on World Tensions. At his suite's desk he read and wrote. Among his visitors was his old friend Adlai Stevenson—Kennedy confidant and the American UN ambassador who had made mincemeat of the Soviets' Cuban missile lies.[40] Pearson ignored the conference and the allure of the Broadway theatres he loved to compose the speech of his life.

Liberal Party organizer Keith Davey had again hired Kennedy's pollster and political advisor Lou Harris. Harris conducted an extensive poll and submitted his report to Davey on January 10. The polling determined that 54 percent of Canadians supported Canada's acquisition of nuclear weapons, with only 34 percent opposed. Further, in vote-rich Quebec and Ontario, support for acquisition was 58 percent and 70 percent respectively. The Harris report argued that old-age pensions and nuclear weapons would be the most important issues in the next campaign, and that if the Liberals supported both they would win a majority.[41] Pearson claimed in a January 29 television interview to have not seen or been influenced by the polls, but later admitted otherwise.[42]

On January 12, 1963, to a gobsmacked audience of friendly Liberals in Scarborough, Ontario, Pearson delivered his bombshell. He began his speech by saying that a new government statement on defence policy was needed due to what he called "the shock of the Cuban crisis and of statements made by NATO leaders and others."[43] Ignoring his past exhortations to the contrary, he continued, "The fact is that the argument for or against nuclear weapons for Canada is a political, not a moral one. . . . War is the evil, the basic immorality."[44] He argued that it was hypocritical for Canada to assume a moral high ground on the issue when nearly all of the uranium used for the building of American nuclear weapons had for years come from Canada—in fact, much of it from his riding. He concluded: "In short, both in NATO and in continental defence, the Canadian government has accepted commitments for Canada in continental and collective defence which can only be carried out by Canadian forces if nuclear warheads are available."[45] In the 1950s, Pearson had been involved in NATO's decision to equip its European forces with nuclear arms, but this was different. Liberal Party policies and his personal opposition to nuclear proliferation and bringing the weapons to Canada were thrown in the ditch.

Over the next few days, Canadians across the country sipped their coffee and read big, bold headlines announcing the startling flip-flop. The *Chronicle-Herald* editorial misled its readers by arguing that the nuclear weapons being debated were all defensive. Then, like many other papers, it stated, "As for the correctness of the policy now offered by the Liberals in this regard, there can be no doubt."[46] The *Globe and Mail* editorial stated, "Coming from Mr. Pearson, this attitude is doubly welcome. He is widely regarded by members of all parties as an eminent authority on foreign affairs."[47] The suggestion, of course, was that Prime Minister Diefenbaker was both an unauthoritative voice on the matter and wrong. The *Ottawa Citizen* stated clearly what Pearson had only hinted: "The Liberals for all their past indecisions can now pose as the champions of NATO and NORAD, the supporters of American military leadership, the pro-Kennedy party."[48]

Pearson later confessed that his astonishing about-face on nuclear weapons was the day he became a politician.[49] Perhaps his abandoning a resolute moral stance for political gain so shortly after the Cuban crisis was a reflection of something he later wrote regarding the 1956 Suez Crisis: "Things can be done under the incentive of terror and fear that cannot be done when the fear disappears."[50] He had indeed captured the significance of the moment. The speech reflected the change in direction that had been signalled by Canadians' reaction first to Kennedy and then to the Cuban crisis. It stated an intention to take Canada further down the road toward greater integration with the United States.

The reaction in Washington to Pearson's speech bordered on gleeful. A curtly phrased January 16 State Department report expected the statement to clear the air. "It is definitely move forward for US interests and improves the possibility that in long run we shall be able to make satisfactory continental air defense arrangements, as well as resolve problem equipping Canadian NATO forces."[51] McGeorge Bundy added a scribbled note saying that the president was relieved and wanted a "ready eye" kept on possible changes to Canada's nuclear stance.

The Americans were happy but Diefenbaker, surprisingly, was happier. As early as 1959, trusted advisor Robert Bryce had recommended that Diefenbaker simply announce the weapons were coming and then weather the political storm.[52] Diefenbaker had rejected the advice to first pursue his two-track nuclear policy and insist on joint civilian control. He then waited for the perfect political climate in which to make the announcement. He ended up waiting for so long—and for so many reasons—that he had assumed the appearance of a dithering procrastinator. He lost control of the narrative. Kennedy's popularity, the Cuban crisis, then Norstad, and then Pearson and the newspapers painted him into a political corner of his own making. But Pearson had just shown him a way to leap out.

Upon hearing the flip-flop news, Diefenbaker exclaimed, "We've got him now!"[53] The next election would be fought, like the last, on the theme of Canadian identity, nationalism, and sovereignty. He would be even better able to present himself as Canada's champion, and Pearson as an American lackey taking direction from Kennedy.[54]

# TWELVE

---

# THE CROSSROADS

DIEFENBAKER'S RE-ELECTION STRATEGY immediately stumbled. Three days after Pearson's Scarborough speech, the Progressive Conservative Party's annual meeting began in Ottawa. Delegates prepared a resolution that supported the acquisition of American nuclear weapons if a global disarmament treaty was not signed within twelve months. Upon hearing of the resolution Diefenbaker ordered all copies destroyed and had another passed stating that the government and not the party would make all nuclear weapons decisions.

He created a new Cabinet subcommittee to examine his government's nuclear policy. The committee quickly and unanimously recommended continuing negotiations with the Americans with the goal of bringing nuclear weapons to Canada and placing them with the Canadian contingent in Europe. Diefenbaker glanced at the report and rejected it. It was exactly what he had wanted before Pearson's speech, but not now. Harkness was furious, the Cabinet was split, the party was confused, and the government was crumbling.

Diefenbaker then did something either brave or bullheaded or both. On January 25, amid withering attacks from the press and Opposition and mounting pressure from within his Cabinet and caucus, he rose in the

House to explain and defend his government's nuclear policy. He was taking a stand in the place he felt most in command, and with wit and words his most reliable weapons. Repeatedly quoting statements he had made in the House since 1957, he outlined the consistency of his policies regarding Canadian-American defence and nuclear negotiations. His government supported changing weapons systems when circumstances changed, but there had never been any question about Canada meeting its NORAD and NATO obligations. Bomarcs and other weapons systems and all Canadian troops were effective even without nuclear weapons. Negotiations were under way to allow the weapons to be placed in Canada with missing parts that would be delivered in a time of crisis. However, it was now prudent for Canada to postpone decisions regarding nuclear weapons because the Kennedy-Macmillan Nassau agreement indicated that NATO was shifting away from the nuclear deterrent and toward a more flexible response involving an increased use of conventional forces. Any decision regarding nuclear weapons, he concluded, should wait until NATO meetings scheduled for May.

Like the weapons he was describing, his speech was both defensive and offensive. Without mentioning Kennedy's name, Diefenbaker argued that his government's policies had always reflected—and would continue to reflect—Canadian interests and not those of "people from outside the country" who cared only for their own national interests. Over and over he painted Pearson as having vacillated on defence issues and he ruthlessly attacked the Opposition leader's change of heart and mind. With Hellyer, Martin, and others yelling from across the floor, Diefenbaker drew toward his conclusion by returning to an old theme: in meeting its security needs and obligations, Canada would be respected and its sovereignty protected. He glared across the aisle at the Liberal front benches and shouted, "We never sold Canada."[1]

With eyes wide, one hand on his hip and the other pointing at the loud and boisterous Opposition, he dramatically fell silent and the big room became eerily quiet. In a quavering voice he said that when the time came for future generations to look back on the decisions he'd made, they would say, "He refused to be stampeded. He refused to act on the impulse of the moment. He and his colleagues together, with the support of the Canadian parliament, brought about a policy, in co-operation with their allies and by influence over their allies, that led to the achievement of peace."[2] Diefenbaker sat down. He glowered at Pearson. Some Liberal and NDP members heckled him as his caucus, seated to either side and behind, rose as one and bathed him in a long and lively standing ovation.

It was a remarkable performance. The mostly extemporaneous speech was long and convoluted in diction and tone. Its use of a prosecutorial style, non sequiturs, and purple prose was typically Diefenbaker. With applause still filling the House, both Harkness and Green rushed to shake Diefenbaker's hand, both sure he had supported their position. The speech would have drawn a smile from Sir John A. Macdonald, who, at the height of the Pacific Scandal, spoke with passion and eloquence to dodge knives being flung and knaves all around. It would have made Mackenzie King, the master of obfuscation, exceedingly proud.

When the House recessed, reporters rushed to Cabinet ministers, seeking to understand what they had just heard. Newspapers wildly contradicted one another in their assessment of what the prime minister said. The *Globe and Mail* paraphrased Winston Churchill in characterizing Diefenbaker's defence policy as "a riddle wrapped in a mystery inside an enigma."[3] A CTV poll released two days later revealed that 58 percent of Canadians supported both Pearson's new determination to bring nuclear weapons to Canada and the fostering of greater co-operation with the United States on major defence issues. A whopping 78 percent opposed Diefenbaker's defence policies and pro-Canadianism.[4] However, when asked which leader was best for Canada, 40 percent of Canadians chose Diefenbaker while only 33 percent picked Pearson.[5] Maybe polls are best left to dogs after all.

Harkness considered what he had heard the prime minister say, or perhaps what he wished he'd heard, and three days later attempted to bring clarity to the lingering confusion by issuing a press release. "Our obligations to equip certain weapons systems with nuclear arms are reiterated, together with the determination to honour those obligations. . . . Should NATO reaffirm for Canada a role involving nuclear weapons, Canada will equip her NATO forces to discharge her obligation . . . nuclear warheads will be made available for our two squadrons of Bomarcs and for the CF101 interceptor squadrons."[6] He was dreaming.

The prime minister summoned Harkness and yet another shouting match ensued. How dare he, Diefenbaker demanded, speak for the prime minister? How could he be so irresponsible as to misstate the government's position? When Harkness yelled back, any vestiges of lingering respect between the two vanished into the blue air. News leaked of this latest high-volume confrontation. The press delighted in seeing Parliament Hill lights burning late, night after night. The take-out food and liquor bills rose as Cabinet ministers and Conservative MPs engaged in secret meetings, trying to determine how to position themselves in the fracturing caucus and save the government from self-destruction. Alliances were made and broken. Promises were made and lies were told. Then the schemers and ambitious dreamers began thinking the unthinkable. They began plotting to get rid of the prime minister.[7]

Just as events were spinning toward a confusing climax, the Americans made it all worse. Since Merchant's retirement as the ambassador to Canada the previous fall, Kennedy had been carefully considering his replacement. Adlai Stevenson had been among those consulted, and he agreed when George Ball said, "Canada is one of the toughest nuts to crack. The one who goes there has to deal with Diefenbaker and Green."[8] The man finally chosen was Walton Butterworth, who had served with

Kennedy's father in the American embassy in London. He counted Pearson among his friends dating back to their days together in Washington. Butterworth was a tough, experienced professional who would doggedly promote Kennedy's agenda in Canada. Among his first acts had been to dispatch a report to Kennedy entitled "Pearson's Nuclear Statement." He praised Pearson's courage and welcomed a potential breakthrough in the file that for years had been frustrating the president.[9] Finally, a Canadian leader was advocating goals consistent with Kennedy's.

From his post in the Canadian embassy in Washington, Basil Robinson had observed American attitudes changing after Pearson's pro-nuclear speech. He noted a great relief among the Americans with whom he was working and hope that the next Canadian election could bring a better prospect of having the president's wishes carried out.[10] Kennedy's Cabinet secretaries McNamara and Rusk cancelled a planned meeting with Green and Harkness. Robinson explained that the Americans believed they should wait until after the election before meeting with Canadians about anything substantive.[11] Waiting would only make sense, of course, if Pearson won.

As all ambassadors do, Butterworth carefully monitored the political landscape and sent home regular reports that summarized the editorial stands of a host of Canadian newspapers.[12] He went further, though, and held regular, secret briefings with a select group of Canadian journalists who were known to be critical of Diefenbaker. He fed them information to augment their pro-Pearson, anti-Diefenbaker articles and editorials.[13]

Butterworth read a transcript of Diefenbaker's January 25 speech. He was appalled. Deciding that the United States had to respond, he drafted a detailed letter to Rusk that took exception to nearly every point Diefenbaker had made.[14] Undersecretary of state George Ball met with a number of State Department officials and the letter was rewritten into a carefully crafted statement. Since all national capitals are leaky vessels, Canadian ambassador Charles Ritchie soon heard that something was up.

He rushed to assistant secretary of state William Tyler's office, told him that he had heard the State Department was considering commenting on Diefenbaker's speech, and urged him to resist doing so. He explained the precarious political situation and that American intervention could negatively affect the government and perhaps the country as a whole.[15]

In a discussion of the draft with Kennedy's special assistant McGeorge Bundy, Ball made the same point: "I wanted to warn you it is possible there will be a little flash back in Ottawa." Bundy responded, "I'll warn the president; and I have kept an eye on those cables and I am quite sure this is the thing to do. There is no problem."[16] Rusk discussed the statement with Kennedy and warned of the political conflagration it would ignite.[17] Bundy returned Ball's call and said, "The President has talked with the Secretary and is concerned about getting into too many fights in one week. Again, the timing is not ours but Diefenbaker's. We can't let these fellows get away with this."[18] In effect, the old PT boat captain had said "damn the torpedoes"—the statement would be released.

The Bundy-Ball telephone conversation also revealed that Rusk and the president had agreed upon a plausible cover-up to address the anticipated Canadian reaction. Referring to Rusk, Bundy said, "He will take the blame."[19] It is thus clear that Kennedy knew the statement was coming, knew it would politically damage the Canadian government, had been offered at least two chances to stop it, but signed off.

Late in the afternoon of January 30, the State Department press release was given to Canadian reporters in Washington. It was astonishing. Point by point, it explained how Diefenbaker's House of Commons speech had misrepresented the efficiency of non–nuclear tipped Bomarc missiles and non-nuclear aircraft; the state of Canadian-American negotiations; the terms of the Nassau agreement; the nature of NATO and NORAD defence arrangements; that having American-owned nuclear weapons in Canada would represent proliferation; and that the missiles threatened Canadian sovereignty.[20] Only three weeks after General

Norstad had told the Canadian people that Diefenbaker was being disingenuous regarding nuclear weapons, Kennedy's State Department, even more bluntly, called their prime minister a liar.

An apoplectic Diefenbaker took the unprecedented step of recalling the Canadian ambassador from Washington. Pearson and NDP leader Tommy Douglas, back in the House after a by-election, both issued statements criticizing the State Department's action. At a Cabinet meeting the next day, Diefenbaker angrily demanded an immediate election based on American interference in Canadian domestic affairs. Cabinet urged him to wait.[21]

In the House that afternoon, Diefenbaker thundered: "[Canada] will not be pushed around or accept external domination or interference in the making of its decisions. Canada is determined to remain a firm ally, but that does not mean she should be a satellite. . . . The Government of Canada does not consider that open public pressures by way of press release or otherwise are appropriate methods of exchanging views between equal sovereign nations or allies."[22] From both sides of the floor, the House erupted with anti-American, anti-Kennedy vitriol. Tommy Douglas said, "I think the Government of the United States should know from this Parliament that they are not dealing with Guatemala."[23] NDP member Doug Fisher said, "It is an insult to me as a Canadian. I see the next election between Diefenbaker and Kennedy, and Kennedy's going to lose."[24]

Pearson did not dispute the State Department's points, but the former diplomat offered that making them in a press release was tactless, provocative, and wrong.[25] He criticized Diefenbaker for disclosing the Nassau agreement's terms, and the fact that Canada and the United States were secretly negotiating a nuclear arms deal. Diefenbaker responded that the American press release sounded suspiciously like Pearson's Scarborough speech.[26] To reporters waiting outside the House, Diefenbaker grumbled, "Canada is not part of the New Frontier and I think the US State Department realizes it."[27]

Canadian newspapers ran the State Department story on their first pages. Most reflected their already established and well-known political bias. Many called for calm while some, such as the *Edmonton Journal*, blamed Diefenbaker for the whole mess.[28] Others noted that the country had just been handed an election issue.[29] Many others, like the *Sudbury Star*, saw red and echoed Diefenbaker's core argument: "The language of the Washington statement, and the manner of its release to the press only a half-hour after it had been handed to the Government, causes many Canadians to wonder if the United States looks on Canada as a satellite."[30]

Some American newspapers wrote of Canadian overreaction but many were highly critical of the Kennedy administration. A *Washington Daily News* editorial, for instance, referenced domestic situations in which toughness had won the day, but argued, "President Kennedy, Secretary of state Dean Rusk and defense secretary Robert S. McNamara, all but led with their chins in the Canadian affair. They forgot Canada is not U. S. Steel and Roger Blough and that Ottawa is not Oxford, Miss."[31]

Seeming to delight in having thrown the fox among the chickens, Ambassador Butterworth supplied the State Department with clippings from a range of Canadian newspapers. The only official reaction to Diefenbaker's response was a short non-apology apology from Secretary of State Rusk. He claimed to be sorry that the State Department's press release was causing unease in Canada but explained that after the prime minister's House of Commons speech, the Kennedy administration was justified in laying out the facts.[32] News of Rusk's statement appeared on the front page of the *New York Times* and was reprinted in papers across Canada. Yet another high-ranking American, the third in three weeks, had just called the Canadian prime minister a liar.

Kennedy put the plan to distance himself from the press release into action. On the night it was given to reporters, he called George Ball and expressed concern about the pressure that was being felt by Butterworth. Ball assured him that the ambassador was fine. "He's the one," Ball said, "who has been pushing it the most."[33] An hour and a half later Kennedy called back and was told that the statement was forcing the House of Commons into an emergency debate. As a result of Norstad's press conference and the State Department release, Ball told the president, the Diefenbaker government could fall. Kennedy worried about being blamed. "I can't make a judgement, but I would think that Diefenbaker would like to be licked on this issue."[34] Sounding tired, he continued, "I think we ought to just say that questions from the press and . . . because of discussions the statement has been made and it is only appropriate that we should give our people and anyone else interested in it the basic facts. We should feed some . . . up there that Diefenbaker's in trouble. We knew that he has always been running against us so it's very important."[35]

That night and the next day, Kennedy called a number of journalists to tell them that he had not approved the statement and that he had been angry when told about it. Among those he contacted was Canadian Max Freedman. Freedman was the *Winnipeg Free Press* Washington correspondent, a Liberal, and one of Pearson's friends and supporters. He was also among Kennedy's press confidants. On many occasions, they enjoyed cigars and drinks together and discussed a wide range of topics, including Diefenbaker, Pearson, and Canada. Kennedy asked Freedman to call the Canadian embassy to say that he had been angry when told of the State Department press release and had nothing to do with it.[36] Freedman did so and also wrote two articles purporting that the president had "blown his top" when informed of the statement.[37]

Sunday, February 3 dawned cold and sunny in Ottawa. At nine o'clock, Cabinet members assembled at Diefenbaker's residence. The obviously tired and still angry prime minister began by recommending an immediate dissolution of Parliament. The meeting quickly fell to pieces. Amid shouts and recriminations, Harkness turned to the prime minister and said, "You might as well know that the people of Canada have lost confidence in you, the party has lost confidence in you, and the cabinet has lost confidence in you. It is time you went."[38] Jaws dropped.

While some Cabinet ministers nodded, others began chirping that Harkness was a traitor. Everyone was suddenly talking and some were shouting wild accusations and insults when Diefenbaker slammed his right palm on the table. He stood, and there was silence. He slowly scanned the faces and then whispered that those who supported him should stand. Nine stood; eleven kept their seats. Diefenbaker glared around the table, shouted that finance minister Donald Fleming should be prime minister, and stormed out. Those around Diefenbaker had long tolerated his moods and eccentricities. Ministers and staff were used to his occasionally snapping in anger. Aides were accustomed to foreign governments being perplexed at not having heard back from Canada and then finding confidential, personal letters in desk drawers or even tossed under the prime minister's bed.[39] Like nearly all in his position, Diefenbaker often expressed the job's stress through waves of anger and pools of morose reflection, but this time it was different. This time it was not a particular decision but the government's very survival at stake. The prime minister had offered not a reasoned strategy but a tantrum, retreat, and petulant pout. He had offered his resignation.

The momentary vacuum was filled with bedlam. Voices were raised and fingers pointed. The leaderless Cabinet took hours to calm itself but by 1:30 p.m. a short resolution had been approved. It called for immediate and direct negotiations between Diefenbaker and Kennedy to resolve the nuclear issue. It stated that the prime minister should neither resign nor ask for dissolution.[40] It was a reasonable step forward but it was not enough for Harkness. Over the previous few weeks he had told several people that he was ready to quit. The time had come. Harkness stood, announced his resignation, shook hands around the table, and went home. Green took the news and resolution to Diefenbaker, who was sitting in the sun-drenched library with Olive, calmly sipping soup.

Diefenbaker arrived at his office the next morning with the resolution in hand but still talking of Fleming becoming prime minister. Cabinet met at nine but little was accomplished beyond accepting the Harkness resignation. At 2:30 p.m., Harkness stood in the House and read his resignation letter. He hit Diefenbaker where it would hurt. "In all defence negotiations concerning nuclear weapons in which I have had a part, the sovereignty of Canada has been protected fully. We have never lost sight of the dignity or independence of this country."[41] He had believed for over two years, he said, that Canada should acquire nuclear weapons for its various systems at home and abroad, but as it had become evident that it would not be happening, he had no option but to resign on a matter of principle.[42] He was the first Cabinet minister to do so since 1944, when two of Mackenzie King's ministers quit over conscription.

Later that afternoon, Pearson rose and stated the obvious. The House no longer had confidence in the government. He moved an amendment on the bill under discussion calling for the government to resign.[43] Diefenbaker's government was in shambles.

Shortly after Pearson had resumed his seat in Ottawa, Secretary of State Rusk appeared before the Senate Subcommittee on Canadian Affairs. He had been called to justify the State Department press release and the aspersions it had cast on Diefenbaker's honesty. He and the senators knew about the Harkness resignation. However, his answers revealed that Rusk also had an accurate knowledge of what had happened at the in-camera meetings in Diefenbaker's home and office. He told the surprised senators that there were at least six or seven Cabinet ministers who had split from the prime minister and supported Harkness. He said that the majority wanted a change in policy rather than an election but that the prime minister was still intent upon calling one in order to launch a campaign based on attacking Kennedy and the United States.[44] Rusk then reiterated everything that the State Department memo had said. For those keeping score, it was the fourth time a senior Kennedy administration official had publicly called Diefenbaker a liar.

Ottawa fell into chaos. There were bizarre meetings, hushed conversations, private deal-making, and public backstabbings. The Social Credit Party secretly offered to vote with the government if Diefenbaker resigned. Minister of trade and commerce George Hees appeared at Diefenbaker's front door with the offer. Diefenbaker suggested that Hees and the Social Credit could both "go to hell."[45]

At 8:15 in the evening on Tuesday, February 5, for only the second time in Canadian history, a government was defeated on a vote of non-confidence. At a caucus meeting the next day, Diefenbaker offered to resign and began walking toward the door. Backslapping, hand-shaking supporters stopped him. He slowly returned to the chair. All those in support of his leadership were asked to stand. There were cheers as the caucus stood as one and wildly applauded. Only Harkness and associate defence minister Pierre Sévigny remained seated, both angrily pushing away hands trying to wrench them to their feet. The Chief would lead the party into one more battle. That afternoon, he visited the governor general. The election was set for April 8.

The news sparked laughter and celebration at the White House.[46] Ambassador Butterworth telegrammed the State Department, gloating about the Americans' role in having brought down Diefenbaker and hoping for a Liberal win in the ensuing election. "In effect we have now forced the issue and the outcome depends on basic common sense of Canadian electorate.... In short, we think Canadian public is with us, even though some liberal politicians may have been afraid we have handed Diefenbaker an issue he can use against them and US.... As this appraisal indicates, we see grounds for optimism that over the long run this exercise will prove to have been highly beneficial and will substantially advance our interests."[47]

Kennedy said nothing publicly about his administration's role in Diefenbaker's fall. McGeorge Bundy later admitted to President Johnson, "I might add that I myself have been sensitive to the need for being extra polite to the Canadians ever since George Ball and I knocked over the Diefenbaker Government by one incautious press release."[48]

Diefenbaker should have been able to run on an impressive record of domestic achievement, the bread-and-butter issues that nearly always sway Canadian voters. But, as Lou Harris predicted with the poll he had done for Pearson, this time would be different. The election would be about something bigger than a new program or tax cut. It would be about Diefenbaker's nationalist vision—a vision that now lay tarnished by Kennedy's celebrity and Cold War fears that had been fanned by the missiles of October. It would be about what Kennedy and the Americans thought of Canada, and about the kind of Canada that Canadians envisioned for themselves.

The election would also be about Diefenbaker. It would question the leadership that had once been so bold but now seemed timid, tired, and confused. The party unity that seemed to revive so quickly in the Conservative caucus room just as quickly fell to pieces. Ontario Conservative Party organizer Eddie Goodman quit. Cabinet ministers George Hees and Pierre Sévigny resigned, stating differences with Diefenbaker over defence policy and relations with the United States.[49] Davie Fulton and Donald Fleming announced they would not run. The Conservative Party's rich, urban, eastern guard had still not accepted that the base had turned rural, populist, and western. They had bankrolled previous campaigns but this time they sat on their wallets. Plus, the Americans moved quickly.

While Kennedy and Newsweek's Washington bureau chief Ben Bradlee had suffered a temporary falling out, they had made up and were back to discussing issues that included Canada and Diefenbaker.[50] On February 18, in the campaign's first week, Newsweek arrived in mailboxes and on newsstands across Canada with an arresting cover. It showed a disturbingly close up and alarmingly unpleasant photograph of Diefenbaker over the headline "Canada's Diefenbaker: Decline and Fall." The accompanying article embarrassed even the prime minister's staunchest critics. Among its sharpest barbs was an unattributed quote from a British politician. "It would be too flattering to dismiss him just as a superficial fellow—he's really much dimmer than that."[51] It claimed that he lacked leadership skills and was unable to make decisions. His administration had been bad for Canada, NATO, America, and the world. The article even insulted his appearance. "Diefenbaker in full oratorical flight is a sight not soon to be forgotten; then the Indian rubber features twist and contort in grotesque and gargoyle-like grimaces; beneath the electric gray V of the hair line, the eyebrows that beat up and down like bats' wings, the agate-blue eyes blaze forth cold fire."[52]

At a news conference the next morning, Diefenbaker was greeted by reporters holding the magazine up over their smiles. He laughed but burned inside. His speeches already included references to eastern elites who controlled much of the media that wanted him gone. He referred to them as Bay Street and St. James Street Tories.[53] The *Newsweek* issue allowed him to add Kennedy and the Americans to those he said were out to unseat him.

Pearson reacted poorly. In a Moncton speech he attacked Diefenbaker for showing disrespect for the United States, or, as he said, "twisting the Eagle's tail feathers." He asked, "Without the U.S., where would we be in the struggle for peace and security in the world?"[54] Afterwards, reporters asked if the Liberals were involved in creating the *Newsweek* article. He said he could answer the charge with a three-letter word—presumably *lie*. A *Toronto Telegram* reporter pushed him further by asking if he received campaign orders from Washington. "That insinuation," he said, "can be answered with the same three-letter word."[55]

Conservative Party officials knew that with Pearson on the defensive, Diefenbaker's nationalist, pro-Canada campaign theme could gain traction. The national office mailed copies of the *Newsweek* article to every Conservative candidate to use as evidence of American interference in the election. Diefenbaker later wrote, "Who, among those who voted in 1963, will ever forget the Kennedy-conceived message conveyed to the Canadian electors by the cover and contents of the 18 February issue of *Newsweek*; its editor was President Kennedy's close friend."[56] The *Newsweek* attack seemed to inspire the fighter within him—the competitor who never seemed happier and more confident than when campaigning as the underdog. A reporter asked him if he would appear on television with his competitors. He said, "I have no competitors."[57]

Trains were a big part of the Diefenbaker campaign. Hearkening back to elections past, he undertook a gruelling whistle-stop tour across an often bone-chillingly cold Canada. The smaller towns drew the bigger crowds. At each stop he stepped onto a windswept platform, delivered a twenty- to thirty-minute speech, and then shook every hand he could before steaming off to do it again. In response to the criticism levelled at him by new opponents and old colleagues, he enjoyed quoting Abraham Lincoln: "If I were to read, much less answer all the attacks made upon me, this office might well be closed for any other business. . . . If the end brings me out all right, what is said about me will not amount to anything; if the end brings me out all wrong, ten angels swearing I was right will make no difference."[58]

The Liberals followed Lou Harris's advice and promoted the Liberal leadership team, but the Progressive Conservative campaign was all about the leader. While Pearson appeared to tire, Diefenbaker grew more energized. He spoke of his domestic record with justifiable pride but always returned to the issue he said mattered most. He promised to save Canada from the economic, cultural, and military power of the United States. He derided Kennedy for interfering in Canadian affairs and for presuming to tell Canadians what was best for them. He insinuated that the United States was a global bully and reminded audiences that, while Canada had contributed to winning two world wars from their opening days, the Americans had stayed out of the fights until the first war was nearly over and until directly attacked in the second.[59]

Kennedy and his people carefully monitored the campaign. Dean Rusk called Canadian ambassador Charles Ritchie and his assistant,

Basil Robinson, to his office on February 21. Rusk was unhappy with Diefenbaker's anti-Americanism. He warned that if Diefenbaker persisted in attacking the president and the United States and continued to misrepresent facts, then he would recommend American intervention. Rusk gave no indication of what form that intervention would take, or that it had already begun.[60]

American embassy and consul officials made themselves conspicuous at many Tory speeches, rallies, and nomination meetings. When Howard Green finished speaking at a Vancouver event, American vice-consul Richard King approached him. He identified himself and asked for a copy of the speech. Green refused. King said he was "officially interested in whatever the Canadian External Affairs Minister said."[61] American diplomatic staff recorded a number of Conservative candidates' speeches and sent tapes and transcriptions to Washington. Rufus Smith, a counsellor at the American embassy in Ottawa, sent a recording of a Diefenbaker speech to the State Department with an observation that betrayed the fact he had been shadowing the prime minister for some time. "His speeches do not conform to prepared texts, which are rarely available in any event, and they are extraordinary mixtures of equivocation, scorn, bombast, pious assertion, heavy-handed wit, snide innuendo, and distortion of fact."[62]

Among the tapes State Department officials heard was Diefenbaker's Prince Albert nomination speech, delivered on March 2. He listed a number of domestic campaign promises but climaxed with the election's primary theme. "We want to maintain Canada's sovereignty. Our nation's future as a political entity depends on that. . . . These northern [radar] lines were established by the previous government, manned in large measure by the Americans, our allies. We took them over, almost all of them, to preserve and maintain Canada's sovereignty."[63]

Ambassador Butterworth also continued to forward Canadian newspaper articles and editorials to Washington. The majority of papers were clearly against Diefenbaker. Among them was the widely read *Toronto Star,* which published over a dozen articles written by Samuel Lubell. They were crammed with quotes gathered from around the country but attributed only to a person's occupation and hometown. Typical of the quotes Lubell published throughout the campaign were these, from an April 2 article: "He's so irresponsible he makes me ashamed I am a Canadian." "I can't stand to look at him on TV." "He's out on a limb sawing off our relations with the United States."[64]

Canadian readers could be excused for not knowing that Samuel Lubell was an American journalist, pollster, and political strategist. During the 1952 and 1960 American presidential elections, he travelled the United States asking ordinary folks their opinions of candidates and issues and then accurately predicted both results. He wrote a book describing his new, non-scientific style of polling. Now he was in Canada doing it again, but with a decidedly anti-Diefenbaker bias. In addition to the articles he had published across Canada, Lubell tried to stir anti-Diefenbaker sentiment and prod Kennedy with more published in American newspapers. A March 25 *Miami Herald* piece accused Diefenbaker of lying about a number of things, including Bomarc missiles, and stated, "Unless these allegations are refuted by someone of the stature of President Kennedy it seems doubtful that any future Canadian government—certainly not one without a party majority—will be able to accept the missiles."[65] The next day, the paper published his "Is Canada Still Our Ally?" It urged Kennedy to directly involve himself to defeat Diefenbaker.[66]

Lubell and McGeorge Bundy were close friends. They saw each other socially and were regular and warm correspondents before and long after the 1963 campaign. After the election, on May 4, Lubell would send a letter to Bundy with the friendly salutation "Dear Mac" and signed "As ever, Sam."[67] The letter reported all he had found regarding Canadian sentiment on nuclear weapons. When Lubell then left for Europe, he carried a letter of introduction from Bundy that stated, "He has been very helpful to the Government on more than one occasion, and he is a very able and disinterested reporter."[68] There is only circumstantial evidence indicating that Lubell was in Canada trashing Diefenbaker at the behest of Bundy or Butterworth, but their efforts were certainly helped by his.

Butterworth continued to "undercut" Diefenbaker to, as he put it, help "our friends who are waging [a] battle for a coherent defense policy."[69] At one point in the campaign, Diefenbaker flew to England to accept investiture as an honorary freeman of the city of London, the first Canadian prime minister to earn the prestigious recognition. Butterworth saw the trip as another opportunity for the administration to "push over the Canadian government" and hoped the British government would join in the fun. He telegrammed, "Finally, Department may want to consider advisability explaining background situation to British Government so that Diefenbaker would be unsuccessful in any effort this weekend [to] obtain from British ammunition to support his subterfuge."[70]

Well aware of the American interference and of Rusk's direct warning to lay off the anti-Americanism, Diefenbaker intensified his attacks. He criticized Pearson's about-face on nuclear weapons. "Never since Saul, at his conversion on the Road to Damascus," he shouted at stop after stop, "had there been such a change in the thinking of one person."[71] He always linked Pearson and the Americans and slammed them both for misrepresenting his government's actions and motives. He reiterated that with him as prime minister, Canadians and not Kennedy would decide Canadian defence policies.

Hitting his stride as the weeks ground on, Diefenbaker revived the evangelical fervour of the 1958 campaign. As his message became simplified, honed, and increasingly anti-Kennedy and anti-American, his crowds grew in size and volume. Assuming the cloak of a Canadian martyr, he repeatedly exclaimed that the rich, the eastern elite, socialists, Liberals, and Kennedy were all allied against him. The only people who were for him, he said over and over, were the people.[72]

Among those who joined Diefenbaker in denouncing Kennedy's interference in Canada and the election was Pierre Trudeau. He had decided to enter the contest as a Liberal candidate, but when Pearson changed his mind about nuclear weapons Trudeau changed his about running. He called Pearson "the unfrocked priest of peace."[73]

In mid-campaign, Trudeau wrote an article that linked recent Canadian events to Kennedy's actions. He lambasted the Liberals for selling out to "les hipsters" in Washington and decried Kennedy's meddling in Canadian affairs. "But how do you think politics works?" Trudeau wrote. "Do you think that General Norstad . . . came to Ottawa as a tourist? . . . Do you think it was inadvertent that on January 30 the State Department gave a statement to journalists reinforcing Mr. Pearson's claims and crudely accusing Mr. Diefenbaker of lying. You think it was by chance that this press release provided the Leader of the Opposition with the arguments he used abundantly? . . . But why do you think that the United States would treat Canada differently from Guatemala when reason of state requires it and circumstances permit?"[74] In a radio interview with journalist Pierre Berton, Trudeau was asked if Quebec separatists were accurate in claiming that Kennedy wanted the province to separate. One could sense the shrug over the radio when Trudeau replied, "Why shouldn't he favour it. It will be a banana republic run by Washington."[75] Turning a charismatic star candidate like Trudeau into an opponent was a blow for Pearson and the party, especially in Quebec.

The Liberals wanted the election in the worst way, and that was exactly how they were running it. They had again fashioned the campaign on White's *The Making of the President 1960*. Many of their policy ideas were inspired by *The Affluent Society*, written by Kennedy's friend and advisor John Kenneth Galbraith.[76] Kennedy's pollster Lou Harris was back offering advice based on information gleaned from five hundred women who worked the phones for him every day. The team was strong but many of their stunts were puerile.

Homing pigeons were released to circle and dramatically return to announce a Pearson speech. They fluttered off and were never seen again.

A three-person "truth squad" led by the bold and brash Chatham-Kent Liberal MP Judy LaMarsh was dispatched to dog Diefenbaker. He transformed the truth squad into a punchline by giving the red-faced Liberals prominent spots at the press table and then introducing and ridiculing them. The truth squad vanished almost as quickly as the pigeons. The Liberals distributed a colouring book that was sophomoric in its attacks on the prime minister and NDP. Diefenbaker claimed it was Pearson's American advisors who were behind all the juvenile tactics: "The Liberal high command seemed to mistake our country for the United States."[77]

Pearson had become a little better on the stump and in crowds, but not much. He still found campaigning an unpleasant chore. Harris encouraged him to do as Kennedy had done in 1960—pick and stick to one theme and one speech a week.[78] Pearson hated repeating himself. He wanted to explain and not preach. He wanted to persuade and not sell. The campaign's first two weeks saw the evaporation of the Liberal's seven-point lead.

Unsatisfied with his regular verbal updates, Kennedy requested a written assessment of the Canadian campaign. The report must have disturbed him. It stated that neither major party was likely to win a majority. "[Diefenbaker] is fighting for his political life and knows it . . . while likening himself to Harry Truman in 1948. . . . It has been brought home to him by his advisors and principal supporters that he should not take an anti-American line, but his 'Made in Canada' policy is often the same thing. . . . [Pearson] simply does not come across to the voter with an image of decisive leadership. His platform manner is dry and undramatic; he is already a two-time loser, his record as Opposition Leader is not clear and purposive."[79]

A few days after Kennedy read the gloomy analysis, his defence department issued a press release. For nearly a year it had been researching the Bomarc missile program. On March 21, it announced that three or four years and about $30 million would be needed to complete the modifications necessary to outfit the Bomarcs with non-nuclear explosive devices. Even then, "the probability of a conventional high-explosive warhead destroying an enemy nuclear warhead is essentially zero. . . . On the other hand there is a high probability of a defensive nuclear warhead destroying an enemy nuclear warhead carried in bomber aircraft."[80] It concluded that the United States Air Force would play no role in developing conventional high-explosive warheads for the Bomarc-B missiles.[81] The report pulled the rug from beneath Diefenbaker's nuclear position. Pearson never got a chance to fully exploit the gift because before that rug was fully removed, it was laid back down.

In February, Kennedy's defence secretary, Robert McNamara, had testified before the House Military Appropriations Subcommittee. His testimony had been kept secret. On March 29, the department released a transcript. It revealed the unflappable McNamara being batted about by Republican congressmen who were unhappy with Kennedy, defence spending, and the apparent inability to defend America against Soviet ICBMs. Republican congressman William Minshall claimed the Bomarcs were useless and asked their cost.

McNamara argued that the $20 million price tag was high but worth it. "At the very least they could cause the Soviets to target missiles against them and thereby increase their missile requirements or draw missiles onto these Bomarc targets that would otherwise be available for other targets."[82] It was a startling admission. One of President Kennedy's most trusted advisors and senior Cabinet secretaries had just characterized Bomarcs as mere decoys, there to draw Soviet nuclear strikes from the United States and upon Canada.

Flamboyant Pennsylvania Democratic congressman "Dapper" Dan Flood was an enthusiastic Kennedy supporter. He sprang to defend McNamara's appraisal: "If we scratch [eliminate] Bomarc, we have stuck the Canadians for a whole mess of them and we have another problem on our border." McNamara agreed and repeated his remarkable assessment of the Bomarcs' value. "As they are deployed, [in Canada] they draw more fire than those Jupiter missiles [in Turkey and Italy] will." Minshall was not buying it. He growled that if all they had ever been intended to be was targets, then the Bomarcs had become very expensive targets indeed. Conceding the point, McNamara replied, "They did, I agree with you fully."[83]

Kennedy was furious. McNamara was not wrong, but he had just offered a gift to Diefenbaker. The defence secretary had committed a textbook political gaffe; that is, he had not spoken an untruth but a truth meant to be unspoken. Kennedy sent him a harshly worded note: "It might be worthwhile to bring to the attention of those who read your testimony on the Bomarc in Canada, that their failure to catch the political significance has strengthened Diefenbaker's hand considerably and increased our difficulties. It would seem to me that every word in those sentences flashed a red light. They should be on the alert for our political, as well as military, security."[84] The White House quickly issued a statement to clarify McNamara's remarks but it was far too little and much too late. It is noteworthy that in his reaction to McNamara's remarks, Kennedy never disputed his secretary's assessment of the facts.

Diefenbaker went on television the day after McNamara's testimony was released. He made great hay from McNamara's gaffe and ended with an attack on American influence in Canada and in the campaign. He expressed the idea that had motivated his life and defined his career.

> We made it abundantly clear . . . Canadian sovereignty . . . must be assured. Only then will we hope to achieve that degree of cooperation with our friends and allies which we want to attain, based on equality and through which we can work together toward fulfillment of our national destiny and international responsibilities. . . . There are bound to be differences . . . and people of our nation . . . must retain the unquestioned right to decide without outside pressure and without interference what is in their best interests. . . . I want Canada's decisions to be made in Canada. I want Canada to be strong not subservient.[85]

Diefenbaker returned to the hustings with the enthusiasm of the redeemed. He shouted to audiences that Pearson and Kennedy wanted to put nuclear weapons in Canada only to attract Soviet missiles. In every speech for the rest of the campaign he explained how McNamara's revelation had laid waste to Pearson's flip-flopping nuclear policy. In speech after speech he referenced the Ontario and Quebec Bomarc bases and exclaimed, "Decoys! . . . North Bay—knocked out. La Macaza—knocked out."[86] The line always drew thunderous applause. Of course, he never reminded voters that he had bought the Bomarcs in the first place. Instead, he argued that he had been consistent in responsibly adjusting defence policies to changing circumstances while Pearson had jumped from one view to the next motivated only by Kennedy and the polls.[87]

While the Americans billowed Diefenbaker's sails, they continued to buffet Pearson's boat. In the campaign's opening weeks Pearson had been forced to deny that Kennedy and the Americans were helping his campaign.[88] The public's distemper worsened after the McNamara bombshell, and Pearson found himself heckled as an American stooge. As he approached the podium to address a large rally in Vancouver, an American flag was unfurled before the stage. He looked down, aghast at what was happening before him, and watched it burn. Pearson was fighting a terrible cold that night as well as an undiagnosed infection that rendered his face red and swollen. He stood bravely before the microphone. Hecklers shouted "American Slave" and "Yankee Lover." A group of young men in the balcony loaded long straws and pelted frozen peas at the side of his aching head. For forty-five minutes Pearson soldiered on. He shouted his speech and ignored the taunts and bombardment. Through it all, Maryon sat stoically on the platform with tears streaming down her cheeks.[89]

Kennedy continued to receive regular election updates. He hinted to *Newsweek*'s Benjamin Bradlee about the private memo he had mistakenly left in Ottawa and that he was still worried about Diefenbaker releasing it. He disingenuously claimed that it lay at the heart of all Canadian-American problems. Bradlee begged for the full story but was told he'd have the exclusive scoop only if Diefenbaker lost. What if he won, Bradlee asked. "Well, then," said the president, "we'll just have to live with him."[90]

Bradlee's question must have haunted Kennedy. A couple of days later, Pearson was about to speak at an Edmonton legion hall when he was told that the White House was on the phone. Max Freedman, a mutual friend of Pearson and Kennedy, had been having dinner with the president and discussing the election. Now the Washington-based Canadian journalist was on the line from the White House pressroom. Pearson was rushed to a janitor's room to take the call. Kennedy wanted to speak with him. It took fifteen minutes for Pearson to convince Freedman that the campaign was struggling mostly because of the perception that he was Kennedy's toady. A direct conversation was out of the question. News that he and Kennedy spoke would inevitably leak, he said, and Diefenbaker would be handed yet another arrow for his bursting quiver. A tired and frustrated Pearson finally shouted, "For God's sake, tell the president not to say anything. I don't want any help from him. This would be awful."[91]

A couple of days later, Lou Harris reported to Kennedy that all the American interference in the Canadian campaign was hurting Pearson and giving credence to Diefenbaker's anti-American crusade. He pleaded with Kennedy to "call off his dogs." "And for God's sake," he pleaded, "keep quiet about Pearson no matter what you're thinking."[92] The chastened president pledged to be silent. He directed Bundy to issue a memo to every department and the embassy in Ottawa. It did not order staff to stop interfering in the election, just to stop getting caught. "The President wishes to avoid any appearance of interference, even by responding to what may appear to be untruthful, distorted, or unethical statements or actions. Will you, therefore, please insure that no one in your Departments, in Washington or in the field, says anything publicly about Canada until after the election without first clearing with the White House."[93]

Just when Kennedy thought he was out, he was pulled back in. Through sources that neither would ever divulge, Canadian journalists Charles Lynch and Peter Trueman learned of the May 1961 Rostow memo. Their articles left readers wondering about the degree to which Kennedy was "pushing Canada." Butterworth sent copies of the articles along with his regular campaign reports to the State Department and confessed that Lynch was among the reporters to whom he had been feeding anti-Diefenbaker tidbits. Despite that admission, he guessed that Diefenbaker had leaked news of the memo.[94] Reporters confronted Diefenbaker. He denied being the leak's source but then, inexplicably, lied about having the memo at all.[95]

Kennedy began every day by reading a number of newspapers, and on March 28, before aides had a chance to warn him of the latest Canadian dust-up, he saw an AP news story about the Rostow memo. He immediately called the State Department and ended up speaking with assistant secretary of state William Tyler. Kennedy read him excerpts from Charles Lynch's *Winnipeg Tribune* story and noted parts that he said were false. He thought the story made the memo out to be much worse than it really was. "Now it seems to me that he may have leaked this—Diefenbaker. It makes him look good and us look lousy . . . he's a liar."[96] Kennedy asked Tyler to see what reaction the story was sparking in Canada. He said, "If it is helping Diefenbaker we ought to knock it down. The question is how."[97]

A Peter Trueman article in the *Montreal Gazette* then made the already juicy story even more salacious. According to Trueman, and confirmed by journalist George Bain in the *Globe and Mail*, the memo contained a note in the margin, scribbled by the president, in which he referred to Diefenbaker using a "derogatory term." Readers had to guess what the president had called the prime minister. The term was soon widely purported to be "SOB."[98]

Kennedy and Bundy discussed the latest bad press and how they could help Pearson without lending credibility to Diefenbaker's claim that they were involved in the campaign. They finally decided that press secretary

Pierre Salinger would call Peter Trueman and deny the SOB rumour. Salinger also called Rostow and asked him to say nothing to the press. He was surprised to find him in Kingston, Ontario, preparing to deliver a lecture. Rostow agreed to offer no comment.[99]

*Time* magazine's Hugh Sidey was another of Kennedy's media confidants. He was ushered into the White House for a previously arranged meeting just after the president had been addressing the Rostow-SOB issue. As they strolled to the Truman balcony, Kennedy declared, "Now I want you to get this damn thing about Diefenbaker correct. I've been in this damn business long enough to know better than that. There are a lot of stupid mistakes I make but that isn't one of them." He added with a smile, "Besides, at the time I didn't know what kind of guy Diefenbaker was."[100] Ben Bradlee later reported that with the Rostow secret suddenly out of the bag, he and Kennedy were free to discuss the sorry mess. Kennedy confided that he did not think Diefenbaker was a son of a bitch; he thought he was a prick.[101]

Pierre Salinger invited a number of correspondents to the White House for a briefing on the Rostow memo. From that meeting came an article by *New York Times* syndicated columnist James Reston. He just happened to be a friend of both Kennedy and Pearson. Reston's piece appeared in the *Montreal Star* on the morning of April 8—Election Day. It argued that Diefenbaker had been wrong to keep the memo, had probably leaked news of its existence, had lied about not having it, and was wrong in using it for political advantage. The story also denied that the president had written "SOB" in the margin.[102] As Canadians went to the polls, Americans were again encouraging them to ponder whether their prime minister was a liar and political rapscallion, and whether the president they admired so much thought their leader was a son of a bitch. The Rostow memo is among Diefenbaker's papers at the University of Saskatchewan. There is nothing at all written in the margins.

Diefenbaker and Olive had returned to Prince Albert. On election day, they walked through a cold sleet to vote, and then to the railcar to await results. A late-spring storm blanketed Ottawa with snow. Pearson and Maryon voted early and then repaired to a Château Laurier suite. Both men were sick. Both were exhausted.

The east-to-west nail-biting wait began again. Newfoundland and the Maritimes reported Liberal gains. Quebec and then Ontario results bolstered the Liberals until momentum stalled at the Manitoba border. The party won only three seats on the prairies and none in Diefenbaker's Saskatchewan. When British Columbia and the territories finally reported, neither Pearson nor Diefenbaker had reason to cheer, but Pearson was at least able to smile.

Social Credit won 24 seats and the New Democratic Party 17. Liberals had gained seats to win 129 and Diefenbaker's Progressive Conservatives had lost seats and held only 95. Pearson had fallen only four seats short of the majority that in February seemed so certain. The Social Credit Party vowed to support the Liberals and so on April 22, Diefenbaker met with Pearson and then visited the governor general. One day shy of his sixty-sixth birthday, Lester Pearson became Canada's prime minister. Canadians had reached a crossroads. In an existential moment of decision they had chosen to turn their fates away from Diefenbaker's nationalist vision.

The Americans could not have been happier. The result was emblazoned above the fold on the front page of the *New York Times* with a photograph of a jubilant Pearson and another of a morose Diefenbaker. It reported that Canadians had rejected Diefenbaker's anti-Americanism: "It was by the same token a triumph for Mr. Pearson's appeal to the Canadian people to honour their obligation to take nuclear arms from the United States as their share in defending North America and Western Europe."[103] *Washington Daily News* columnist Richard Starnes noted, "It is an irony of history that President Kennedy's Administration while

properly charged with failures in Cuba, Laos and Europe is prevented by
the rules of the game from claiming credit for a skilfully executed triumph elsewhere. The victory occurred in Canada where adroit statecraft
by the American State Department brought down the bumbling crypto
anti-Yankee government of Prime Minister John Diefenbaker and
replaced it with a regime which promises to be faithful to the concept of
Canadian-American interdependence . . . the Kennedy Administration
must congratulate itself in private for its coup."[104] The Starnes column
was passed around the State Department with readers adding smug handwritten notes to its cover page. Assistant Secretary of State Tyler wrote to
McGeorge Bundy, "Mac, You see how smart we I mean you are!" Another
note to Bundy that is illegibly initialled said, "Tyler will give credit where
credit is due however Starnes does not."[105]

Southam syndicated columnist Charles Lynch made a career of writing what many others would not. In a column that appeared in papers
across Canada he wrote, "Diefenbaker was defeated by Kennedy."[106] His
observation was echoed even in France, where the *Paris-Presse* headline
was succinct: "Canada has voted American."[107]

# THIRTEEN

## PEARSON AND KENNEDY

Good politics often makes for lousy policy. Kennedy discovered as much when the mythical missile gap with which he had pummelled Nixon informed a massive military expansion. Similarly, after singing the praises of the North's potential, Diefenbaker oversaw a discouraging pace of development and return on investment. Pearson learned the truth of the adage when trying to implement his campaign pledge to quickly pass an ambitious legislative agenda in what he called Sixty Days of Decision. It was a great slogan. Walter Gordon and Keith Davey had originally wanted it to be 100 days, but Maryon thought it conjured thoughts of FDR and so was too American. Pearson worried about equating it to the 100 days between Napoleon's escape from Elba and Waterloo defeat.[1] The former baseball player's many unforced errors suggest that 100 days would have indeed been better, or maybe even 200.

Pearson quickly assembled a Cabinet that boasted education, talent, intellect, and experience. With the belief that he needed to quickly repair relations with Canada's allies, he rushed to Britain. Pearson knew Macmillan from his years in London. Their conversation focused on broad international issues and the state of the Cold War. Ironically, given their recent decisions to build nuclear arsenals, both leaders expressed hope that substantive negotiations regarding a nuclear test ban treaty would soon begin. Pearson enjoyed a dinner with the Queen and a night at Buckingham Palace before returning to Ottawa. He then allowed himself only a couple of days to address domestic decisions before turning to Canada's frayed relations with the United States.

Canada's diplomatic corps, especially those in the United States, had celebrated Diefenbaker's demise. On the day after the election, Canada's ambassador in Washington, Charles Ritchie, had confided to his diary, "I must write at once to Howard Green to express my respect for his steady support. I shall not be writing to Diefenbaker. I consider his disappearance a deliverance; there should be prayers of thanksgiving in the churches."[2] American newspapers echoed Ritchie's sentiment. The *New York Times* front-page story, for instance, reported, "In Mr. Pearson, Canada has a man of the highest international stature, admired and trusted by the United States more than any Canadian statesman of modern times."[3]

Kennedy, of course, was overjoyed. He called Lou Harris to the White House to thank and congratulate him. In a complimentary letter to Pearson, the president emphasized that re-establishing close relations with Canada was very important to him and his administration.[4] He invited Pearson to visit him not in the formality of Washington but at his family's summer home at Hyannis Port, Massachusetts. Both men began preparations for what would be an important set of meetings.

Kennedy rocked in his Oval Office chair and led his senior staff in a long discussion about the new dawn in Canadian-American relations. Bundy followed with a National Security Council memo to all Cabinet members. "The advent of the new government in Canada has naturally stirred nearly all branches of the government to a new hope that progress can be made in effective negotiations with this most important neighbor on all sorts of problems."[5] He added that Cabinet secretaries should consider ways in which all outstanding issues related to their departments could be addressed in Hyannis Port. Bundy's memo concluded with an admonition sure to capture attention: "It is the President's wish that these negotiations should be most carefully coordinated under his personal direction through the Department of State."[6]

The memo suggested a realization that after scrapping unsuccessfully with Diefenbaker for two years, Washington needed to rethink relations with Canada. While American foreign policy related to every other country and region was strategically based, it had always been ad hoc, reactive, and even dismissive with respect to Canada. St. Laurent and Pearson had tried to address that casualness, and Diefenbaker redoubled the effort by overtly demanding to be treated as a sovereign ally. Kennedy finally seemed to be getting the message. Pearson's election offered a chance for both countries to reset the relationship, and for Kennedy to stop bullying and begin bargaining, and to offer respect rather than assume obedience. In other words, to interact with Canada as Diefenbaker had asked.

On May 2, Kennedy met with Bundy, Ball, McNamara, and others to prepare for Pearson's visit. Among the items discussed was consultation with Canada in times of military emergency. Bundy suggested that there must be consultation. Kennedy asked if a Canadian prime minister could withhold permission for his forces to go to DEFCON 3 or 2 if American forces were so ordered. NORAD commander in chief General John Gerhart replied that a prime minister "is not supposed to," but, because elevating an alert is a political decision, the president should ensure that the prime minister is properly consulted.[7] Kennedy left the general's interpretation unchallenged.

The next day, a sanitized but still top-secret summary of the conversation was sent to Pearson. Among its statements was this admission that reiterated the terms of the NORAD agreement: "In the event of a surprise attack, NORAD should be able to employ its forces immediately. In a time of heightened tension NORAD normally would consult with both governments before increasing its readiness posture."[8] This oblique reference to the week in which the president and his advisors debated options regarding Cuba was as close as Kennedy would ever come to an admission of error.


Kennedy met Pearson at the Otis Air Force Base in Falmouth, Massachusetts, on Friday, May 10. In his brief welcome he made a point of twice referring to his guest as "a great friend of the United States."[9] A short time later, a brisk wind was blowing in from the roiling Atlantic as Pearson's helicopter touched down on the manicured lawn of the six-acre Kennedy compound. Canada's Red Ensign flapped alongside the Stars and Stripes. Pearson and Kennedy chatted like old friends through a clam chowder lunch. Kennedy offered a couple of remarks at Diefenbaker's expense and asked if his State Department's press release had been helpful in the election. Pearson replied, "It probably cost me fifty seats."[10] Kennedy changed the subject.

Canadian and American officials disappeared into various rooms to discuss the matters to which they had been assigned. Kennedy smiled as his assistant Dave Powers was quizzing Pearson on arcane baseball statistics and running up against the prime minister's encyclopedic knowledge of the game. Thinking he finally had him, Powers asked about a Detroit pitcher who threw a no-hitter but lost the game—a remarkable rarity. Pearson instantly named Ken MacKenzie. Kennedy laughed at Powers' shock and declared the contest over. Pearson did not reveal that he was so quick to answer because MacKenzie was not only Canadian but also from Manitoulin Island, in Pearson's riding.[11]

Ambassador Ritchie was among Pearson's staff at Hyannis Port. He recorded in his diary, "The meeting between the President and Mike was tinged with euphoria. The atmosphere was that of clearing skies after a storm—the clouds of suspicion covering Canada-U.S. relations had parted, the sunshine of friendship shone."[12]

Among the topics discussed over two busy days was a renegotiation of the Columbia River Treaty. The need for an American-Canadian agreement was first recognized in the 1930s, when hydroelectric development began on the powerful 1,200-mile river that thunders over the British Columbia-Washington border. One of Eisenhower's last acts as president was to sign the Columbia River Treaty with Diefenbaker. Their countries would share the costs and benefits of building several new dams to create power and manage flood control. The treaty was ratified by the American Senate, but British Columbia's premier, W.A.C. Bennett, objected to the terms and to not being included in the negotiations. Progress ground to a halt.

Diefenbaker had refused to give in to Bennett's demands and so put the project on a back burner. Pearson, on the other hand, agreed with Bennett that the treaty's terms unfairly favoured the Americans and that the construction schedule was too ambitious. His request for the treaty to be renegotiated initiated the first tension of the day as Kennedy pushed back. He would not risk sending an altered treaty to the Senate for another process of ratification. When Pearson refused to give ground, Kennedy agreed to implement the necessary changes through executive orders.[13]

The Columbia River Treaty issue had been simmering for three years; it was dispatched in minutes. Both sides hoped a number of other files that had soured bilateral relations could be addressed at the same pace. Other topics discussed included trade in lumber, wheat, and oil, Great Lakes shipping regulations, air-traffic routes, and fishing matters. In all cases, plans were made to seek solutions.

Not surprisingly, Canada's acceptance of American nuclear warheads for its weapons systems at home and in Europe was of special interest. Pearson said that at its first meeting, his Cabinet consented to the draft agreement that was on the table at Diefenbaker's defeat. Canada would take the nukes. Pearson said that with Parliament reconvening soon, it would take only three or four weeks to complete the political process and ready the agreement for a final signature. Kennedy quibbled only about wording. He asked, and Pearson agreed, that the reference to moving a "nuclear stockpile" to Canada be changed. Pearson noted that there might still be negative political reaction in Canada, especially when it became known that there would be more nuclear-armed American planes in Canada's sky and more American military personnel on Canadian soil.[14] But he would handle it.

The nuclear question returned on Friday evening. Before a crackling fire, Kennedy rocked while Pearson slouched in a wingback chair. They spoke of the two-key system that Macmillan had demanded for Britain and that Diefenbaker had discussed. Kennedy did not reveal the growing consensus in Washington that the system was, as some had long suspected, a sham. It was designed to mitigate an accidental launch and not to ensure an allied agreement to fire. In the spring of 1961, defence expert and former first secretary of the air force Senator Stuart Symington had dismissed the system at a secret Senate hearing as "just a lot of nonsense." He worried that it could lead to an allied general "knocking an American general on the head" and starting a nuclear war.[15]

Kennedy had responded by ordering greater security at American nuclear bases and asking for more information. Walter Rostow reported in February 1963. He shared Symington's concerns about a rogue nation or general but said it didn't matter; even with the two-key system, Americans retained total control over when and whether missiles were launched. The report was a relief to Kennedy but proved that the system he had offered to Diefenbaker and was now presenting to Pearson as a protection for Canadian sovereignty was worthless. Like the dancing diction of offensive versus defensive nuclear weapons, the two-key system provided nothing but political cover.[16] As he warmed himself by the fire, Pearson was unaware of this fact. Kennedy didn't tell him.

By midsummer the nuclear deal was done. Pearson's announcement was approved and coordinated through the White House and State Department.[17] In August, he declared that Canadian-based Bomarcs and Voodoo interceptors would get their American nuclear arms. In Europe, the Honest John rockets would be emptied of their sand and armed while the Starfighter jets would be retooled to accept American nuclear-tipped missiles. In addition, American nuclear weapons would be accepted at American bases in Canada and Canadian storage sites. Most nukes would arrive in time for Christmas.

During their Hyannis Port meetings, Pearson and Kennedy also discussed the growing crisis in Vietnam. By that point, Canada had been involved for seven years and was still a member of the International Control Commission. The Vietnam ICC was continuing its vain struggle to oversee a ceasefire that had never really existed. Kennedy was still trying to deal with the tinderbox of an undeclared but increasingly Americanized war. In June 1962, Canada and India had issued a special report—over the objection of the Poles—that condemned the North Vietnamese for "inciting, encouraging, and supporting hostile activities in South Vietnam." In fact, at that point there were only about four hundred North Vietnamese soldiers in the South. The ICC found that much of the increasingly deadly and frequent violence involved one South Vietnamese faction fighting another.[18] The report acknowledged this fact while criticizing the Americans, whose money and advisors were enabling an increasingly corrupt South Vietnamese President Diem to attack his enemies and fill his pockets.[19] Meanwhile, communist guerrillas—the Viet Cong—were regularly defeating sadly inept South Vietnamese army units that, even when supported by American helicopter gunships, seemed unable to defeat their growing number of enemies or defend their shrinking number of friends.

Canada's role as America's apologist was expressed again in March 1963 when External Affairs Minister Green had said in the House, "The main blame for the trouble in South Vietnam rests surely on the shoulders of the communists and not on the United States at all. Any action the United States has taken has been in a measure of defence against communist action."[20] The Vietnam ICC special report was released in June. It was the last gasp for the multinational commission. India became less willing to co-operate and even withdrew its consent to publish the report. Its one-sided, pro-Western perspective stretched credulity to the breaking point.

Like Eisenhower before him, Kennedy fully understood the quagmire into which he was leading America. In the fall of 1961, Kennedy had gone off the record with *New York Times* reporter Arthur Krock and said, "United States troops should not be involved on the Asian mainland. . . . The United States can't interfere in civil disturbances, and it is hard to prove that this wasn't largely the situation in Vietnam."[21] By March 1963, however, Kennedy had approved more money, men, arms, and support for the unreliable Diem. Nothing positive had come of it. In the sprawling summer home he had known since childhood, he leaned forward in his rocking chair and asked Pearson what he should do about Vietnam. Pearson replied without hesitation: "I'd get out." Kennedy shook his head and said, "Any damn fool knows that. The question is, how?"[22]

Kennedy was a different man and a different president than the one Diefenbaker had met in 1961. Struggles with Khrushchev and his own generals had hardened him. They'd made him more reflective and more dedicated to clear communications in the cause of peace. Despite the Canadian External Affairs opinion written shortly after the Cuban Missile Crisis that argued otherwise, the close call encouraged Kennedy to deal more directly with allies and enemies alike. Kennedy asked Pearson for a secret "heads of government" channel, hoping it would help to avoid misunderstanding by keeping communications away from the bureaucracy and press.[23] Kennedy said he wanted a direct back channel to Pearson to keep the prime minister informed of not just bilateral issues but of discussions he and others in his administration were having regarding the Soviet Union, disarmament, and a possible test ban treaty.[24] In a subsequent meeting with Pearson a few days later, Butterworth added that the president believed their secret communications should not be shared with either Cabinet.[25] The back channel afforded Pearson the respect that Diefenbaker had insisted Canada's prime minister, and Canada itself, deserved.

The two days at Hyannis Port allowed Pearson and Kennedy to agree on a great deal, and the closeness they already felt to grow. In addition to the two leaders, the ambassadors, special advisors, and Cabinet members who took part all agreed that it was as if the air had been cleared.[26] Many shared Diefenbaker stories. Jokes were made at his expense. At one point during a reception for the media, for instance, a piece of paper being handed to the president was dropped. As reporters—including Peter Trueman, who had broken the Rostow memo's SOB controversy—looked on, Pearson picked it up and said, "I'm just going to make some marginal notations on it." As laughter filled the room, he handed it to Kennedy and said, "I just happened to find this on the floor."[27]

When it was all over, Kennedy braved a cold wind and drizzling rain to walk Pearson to the helicopter. Without raincoats they stood as a Marine guardsman lowered the presidential flag, carefully folded it, and brought it to the president. He presented it to the prime minister with a warm handshake.

The Canadian press reaction to the meeting was effusive. All made reference to a new spirit of friendship and hoped it would allow greater co-operation between the two countries. An *Ottawa Citizen* editorial was typical: "The Hyannis Port conference has taken Canadian-American relations back to sanity. The ugly atmosphere created by the Diefenbaker government over the past few months has blown away like fog from the Massachusetts coast and the two neighbours are at work on problems they face together."[28]

The American press was equally pleased with the progress made and with the new and positive mood. Many editorials noted a welcome end to Canada's obdurate insistence on autonomy. The influential Walter Lippmann wrote in the *Washington Post*, "The general effect of the meeting at Hyannisport between the Canadian prime minister and the USA president has been that of a good scrubbing and a cool shower after a muddy brawl. . . . The prime minister for his part scrubbed out the suspicious nationalism of his predecessor by his very presence at Hyannisport."[29] The next few months would bear out Lippmann's observation and make clear that the crossroads of Canadian nationalism had indeed been reached and was now in the rear-view mirror.

While Kennedy and his people, along with Lippmann and his fellow American and Canadian scribblers, shared a moment of joy at the defeat of the nationalist prime minister, they ignored an important fact. Pearson's finance minister, Walter Gordon, was as much an unrepentant and unapologetic Canadian nationalist as Diefenbaker had ever been. He first came to President Kennedy's attention when running Pearson's 1963 national campaign while also contesting for a seat in Toronto's Davenport riding. Frustrated with Kennedy's interventions, he blew up at Lou Harris. "Tell the silly bastard to keep his mouth shut!" Gordon yelled. "I thought he was a pro. He's not even an amateur."[30] Gordon was among the Canadian contingent at Hyannis Port. Upon meeting the president, he sheepishly offered that perhaps Kennedy had heard of him. Kennedy smiled and said that Harris had given him the message straight and that Gordon had been right—nothing should have been said.[31]

In 1935, Gordon had formed what became a successful accounting firm, and during the Second World War he had served in the Finance Department and with the Bank of Canada. In 1955, he chaired the Royal Commission on Canada's Economic Prospects. Its 1957 report lamented the degree to which Americans controlled Canada's economy. Its observations and recommendations formed the core of a new wave of Canadian economic nationalism. The idea found expression in Diefenbaker's attempts to fight the continental pull of the United States by exploiting untapped northern resources, diverting trade, cultivating ties with China and Cuba, and forging a more independent foreign policy.

As Pearson's finance minister, Gordon was responsible for designing the Liberal government's first budget. With Pearson's self-imposed Sixty Days of Decision, he had little time to move his ideas to policies. The House would resume sitting on May 16 and the budget deadline was set for June 13. Upon his return from Hyannis Port, Gordon got to work. Due to time constraints and his not really trusting his department's bureaucrats, he employed three outsiders to help draft the budget. Among them was Geoffrey Conway, a PhD candidate at Harvard.[32]

Gordon presented his draft budget to Pearson, who expressed only minor reservations. He then showed it to the governor of the Bank of Canada, Louis Rasminsky, who offered more pointed concerns. Among other things, Rasminsky worried that it would irk the Americans and invite blowback. Pearson and the Cabinet nonetheless approved the budget and the speech to present it. On June 13, Gordon followed budget-day tradition by taking reporters with him to purchase a new pair of shoes. Then, on that warm afternoon, he stood in the House to present what became a thunderbolt.

The budget contained measures to fight unemployment, block tax loopholes, and raise revenues by ending some ineffective tax exemptions. Other innovations, however, were clear expressions of Gordon's economic nationalism. The budget stated a goal of establishing 25 percent Canadian ownership of all companies operating in Canada. To pursue the goal, it pledged to create a 30 percent takeover tax on each share of a Canadian-owned company purchased by a foreign buyer. Plus, the withholding tax would be increased from 15 percent to 20 percent on all dividend payments made to foreigners by companies with less than 25 percent Canadian ownership. Companies with more than 25 percent Canadian ownership would be rewarded with tax benefits on their depreciation allowances.[33]

As Opposition leader, Diefenbaker offered some barbs about the budget, but because its nationalist foundation mirrored his thinking, he remained relatively quiet. He did not dispute whether Gordon's budget was a nationalist flag being planted on the Hill—it clearly was; he questioned only whether Pearson would allow that flag to stand when it was battered by the inevitable hurricane of American criticism.[34]

Canadian markets began to wobble. On June 18, president of the Montreal and Canadian stock exchanges, Eric Kierans, issued a blistering statement arguing that the withholding tax and dividend taxes would hamper Canada's economic growth and tarnish its reputation in the United States. He predicted that American investors would withdraw funds from Canada at such a rate that all sectors of the economy and all Canadians would suffer. He recommended that international investors should either not buy Canadian bonds or buy short.[35]

Proving that their problem had not really been with Diefenbaker as much as his nationalist, pro-Canadian stands, the American press quickly turned on Pearson and Gordon. Typical of the anti-Canadian rhetoric was a column in the journal *Challenge* that urged its readers to recall that Canada was built on a foundation of losers who fled the War of Independence. Furthermore, it continued, the country was now under the influence of a finance minister who was rich "by Canadian standards" and displayed "ineptitude" with his budget. "What forces the Canadian government to such policies is not a real balance of payments problem," the *Challenge* piece observed, "but a political mythology about American domination, with an erroneous view of how to prevent it."[36] The *New York Times* June 24 editorial repeated the same criticism it had levelled at Diefenbaker: "By resorting to blatant nationalism, Canada will hurt itself most of all. . . . Until it initiated its anti-American proposals, Canada was the preferred nation among investors and reaped the benefits in terms of solid economic achievement."[37]

Kennedy was briefed and he was angry. Pearson had mentioned American ownership of the Canadian economy just a few weeks before at Hyannis Port. He'd warned the president that his finance department was considering ways to encourage more Canadians to invest in their own companies. While Kennedy had been well-prepared and actively engaged in all other matters, this point had appeared to leave him rather puzzled. He asked Pearson what actions were being contemplated and was told that only moral suasion would be used to ask American subsidiaries to appoint more Canadians to senior management positions. Regulations would also be employed to address the still lingering practice of American laws being applied to American companies in Canada. Kennedy listened but said little. Now, though, with Gordon's new tax schemes about to help Canadians by hurting Americans, he found his voice.[38]

Kennedy took the budget personally. He could not believe that his friend would act in the same nationalist fashion as his old nemesis, but he agreed to react through a lower-level channel.[39] Assistant secretary of state Griffith Johnson called the Canadian embassy to report that Kennedy was upset about the new anti-American taxes and about not having been consulted before the budget was presented.[40] The State Department's Willis Armstrong spoke to Basil Robinson at the Canadian embassy; Kennedy's main objection, Armstrong said, was that the budget was "economically nationalist."[41] He assured Robinson that the president understood the political crisis that Pearson had created for himself and would stay quiet for now—but not, he added, rather ominously, for long.[42] The State Department's Bill Anderson met with Ambassador Ritchie and resorted to insults. "What Canadians need in financial questions," he advised, "is a psychoanalyst's couch."[43]

The State Department informed Ambassador Butterworth that Kennedy was "extremely unhappy" and that he was to let the appropriate Canadians know it. The telegram began with an expression of anger and disappointment that America's special friend, neighbour, and ally would produce such a clearly anti-American, discriminatory budget. It expressed worry that the new and unfair taxes would force American subsidiaries operating in Canada into untenable positions. It also expressed fear that the Canadian action would inspire smaller, developing countries to take similar anti-American actions.[44]

Despite having asked for the establishment of a secret and direct communication link, Kennedy chose not to call Pearson, and so Pearson avoided the temptation to call the White House. Instead, the prime minister asked Robinson to hurry over to the State Department and request that the Americans refrain from any public statements. Bundy was able to tell Kennedy that Robinson or Pearson himself would gladly speak with Rusk or any other official to clarify what was going on.[45] Bundy promised the president that changes to the budget were on the way.[46]

Pearson later observed, "I do not think I have ever known in my years in Ottawa anything quite so violent and so bitterly hostile to a particular clause in any budget."[47] The quick and overwhelmingly negative reaction from both sides of the border and from bond traders around the world led to a series of meetings with Gordon, Rasminsky, and a revolving door of finance department officials. They considered the economic ramifications of keeping, amending, or ditching the controversial proposals.

On June 19, Walter Gordon withdrew or redrew every aspect of the budget that had been designed to bolster Canadian ownership of the Canadian economy. He announced the changes in the House and concluded, "They do not alter the objectives of the budget."[48] It was not true and he knew it. Gordon's speech was poorly timed; the markets were still open. The quick-witted made small fortunes buying up stock from those selling to avoid the taxes they did not know had just been rescinded.

The *Globe and Mail* and other newspapers declared Gordon incompetent and called for his head.[49] Several of Pearson's advisors and even his wife, Maryon, who had not wanted Gordon in the portfolio in the first place, said he must go. Gordon offered to quit. Even though Pearson had just emasculated his friend's core principles, he would not accept his resignation. Withdrawing the budget's primary provisions was sufficient to announce that Pearson was unwilling to weather Kennedy's criticism, or the cost of economic nationalism. Pearson later explained, "We can maintain our economic sovereignty if we are willing to pay the price, and the price would be nationalist policies which would reduce our standard of living by perhaps 25 to 30 percent. Not many Canadian are willing to do that and I don't think Canadians should have to do that."[50]

Kennedy said nothing publicly about the budget. Ambassador Butterworth observed, "Walter Gordon's temporary withdrawal yesterday of his budget tax resolution designed to prevent foreign takeovers has provided a humiliating rather than triumphal conclusion to the Liberal Gov'ts '60 Days of Decision.'"[51] Former American secretary of state Dean Acheson was as astute but less polite when he privately joked that Pearson had committed a "boner on the budget." He wrote to a friend, "It was as stupid as our performance at the Bay of Pigs." Acheson expressed agreement with Butterworth, who had said that Canada was "a tribal society, naïve, terribly serious about the wrong things and not at all aware of their real problems. . . . Their best move would be to ask us to take them over; and our best move would be to say, no."[52] The Gordon budget had surprised Kennedy. A month later, Kennedy pulled a surprise of his own.

The American economy had recovered from the late 1950s recession, but a number of issues lingered. Among them was a balance of payments problem caused by too many American dollars leaving the country. To encourage Americans to invest at home, Kennedy proposed the Interest Equalization Tax. It imposed a 15 percent tax on foreign securities sold in the United States.

Treasury Secretary Dillon sent a representative to warn Walter Gordon of the new measure on Thursday, July 18. Gordon could not believe it. The new tax would help the American economy at the expense of Canadian companies and the federal and provincial governments by increasing the cost of borrowing in the United States. To counter the tax, a Canadian seller hoping to attract American investors would need to raise their bond's rate of return and so accept less net revenue. The tax's effects could lead investors to become jittery about the Canadian dollar and dump it for gold or more stable currencies. It could cause the second run on the dollar in fourteen months.

Pearson called Dean Rusk and asked that the White House issue a statement saying that Kennedy had not created the tax in retaliation for the nationalist Gordon budget. Ambassador Ritchie hastily arranged to meet with Rusk and George Ball. Ball said that he understood the irony of Canadians feeling all right about surprising Kennedy and threatening to hurt America with the Gordon budget but upset when the same thing was done to them.[53] Ball called Bundy and then Dillon; all agreed there should be a response.[54] The thankless task fell to undersecretary for monetary affairs Bob Roosa, who made a brief and largely ignored statement that simply reiterated the purpose of the new tax.

Bank of Canada governor Rasminsky cut short a salmon fishing holiday to rush back to Ottawa. He met with Pearson, Gordon, and finance department officials and shortly afterwards was on a plane to Washington. Along with two staff from External Affairs, Rasminsky sat with Roosa and Dillon. When asked directly if the new American tax was in retaliation to Gordon's budget, Roosa diplomatically assured the Canadians that it was not. Further, the president had shown great restraint in not taking retaliatory actions against the anti-American elements in Gordon's budget; however, he added with the hint of a threat, they were still available to him.[55] Besides, Kennedy's new tax applied to twenty-two countries and did not specifically target Canada.

Rasminsky argued that in attempting to fix the American balance of payments problem, Kennedy would negatively impact Canada's. He conceded that the export of American dollars to other countries was an issue, but argued that Canada's relationship with the United States was unique because of the enormous amount of American goods and services purchased by Canadians each year that returned dollars to the United

States. No other country could say the same. Canada, therefore, should be exempted from the new tax.

For two days, Rasminsky schooled the Americans on the integration of the Canadian and American economies and the importance of the relationship to the stability and growth of each. Dillon expressed surprise at much of what he heard and at the fact that pain inflicted on the Canadian economy would soon be felt in the United States.[56] Late Sunday afternoon an agreement was hammered out and phone calls made to Kennedy and Pearson. Canada would be exempted from the Interest Equalization Tax if in return it created an exchange fund ceiling. The measure would limit the number of dollars Ottawa could borrow from the United States to deposit in its foreign capital reserve fund. Kennedy agreed to act through an executive order so the agreement could be announced before markets opened on Monday morning.

It is possible that in creating the Interest Equalization Tax, Kennedy had not acted with a mind to punish Canada. In fact, it's possible that Canada had not even crossed his mind. Or, perhaps, beneath his suave exterior, he was still the grandson of old Honey Fitz, the Boston street fighter, who knew exactly what the tax would do and was reminding Canadian nationalists of his power. Walter Gordon believed the truth lay somewhere in between, observing, "We had been given a sharp reminder of Canada's dependency on the United States."[57] Gordon later wrote that in agreeing to trade the tax exemption for the exchange fund ceiling, the immediate problem was averted, but "this caused us considerable embarrassment in the management of our exchange reserves and placed another limitation upon the flexibility and freedom of Canadian monetary policy."[58] Another sliver of economic autonomy had been traded away.

Pearson quickly learned that surrendering to American pressure was not enough for the Kennedy administration. Two weeks later, on August 2, Walter Gordon travelled to Washington to meet with Treasury Secretary Dillon. George Ball asked to see him as well. Gordon and Ball had known each other for years. They were members of the exclusive Bilderberg Group, comprising international business, academic, and political leaders. Their meeting, however, was short on friendly chat. Ball launched into a tirade replete with insults directed at the Canadian government and Canadians. He scolded Gordon for his June budget. After twenty minutes, Gordon stood and gave it back to him. He corrected inaccurate facts and false assumptions. Ball was chastened. He apologized.

Gordon was back in Washington for a September 19 meeting of the annual Joint Canada–United States Committee on Trade and Economic Affairs. Americans around the table included a number of senior Kennedy officials and the secretaries of state, commerce, agriculture, and the treasury. Apparently forgetting all that Gordon had told him a month before, Ball began the meeting by taking up his attack on Canada and the economic nationalism of Gordon's abandoned budget measures.[59] No matter how many times Gordon contextualized his budget's goals with explanations of Canada's balance of payments problems, the criticism continued.

Ball's frustration with Canadians was perhaps born of his history with Diefenbaker and his dismissive view of Canada in general. In preparation for the September joint Cabinet meeting, Ball had discussed with McGeorge Bundy the possibility of establishing free trade with Canada, or even a customs union that would, for all intents and purposes, eliminate the border. He believed that while such an arrangement would be beneficial to Canadians, they would not accept it because of their desire to maintain what he dismissively referred to as their "integrity."[60]

In his 1968 memoir Ball wrote, "Canada, I have long believed, is fighting a rear-guard action against the inevitable . . . the desire to maintain their national integrity is a worthy objective. But the Canadians pay heavily for it . . . there is a danger that the efforts of successive Canadian governments to prevent United States economic domination will drive them toward increasingly restrictive nationalistic measures that are good neither for Canada nor for the health of the whole trading world. . . . The result will inevitably be substantial economic integration, which will require for its full realization a progressively expanding area of common political decision."[61]

In 1914 there were thirty-two independent Canadian-owned car manufacturers. By the 1920s, Ford, Chrysler, and General Motors had starved or swallowed nearly all of them. The "Big Three" established Canadian branch plants, with a great deal of product exported to the United States, while many American-built parts and cars were sold in Canada. As the companies grew, the American and Canadian governments imposed a number of tariff and non-tariff restrictions. In 1936, for example, the Canadian government established a 17.5 percent tariff on imported American-made cars, and a complex system of tariffs on American-made parts. American tariffs on cars, trucks, and parts went up and down but were generally lower than Canadian trade impediments. The companies continued to hop the tax and tariff walls by building and growing more Canadian branch plants.

By the 1950s, Canadian consumers were inundated every year by American advertising that touted new and exciting models. Canadians may have loved the tailfins and chrome, but Canadian branch plants saw profit margins shrink when they undertook short runs of the various models to try and meet demand. At the same time, British, European, and Asian recovery from the Second World War was adding competitive pressure. By 1960, one-third of the cars sold in Canada were imports. That fact hurt the car industry, but the growing number of Canadian dollars leaving the country to buy more foreign cars hurt the whole economy.[62]

Diefenbaker felt pressure from a number of quarters, including the United Automobile Workers Union and the Canadian Automobile Chamber of Commerce, who for once saw their interests aligned. Both asked for government help. Their representations spoke to Diefenbaker's concerns about economic sovereignty. He appointed a one-man Royal

Commission to examine the automotive sector. Vincent W. Bladen's April 1961 report detailed the extent to which Americans controlled Canadian car manufacturers and thousands of direct and related jobs. Even the unions protecting Canadian workers from decisions largely made in Detroit were American. Bladen concluded that Canada's car industry needed to grow and become more independent. He recommended a host of tariff and tax changes.[63]

Diefenbaker shelved all but a couple of Bladen's recommendations. He removed a 7.5 percent excise tax and tinkered with the sales tax on cars; both were raising prices for Canadian consumers while doing nothing to help manufacturers. In October 1962, Diefenbaker approved a pilot project. It placed a 25 percent duty on each automatic transmission that Canadian manufacturers imported from the United States. The government would repay them the duty when they exported their first ten thousand Canadian-made engine blocks to the United States. The duty-remission pilot project led to an increase in the manufacture and export of Canadian engine blocks to the United States and a rise in the number of Canadian-made transmissions. The pilot also led to an increase in the number of Canadian automotive jobs, a boost to Canadian-based car and part companies, and overall relief for Canada's trade deficit. It elicited no complaint from the Kennedy White House.

Within the year, the Liberals came to power. Like Diefenbaker, Finance Minister Gordon sought ways to make Canada's automotive industry more Canadian. On October 31, 1963, he extended Diefenbaker's pilot project and renamed it the full-duty remission program. It no longer included just a few but all imported vehicles and parts. It was a Halloween trick or treat the Americans could not and would not ignore.

Advised that American jobs were threatened, Kennedy ordered that something be done.[64] In short order, George Ball was appointed chair of the Canadian Task Force, charged with responding to Gordon's initiative. Ball was soon as upset as the president. In a telephone conversation with

McGeorge Bundy's deputy, he vented his anger, discussed several retaliatory options, and predicted a greater crisis in Canadian-American relations
than they had ever seen.[65]

Ball and Dillon determined that Canada's full-duty remission program was nothing more than a subsidy being offered to Canadian-based
manufacturers. They guessed that it would affect the production of $150
to $200 million in American-made parts and lead to significant American
job losses. They considered a number of responses: tariffs, countervailing duties, and new trade restrictions on other goods.[66] Ball met with
Kennedy and recommended that he call Pearson to protest the program.
Kennedy declined but encouraged Ball to continue to see what could be
done to counter or end it. Ball and Dillon agreed that the best course
of action would be to encourage American manufacturers to write to
Kennedy demanding that action be taken. The president could then
claim to be acting under pressure from his business community.[67]

Ball was soon able to report to the treasury secretary that he had
"drummed up four companies asking for countervailing duties."[68] Franklin
Roosevelt Jr. played an important role in gathering the companies willing to participate in the devious plot. In a telephone conversation with
Roosevelt, a worried Ball asked, "Do you think there's any danger that
these guys are going to get back to the Canadian government that this was
in effect stirred up by the U. S. government?"[69] Roosevelt was confident
in the discretion of his pliant conspirators.

Ball and Bundy brought Kennedy up to date on the clandestine
manoeuvrings late in the afternoon on November 5. They urged the president to call Pearson but he again declined. He did not want every call to
be about something undesirable.[70] Instead, Ball called Walter Gordon and
fed him the line about the mounting pressure Kennedy was feeling from
American manufacturers. He said they were demanding countervailing
duties to fight the Canadian subsidy. Taking the bait, Gordon agreed to
send representatives to Washington to discuss options.[71]

On the morning of November 21, Kennedy met with his Cabinet for what would be the last time. The agenda's final item was Canada. It was agreed to create a new National Security Council subcommittee to examine ways to further integrate the Canadian and American economies. George Ball was appointed committee chair. Later that day, President Kennedy left for a short trip to Texas.

In the last months of Kennedy's life, defence, cars, and taxes were not the only Canadian-related issues demanding his attention. He also faced violence on the border.

The Great Lakes are nature's highway. They link Canadian and American Midwest farms to central and eastern cities, and through them to the world. Canadian shipping companies exploited post–Second World War prosperity and the sale of surplus navy and merchant marine vessels at garage-sale prices to grow in size and wealth. The biggest and most influential became Canada Steamship Lines. By the late 1940s, the companies grew rich while sailors and dockworkers grew angry. Ships often resembled floating sweatshops and the docks were jungles. Unions fought the companies to improve pay and work conditions. They also fought each other for fee-paying members, and their turf wars were intensified by communist infiltration that ignored the border and often members' best interests.[72] Strikes, intimidation, beatings, and gangsterism often resulted in ships stranded in ports, suddenly without crews and unable to be loaded or unloaded.

In an attempt to wrest order from the growing chaos while simultaneously fighting domestic communists, the St. Laurent government condoned the Americanization of Canadian maritime unions. It supported the pressure that the American Federation of Labor-Congress of Industrial Organizations (AFL-CIO) exerted on its Canadian counterpart, the Trades and Labour Congress of Canada, to merge the Canadian Seaman's

Union with the American-based Seafarers' International Union (SIU). In 1949, the SIU appointed Hal Banks to preside over its Canadian branch.

Hal Banks was a thug. He was born in Iowa and grew up in California. He had been arrested for passing bad cheques and came to know the cold, grey walls of San Quentin. He was later accused of murder, kidnapping, and numerous rapes before becoming a sailor and then a union enforcer.[73] He was deemed the perfect man to build the SIU in Canada. From his opulent office in Montreal, Banks became a tyrant. He bribed, bought, or had beaten up all those who opposed him or the SIU. He established "Do Not Ship" lists that banned certain workers, ships, and companies. Happy that a semblance of order had been established, the ships were moving, and the communists were gone or hiding, the shipping companies and the Canadian and American governments turned a blind eye when Banks and his gangsters broke laws and bones.[74]

The violence and growing influence of American maritime unions in Canada finally became too much to ignore. In 1962, Diefenbaker created a commission of inquiry led by the hot-tempered but determined British Columbia Court of Appeal justice Thomas G. Norris. Beginning in July, the Norris inquiry laid bare the stench of what was being perpetrated in the name of profit, politics, and power.

The inquiry was completing its work when Lester Pearson became prime minister. He was dragged into the morass of violently competing interests when the Canadian Great Lakes freighter *James Norris* steamed into the Chicago harbour and a labour spat led to a gun battle. A union standoff stranded the ship. Pearson promised the House of Commons that he would do something about the *Norris* incident and the larger crisis that was terrorizing workers and hurting business.[75]

At their Hyannis Port meeting, Pearson and Kennedy left their advisors to enjoy a short stroll. With the ocean pounding the shore, Pearson broached the violence on the lakes. He explained that the problem was being blamed on the actions of American unions in Canada. He wondered what could be done. Kennedy shook his head and, using language that Banks and his men would have appreciated, said, "I don't know what I can do about those fuckers!"[76]

They agreed that the solution, like the problem, needed to ignore the border. A committee was struck comprising two Canadians, Labour Congress president Claude Jodoin and minister of labour Allan MacEachen, and two Americans, AFL-CIO president George Meany and labour secretary Willard Wirtz. Dubbed the Committee of Four, they met in Washington a week later but quickly fell apart. Meany and Jodoin screamed accusations at each other about SIU activities in Canada, which union was legitimate, and whose men were scabs. Meany was not about to surrender a scintilla of AFL-CIO or SIU power regardless of what the Canadians wanted. Perhaps George Ball was right when he confided in a telephone conversation with Bundy, "I must say if the Prime Minister thinks he can control our angry labour unions, he is not as smart as I think he is."[77]

Thomas Norris finally released his report in July 1963. It placed a preponderance of blame for the Great Lakes mess on Banks and the SIU. Its most important recommendations were that Banks be deported and government-appointed trustees be empowered to merge the maritime unions to better serve workers, shipping companies, and Canada.[78] Following a series of lively debates in the House of Commons, Allan MacEachen announced that the government would create a trusteeship council after the upcoming parliamentary recess.

Angry SIU workers who were loyal to their leader and wanted no part of government telling them how to run their union reacted by planting a bomb on a Canadian ship that new labour strife had stranded in Chicago. The bombing led Pearson to call Kennedy. The president was in a tough spot. He had spoken at the AFL-CIO convention the year before and wandered off his prepared text to praise organized labour's contributions to the country's well-being and progress. To great applause George Meany responded, "We are delighted that we have a Chief Executive in the White

House who understands the ideals and the aspirations of our people . . . and merely say to you, don't worry about us. We will cooperate 1,000 percent."[79]

Meany mattered. If the crisis on the lakes was to be solved, Kennedy needed his help. Meany was America's most powerful advocate for organized labour. To many Americans, his opinions reflected those of working people in general.[80] Further, the AFL-CIO was a major contributor to Kennedy and his Democratic Party. It was hard to tell which president needed the other more. It was perhaps with this quandary in mind that at Hyannis Port, Kennedy had told Pearson, "Meany will do a lot of things I ask him to do," but after a long pause added, "and I'll do a lot he asks me to do."[81] Now, on the phone with Pearson, Kennedy again promised to do what he could with Meany.[82] After hanging up he grumbled to an aide that it would be a shame if this union trouble jeopardized all the hard work he had done at Hyannis Port to rebuild trust with Canada.[83]

Although Meany did not attend, the Committee of Four met several more times over the following weeks but accomplished nothing. Jodoin wanted to co-operate with the AFL-CIO in the hope that it would help reduce the harassment of Canadian ships and workers in American ports. He made an appointment to see Meany and flew to his office in Washington. He spent two infuriating hours reading old magazines in Meany's waiting room. He finally left in disgust.[84]

MacEachen was good to his word, and with Parliament's resumption he ignored the Committee of Four impasse and introduced legislation to create an all-Canadian trusteeship council to oversee Canadian maritime unions and Canadian subsidiaries of American maritime unions. Meany erupted. He told a hastily called press conference, "I am just as much opposed to government controlled unions in Canada as I am to government controlled unions in Honduras, or Peru or any other place on the face of the earth. I am absolutely opposed to it."[85]

American Labor Secretary Wirtz rushed to the White House. He believed the trouble with the Canadian unions was a Canadian matter that

Pearson was trying to get his department, the president, or Meany to solve. He blamed what he characterized as Diefenbaker's "anti-American questions" in the House and the anti-American views of many Canadian newspapers for forcing Pearson to be harder on the issue than he really wanted to be. He told Kennedy that only Meany was acting in good faith.[86]

Wirtz left the Oval Office and called a press conference. He proclaimed his support for Meany and said the Canadians were wrong in wanting government-appointed trustees to reorganize and oversee maritime unions. The Canadian government should not, he insisted, be allowed to exert such influence over American business, ports, or organized labour.[87] Pearson again called Kennedy. While not mentioning his meeting with Wirtz, the president apologized for any embarrassment caused by the Wirtz press conference. He characterized the unreserved praise for the AFL-CIO as "unfortunate." They read statements to each other that they would make and agreed that Ambassador Ritchie would coordinate their timing.[88]

MacEachen's Trustee Act became law on October 18. It afforded government-appointed Canadian trustees the power to oversee and influence union property, finances, management, and rules. In a section quickly dubbed the "Hal Banks provision," it allowed trustees to suspend or fire a union employee. Banks responded by having SIU members in Canadian and American ports drop their tools. On October 21, two thousand SIU members shouted slogans on Parliament Hill and then cheered when Banks pulled up in his brand new, gleaming white Cadillac. Someone yelled, "You're a goddam crook!" Banks shouted back, "I agree."[89]

Pearson again called Kennedy. With the raucous protest roaring outside his office windows, he told the president about the havoc in Ottawa and the ships stuck in ports. In Montreal's harbour alone, for instance, armed union men had trapped twenty-eight vessels. Pearson warned that he would quickly establish the trusteeship council to quell the violence, end the illegal strikes, and restore calm, all by taking control of the

Canadian branch of the SIU. Kennedy would not agree to call Meany but did pledge to remain silent about Pearson's proposed plan.⁹⁰

Diefenbaker made no such promise. Later that afternoon, with protesters bluing the air outside, he filled the Commons with accusations of his own. He cried that there was too much American power in all Canadian unions, and especially the maritime unions. He slammed the government's handling of the whole affair, saying Pearson was causing "chaos approaching anarchy." He then moved a motion of non-confidence.⁹¹ Pearson jumped to his feet. He slammed Diefenbaker and took shots at Meany and Banks. He praised Kennedy for working in good faith to help resolve the dispute. As expected, Diefenbaker's motion failed.

The next day, however, a number of Canadian newspapers echoed Diefenbaker's point. The *Globe and Mail* was particularly harsh on Wirtz and Kennedy for backing the American union that, its editorial claimed, was primarily responsible for the current problems. Entitled "Diplomacy by Bully," it hinted that Kennedy could quickly solve the whole mess but was choosing not to. It noted a number of examples of Americans using the press to push Canada around. Among them was the State Department's January press release besmirching Diefenbaker, and the more recent Wirtz press conference. The column ended with a line that could have been ripped from one of Diefenbaker's campaign speeches: "Frankness between friends is a virtue. But the kind of frankness in which US leaders have lately been indulging is that of neighbourhood bully—'You do it my way or else!'"⁹²

The trustees were appointed on October 23. Among their first acts was to summon Hal Banks to Ottawa. He was told to end the SIU strike action or face prosecution. He caved. Three days later the men returned to work and the ships resumed their journeys. The truce was only temporary. At the AFL-CIO convention held just a few weeks later in New York, Banks delivered a blistering address in which he promised to fight the Canadian government and increase his union's power by having only SIU members on every ship on the Great Lakes. SIU strikes and threats of violence soon had every ship moving at a glacial pace or stopped completely.[93]

Pearson called Kennedy. The president agreed to have Wirtz investigate the latest flare-up. He again promised to do what he could to influence Meany and American SIU president Paul Hall.[94] Wirtz told Kennedy that Meany and Hall would do nothing unless he personally asked them to do so. Issuing such a request would certainly help Canada but would leave Kennedy in the unattractive position of being even more beholden to the unions and their leaders than he was already. Further, Kennedy knew that he would soon be asking for maritime union support for a plan he had yet to announce, whereby American wheat would be shipped to the Soviet Union in Soviet as well as American ships. Once again, Kennedy's admiration for Pearson and their personal friendship did not matter. He would do what was best for America. He did nothing.

With the shipping season almost over, Kennedy and Wirtz agreed to allow the troubles to play themselves out over the winter and then contemplate action in the spring.[95] Pearson was left to carry on with Canadian trade stopped up, American unions still dominating Canadian unions and hurting shipping companies, and without Kennedy's help to do anything substantive about it.

Just as it appeared that things could not get worse for Pearson, he sat for a TV interview with Pierre Berton. He was asked about a *Toronto Star* story claiming that in the recent election, Hal Banks and his union had made substantial contributions to the Liberal Party. Pearson admitted the story to be true.[96] The revelation could have sparked a scandal but it was ignored. The interview aired on the morning of November 22. Before anyone had time to react to it, gunshots shattered a beautiful afternoon in Dallas.

# F O U R T E E N

---

# MYTHS, MOURNING, AND
# THE ROAD TAKEN

ON JUNE 10, 1963, IN A SPEECH AT American University that must
have thrilled Howard Green, President Kennedy announced a major step
toward disarmament with the unilateral suspension of American atmos-
pheric nuclear testing. With phrases and a tone he had never employed
before, Kennedy acknowledged American and Soviet sacrifices in the
Second World War, blamed both sides for the Cold War, and offered the
acknowledgement of a shared humanity as the first step toward peace.[1]

Kennedy had not changed his mind about communism. He called it
"profoundly repugnant as a negation of personal freedom and dignity."[2]
This conviction made the speech even more remarkable, for he was reach-
ing out to an enemy he still despised to end the competition that had cost
so many dollars and lives. He had come full circle to Eisenhower's goal of
peace through coexistence. The speech led to the establishment of the
Limited Nuclear Test Ban Treaty. It sought to check the balance of terror
under which the world had lived for so long. In August, Kennedy thanked
Pearson for Canada being one of the treaty's first signatories.[3]

Only a day after this extraordinary speech, Kennedy delivered
another. From his desk in the Oval Office, he declared racial equality a
moral issue.[4] After years of reluctantly and incrementally supporting the

civil rights movement, the president's words were a ringing declaration that his administration was now its partner. The speech announced his introduction of the Civil Rights Act. It sought to drive another nail into the coffin of old Jim Crow—those laws, practices, and understandings that separated black from white and America from its creed.

The two speeches and the actions they endorsed represented bold leaps that Kennedy had never before dared to take. He was praised and condemned for his political courage. At a meeting with African-American leaders, he removed a small piece of paper from his pocket and said that as a result of his civil rights speech and related legislation, support for his presidency had plummeted from 60 percent to 47 percent. He had especially angered southern Democrats. Kennedy smiled and said, "I may lose the next election because of this. I don't care."[5]

While these were positive steps toward a brighter future, his actions in Vietnam represented a slow descent into darkness. Throughout the summer and fall, the region had become increasingly violent and chaotic. Kennedy had replaced America's South Vietnamese ambassador with his former Republican opponent Henry Cabot Lodge. Lodge supported CIA and military advisors who believed that South Vietnam's corrupt president Diem had to go. Kennedy's tacit approval allowed a CIA-supported coup on November 2. Diem was assassinated.

Canadian Vietnam ICC ambassador Gordon Cox told Lodge and Prime Minister Pearson that having Diem killed was a tragic error. Lodge dismissed Cox as incompetent and disloyal.[6] Cox was vindicated, however, when the assassination resulted in more frenzied violence than ever before. The new competition for hearts, minds, and power led to a massive American intervention only ten months later. Canada would soon welcome an estimated thirty-two thousand American draft dodgers and deserters fleeing the war's horrors. The war eventually led to the deaths of 58,200 Americans. When one considers Vietnamese and Cambodians, the number of lost lives rises to over five million.[7]

In his final months, Kennedy suffered personal tragedy. On August 7, six weeks before she was scheduled to give birth, Jacqueline was admitted to hospital. Kennedy rushed to her side but the baby was born before he arrived. Something was wrong. The child, Patrick, suffered from respiratory distress syndrome. Jacqueline held the baby only once before he was moved to Boston for specialized care. He lingered but doctors could do little. At two in the morning, Kennedy was awoken at his nearby hotel. Striding down the hospital corridor toward his dying son's room, he glanced through an open doorway and saw a young mother comforting a severely burned little boy. He stopped and asked a nurse for the mother's name and that she deliver a note. On a small piece of paper he wrote, "Keep up your courage. John F. Kennedy."[8]

While the president sat on a hard-backed wooden chair and held his son's tiny hand in his own, Patrick died. For a moment he was no longer the president but a young father. He hid in a nearby boiler room and for ten minutes he sobbed uncontrollably. He then returned to Jackie and they cried together.[9]

World and domestic events did not allow Kennedy to grieve for long. His civil rights legislation was splitting the Democratic Party, and nowhere was this more evident than Texas. Not even vice president Lyndon Johnson's backslapping, hand-gripping, aggressive politicking could heal the rift in his home state. Although the presidential election was a year away, Kennedy needed to begin stitching his party back together if he hoped for a second term. He could not forget that he had won his first by such a slim margin. On a mild and windy November 21 afternoon, Kennedy and Jacqueline arrived in Texas for a two-day five-city whirlwind fence-mending tour.

The reception at the San Antonio airport and along the motorcade route was positive and rambunctious. There were similarly positive receptions in Houston and Fort Worth. At a Fort Worth breakfast speech, Kennedy appeared in fine spirits. He joked about having the same feeling in Texas as he had experienced in Paris; that is, he seemed to be simply the man escorting Jacqueline Kennedy. No one ever seemed to wonder, he quipped, what he and Lyndon were wearing.[10]

He then shifted from fun to fear. He listed the city's contributions to national defence and noted that Canadian pilots had trained in Fort Worth before the United States had entered the First World War. He reminded the business audience of the many benefits of federal defence contracts. He then detailed the massive increase in military capacity that his administration had overseen:

> We have increased our defence budget by over 20%; increased the program for the acquisition of Polaris submarines from 24 to 41; increased our Minute Man missile purchase by more than 75%; doubled the number of strategic bombers and missiles on alert; doubled the number of nuclear weapons available for the strategic alert force; increased the tactical nuclear forces available in Europe by 60%; added 5 combat ready divisions and 5 tactical fighter wings to the armed forces; increased our strategic air lift capacities by 75%; increased our special counter-insurgency forces by 600%. . . . We intend to maintain that capacity until peace and justice are secure.[11]

The speech left no question of Kennedy's long-held belief in peace through strength. Further, it was an unapologetic reaffirmation of his willingness to conscript the military-industrial complex into that effort. The brandishing of strength and brute power stood in sharp contrast to the conciliatory words he had spoken in favour of peace in his June speech at American University and the spirit of the nuclear test ban treaty he had signed in August.

Back at their hotel, preparing to leave for the short trip to Dallas, Kennedy showed Jacqueline a full-page *Dallas Morning News* advertisement.

In blunt, crude language it called his presidency a failure and character-ized him as a weakling and communist sympathizer. He said, "Oh, you know, we're heading into nut country today. But, Jackie, if somebody wanted to shoot me from a window with a rifle, nobody can stop it, so why worry about it."[12]

The Dallas welcome was as exuberant as the others. The sun-drenched motorcade route was lined with cheering people and many waved from open windows and rooftops. Then, with the president's black Lincoln Continental limousine slowly moving through Dealey Plaza, a shot was heard. The bullet entered Kennedy's upper back and exited through his throat. It was a ghastly but survivable wound. At that point, any other person would have collapsed onto the wide seat and been sheltered from other shots. His hands went automatically to his throat, but he remained erect.

After Prime Minister Diefenbaker had forced Kennedy to plant the ceremonial tree in Ottawa in May 1961, the president's reinjured back had been a source of constant agony. Even the daily cocktail of painkillers couldn't numb the sting. He was fitted for a new, larger, stiffer back brace. It extended from under his arms to his hips. While the last few months had seen an improvement in his overall health, on the last morning of his life, Kennedy had followed his regular routine. He slowly fastened the brace's buckles and straps and then wrapped a long bandage around the entire affair before stiffly and uncomfortably slipping into his white dress shirt. The brace would enable him to endure the motorcade's bumps and keep smiling and waving.

Tragically, though, when he was hit by the first shot, the brace held him bolt upright in the limousine's back seat—he could not slump down.[13] Held firmly in place, Kennedy remained a target for the second, fatal, shot.

It tore time. For millions of people, the assassination was an irreparable rending that forever split before and after. The violence in Dallas was visited not just upon the man but also on the very idea that everything was possible and all problems solvable. For in the final analysis, Kennedy's gift was not his programs and policies but himself. His most important contribution was the courageous determination that idealism is not naive, hope is not foolish, hardship and challenge is incentive, and community can extend beyond one's family, city, or even country.

The public murder of a man who represented so much to so many, and by such a puny assassin, was incomprehensible and overwhelming. People who had never met or even seen him wept as if a family member had passed away. In London, famed actor Sir Laurence Olivier interrupted a performance and had the audience stand as the orchestra played the American national anthem. Other Londoners stood in the multi-coloured neon glow of Piccadilly Circus and openly sobbed. Charles de Galle said, "I am stunned. They are crying all over France. It is as if he were a Frenchman, a member of their own family."[14]

Canada declared November 23 to 29 an official period of mourning. Churches in Poland were crowded on its national day of mourning, and the Nicaraguan government declared a week of mourning as well.[15] Flags were dropped to half-staff in Ottawa and other world capitals, including Moscow. In the United States and around the globe, airports, schools, streets, libraries, public squares, and more were named after him. In the Canadian Yukon, a fourteen-thousand-foot snow-peaked mountain became Mount Kennedy.

Myths are important in all societies. They help create, define, and preserve the values and institutions deemed important. In so doing, they provide structure and stability. Kennedy's youth, looks, vigour, and promise, and the degree to which he inspired hope and optimism, coupled with the Shakespearean tragedy of his bloody and public death, rendered the myth inevitable. Jacqueline Kennedy instinctively understood. She was shattered but still managed to take charge. She arranged for the state funeral to reflect Lincoln's. She insisted on an eternal flame at his grave and that he would be buried not back home, but at Arlington National Cemetery, just across the Potomac River from Washington, which since the Civil War had become a revered burial place for veterans. She chose a hilltop location overlooking Washington that the president had actually visited and declared a fine spot to be placed at rest.

From a popular play addressing the legend of King Arthur, she took the name Camelot—that mystical place of missed opportunity—to describe her husband's thousand-day presidency. Kennedy's brother, Robert, also moved quickly. He ordered files to be removed from the White House, and Oval Office tapes and other records to be taken and squirrelled away. The myth could grow properly only if the legacy was carefully sculpted.

As the myth grew, Kennedy transcended politics and entered popular culture. In March 1960, Senator Kennedy had met former British intelligence officer Ian Fleming, who wrote the James Bond adventure novels. Long before Kennedy had conceived Operation Mongoose, Fleming suggested that the United States should use clandestine tricks to attack and discredit Castro.[16] A year later, *Life* magazine listed Fleming's *From Russia with Love* as among the president's favourite books. The endorsement led Fleming's American publisher to push the previously underperforming titles and to Sean Connery taking the British rogue to the big screen. The favour was returned when a character in 1962's *The Spy Who Loved Me* said, "We need some more Jack Kennedy. . . . They ought to hand the world over to young people who haven't got the idea of war stuck in their subconscious."[17] It was a meeting of myths.

Kennedy had created the President's Council on Physical Fitness. In the summer of 1963, DC Comics worked with the White House to promote it. A story was written based on Kennedy asking for Superman's help to urge Americans to take better care of themselves through diet and exercise. The project was shelved after the assassination but President Johnson lent his support and so the comic book was published in July 1964. The cover showed a ghostly JFK towering over the Capitol Building and Superman in mid-flight, glancing sadly back—one mythical hero in awe of another.

The Beatles' second album was released on the day Kennedy died. Three months later, they arrived for their first American tour and fifty thousand kids screamed their welcome at the newly named JFK airport. While Elvis had offered sex and daring, the Beatles offered love and fun. Their first American television appearance was so popular that the crime rate actually dipped while they performed. Even criminals had stopped to watch. In September they toured Dallas. They smiled and waved from an open limousine as they passed through Dealey Plaza. Many of those trying to understand the band's unprecedented popularity claimed their songs and wit personified the same youthful enthusiasm as the Kennedy promise. They renewed that promise while providing a welcome tonic to America's grief. They allowed the black bunting to be removed and the country to smile again.[18]

The myth might not have happened. Diefenbaker could have skipped the tree ceremony and Kennedy might not have been wearing the brace. Kennedy's handlers could have chosen a different route and avoided Dealey Plaza. It might have rained in Dallas and so the limousine's roof would have been affixed, stealing Oswald's target. Oswald could have missed.

These scenarios lead one to ponder not the myth but the legacy had Kennedy lived. No one can be sure whether the flames in American cities or Vietnamese villages, or the generational divisions on college campuses and around kitchen tables could have been avoided. If Kennedy had lived, the Democratic Party, which he had largely ignored to wage his 1960 victory, and which many of his policies had divided, might not have rallied for his re-election efforts in 1964. The reason may rest not with his public policies but his private life.

In July 1963, FBI director Hoover informed Attorney General Robert Kennedy that among the women with whom his brother was cavorting was a twenty-seven-year-old East German named Ellen Rometsch. She had been a communist in her youth and the FBI suspected she was a spy. The attorney general had her immediately deported. On August 21, she left Andrews Air Force base aboard an air force plane accompanied by one of his aides.[19]

Unfortunately for the president, the Senate Rules Committee was already investigating Bobby Baker. He had resigned as secretary to Senate majority leader Mike Mansfield due to shady business affairs. The ensuing investigation led to the discovery that he had also been arranging women for many high-profile men around Washington. Rometsch was one of those women. The president sat through a humiliating lunch in which he stretched the law by asking Hoover to keep the connection between him and Rometsch from the committee.[20] In October, the Senate committee announced that it would be calling a number of women to testify, including Ellen Rometsch.[21]

At that point, the public was still seeing Kennedy through the carefully staged television appearances and photo opportunities that depicted him as a loving husband and father. The Rometsch testimony would have shattered that image. It could have persuaded reporters who had known about the parade of sexual partners and of the president's nude romps with naked young women in the White House swimming pool to break their silence.[22] Her testimony could have suggested that the president's reckless behaviour was not just the product of an insatiable libido but perhaps a threat to national security. Hoover's voluminous files going back to the 1940s could have been subpoenaed or, given his disdain for John's behaviour and hatred for Joe and Robert, he might have volunteered them.

Had the scandal broken, Kennedy might not have contested the 1964 presidential race. He could have been impeached. The myth would be stillborn and the legacy in tatters. He could have been reduced to a man of ability who had spoken well and acted boldly but ultimately left a miserable legislative record and the presidency in disgrace. The assassination rendered the Rometsch testimony unseemly. It never happened. She remained in Germany and the myth remained intact. Iconoclasts and revisionists would chip away for decades but never break it.

The enduring Kennedy myth and legacy affected Canada. He joined Macdonald, Lincoln, and Churchill as standards against which future Canadian leaders were measured. When Pierre Trudeau rode his relative youth and undeniable charisma to power in 1968, he was complimented for the degree to which his intellectual cool and magnetism reminded Canadians of Kennedy. A Trudeau biographer observed: "The mood was conditioned by nearly a decade of jealousy. Canadians had enviously watched the presidency of John Kennedy, and continued to wish for a leader like him."[3] The age of the televised, celebrity politician had arrived.

President Johnson committed to advance the domestic and foreign policy shifts that Kennedy had initiated. Similarly, changes that had altered Canada's national trajectory continued. Diefenbaker's stubborn civic nationalism had offered Canadians a chance to turn toward greater autonomy, emboldened through a deep-seated national identity. Blinded by Kennedy's light, and chagrined by Diefenbaker's darkness and sovereignty's costs, Canadians said no. Now, Kennedy's ghost haunted two nations.

Aboard a plane in Dallas, Lyndon Johnson took the oath of office to become president of the United States. A stunned Jacqueline Kennedy stood at his side with her husband's blood spattered on her pretty pink suit. She had refused to change, saying, "Let them see what they have done."[4] Johnson kept Kennedy's staff and Cabinet. Johnson was as unlike Kennedy as Diefenbaker, but his gruff, homespun demeanour hid a brilliant political mind. He shamelessly exploited the grief felt for the fallen president to bend Congress to his will. Kennedy's education bill, civil rights legislation, and programs to fight poverty all moved ahead surer and swifter than they would have if Kennedy had lived.

Among the foreign affairs issues that Johnson needed to address was America's relationship with Canada. He and Pearson chatted briefly at Kennedy's funeral. Johnson expressed hope that the good relations that had begun to be re-established after the 1963 Canadian election would continue. He claimed to understand that Canadians often took independent points of view. Pearson offered a mild joke in replying that, as a Texan, Johnson would understand independent thinking.[25] They were nice thoughts, politely expressed. Minutes later, though, Johnson rushed into a meeting of state governors and, in apologizing for his tardiness, blurted something that would bring shudders to Canadian nationalists. "Canada is such a close neighbor and such a good neighbor that we always have plenty of problems there. They are kind of like problems in the hometown."[26]

Pearson arranged to visit the new president in January. Secretary of state Dean Rusk's long and detailed pre-visit briefing report began:

> The Canadians have maneuvered themselves into an impossible dilemma. Their economic prosperity depends on the continual inflow of U.S. capital. This necessarily brings with it control of their enterprises by U.S. management. They could undoubtedly improve their standard of living if they accepted the full consequences of this situation and permitted a gradual integration of the Canadian market with our own. But because they are so conscious of the overwhelming size and power of the United States, they tend to pursue highly nationalistic policies—fearing that otherwise Canada would become, if not the 51st State, at least a neighbor heavily dependent on the U.S. Colossus.[27]

Rusk had missed the point of the past few months. When Canadians relegated Diefenbaker to the Opposition benches, they had signalled, in part, a willingness to trade sovereignty for security and autonomy for integration. The "acceptance of the full consequences of their situation" had already happened. Pearson had made the point clear in a number of decisions and reactions to American pressure and did so again in a 1965 article he wrote for the respected American journal *Foreign Affairs*. Most of the piece explained Canada to Americans in the tone of a patient teacher addressing an inattentive pupil. When he came to Canada's place in the world he conceded, "We accept obligations even if we cannot determine developments."[28] Diefenbaker never would have said such a thing.

A turn had been taken. In the 1963 spring election, John Diefenbaker had tried to stand against the decades-long shift toward continentalism and proposed a renewed concern for Canadian sovereignty to protect the country against the "American Colossus" and, most immediately, Kennedy's desire to "push Canada around." It was similar to the nationalist campaign Macdonald had run in 1891 and Borden had waged against Laurier and free trade in 1911. Macdonald won. Borden won. Diefenbaker's crusade was the first time that a campaign promising to stand against American dominance had lost. Canadians, of course, considered a host of issues when making their ballot-box decision in 1963. But, in the end, they supported Pearson and continentalism. In looking ahead, Rusk had missed what was larger than it appeared in the rear-view mirror.

On January 21, 1964, Pearson and his wife, Maryon, arrived at Andrews Air Force base. They helicoptered to the oddly snow-free White House lawn where they shook hands with President Johnson in a brief ceremony. Pearson hosted an uneventful black-tie dinner that evening at the Canadian embassy residence. He erred by gossiping with Dean Rusk, which caused the always-sensitive Johnson to feel slighted.[29] The uncomfortable dinner marked the beginning of a sour relationship between Pearson and the new president. The next morning the Canadian party toured Arlington National Cemetery and laid a wreath at Kennedy's grave. They entered the White House North Portico just before ten o'clock.

The Canadian embassy's Basil Robinson had warned Pearson that Johnson had not spent much time preparing for the meeting and had little knowledge of Canadian-American issues or, for that matter, curiosity about Canada.[30] The meeting was brief and merely touched on a list of bilateral irritants while resolving nothing. In a televised ceremony afterwards, Pearson and Johnson signed the important but already concluded Columbia River Treaty and an agreement to create an international park for Franklin Roosevelt's summer home on Campobello Island, New Brunswick. The joint communication issued afterwards was typically bland. A telling phrase hinted at the renewed continentalist orientation of the relationship: "The Prime Minister and the President discussed at some length the practicality and desirability of working out acceptable principles which would make it easier to avoid divergences in economic and other policies of interest to each other."[31]

Neither Pearson nor Johnson mentioned nuclear weapons—they didn't need to. Pearson had promised the Canadian people, and then Kennedy at their Hyannis Port meeting, that Canada would accept the American weapons. They had arrived in Canada and Europe over the winter and spring. Pearson had not requested of Kennedy or Johnson any additional assurance of consultation regarding their use beyond the NORAD and NATO agreements.[32] In March 1964, with the weapons in Canada and with Canadian troops in Europe, Johnson informed Pearson that he had asked NORAD's commander in chief Gerhart to initiate discussions with Canadian military leaders regarding their deployment in an emergency. Johnson said he was writing only as a courtesy and would contact Pearson again when he was satisfied with whatever agreement the generals worked out.[33]

Paul Hellyer, who had helped change Pearson's mind on the nuclear issue, was now his defence minister. Hellyer informed the Canadian Chiefs of Staff that until a final agreement was reached, NORAD commanders had pre-authorized permission to use nuclear weapons when there was unmistakable evidence that an attack on North America had been launched.[34] Hellyer's directive meant that while negotiations regarding a Canadian-American consultation process were ongoing, the prime minister would not need to be consulted or even informed before American nuclear weapons were fired from or over Canada. The final deal afforded Canadian and American generals great latitude in their use of the weapons in both American and Canadian airspace.[35]

Other decisions were made that affected Canada's economic independence. The most significant involved cars. In the fall of 1963, Pearson had been advancing the goal of gaining more access to the American automobile market while creating more car and car parts jobs in Canada. Walter Gordon's full-duty remission program was working.[36] In fact, it was working too well. Just three days before the assassination, George Ball told Kennedy of growing American worries that the program was so successful that American sales and jobs were under threat. It was suggested that Kennedy might consider imposing countervailing duties on the Canadians.[37]

Ball's prediction proved correct. In January 1964, the Studebaker car company closed a plant in Indiana and immediately expanded its facility in Hamilton, Ontario. The move led President Johnson to call Pearson twice to express the concerns of congressmen worried that the American market was about to be flooded by cheaper Canadian cars.[38] With the American Treasury Department under pressure to stem the loss of American capital, jobs, and business, and congressmen threatening countervailing duties on cars and a broader trade war, Canadians and Americans found themselves at the bargaining table.

Over the summer of 1964, numerous meetings led to no resolutions. Political considerations entered the picture as November's presidential election drew nearer. The Canadians also warned that if a trade war ensued, it could bring down the American-friendly Pearson government and put the Canadian-nationalist Diefenbaker back into power. That was a scenario and bogeyman the Americans did not care to contemplate.[39]

By the end of September, the bare bones of an automobile deal took shape. Over the fall and early winter, Ford, Chrysler, and General Motors, the Big Three car companies, came on board. The agreement was finalized in January 1965. It allowed companies to move product between their Canadian and American operations without duties. With respect to the automotive industry, the Canadian-American border had been erased.

Pearson and secretary of state for external affairs Paul Martin flew to Johnson's Texas ranch to sign the Auto Pact agreement. Pearson arrived in his business suit to find Johnson in an ersatz cowboy outfit. Making matters even more uncomfortable, the president stepped before the microphones and reporters and welcomed "Prime Minister Wilson," the surname of the current British prime minister. Johnson then insisted upon loading the press and his Canadian guests into three cars and bouncing them through a tour of his ranch. The differences between the suave and classy Kennedy and somewhat boorish Johnson disturbed Pearson; but, even if the two leaders would not get along, they were able to advance their respective agendas.[40]

A trade war had been averted and a major boost given to the Canadian economy—especially manufacturing-rich Ontario. At the same time, another step had been taken along the road toward economic integration. Pearson said throughout the Auto Pact negotiations and afterwards that he was eager to discuss similar sector-by-sector free-trade zones involving other industries and argued that the economic benefits of the deal outweighed threats to economic independence.[41] Pearson's emasculated finance minister, Walter Gordon, later wrote that he did not like the Auto Pact in principle, but accepted it in acknowledging the economic facts of life.[42]

By 1965, the Americanized war in Vietnam was devolving into the quagmire Kennedy had feared and hoped to avoid. Johnson was taking his lead not from Kennedy's post–Cuban Missile Crisis notion of greater accommodation with communist opponents, but his earlier strategy of confrontation. He escalated the Vietnam war with a massive infusion of American troops and devastating bombing campaigns. In April, Pearson travelled to Philadelphia to receive the Temple University World Peace Award. Against the advice of Ambassador Ritchie and Paul Martin, he seized the opportunity to criticize President Johnson's handling of the war. His acceptance speech specifically called for an end to the bombing of North Vietnamese cities.[43] Upon leaving the stage, he was told Johnson wanted to see him. A helicopter was dispatched and the next day Pearson was at the president's Camp David retreat.

A sumptuous lunch was laid out on a long table. Pearson nibbled politely as Johnson ignored him. He tried to make small talk with Johnson's wife while the president, with his normal use of vulgar language and Texas-based metaphors, shouted into the phone at McNamara about Vietnam. With the awkward lunch finally over, they moved to the terrace where Johnson turned his rage on Pearson. Unable to get a word in, Pearson cowered in stunned silence as the towering Johnson moved menacingly close, leaned down into his face, and launched into a profanity-laden tirade. Shouting about the Temple speech, he grabbed Pearson by his shirt collar and yelled, "You pissed on my rug."[44]

Pearson said nothing of Johnson's insulting him, the office of prime minister, and Canada. On the contrary, once back in Ottawa, Pearson wrote a long letter to Johnson explaining, "I want to assure you that my government, and I particularly as its leader, want to give you all possible support in the policy, difficult and thankless, you are following in Vietnam in aiding South Vietnam to resist aggression."[45]

At their January 1964 White House meeting Johnson and Pearson had agreed to undertake a study of Canadian-American relations. Based on their keen intelligence and years of diplomatic experience, former ambassadors Arnold Heeney and Livingston Merchant were chosen to lead the effort. The operative word that informed nearly all of the 1965 Merchant-Heeney Report's recommendations was "partnership." Entitled *Canada and the United States: Principles for Partnership*, the report addressed economic, social, and defence issues. It made the case that a partnership between sovereign states demands respect that must be demonstrated through open and timely consultation. Merchant and Heeney acknowledged, no doubt with the Cuban Missile Crisis in mind, that in some cases consultation must be "telescoped."[46] But even then, they argued, there is no excuse for an absence of consultation.

They contended that Canada must recognize America's leadership in NATO and North American defence: "This is not to say that the Canadian Government should automatically and uniformly concur in foreign policy decisions taken by the United States Government. . . . The Canadian Government cannot renounce its right to independent judgement and decision in the 'vast external realm.'"[47] The report expressed Diefenbaker's full argument and something that Kennedy never seemed to completely accept: all dealings between the two countries must rest on an acknowledgement of both America's power and Canada's sovereignty. Pearson read but largely ignored the report.[48]

While millions mourned and mythologized Kennedy, Diefenbaker sank into a pool of bitter resentment while plotting his return to power, and Pearson moved Canada further along the continentalist road. For their part, journalists and scholars tried to make sense of what had just transpired. Their understanding was coloured by the publication of two books.

The first, entitled *Renegade in Power: The Diefenbaker Years*, was written by *Maclean's* magazine columnist Peter C. Newman and published in October 1963. It was based on interviews with politicians, bureaucrats, and other reporters. Rich in anecdotes, rumours, and insider scoops, it was the first Canadian book of its kind and became a runaway bestseller. A vicious and scathing attack on Diefenbaker as a leader and a man, *Renegade in Power* derided his actions, questioned his motives, and trivialized his accomplishments. Somewhat lost in the flinging mud were the ideas he championed, the Canada he envisioned, and the nationalist option he proposed.

Two years later, McMaster University philosophy professor George Grant published a small and provocative book entitled *Lament for a Nation: The Defeat of Canadian Nationalism*. Grant ignored the muck of Diefenbaker's administration that had so entranced Newman. He focused instead on the ideas that had guided it. He argued that even before Canada's creation in 1867, Canadians were aware and proud of their unique, conservative, Burkean, un-American founding ideas and had fought to preserve them. Early in the twentieth century, however, the Liberal Party had given up the fight and adopted American-style liberalism. That change led the party to promote pro-American, continentalist economic, cultural, and foreign policies. Grant contended that Diefenbaker stood opposed to that ideological leaning and the policies it inspired. His 1957 election represented an attempt to re-establish the country's original vision and seek a more Canadian, un-American future. The Diefenbaker moment was Canadian nationalism's last gasp.[49] Grant called the defence crisis of 1963 "the strongest stand against satellite status that any Canadian government ever attempted."[50]

Grant's more nuanced analysis was embraced by those who had been repulsed by Newman's smashing broadside, those seeking a fuller understanding of the tumultuous time just passed, and those who had supported Diefenbaker, opposed Pearson, and seen through Kennedy's celebrity. The book was not without problems. Its wide brush tarred too many well-intentioned Canadians as sellouts, especially his old friend Pearson and those of the external affairs department who, interestingly, included his brother-in-law George Ignatieff. Pearson was no sellout. His perspective on Canada's best interests simply had no time for either Diefenbaker's civic nationalism or Gordon's economic nationalism, with their demands for greater sovereignty. As Pearson's advisor Tom Kent admitted, "The nationalist issue as such was just never faced up to."[51]

*Lament for a Nation* also downplayed the fact that Canada was born of not just British, but also French and Aboriginal traditions. This was the complexity at the heart of the Canadian identity that Diefenbaker envisioned and expressed as One Canada. Losing British connections—a major element of Grant's lament—did not, as he contended, represent a loss of all emotional and historic ties.

Linked to that oversight, Grant downplayed the fact that the day before Pearson became prime minister, a bomb shattered a Montreal afternoon and killed a janitor working in an army recruitment centre. It was the first of many bombs that rocked Quebec and shaped the debate regarding the establishment of an independent state to house the Québécois nation. Pearson had to fight the narrow tribalism at the core of the separatist argument. Lost for too long in that fight were the central ideas of Diefenbaker's civic nationalism: the pan- and pro-Canadianism that rejected Quebec's notion of "pure wool" people like it did prairie nativism and the banal racism of city streets and country lanes that feared differences rather than embracing the unity of citizenship based not on blood but law.

Grant also failed to predict the imminent uptick in patriotism, or, as Liberal Jack Pickersgill called it, status nationalism.[52] While Canadians were digesting Grant's new book, in 1965 most also welcomed Pearson's new flag. The bold red and white design became a symbol around which those professing their love of Canada could rally. Stories soon circulated of the flag festooning the backpacks of American travellers wishing to avoid anti-Americanism when they went abroad. Grant could also not foresee the national pride engendered by Expo 67, the world's fair celebrating Canada's 100th birthday in 1967, which Pearson hosted in Montreal.

While Grant did not predict the waves of patriotism, he would have been quick to dismiss them. While flags and fairs are great, the emotions they inspire are shallow and transitory. Sparks of showy patriotism always flare and fizzle. Patriotism is about celebration. It can dance merrily along without autonomy, but nationalism demands it. Nationalism is about identity. Unlike the bread and circuses of patriotism or jingoist chest-thumping or empty-headed chauvinist aggression, civic nationalism reflects a quiet confidence in what is unique, valued, and valuable. It isn't easy. It demands work. If you don't believe it, you won't see it. That is the pro-Canadian, historically based civic nationalism that Diefenbaker proposed. It is the same civic nationalism against which Kennedy fought and that was left behind at the crossroads.

Diefenbaker was not promoting an end to Canadian internationalism, but a re-evaluation of national self-interest as a determining factor in the pursuit of the country's priorities. He was not demanding an end to America's leadership in the Western alliance or continental defence, but the respect accorded a partner. He was not suggesting a withdrawal of American investment from Canada, but greater autonomy in determining the country's economic future. Flaws in Diefenbaker's character and leadership are undeniable. As George Grant observed, "The country he thought about was not the country he was required to govern."[53] But Diefenbaker's failings and ultimate failure to convince enough Canadians to share his nationalist vision does not subtract from its legitimacy or value.

CBC Radio personality Peter Gzowski once entertained Canadians with a contest. He offered a prize to whoever could create the Canadian equivalent to "As American as apple pie." There were thousands of entrants and the winner was: "As Canadian as . . . possible under the circumstances."[54] It was as cute as it was sad. Kennedy might well have smiled and Pearson might have grinned but Diefenbaker would not have been amused. Diefenbaker wanted more for Canada, and he fought Kennedy and Canadians who wanted less.

# N O T E S

---

## PROLOGUE

1   *Globe and Mail*, November 15, 1957.

2   *Varsity*, University of Toronto, November 15, 1957.

3   Lewis later became leader of Ontario's New Democratic Party (1970–78), Canadian Ambassador to the United Nations (1984–1988), and an influential advocate in the fight against HIV-AIDs in Africa.

4   Cameron Smith, *Unfinished Journey*, p. 382.

5   *Globe and Mail*, November 15, 1957.

6   Stephen Lewis, Interview with Steve Paikin, TVO's *Agenda*, November 22, 2013.

7   *Toronto Star*, November 15, 1957.

8   C. P. Stacey, *Canada and the Age of Conflict*. Vol. 2, p. 61.

## ONE: CHARACTER AND PRINCIPLES: KENNEDY, PEARSON, AND DIEFENBAKER

1   Robert Dallek, *An Unfinished Life*, pp. 30–31.

2   David Nasaw, *The Patriarch*, pp. 372–73, 508.

3   Ibid., p. 264.

4   John F. Kennedy, *Why England Slept*, pp. 215–16.

5   *New York Times*, August 20, 1943.

6   Lester B. Pearson, *Mike*. Vol. 1, p. 25.

7   John English, *Shadow of Heaven*, p. 101.

8   Ibid., pp. 92–93.

9   Pearson, *Mike*. Vol. 1, p. 52.

10  Ibid., pp. 123–25

11  Andrew Cohen, *Lester B. Pearson*, p. 70.

12  Pearson, *Mike*. Vol. 1, p. 211.

13  Cohen, *Lester B. Pearson*, p. 88.

14  Andrew Cooper, *Canadian Foreign Policy*, p. 36.

15    Pearson, *Mike*. Vol. 1, p. 280.

16    John G. Diefenbaker, *One Canada*. Vol. 1, p. 75.

17    Ibid., p. 71. See also Denis Smith, *Rogue Tory*, pp. 21–31.

18    Diefenbaker, *One Canada*. Vol. 1, p. 75.

19    Peter Stursberg, *Leadership Gained, 1956–1962*, p. 26.

20    As told by former prime minister John Turner at the opening of the R. B. Bennett Centre in Hopewell Cape, New Brunswick, July 19, 2010.

21    Diefenbaker, *One Canada*. Vol. 1, pp. 163–64. See also Smith, *Rogue Tory*, pp. 77–79.

22    Diefenbaker to Long, January 22, 1935. USkUASC. *Diefenbaker Papers*. MG II/ II/141/9150.

23    Smith, *Rogue Tory*, p. 84.

24    Cohen, *Lester B. Pearson*, p. 103. See also John English, *The Worldly Years*, p. 66.

25    *National Post*, December 19, 2011. Also, John George Dryden, telephone conversation with author, December 16, 2013.

26    *The Star Pheonix*, December 14, 2013.

27    Jason Gregory Zorbas, *Diefenbaker and Latin America*, pp. 15, 28.

28    Diefenbaker, *One Canada*. Vol. 1, p.180.

29    John F. Kennedy, April 3, 1945, and May 4, 1945. *JFK Articles 1941–1949*. JFKLM. PPP. Digital File: JFKPOF-129-003.

30    Diefenbaker, *One Canada*. Vol. 1, p. 217.

31    *Look*, June 11, 1946.

32    Reg Whitaker and Gary Marcuse, *Cold War Canada*, pp. 38–40.

33    George Kennan, "The Success of Soviet Conduct," pp. 566–82.

34    Pearson, *Mike*. Vol. 1, pp. 233–234.

35    Cited in Spencer Warren, *Churchill's Iron Curtain Speech Fifty Years Later*, p. 100.

36    Edelgard Mahant and Graeme S. Mount, *Invisible and Inaudible in Washington*, p. 31.

37    Theodore Sorensen, *Kennedy*, p. 29.

38    Mahant and Mount, *Invisible and Inaudible in Washington*, p. 119.

39    Nasaw, *The Patriarch*, p. 669.

40    Ralph Martin and Ed Plaut, *Front Runner, Dark Horse*, p. 178.

41    John F. Kennedy, Remarks at the University of Montreal, December 4, 1953. JFKLM. Kennedy Papers, PPP. Box 102.

42    Ibid.

43    Ibid.

44    John F. Kennedy, Remarks on the Saint Lawrence Seaway before the Senate, January 14, 1954. JFKLM. PPP. Box 102.

45    Ibid.

46   Ibid.

47   Ibid.

48   *Boston Post*, January 15, 1954.

49   John F. Kennedy, *Meet the Press* interview, February 14, 1954. JFKLM. *PPP*. Box 920A.

50   The best description of Kennedy's myriad medical issues is found throughout Dallek, *An Unfinished Life.*

51   John F. Kennedy, *Profiles in Courage*, p. 213.

52   Stephen H. Browne, *Edmund Burke and the Discourse of Virtue*, p. 68.

53   Edmund Burke, *Reflections on the Revolution in France*, p. 29.

54   Sorensen, *Kennedy*, p. 15.

55   Paul Healy, "The Senate's Gay Young Bachelor," June 13, 1953.

56   Ibid.

57   Peter Collier and David Horowitz, *The Kennedys*, p.233.

58   Ibid., p. 258.

59   Cohen, *Lester B. Pearson*, p. xiii.

60   Lester Bowles Pearson, Acceptance Speech, Nobelprize.org. Nobel Media AB 2013. Accessed October 29, 2013.

61   Ibid.

62   See Andrew Cohen, *While Canada Slept*. See also Don Munton, "Myths of the Golden Age."

63   George Ignatieff, *The Making of a Peacemonger*, p. 109. See also Adam Chapnick, "The Golden Age," pp. 217–218.

64   R. A. Spencer, "Triangle into Treaty," p. 88.

65   Geoffrey Pearson, *Seize the Day*, p. 29.

66   Reginald C. Stuart, *Dispersed Relations*, p. 233.

67   Denis Stairs, *The Diplomacy of Constraint*, p. 47.

68   John Holmes, "The Unquiet Diplomat," p. 298.

69   Pearson, *Mike*. Vol. 2, p. 180.

70   Pearson to A.R.M. Lower, October 12, 1950. LAC. *Pearson Papers*. MG26, N.1, Vol. 7.

71   Robert Bothwell, *Alliance and Illusion*, p. 95.

72   Pearson, *Seize the Day*, p 98

73   Recollection of George Ignatieff reported in Peter Stursberg, *Lester Pearson and the American Dilemma*, pp. 176–77.

74   Cohen, *Lester B. Pearson*, p.113.

75   House of Commons, *Debates*. January 31, 1956.

76   Peter Stursberg, *Leadership Lost, 1962–1967*, p. 161.

77   Ibid., p. 179.

78 Robert Bothwell, "The Canadian Isolationist Tradition," p. 83.

79 Cohen, *Lester B. Pearson*, p. 123.

80 Diefenbaker, *One Canada*. Vol. 1, p. 240.

81 Diefenbaker to Murray, January 29, 1945. LAC. *Murray Papers*. MG30-E186, Vol. 14. See also *Montreal Gazette*, June 8, 1945.

82 Smith, *Rogue Tory*, p. 205.

83 Ibid., p. 206.

84 Brian Mulroney, *Memoirs*, pp. 36–38.

85 *Globe and Mail*, December 15, 1956.

86 English, *The Worldly Years*, p. 159.

87 John Meisel, *The Canadian General Election of 1957*, p. 73.

88 John G. Diefenbaker, "Major Campaign Speech No. 1," April 25, 1957. USkUASC. *Diefenbaker Papers*. MG 01/XXI/589.

89 Ibid.

90 Ibid.

91 Richard Gwyn, *The Man Who Made Us*, p. 354.

92 Christopher MacLennan, *Toward the Charter*, p. 122.

93 Peter C. Newman, *Renegade in Power*, pp. 51–52.

94 John G. Diefenbaker, "Colony or Nation," Speech, April 30, 1957. USkUASC. *Diefenbaker Papers*. MG 01/ XII/A380.2

95 Peter C. Newman, *Here Be Dragons*, p. 260.

96 Robert Bothwell, Ian M. Drummond, John English, *Canada Since 1945*, p. 118. See also Gerald Friesen, *Citizens and Nation*, pp. 224–25.

97 Diefenbaker was assisted in the creation of his vision and the manner in which it was communicated by a number of advisors, most importantly economist Merril Menzies. The challenge to the liberal consensus was helped a great deal by Donald Creighton's bestselling two-volume biography of Sir John A. Macdonald. Its publication in 1952 and 1956 placed Sir John and his conservative ideas at the centre of Canada's creation and growth.

98 John Duffy, *Fights of Our Lives*, p. 176.

99 Diefenbaker, *One Canada*. Vol. 2, p. 2.

## TWO. THE COLLISION

1 Peter Dempson, *Assignment Ottawa*, p. 95.

2 Donald M. Fleming, *So Very Near*. Vol. 1, p. 345.

3 Smith, *Rogue Tory*, pp. 250–51.

4 Ibid.

5    Ibid, p. 253.

6    John G. Diefenbaker speech at Dartmouth College. "Great Issues in the Anglo-Canadian-American Community," September 7, 1957. USkUASC. *Diefenbaker Papers*. MG XXI/18/619.

7    Fleming, *So Very Near*. Vol. 1, pp. 509–20.

8    John F. Kennedy, Remarks at University of New Brunswick, Fredericton, New Brunswick, Canada, October 8, 1957. JFKLM. *PPP.* Box 102.

9    Ibid.

10   Ibid.

11   Ibid.

12   Garry Wills, *Nixon Agonistes*, p. 118.

13   Herman S. Wolk, "The New Look," p. 5.

14   Jean Edward Smith, *Eisenhower in War and Peace*, p. 642.

15   Lawrence Martin, *The Presidents and the Prime Ministers*, p. 9.

16   Joint Statement Following Discussions with Prime Minister St. Laurent of Canada, November 14, 1953. *Eisenhower Papers*, p. 248.

17   Pearson, *Mike*. Vol. 2, p. 69.

18   Ibid., p. 68.

19   English, *The Worldly Years*, p. 121.

20   Memorandum for the Cabinet: Canada-United States Agreement on Overflights, June 19, 1957. USkUASC. *Diefenbaker Papers*. MG XII/1/A/18.

21   Memorandum for Mr. Diefenbaker and Memorandum for the Minister, June 20, 1957. USkUASC. *Diefenbaker Papers*. MG XII/1A/18.

22   Joseph T. Jockel, *No Boundaries Upstairs*, p. 111.

23   Defence and Security Issues, Section A. Continental Air Defence. December 8, 1954. USkUASC. *Diefenbaker Papers*. MG XII/F/335.

24   Cabinet Conclusions, July 31, 1957. LAC. *PCO*. RG 2.

25   Memorandum from Under-Secretary of State for External Affairs to Secretary of State for External Affairs, December 2nd, 1957. LAC. *DEA*. 50309-40.

26   Memorandum from Under-Secretary of State for External Affairs to Secretary of State for External Affairs, February 11, 1958. LAC. *DEA*. 50210-F-40.

27   Smith, *Rogue Tory*, p. 265.

28   Ignatieff, *The Making of a Peacemonger*, p. 186.

29   Pearkes to Diefenbaker, June 8, 1965. USkUASC. *Diefenbaker Papers*. MG, XIV/E/222/E/13.

30   Ibid.

31   Ignatieff, *The Making of a Peacemonger*, p. 188.

32    Holmes to Robinson, August 1, 1958. LAC. *Robinson Papers.* MG31, Vol. 3A.

33    John Hilliker, "The Politicians and the 'Pearsonalities,'" pp. 152–67.

34    H. Basil Robinson, *Diefenbaker's World*, p. 21.

35    House of Commons, *Debates.* December 21, 1957.

36    John F. Kennedy, "Speech to National Conference of Christians and Jews in Chicago," December 3, 1957. JFKLM. *PPP.* Box 102.

37    Ibid.

38    House of Commons, *Debates.* January 20, 1958.

39    Ibid.

40    Smith, *Rogue Tory*, p. 278.

41    Pearson, *Mike.* Vol. 3, p. 33.

42    Dick Spencer, *Trumpets and Drums*, p. 53.

43    Ibid., p. 54.

44    Peter Stursberg, *Lester Pearson and the Dream of Unity*, p. 54.

45    Nixon to Diefenbaker, April 1, 1958. LAC. *Diefenbaker Papers.* Reel M-9378.

## THREE. IKE, THE CHIEF, AND THE CANDIDATE

1    Statement by the Honourable Livingston T. Merchant, United States Ambassador to Canada, before the Senate Foreign Relations Committee on United States Relations with Canada, May 16, 1958. USkUASC. *Diefenbaker Papers.* MG 01/XII/A/295.

2    Ibid.

3    Robinson, *Diefenbaker's World*, p. 50.

4    See Ron Dart, *The Red Tory Tradition*, and Charles Taylor, *Radical Torys.*

5    Sean Maloney, *Learning to Love the Bomb*, p. 60.

6    Crepault to Diefenbaker, July 26, 1957. LAC. *Robinson Papers.* MG31, Vol. 8. File 8.1.

7    Cabinet Conclusions, May 8, August 1, September 8 and September 22, 1958. LAC. *PCO.* RG 2.

8    Cabinet Conclusions, January 13, 1958. LAC. *PCO.* RG 2.

9    Ibid., April 29, 1958.

10    "Agreement between The Government of Canada and The Government of the United States of American concerning the Organization and Operation of the North American Air Defence Command (NORAD), May 12, 1958," pp. 3–4. USkUASC. *Diefenbaker Papers.* MG XII/20/A/556.

11    House of Commons, *Debates.* June 10, 1958.

12    Robinson, *Diefenbaker's World*, p. 51.

13    Ibid.

14    House of Commons, *Debates*. September 23, 1958.

15    Ernie Regehr, *Arms Canada*, p. 47.

16    Notes on Meeting between Dulles and Smith. July 8, 1958, LAC. *Robinson Papers*. MG31, Vol. 1, File 1.14.

17    Memorandum to Cabinet: CF105 Avro Arrow Program, March 8, 1960. LAC. *Harkness Papers*. MG 32. Vol. 57. File 19. See also George Pearkes interview with Dr. Reginald Roy, April 5, 1967. ACC 74-1, Box 5, Interview #61.

18    Memorandum for the Prime Minister, September 5, 1958. USkUASC. *Diefenbaker Papers*. MG XIV/D/23.

19    Cabinet Conclusions, September 22, 1958. LAC. *PCO*. RG 2.

20    Cabinet Conclusions, February 17, 1959. LAC. *PCO*. RG 2.

21    The Arrow decision remains controversial and many are still not able to forgive Diefenbaker for his decision. For interesting views on the decision see Palmiro Campagna, *Storms of* Controversy, Daniel Wyatt, *The Last Flight of the Arrow*, and Michael Bliss, *Northern Enterprise*, pp. 474–77.

22    Campagna, *Storms of Controversy*, 66.

23    Memorandum for the Minister, Nuclear Arms Policy, April 20, 1963. LAC. *Green Papers*. MG 31. E-83. Vol. 9.

24    House of Commons, *Debates*. February 20, 1959.

25    Robertson to Chiefs of Staff and Secretary to the Cabinet, "Acquisition of Nuclear Weapons." October 20, 1958. LAC. *Robinson Papers*. MG31, Vol. 8. File 8.2.

26    McCardle Memorandum for Minister, October 15, 1958. USkUASC. *Diefenbaker Papers*. MG O1/XIV/D/26.2.

27    Patricia McMahon, *Essence of Indecision*, p. 55.

28    Cabinet Conclusions, August 27, 1959. LAC. *PCO*. RG 2.

29    Eisenhower to Diefenbaker, August 30, 1959, LAC. *Heeney Papers*. MG 30, E 144. Vol. 1.

30    Heeney to Diefenbaker, "Lessons from Sky Hawk." September 4, 1950. LAC. *Heeney Papers*. MG 30, E 144. Vol. 1.

31    House of Commons, *Debates*. January 19, 1960.

32    Dwight D. Eisenhower, *Waging Peace, 1956–1961*, p. 580.

33    Ibid., p. 581.

34    John G. Diefenbaker, Address by the Prime Minister, before the United States General Assembly, September 26, 1960. USkUASC. *Diefenbaker Papers*. MG XII/77/C/435.

35    Ibid.

36    Robinson, *Diefenbaker's World*, p. 155.

37    Smith, *Rogue* Tory, p. 377.

38    Robinson, *Diefenbaker's World*, p. 156.

39    Memorandum of Conversation with the Prime Minister in Ottawa, Tuesday, August 30, 1960 and Wednesday August 31, 1960. LAC. *Heeney Papers*. August 30, 1960. MG 30, E 144 Vol. 1.

40    Ibid.

41    Richard Nixon, *RN*. Vol. 1, p. 270.

42    Herbert S. Parmet, "The Kennedy Myth and American Politics," p. 32.

43    Martin and Plaut, *Front Runner, Dark Horse*, p. 461

44    John F. Kennedy, Remarks in the Senate, August 14, 1958. JFKLM. *PPP*. Box 102.

45    Ibid.

46    Ibid.

47    Galbraith to Harris, September 27, 1960. JFKLM. *John K. Gailbraith Papers*. Box 74.

48    Daryl G. Press, *Calculating Credibility*, p. 87.

49    Sheldon M. Stern, *The Week the World Stood Still*, p. 21.

50    Christopher A. Preble, *John F. Kennedy and the Missile Gap*, p. 109. See also Ronald E. Powaski, *March to Armageddon*, p. 94.

51    Christopher A. Preble, "Who Ever Believed the Missile Gap?" p. 801.

52    Smith, *Rogue Tory*, p. 378.

53    Robinson, *Diefenbaker's World*, p. 165.

54    Ibid.

55    Nixon, *RN*. Vol. 1, p. 277.

56    Robinson, *Diefenbaker's World*, p. 166.

57    Kennedy to Diefenbaker, November 21, 1960. USkUASC. *Diefenbaker Papers*. MG 01/XII/A/268.

58    Robinson, *Diefenbaker's World*, p. 51.

## FOUR. THREE HOURS IN WASHINGTON—FEBRUARY 20, 1961

1    G. Scott Thomas, *A New World to the Be Won*, p. 35.

2    Merle Miller, *Plain Speaking*, p. 187.

3    Heeney to Green, January 9, 1961. LAC. *Green Papers*. MG 30, E 144, Vol. 7. File 3.

4    Heeney to Green, January 9, 1961. LAC. *Robinson Papers*. MG 32. B-13. Vol. 7. File 2.

5    Conversation with Arnold Heeney, January 17, 1961. USkUASC. *Diefenbaker Papers*. MG O1/XII/D/149.

6    Diefenbaker, John (George) Prime Minister, Memorandum, Department of State. December, 1960. JFKLM. *POF*. Box 113. File: Canada – Security 1961.

7   Rusk to Kennedy, Memorandum for Meeting with Prime Minister Diefenbaker. February 17, 1961. JFKLM. *Kennedy Papers*. *POF*. Box 113. File: Canada – Security 1961.

8   Ibid.

9   Ibid.

10  Ibid.

11  Green, Howard (Charles), Secretary of State for External Affairs, Memorandum, Department of State, undated. JFKLM. *POF*. Box 113. File: Canada – Security 1961.

12  Rusk to Kennedy, Memorandum for Meeting with Prime Minister Diefenbaker. February 17, 1961. JFKLM. *Kennedy Papers*. *POF*. Box 113. File: Canada – Security 1961.

13  Diefenbaker, John (George) Prime Minister, Memorandum, Department of State, December, 1960. JFKLM. *Kennedy Papers*. *POF*. Box 113.

14  Rusk to Kennedy, Memorandum for Meeting with Prime Minister Diefenbaker. February 17, 1961. JFKLM. *Kennedy Papers*. *POF*. Box 113. File: Canada – Security 1961.

15  Thomas Patterson, "Introduction," in Patterson (ed.), *Kennedy's Quest for Victory*, p. 5.

16  Conversations between the President of the United States and the Prime Minister of Canada, February 20, 1961. JFKLM. *POF*. Box 113. File: Canada – security 1961. See also Heeney to Green, February 23, 1961. LAC. *Robinson Papers*. MG 32. B-13. Vol. 7. File 4.

17  Ibid.

18  James Fetzer, "Clinging to Containment: China Policy," in Paterson (ed.), *Kennedy's Quest for Victory*, p. 179.

19  Bothwell, *Alliance and Illusion*, p. 154.

20  Memorandum of Conversation, State Department, April 28, 1961. JFKLM. *NSF*. Countries Files: Canada. Box 18. File 2.

21  Arnold Heeney, Conversations between the President of the United States and the Prime Minister of Canada, the White House, Washington, February 20, 1961. USkUASC. *Diefenbaker Papers*. MG XIV/D/222/5.

22  John F. Kennedy, Remarks at University of New Brunswick, Fredericton, New Brunswick, Canada, October 8, 1957. JFKLM. *PPP*. Box 102.

23  Arnold Heeney, Conversations between the President of the United States and the Prime Minister of Canada, the White House. Washington, February 20, 1961. USkUASC. *Diefenbaker Papers*. MG XIV/D/222/5.

24  Ibid. See also Greg Donaghy and Michael Stevenson, "The Limits of Alliance," p. 33.

25  Robinson, *Diefenbaker's World*, p. 51.

26  Arnold Heeney, Conversations between the President of the United States and the Prime Minister of Canada, the White House. Washington, February 20, 1961. USkUASC. *Diefenbaker Papers*. MG XIV/D/222/5.

27  Cabinet Conclusions, February 21, 1961. LAC. *PCO*. RG 2. See also Fleming, *So Very Near*. Vol. 1, p. 256.

28  Conversations between the President of the United States and the Prime Minister of Canada, February 20, 1961. JFKLM. *POF*. Box 113. File: Canada – Security 1961.

29  Cabinet Conclusions, February 21, 1961. LAC. *PCO*. RG 2. See also Bryce to Harkness, March 2, 1961. LAC. *Green Papers*. MG 31. E-83. Vol. 9. File 7.

30  Arnold Heeney, Conversations between the President of the United States and the Prime Minister of Canada, the White House. Washington, February 20, 1961. USkUASC. *Diefenbaker Papers*. MG XIV/D/222/5.

31  A. DeVolpi, V.E. Minkov, G.S. Stanford, and V.A. Simonenko, Alexander DeVolpi, Vladimir Minkov, Vadim Simonenko, George Stanford, *Nuclear Shadowboxing*, pp. III–37. See also Ike Jeanes, *Forecast and Solution*, p. 309.

32  Conversations between the President of the United States and the Prime Minister of Canada, February 20, 1961. JFKLM. *Kennedy Papers*. *POF*. Box 113. File: Canada – Security 1961. See also Notes for Conference in Washington with President Kennedy, February 20, 1961. LAC. *Robinson Papers*. MG31, Vol. 4. File 2.

33  Knowlton Nash, *Kennedy and Diefenbaker*, p. 95.

34  Robinson, *Diefenbaker's World*, p. 172.

35  Nash, *Kennedy and Diefenbaker*, p. 95.

36  Ibid.

37  Department of State Memorandum of Conversation, February 20, 1961. JFKLM. *NSF*. Countries Files: Canada. Box 18. File 1.

38  Heeney to Diefenbaker, February 20, 1961. LAC. *Heeney Papers*. MG 30. E-144. Vol. 1.

39  House of Commons, *Debates*. February 20, 1961.

40  Ibid.

41  Smith, *Rogue Tory*, p. 382.

## FIVE: THE TRIUMPHANT AND TERRIBLE SPRING

1  Diefenbaker, *One Canada*. Vol. 2, p. 173.

2  Alex Thomson, *U.S. Policy Towards Apartheid South Africa, 1948–1994*, pp. 28–29.

3  House of Commons, *Debates*. April 27, 1960.

4  Ignatieff to External Affairs, April 11, 1960. USkUASC. *Diefenbaker Papers*. MG XII/100/F/69.

5  Diefenbaker, *One Canada*. Vol. 2, pp. 209–211.

6  Fulton and Davie Press Conference, March 13, 1961. USkUASC. *Diefenbaker Papers*. MG XII/55/C/110.

7   Arthur E. Blanchette, *Canadian Foreign Policy, 1945–2000*, pp. 184–85.

8   Robinson, *Diefenbaker's World*, p. 185.

9   Joe Clark, *How We Lead*, p. 106.

10  James A. Nathan, *Anatomy of the Cuban Missile Crisis*, p.26.

11  Dwight D. Eisenhower, *Eisenhower Diaries*, p. 379.

12  Thomas G. Paterson, "Fixation with Cuba," in Paterson (ed.), *Kennedy's Quest for Victory*, p. 126.

13  Lawrence Freedman, *Kennedy's Wars*, p. 128.

14  Pero Gleijeses, *Conflicting Missions*, p. 14.

15  Dallek, *An Unfinished Life*, p. 357.

16  Ibid., p. 358.

17  Robert Wright, *Three Nights in Havana*, p. 38.

18  John M. Kirk, *Canada-Cuba Relations*, p. 31.

19  Nash, *Kennedy and Diefenbaker*, p. 103.

20  Wright, *Three Nights in Havana*, p. 70.

21  Heeney to Diefenbaker, March 12, 1960. LAC. *Heeney Papers*. MG 30 E144, Vol. 2. File 3.

22  Sorensen, *Kennedy*, p. 309.

23  House of Commons, *Debates*. April 20, 1961.

24  Heeney to Diefenbaker, April 22, 1961. LAC. *Heeney Papers*. MG 30 E144, Vol. 2. File 5.

25  Paterson, "Fixation with Cuba," p.141.

26  Stern, *The Week the World Stood Still*, p. 16.

27  Benjamin Bradlee, *Conversations with Kennedy*, p. 122.

28  Cohen, *Lester B. Pearson*, p. 137.

29  Study Conference on National Problems (Summary of Discussions). LAC. *Pearson Papers*. MG 26 N1, Vol. 108. File: Study Conference, Part 3.

30  English, *The Worldly Years*, 203.

31  Pearson to Hutchison, September 14, 1960. LAC. *Pearson Papers*. MG 26 N1, Vol. 107. File: Liberal Party Policy.

32  John F. Kennedy, "The Terrain of Today's Statecraft," August 1, 1959.

33  Ibid.

## SIX: THREE DAYS IN OTTAWA—MAY 16 TO 18, 1961

1   Robinson. *Diefenbaker's World*, p. 194.

2   *Globe and Mail*, May 17, 1961.

3   *Ottawa Citizen*, May 17, 1961.

4     *Globe and Mail*, May 17, 1961.

5     Dalleck, *An Unfinished Life*, p. 336.

6     Ted Sorensen, *Kennedy*, p. 364.

7     Merchant to Secretary of State, April 12, 1961. JFKLM. *NSF*. Countries Files: Canada. Box 18. File 2.

8     Suggested Program for the President's Visit to Ottawa, May 16–18, 1963. JFKLM. *NSF*. Countries Files: Canada. Box 18. File 2.

9     *Ottawa Citizen*, May 17, 1961.

10    *Globe and Mail*, May 17, 1961.

11    Nash, *Kennedy and Diefenbaker*, p.128.

12    *Life*, May 26,1961.

13    Nash, *Kennedy and Diefenbaker*, p.128.

14    Hugh Brewster, "JFK and Jacqueline Kennedy's Visit to Canada," November 21, 2013.

15    *New York Herald*, May 15, 1961. Reprinted in the *Ottawa Citizen*, May 16, 1961.

16    Merchant to Rusk, May 28, 1961. JFKLM. *NSF*. Countries File: Canada. Box 18. File 4.

17    Robinson, *Diefenbaker's World*, p.201.

18    Merchant to Rusk, May 28, 1961. JFKLM. *NSF*. Countries File: Canada. Box 18.

19    Robinson, *Diefenbaker's World*, p. 202.

20    Merchant to Rusk, May 28, 1961. JFKLM. *NSF*. Countries File: Canada. Box 18.

21    James Francis Rochlin, *Discovering the Americas*, p. 46.

22    Asa McKercher, "Southern Exposure," pp. 64–65.

23    Merchant to Rusk, May 28, 1961. JFKLM. *NSF*. Countries File: Canada. Box 18.

24    Robinson, *Diefenbaker's World*, p. 201.

25    Pearson to Lett, August 22, 1954. LAC. *DEA Papers*. RG 25/4629/50052-A-40(1).

26    Robert Bothwell, "The Further Shore," p. 98.

27    David Kalser, *American Tragedy*, p. 34.

28    "Trends in Canadian Foreign Policy." May 2, 1961. JFKLM. *POF*. Countries File: Canada – Kennedy Trip to Ottawa 5/61. Box 113.

29    Rostow to White, May 15, 1961. JFKLM. *NSF*. Countries File: Canada. Box 18. File 3.

30    Merchant to Rusk, May 28, 1961. JFKLM. *NSF*. Countries File: Canada. Box 18. File 4.

31    "Visit of President Kennedy to Ottawa, May 16–18, 1961." LAC. *Robinson Papers*. Vol. 5. File 7.

32    "General Colour on Hyannisport Meeting," May 15, 1963. LAC. *Robinson Papers*. MG31. E31. Vol. 12. File 9.

33    Kristian Steinnes, "The European Challenge," *Contemporary European History*, Vol. 7, no. 1 (March 1998), p. 72.

34    Arthur Schlesinger Jr., *A Thousand Days*, pp. 704–705.

35    Stuart Ward, "Kennedy, Britain and the European Community," p.322. See also
      Steinnes, "The European Challenge," p.72.

36    "Memoranda of Conversation, Trip to Ottawa, May 17, 1961." JFKLM. *NSF.* Box
      18. File: Canada – General – Ottawa Trip 5/17/61.

37    "Visit of President Kennedy to Ottawa," May 16–18, 1961. LAC. *Robinson Papers.*
      MG31, Vol. 5. File 7.

38    Julian Lindley-French and Neil Macfarlane, *The North Atlantic Treaty Organization,*
      p. 33.

39    "A Review of North Atlantic Problems for the Future." March 1961. JFKLM. *NSF.*
      Regional Security: NATO. Box 220.

40    Burgess for the President, May 4, 1961. "President's Trip to Ottawa. May 16–18,
      1961. Continental Defense Background Paper." JFKLM. *POF.* Box 113.

41    Merchant to Rusk, May 28, 1961. JFKLM. *NSF.* Countries Files: Canada. Box 18.

42    "Visit of President Kennedy to Ottawa, May 16–18, 1961." LAC. *Robinson Papers.*
      MG 31 E31,Vol. 5. File 7.

43    Harkness to Diefenbaker, February 23, 1961. USkUASC. *Diefenbaker Papers.* MG
      01/VI/R/89.

44    McMahon, *Essence of Indecision,* p. 107.

45    Brian Bow, *The Politics of Linkage,* p. 48.

46    English, *The Worldly Years,* p. 245.

47    Robinson, *Diefenbaker's World,* p. 144.

48    Burgess for the President, May 4, 1961. "President's Trip to Ottawa. May 16–18,
      1961. Continental Defense Background Paper." JFKLM. *POF.* Box 113.

49    "Visit of President Kennedy to Ottawa, May 16–18, 1961." LAC. *Robinson Papers.*
      Vol. 5. File 7.

50    Charles Ritchie interview cited in Gwynne Dyer, *Canada and the Great Power Game,*
      *1914–2014,* p. 358.

51    Cabinet Defence Committee Minutes, January 23, 1961. LAC. *Green Papers.* MG 31.
      E-83. Vol. 9. File 1.

52    Ibid.

53    Visit of President Kennedy to Ottawa, May 16–18, 1961. LAC. *Robinson Papers.* Vol. 5.
      File 7.

54    Ibid.

55    "Defence Policy," January 1961. LAC. *Kent Papers.* Vol. 6. File: National Rally Text
      and Follow Up.

56    Visit of President Kennedy to Ottawa, May 16–18, 1961. LAC. *Robinson Papers.* MG
      31 E83, Vol. 5. File 7.

57 M. J. D. to Prime Minister, May 9, 1961. USkUASC. *Diefenbaker Papers*. MG XIV/E/ 9008/853.

58 John F. Kennedy, Address before the Canadian Parliament in Ottawa. May 17, 1961. JFKLM. *POF*. Digital File: JFKWHA-031.

59 Ibid.

60 Ibid.

61 Ibid.

62 Peyton V. Lyon, *Canada in World Affairs, 1961–1963*, p. 523.

63 House of Commons, *Debates*. September 11, 1963.

64 McKercher, "Southern Exposure," p. 58.

65 Joint Communiqué Issued by President Kennedy of the United States and Prime Minister Diefenbaker of Canada, Following Discussions Held on May 17, 1961, in Ottawa. USkUASC. *Diefenbaker Papers*. MG XVI/E/9008/853.

66 Memorandum to the President from WWR, What We Want from the Ottawa Trip, May 16, 1961. USkUASC. *Diefenbaker Papers*. MG 01/XII/D/113.

67 Robinson, *Diefenbaker's World*, p. 206.

68 *Ambassador in United States to Secretary of State for External Affairs*, May 8, 1961. LAC. *DEA Papers*. Telegram 1473 320. DEA/1415-N-40.

69 Richard Reeves, *President Kennedy*, p. 595.

70 Diefenbaker, *One Canada*. Vol. 2, p. 184.

71 Fairlcough to Diefenbaker, May 9, 1963. USkUASC. *Diefenbaker Papers*. MG XVI/E/9008/853.

72 John Diefenbaker to Elmer Diefenbaker, May 18, 1961. USkUASC. *Diefenbaker Papers*. MG V/4/2135.

73 Merchant to Secretary of State, May 19, 1961. JFKLM. *Kennedy Papers*. NSF. Box 18. File: Canada.

74 Diefenbaker to Kennedy, June 9, 1961. JFKLM. *Kennedy Papers*. Digital File: JFKPOF-140-001.

75 Kennedy to Diefenbaker, June 9, 1961. LAC. *Diefenbaker Papers*. Reel M-9378.

76 Nash, *Kennedy and Diefenbaker*, p. 110.

## SEVEN. TRIPPING INTO WAR—VIENNA AND BERLIN

1 Nolting to State Department, May 16, 1961. JFKLM. *Kennedy Papers*. NSF. Box 18. File: Canada.

2 Merchant to State Department, June 2, 1961. JFKLM. *Kennedy Papers*. NSF. Box 18. File: Canada.

3 Ibid.

4    *Star Phoenix*, January 24, 1981.

5    *Globe and Mail*, February 16, 1966.

6    Robert Dallek, *Flawed Giant*, p. 10.

7    Phillip A. Goduti, *Robert F. Kennedy and the Shaping of Civil Rights, 1960–1964*, p. 5.

8    John F. Kennedy, Special Message to the Congress on Urgent Nation Needs, May 25, 1961. JFKLM. *POF.* Digital File: JFKPOF-034-030.

9    Ellis to Kennedy, February 11, 1961. JFKLM. *POF.* Box 113. File: 1.

10   Martin Mann, "Plain Facts about Fall Out Shelters," p. 56.

11   Ibid., p. 60.

12   Dallek, *An Unfinished Life*, p. 391.

13   Francis X. Winters, *The Year of the Hare*, p. 136.

14   John G. Diefenbaker, "Speech on CBC Radio International," May 5, 1961. USkUASC. *Diefenbaker Papers.* MG 01/XIX/10.

15   Walter Moss, *A History of Russia*. Vol. 2, p. 262.

16   Frederick Kempe, *Berlin 1961*, p.7.

17   Dallek, *An Unfinished Life*, pp. 398–99.

18   Michael Beschloss, *The Crisis Years*, pp. 189–90.

19   Reeves, *President Kennedy*, p. 159.

20   Kenneth P. O'Donnell and David F. Powers with Joe McCarthy, *Johnny We Hardly Knew Ye*, p. 342.

21   Beschloss, *The Crisis Years*, p. 205. See also Dallek, *An Unfinished Life*, pp. 398–99, 408.

22   Bothwell, *Alliance and Illusion*, p. 164.

23   Reeves, *President Kennedy*, p. 171.

24   Ibid., p. 116.

25   Dallek, *An Unfinished Life*, pp. 398–99, 414.

26   Michael Dobbs, *One Minute to Midnight*, p. 7.

27   Dallek, *An Unfinished Life*, pp. 398–99, 415.

28   John F. Kennedy, Radio and Television Report to the American People on Returning From Europe, June 6, 1961. JFKLM. *POF.* Digital File: JFKWHA-037.

29   Ibid.

30   Harris Wofford, *Of Kennedy and Kings*, p. 379.

31   Beschloss, *The Crisis Years*, pp. 245, 237.

32   Merchant to Secretary of State, May 23, 1961. JFKLM. *NSF.* Box 18. File: Canada – General.

33   House of Commons, *Debates.* June 12, 1961.

34  John F. Kennedy, "Telephone Conversation with the Prime Minister of Canada on the Opening of a New Mutual Defense Communication System," July 22, 1961. JFKLM. *POF.* Digital File: JFKWHA-044-005.

35  Cabinet Conclusions, July 24, 1961. LAC. *PCO.* RG 2.

36  Ibid.

37  Ibid.

38  Ibid.

39  John F. Kennedy, Radio and Television Address to the American People on the Berlin Crisis, July 25, 1961. JFKLM. *POF.* Digital File: JFKWHA-045.

40  Ibid.

41  Ibid.

42  Ibid.

43  John G. Diefenbaker, "Speech to Canadian Weekly Newspapers Association," August 15, 1961. USkUASC. *Diefenbaker Papers.* MG 01/XXII/A/215. See also McMahon, *Essence of Indecision*, pp. 117–18.

44  *Halifax Chronicle-Herald*, July 23, 1961.

45  Kennedy to Diefenbaker, August 3, 1961. JFKLM. *NSF.* Countries Files: Canada. Box 20. File 2.

46  Diefenbaker to Kennedy, August 11, 1961. JFKLM. *NSF.* Countries Files: Canada. Box 20. File 2.

47  McMahon, *Essence of Indecision*, p. 117.

48  Cabinet Conclusions, August 17, 1961. LAC. *PCO.* RG 2.

49  Escott Reid, *Radical Mandarin*, p. 318.

50  Roy MacLaren, *Commissions High*, p. 467.

51  Cabinet Conclusions, August 23, 1961. LAC. *PCO.* RG 2.

52  Heeney to Robertson, August 28, 1961. LAC. *Heeney Papers.* MG 30. E-144. Vol. 1.

53  *Globe and Mail*, September 4, 1961.

54  John G. Diefenbaker, "Speech to Canadian Bar Association," September 1, 1961. USkUASC. *Diefenbaker Papers.* MG 01/XXII/A/215.

55  Peter Haydon, *The 1962 Cuban Missile Crisis*, p. 179.

56  Armstrong to Secretary of State, September 15, 1961. JFKLM. *NSF.* Countries Files: Canada. Box 20.

57  *Montreal Gazette*, September 20, 1961.

58  Ibid.

59  Armstrong to Secretary of State, October 12, 1961. JFKLM. *NSF.* Countries Files: Canada. Box 20.

60  Notes for Nation's Business, September 20, 1961. USkUASC. *Diefenbaker Papers*. MG 01/XIV/E/222.

61  Bradlee, *Conversations with Kennedy*, pp. 165, 170.

62  John F. Kennedy, "Address in New York City Before the General Assembly of the United Nations," September 25, 1961. JFKLM. *POF.* Digital File: JFKPOF-035-048.

63  Ibid.

64  Robinson, *Diefenbaker's World*, p. 232.

65  Robinson to Undersecretary, "Meeting with VOW," October 5, 1961. LAC. *Robinson Papers*. Vol. 9. File 1.

66  Ibid.

67  Nash, *Kennedy and Diefenbaker*, p. 141.

68  McMahon, *Essence of Indecision*, p. 127.

69  Ibid., p. 128.

70  Cabinet Conclusions, November 21, 1961. LAC. *PCO*. RG 2.

71  *Montreal Gazette*, November 3, 1961. Also see *Washington Post*, November 2, 1961.

72  Armstrong to Rusk, October 12, 1961. JFKLM. *NSF*. Countries Files: Canada. Box 18.

73  Ibid.

74  Jamie Glazov, *Canadian Policy Toward Khrushchev's Soviet Union*, p. 109.

75  Merchant to State Department, November 27, 1961. JFKLM. *NSF*. Countries Files: Canada. Box 18.

76  Merchant to State Department, December 30, 1961. JFKLM. *NSF*. Countries Files: Canada. Box 18.

## EIGHT: OVERSTEPPING BOUNDS IN THE 1962 ELECTION

1  Bradlee, *Conversations with Kennedy*, p. 29. See also Gretchen Rubin, *Forty Ways to Look at JFK*, p. 157.

2  Robinson, *Diefenbaker's World*, p. 237. See also Smith, *Rogue Tory*, p. 477.

3  Pearson to Geoffrey Pearson, May 25, 1960. LAC. *Pearson Papers*. MG26. N.2. Vol. 53.

4  Harold Macmillan, *Pointing the Way*, p. 356.

5  John F. Kennedy, Summary of the President's Remarks to the National Security Council, January 18, 1962. JFKLM. *NSF*. Box 313.

6  John F. Kennedy, State of the Union Address to Joint Session of Congress, January 11, 1962. JFKLM. *POF.* Digital File: JFKWHA-066.

7  Ward, "Kennedy, Britain and the European Community," p. 317.

8  Dean Rusk Telegram from the Department of State to Embassy in Germany, January 15, 1962. JFKLM. FRUS Department of State, Central Files, 611.42.1-1562. Conference Files: Lot 65 D 533, CF 2028.

9   Robinson, *Diefenbaker's World*, p.132.

10  John G. Diefenbaker, "Speech to Montreal Real Estate Board," January 25, 1962. USkUASC. *Diefenbaker Papers*. MG XIV/E/222/8.

11  Robert William Reford, *Canada and Three Crises*, p. 165.

12  House of Commons, *Debates*. January 31, 1962.

13  *Globe and Mail*, February 1, 1962.

14  Text of Statement by United States Senator Kenneth Keating, February 7, 1962. USkUASC. *Diefenbaker Papers*. MG 01/XII/C/120.

15  Charles Ritchie, *Storm Signals*, p. 2.

16  Ibid.

17  Ibid., p. 6.

18  House of Commons, *Debates*. February 15, 1962.

19  John F. Kennedy, State of the Union Address to Joint Session of Congress, January 11, 1962. JFKLM. *POF*. Digital File: JFKWHA-066.

20  Ibid.

21  Embassy in Canada to the Department of State, February 26, 1962. JFKLM. *FRUS*, 1961–1963. Department of State, Central Files, Document 429. 742.5611/3-862.

22  Ibid.

23  Ibid.

24  House of Commons, *Debates*. February 28, 1962.

25  McMahon, *Essence of Indecision*, p. 134.

26  Embassy in Canada to the Department of State, Document 431. Foreign Relations of the United States, 1961–1963. Department of State, Central Files, 742.5611/3-862.

27  Le Pan to Pearson, February 21, 1962. LAC. *Pearson Papers*. MG 26 N2, Vol. 49. File 802.

28  Adam Chapnick, *Canada's Voice*, pp. 110–112.

29  Kennedy to Diefenbaker, April 1, 1962. USkUASC. *Diefenbaker Papers*. MG 01/XII/A/268.

30  Kennedy to Diefenbaker, April 14, 1962. JFKLM. *NSF*. Countries Files: Canada. Box 20. File 2.

31  Armstrong to Diefenbaker, April 15, 1962. USkUASC. *Diefenbaker Papers*. MG 01/XII/A/268.

32  Peter Regenstreif, *The Diefenbaker Interlude*, pp. 72–76.

33  Interview with Carolyn Smart, October 16, 2013.

34  Interview with Brian Gallagher, September 18, 2014.

35  Stursberg, *Lester Pearson and the American Dilemma*, p. 181.

36  Robinson, *Diefenbaker's World*, p. 267.

37   Ibid.

38   Nash, *Kennedy and Diefenbaker*, p. 157.

39   John F. Kennedy. Remarks at a Dinner Honoring Nobel Prize Winners of the Western Hemisphere. April 29, 1962. JFKLM. *POF.* Digital File: JFKPOF-037-042.

40   *Ottawa Citizen*, May 6, 1962.

41   Bundy and Ball, Telcon. May 7, 1962. JFKLM. *Ball Papers*. Box 2. File: Canada.

42   Merchant to Ball, May 5, 1962. JFKLM. *NSF.* Box 18.

43   Ibid.

44   Ibid.

45   Nash, *Kennedy and Diefenbaker*, p. 160.

46   Ibid.

47   Ibid.

48   Bundy and Ball, Telcon, May 7, 1962. JFKLM. *Ball Papers*. Box 2. File: Canada.

49   Ibid.

50   Merchant to Rusk and Ball, May 13, 1962. JFKLM. *NSF.* Countries File: Canada. Box 18.

51   Nash, *Kennedy and Diefenbaker*, p. 161.

52   Penny Bryden, *Planners and Politicians*, p. 54.

53   English, *The Worldly Years*, p. 234.

54   Theodore White, *The Making of the President 1960*, p. 51.

55   Lou Harris, Interview in *Guelph Mercury*, November 21, 2013.

56   Ibid.

57   Ibid.

58   Ibid.

59   Stursberg, *Lester Pearson and the American Dilemma*, p. 87.

60   Dillon and Ball, Telcon, June 21, 1962. JFKLM. *Ball Papers*. Box 2. File: Canada.

61   Dillon and Ball, Telcon, June 24, 1962. JFKLM. *Ball Papers*. Box 2 File: Canada.

62   Macmillan to Diefenbaker, July 2, 1962. LAC. *Diefenbaker Papers*. Reel M-9378.

63   Michael Bordo, Tamara Gomes, and Lawrence Schembri, *Canada and the IMF*, p. 23.

64   "Do as the Doukhobors Do," Malvina Reynolds. http://people.wku.edu/charles .smith/ MALVINA/mr213.htm.

65   N. Caiden, "The Canadian General Election of 1962," pp. 76, 82.

66   English, *The Worldly Years*, p. 242.

## NINE. CUBAN MISSILES AND CANADIAN COUP D'ÉTAT

1   Stern, *The Week the World Stood Still*, p. 22.

2   Dobbs, *One Minute to Midnight*, p. 3.

3    Stern, *The Week the World Stood Still*, p. 40.

4    Ibid., p. 43.

5    Ibid.

6    Beschloss, *The Crisis Years*, p. 435.

7    Ibid.

8    Stern, *The Week the World Stood Still*, p. 48.

9    Don Munton and David A. Welch, *The Cuban Missile Crisis*, p. 10.

10    Herbert S. Dinerstein, *The Making of a Missile Crisis: October 1962*, p. 156.

11    John Jacob Nutter, *The CIA's Black Ops*, p. 115.

12    Munton and Welch, *The Cuban Missile Crisis*, p. 20.

13    James G. Hershberg, "Before the Missiles of October," p. 250.

14    Munton and Welch, *The Cuban Missile Crisis*, p. 26.

15    Ibid., p. 27.

16    Dobbs, *One Minute to Midnight*, p. 37. See also Munton and Welch, *The Cuban Missile Crisis*, pp. 21–27.

17    Munton and Welch, *The Cuban Missile Crisis*, p. 33.

18    Ibid., p. 40.

19    Ibid., p. 42.

20    Ibid., p. 44.

21    Ibid., p. 45.

22    Interview with Robert Ough, May 5, 2014.

23    Asa McKercher, "A 'Half-hearted Response'?," p. 337.

24    Robinson to Diefenbaker, October 4, 1963. LAC. *Diefenbaker Papers*. Reel M-9378.

25    Robertson to Green, October 4, 1962. LAC. *DEA* Box 5077, File 4568-40.

26    Kennedy to Diefenbaker, October 20, 1962. USkUASC. *Diefenbaker Papers*. MG 01/XII/A/268.

27    Diefenbaker to Kennedy, October 30, 1962. JFKLM. *NSF*. Countries Files: Canada. Box 20. File 4.

28    Ibid., unsigned attachment.

29    Kennedy to Diefenbaker, undated. JFKLM. *NSF*. Countries Files: Canada. Box 20. File 4.

30    Robinson, *Diefenbaker's World*, p. 284.

31    Ibid.

32    Harold Macmillan, *At the End of the Day*, p. 186.

33    Frank Costigliola, "Nuclear Arms, Dollars, and Berlin," in Paterson (ed.), *Kennedy's Quest for Victory*, p. 47.

34    Joseph T. Jockel, *Canada in NORAD, 1957–2007*, p. 55.

35    Memoradum for the Prime Minister, October 22, 1962. USkUASC. *Diefenbaker Papers*. MG XII/88/D/204.

36    Kennedy to Diefenbaker, October 22, 1962. JFKLM. *NSF.* Countries Files: Canada. Box 20. File 4.

37    Ibid.

38    Rusk to Kennedy, Memorandum for Meeting with Prime Minister Diefenbaker, February 17, 1961. JFKLM. *POF.* Digital File: JFKPOF-113-004.

39    "The Cuban Situation," May 12, 1961. JFKLM. *NSF.* Countries Files: Canada. Box 20. File 4.

40    Merchant to Department of State, Memorandum of Conversation, November 5, 1962. JFKLM. *NSF.* Countries Files: Canada. Box 20. File 5. See also Nuclear Arms Question. LAC. *Harkness Papers.* MG 32. Vol. 14. File 2.

41    Ibid.

42    Ibid.

43    Merchant to Rusk, October 22, 1962. JFKLM. *FRUS.* Box 441.

44    McKercher, "A 'Half-hearted Response'?," p. 338.

45    John F. Kennedy, Report to the American People on the Soviet Arms Buildup in Cuba, October 22, 1962. JFKLM. *POF.* Digital File: JFKWHA-142-001.

46    Ibid.

47    Ibid.

48    Munton and Welch, *The Cuban Missile Crisis*, p. 64.

49    Dobbs, *One Minute to Midnight*, p. 43.

50    House of Commons, *Debates*. October 22, 1962.

51    Ibid.

52    Merchant to Rusk, October 22, 1962. JFKLM. *NSF*. Countries Files: Canada. Box 40.

53    White to Rusk, October 23, 1962. JFKLM. *NSF*. Countries Files: Canada. Box 40A.

54    Robert Kennedy, *Thirteen Days*, p. 40.

55    Stern, *The Week the World Stood Still*, p. 71.

56    Haydon, *The 1962 Cuban Missile Crisis*, p. 128.

57    Douglas Harkness, Nuclear Arms Question. LAC. *Harkness Papers.* MG32 B19, Volume 57. File 2. See also *Ottawa Citizen*, October 22, 24, 25, 1977.

58    Smith, *Rogue Tory*, p. 458.

59    Douglas Harkness, Nuclear Arms Question. LAC. *Harkness Papers.* MG32 B19, Volume 57. File 2.

60    Diefenbaker handwritten note, August 7, 1961. USkUASC. *Diefenbaker Papers.* MG XIV/E/161.

61    Macmillan, *At the End of the Day*, p. 190.

62 Cees Wiebes and Bert Zeeman, "Political Consultation during International Crises," pp. 94–95.

63 Haydon, *The 1962 Cuban Missile Crisis*, p. 124.

64 Interview with Robert Ough, May 5, 2014.

## TEN. THE DEEPENING CRISIS

1 Dobbs, *One Minute to Midnight*, pp. 58, 66.

2 Alice L. George, *The Cuban Missile Crisis*, p. 58.

3 Stern, *The Week the World Stood Still*, p. 79.

4 Douglas Harkness, Nuclear Arms Question. LAC. *Harkness Papers*. MG32 B19, Volume 57. File 2.

5 Cabinet Conclusions, October, 23, 1962. LAC. *PCO*. RG2.

6 Ibid.

7 Patrick Nicholson, *Vision and Indecision*, p. 159.

8 Cabinet Conclusions, October 23, 1962. LAC. *PCO*. RG2.

9 Douglas Harkness, Nuclear Arms Question. LAC. *Harkness Papers*. MG32 B19, Volume 57. File 2.

10 Stursberg, *Leadership Lost, 1962–1967*, pp. 16–17.

11 English, *The Worldly Years*, p. 247.

12 Diefenbaker, *One Canada*. Vol. 3, p. 69.

13 English, *The Worldly Years*, p. 248.

14 House of Commons, *Debates*. October 23, 1962.

15 Cohen, *Lester B. Pearson*, p. 145.

16 Munton and Welch, *The Cuban Missile Crisis*, p. 66.

17 Sheldon Stern, *The Cuban Missile Crisis in American Memory*, p. 75.

18 Smith, *Rogue Tory*, p. 459. See also Robinson, *Diefenbaker's World*, p. 288.

19 Stern, *The Week the World Stood Still*, p. 77.

20 Peter Haydon, "Canadian Involvement in the Cuban Missile Crisis Reconsidered," p. 56.

21 Haydon, *The 1962 Cuban Missile Crisis*, p. 99.

22 Ibid., p. 240.

23 Lyon, *Canada in World Affairs, 1961–1963*, p. 42.

24 Haydon, "Canadian Involvement in the Cuban Missile Crisis Reconsidered," p. 58.

25 Ibid.

26 Svetlana Savranskaya, "New Sources on the Role of Soviet Submarines in the Cuban Missile Crisis," p. 246.

27 Haydon, "Canadian Involvement in the Cuban Missile Crisis Reconsidered," p. 49.

28  Dobbs, *One Minute to Midnight*, pp. 92–93.

29  Ibid., p. 73.

30  Ibid., p. 87.

31  Jocelyn Maynard Ghent, "Canada, the United States, and the Cuban Missile Crisis," p. 76.

32  Cabinet Conclusions, October 24, 1962. LAC. *PCO*. RG2.

33  Douglas Harkness, Nuclear Arms Question. LAC. *Harkness Papers*. MG32 B19, Volume 57. File 2.

34  House of Commons, *Debates*. October 25, 1962.

35  Ibid.

36  Record, October 26, 1962. LAC. *DEA*. Volume file: 244-40.

37  Alice L. George, *Awaiting Armageddon*, p. 73.

38  Ghent, "Canada, the United States, and the Cuban Missile Crisis," p. 184.

39  Khrushchev to Kennedy, October 25, 1962. JFKLM. *FRUS*. Vol. 6. File 127-7.

40  Dobbs, *One Minute to Midnight*, p. 113.

41  Munton and Welch, *The Cuban Missile Crisis*, p. 71.

42  Paterson, "Fixation with Cuba," p. 151.

43  Munton and Welch, *The Cuban Missile Crisis*, pp.76–77.

44  Dobbs, *One Minute to Midnight*, pp. 308–309.

45  Jonathan M. House, *A Military History of the Cold War, 1944–1962*, p. 435.

46  Munton and Welch, *The Cuban Missile Crisis*, p. 82.

47  Ibid.

48  Robert A. Divine, *The Cuban Missile Crisis*, p. 58.

49  Munton and Welch, *The Cuban Missile Crisis*, p. 93.

50  *Globe and Mail*, November 23, 1962.

51  CTV Bulletin, December 24, 1963. USkUASC. *Diefenbaker Papers*. MG 01/XII/B/350.

52  D. B. Dewar to Bryce, November 20, 1962. LAC. *PCO Records*, RG2-B-2, file F-2-8 (a).

53  Cabinet Conclusions. January 9, 1962. *PCO Records*, RG2-B-2, file F-2-8(a), LAC.54 Ignatieff, *The Making of a Peacemonger*, p. 206.

55  Ghent, "Canada, the United States and the Cuban Missile Crisis," p. 182.

56  ABC and CBS Interview, December 17, 1962. JFKLM. *POF*. Digital File: JFKWHA-153.

57  "USIA Summary of Foreign Press," October 23, 1962. JFKLM. *POF:* Countries File: Cuba.

58  *Washington Post*, October 27, 1962.

59   Robertson to Diefenbaker, November 2, 1962. LAC. *Green Papers*. MG 31. E-83. Vol. 9.

60   John G. Diefenbaker, Diefenbaker Speech to Zionist Organization of Canada. November 5, 1962. USkUASC. *Diefenbaker Papers*. MG 01/XII/C/342.

61   Butterworth to Department of State, February 3, 1963. JFKLM. *FRUS*. Box. 13. File: 1196-9.

## ELEVEN: TOPPLING A GOVERNMENT

1    ABC and CBS Interview, December 17, 1962. JFKLM. *POF.* Digital File: JFKWHA-153.

2    Sorensen, *Kennedy*, p. 636.

3    Memorandum to the Prime Minister, Telephoned from B. T. Richardson, December 20, 1962. USkUASC. *Diefenbaker Papers*. MG 01/XII/C/291.

4    Memorandum from United States Division to Assistant Under-Secretary of State for External Affairs. December 13, 1962. USkUASC. *Diefenbaker Papers*. MG 01/XII/C/291.

5    En Route Nassau Notes, December 20, 1962. USkUASC. *Diefenbaker Papers*. MG 01/XII/C/291.

6    Peter Calvocoressi, *World Politics Since 1945*, p. 191.

7    Nash, *Kennedy and Diefenbaker*, p. 217.

8    Ibid.

9    Bahamas Meetings, December 21–22, 1962. USkUASC. *Diefenbaker Papers*. MG 01/XII/C/291.

10   General Colour on Hyannisport Meeting, May 15, 1963. LAC. *Robinson Papers*. MG31. E31. Vol. 12.

11   Nuclear Arms Discussions with Prime Minister Macmillan, Nassau, December 21–22, 1962. USkUASC. *Diefenbaker Papers*. MG 01/XII/C/291.

12   Cadieux to Minister, December 28, 1963. LAC. *Robinson Papers*. MG31. E-44. Vol. 1.

13   Cabinet Conclusions, October 30, 1962. LAC. *PCO*. RG2.

14   Douglas Harkness, Nuclear Arms Question. October 26, 1962. LAC. *Harkness Papers*. MG 32 B19, Vol. 57. File 9.

15   Ibid.

16   *Ottawa Citizen*, October 22, 1977.

17   Press Conference, General Lauris S. Norstad, January 3, 1963. USkUASC. *Diefenbaker Papers*. MG. VI/2/108.

18   *Ottawa Citizen*, January 4, 1963.

19   *Montreal Gazette*, January 7, 1963.

20   *Halifax Chronicle-Herald*, January 5, 1963.

21   *Toronto Telegram*, January 5, 1963.

22   *Globe and Mail*, January 5, 1963.

23   Jocelyn Maynard Ghent, "Did He Fall or Was He Pushed?," p. 255.

24   John F. Kennedy, Remarks on Presenting Distinguished Service Medal to General Lauris Norstad, January 9, 1963. JFKLM. *POF.* Digital File: JFKPOF-042-018 JFKLM.

25   Diefenbaker, *The Tumultuous Years*, 3.

26   Nash, *Kennedy and Diefenbaker*, p. 225.

27   English, *The Worldly Years*, pp. 246–48.

28   Ignatieff, *The Making of a Peacemonger*, p. 207.

29   Paul Hellyer, Following the NATO Parliamentary Conference held in Paris, November 29, 1962. *Pearson Papers.* MG 26 N1, Vol. 55. File: NATO Parliamentary Conference. See also White to Secretary of State, November 23, 1962. JFKLM. *NSF.* Regional Security. Box 225. File 2.

30   White to Secretary of State, November 23, 1962. JFKLM. *NSF.* Regional Security. Box 225. File 2.

31   Howard H. Letner, "Foreign Policy Decision Making," p. 34.

32   Paul Hellyer, *Damn the Torpedos*, p. 25.

33   *Saint John Telegraph Journal*, October 12, 1960.

34   Sharp to Pearson, November 29, 1962. LAC. *Pearson Papers.* MG 26 N1, Vol. 94. Leader of Opposition files, Nuclear Policy, Part 2.

35   Pickersgill to Pearson, January 3, 1963. LAC. *Pearson Papers.* MG 26 N1, Vol. 94. Leader of Opposition files, Nuclear Policy, Part 2.

36   *Toronto Telegram*, February 20, 1961.

37   *Toronto Telegram*, May 1, 1962.

38   Campaign Promises of Liberal Party Leader Lester Pearson, April 25–June 15, 1962, by topic. June 20, 1962. USkUASC. *Diefenbaker Papers.* MG 01/VII/A/1720.

39   Department of National Defence, Debate Material. June 10, 1963. LAC. *Pearson Papers.* MG 26 N1, Vol. 164. Leader of the Opposition files.

40   Denis Smith, *Gentle Patriot*, p. 120.

41   McMahon, *Essence of Indecision*, pp. 160–61

42   Inquiry, January 20, 1963 CBCTV. LAC. *Pearson Papers.* Speeches. MG 26 N1. Vol. 23. File 1. See also Lester B. Pearson. John A. Munro, John A. and Alex I. Inglis, Alex I. (ed.) *The Memoirs of the Right Honourable Lester B. Pearson. Volume 3, 1957-1968*, p. 71.

43   Lester B. Pearson, Text of an Address by the Honourable Lester B. Pearson Delivered at a Luncheon Meeting of the York-Scarborough Liberal Association, January 12, 1963. *Pearson Papers.* Speeches. MG 26 N1. Vol. 23. File 1.

44   Ibid.

45   Ibid.

46   *Halifax Chronicle-Herald*, January 15, 1963.

47   *Globe and Mail*, January 14, 1963.

48   *Ottawa Citizen*, January 14, 1963.

49   English, *The Worldly Years*, p. 162.

50   Pearson. *Mike*. Vol. 2, p. 272.

51   Butterworth to Secretary of State, January 16, 1963. JFKLM. *NSF.* Regional Security. Box 225. File 3.

52   Memorandum from Secretary to Cabinet to Prime Minister. PERSONAL [Ottawa], Nuclear Weapons; Policy Statement. January 8, 1961. USkUASC. *Diefenbaker Papers.* MG 01/XII/F/100.

53   McMahon, *Essence of Indecision*, p. 161.

54   *Ottawa Citizen*, October 22, 1977.

## TWELVE: THE CROSSROADS

1   House of Commons, *Debates*. January 25, 1963.

2   Ibid.

3   *Globe and Mail*, January 31, 1963.

4   CTV Poll, January 27, 1963. LAC. *Harkness Papers*. Vol. 57. B 19.

5   *Winnipeg Free Press*, February 10, 1963.

6   Department of National Defence Statement by the Honourable D. S. Harkness Minister of National Defence, January 28, 1963. LAC. *Harkness Papers*. MG 32 B19, Vol. 57. B 19.

7   Newman, *Renegade in Power*, p. 368.

8   Stevenson and Ball, Telcon, August 22, 1962. JFKLM. *Ball Papers*. Box 2. File: Canada.

9   Butterworth, Pearson's Nuclear Statement, January 14, 1963. JFKLM. *POF.* Countries Files: Canada. Box 18.

10  Robinson, *Diefenbaker's World*, p. 304.

11  Ibid., p. 305.

12  Butterworth to State Department, February 13, 1963. JFKLM. *POF.* Countries Files: Canada. Box 113.

13  Stursberg, *Lester Pearson and the American Dilemma*, p. 184.

14  Butterworth to Rusk, January 27, 1963. JFKLM. *NSF.* Countries Files: Canada. Box 18.

15  Tyler to Ball, Telcon, January 29, 1963. JFKLM. *Ball Papers*. Box 2. File: Canada.

16  Ball to Bundy, Telcon, January 30, 1963. JFKLM. *Ball Papers*. Box 2. File: Canada.

17  Martin, *The Presidents and the Prime Ministers*, p. 203.

18  Bundy to Ball, Telcon, January 31. 1963. JFKLM. *Ball Papers.* Box 2. File: Canada.

19  Ibid.

20  Department of State for the Press, No. 59. June 10, 1963. JFKLM. *NSF–Regional Security.* Box 225. File 2.

21  Cabinet Conclusions, January 31, 1963. LAC. *PCO.* RG2.

22  House of Commons, *Debates.* January 31, 1963.

23  Ibid.

24  Ibid.

25  Ibid.

26  Ibid.

27  *Globe and Mail,* February 1, 1963.

28  *Edmonton Journal,* January 30, 1963.

29  *Peterborough Examiner,* February 2, 1963.

30  *Sudbury Star,* February 2, 1963.

31  *Washington Daily News,* February 25, 1963.

32  *New York Times,* February 1, 1963.

33  Kennedy and Ball, Telcon, January 31, 1963. JFKLM. *Ball Papers.* Box 2. File: Canada.

34  Ibid.

35  Ibid.

36  Nash, *Kennedy and Diefenbaker,* pp. 252–53.

37  *Winnipeg Free Press,* February 2, 1963.

38  Smith, *Rogue Tory,* p. 478.

39  Stursberg, *Leadership Lost, 1962–1967,* p. 122.

40  Fleming, *So Very Near.* Vol. 1, pp. 597–601. See also Patrick Nicholson, *Vision and Indecision,* pp. 230–36.

41  House of Commons, *Debates.* February 4, 1963.

42  Ibid.

43  Ibid.

44  Ghent, *"Canada, the United States, and the Cuban Missile Crisis."* 161.

45  Smith, *Rogue Tory,* p. 483.

46  Martin, *The Presidents and the Prime Ministers,* p. 203.

47  Butterworth to Department of State #445, February 5, 1963. JFKLM. *FRUS 1961–1963;* XIII 1196–1199.

48  Bundy to Johnson, May 1, 1964. Cited in Martin, *The Presidents and the Prime Ministers,* p. 203.

49  Newman, *Renegade in Power,* pp. 379–81.

50  Bradlee, *Conversations with Kennedy,* pp. 165–66, 170–74.

51   Dwight Martin, "Canada's Diefenbaker: Decline and Fall," *Newsweek*, February 18, 1963.

52   Ibid.

53   Diefenbaker, *One Canada*. Vol. 3, pp. 178–79.

54   *Toronto Telegram*, May 21, 1963.

55   Ibid.

56   Diefenbaker, *One Canada*. Vol. 3, p. 107.

57   Newman, *Renegade in Power*, p. 384.

58   John Diefenbaker, February 19, 1963. Address to the Annual Meeting of the Progressive Conservative Association of Ontario, Toronto. USkUASC. *Diefenbaker Papers*. MG XIVE222/1968/10.

59   *Globe and Mail*, March 23, 1963.

60   Robinson, *Diefenbaker's World*, p. 309.

61   Peterson to Secretary of State, March 4, 1963. JFKLM. *NSF*. Countries Files: Canada. Box 18A. File 1.

62   Smith to Secretary of State, March 13, 1963. JFKLM. *NSF*. Countries Files: Canada. Box 18A. File 1.

63   Ibid.

64   *Toronto Star*, April 2, 1963.

65   *Miami Herald*, March 25, 1963.

66   *Miami Herald*, March 26, 1963.

67   Lubell to Bundy, May 4, 1963. JFKLM. *NSF*. Countries Files: Canada. Box 18A. File 4.

68   Bundy to Battle, July 15. 1963. JFKLM. *NSF*. Countries Files: Canada. Box 19. File 1.

69   Butterworth to Secretary of State, February 20, 1963. JFKLM. *NSF*. Countries Files: Canada. Box 18A. File 1.

70   Ibid.

71   John G. Diefenbaker, Excerpt from Election Speech by Prime Minister Diefenbaker at Vineland, Ontario, March 6, 1963. LAC. *Green Papers*. MG XXX1/E-83/9/3.

72   English, *The Worldly Years*, p. 262. See also Smith, *Rogue Tory*, pp. 499–504.

73   English, *The Worldly Years*, p. 251.

74   Nash, *Kennedy and Diefenbaker*, pp. 255–56.

75   A. B. McKillop, *Pierre Berton*, p. 418.

76   English, *The Worldly Years*, p.238.

77   Ibid., p. 262.

78   Nash, *Kennedy and Diefenbaker*, p. 278.

79   Butterworth to Secretary of State, March 11, 1963. JFKLM. *NSF*. Countries Files: Canada. Box 18A. File 1.

80   Report to Secretary of State, March 21, 1963. JFKLM. *NSF.* Countries Files: Canada. Box 18A. File 1.

81   Ibid.

82   Canadian Embassy to External Affairs, Verbatim Extract from Transcript of Hearing During Secretary McNamara's Appearance February 6 Before Subcommittee of Committee on Appropriations of House of Representatives, March 29, 1963. LAC. *Green Papers.* MG 31. E-83. Vol. 9.

83   Ibid.

84   Kennedy to McNamara, April 2, 1963. JFKLM. *NSF.* Countries Files: Canada. Box 18A. File 3.

85   Butterworth to Secretary of State, April 5, 1963. JFKLM. *NSF.* Countries Files: Canada. Box 18A. File 3.

86   Smith, *Rogue Tory*, p. 504.

87   *Globe and Mail*, March 4, 1963.

88   *Toronto Telegram*, March 21, 1963.

89   English, *The Worldly Years*, p. 264.

90   Bradlee, *Conversations with Kennedy*, p. 166.

91   Nash, *Kennedy and Diefenbaker*, pp. 278–79.

92   Ibid., p. 279.

93   Bundy to Secretary of State and Secretary of Defense, April 1, 1963. JFKLM. *NSF.* Countries Files: Canada. Box 18A. File 3.

94   American Embassy in Ottawa to State Department, March 27, 1963. JFKLM. *POF.* File: Canada–Rostow memorandum.

95   *Ottawa Citizen*, March 27, 1963.

96   Kennedy and Tyler, Telcon, March 28, 1963. JFKLM. *POF.* Digital File: JFKPOF-TPH-16A-5.

97   Ibid.

98   *Montreal Gazette*, April 5, 1963. *Globe and Mail*, April 6, 1963. *New York Times*, April 8, 1963.

99   Smith, *Rogue Tory*, p. 506.

100  Martin, *The Presidents and the Prime Ministers*, pp. 209–210.

101  Bradlee, *Conversations with Kennedy*, p. 183.

102  *Montreal Star*, April 8, 1963.

103  *New York Times*, April 9, 1963.

104  *Washington Daily News*, April 23, 1963.

105  Assistant Secretary of State to Bundy, April 24, 1963. JFKLM. *NSF.* Countries Files: Canada. Box 18A. File 4.

106   *Winnipeg Free Press*, April 23, 1963.

107   *Paris-Presse*, April 9, 1963. Cited in Dyer, *Canada in the Great Power Game, 1914–2014*, p. 357.

## THIRTEEN: PEARSON AND KENNEDY

1     Pearson, *Mike*. Vol. 3, p. 83.

2     Ritchie, *Storm Signals*, p. 47.

3     *New York Times*, April 9, 1963.

4     Kennedy to Pearson, April 9, 1963. JFKLM. *NSF.* Box 19A. File: Canada.

5     Bundy Memorandum, April 18, 1963. JFKLM. *NSF.* Box 340.

6     Ibid.

7     Memorandum for Record, Meeting with the President on Canada, May 2, 1963. File: Canada JFKLM. *NSF.* Box 19A.

8     Department of State to Embassy Ottawa, May 3, 1963. File: Canada JFKLM. *NSF.* Box 19A.

9     John F. Kennedy, Welcoming Remarks to Prime Minister Pearson of Canada, at Otis Air Force Base, Falmouth, Massachusetts, May 10, 1963. JFKLM. *POF.* Digital File: JFKWHA-184-001.

10    Nash, *Kennedy and Diefenbaker*, p. 307.

11    Pearson, *Mike*. Vol. 3, p. 83.

12    Ritchie, *Storm Signals*, p. 49.

13    Pearson, *Mike*. Vol. 3, p. 112.

14    Ritchie to External Affairs, May 14, 1963. LAC. *Robinson Papers.* MG31. E31. Vol. 12.

15    Costigliola, "The Pursuit of Atlantic Community," p. 32.

16    Rostow to President, February 19, 1963. JFKLM. *POF.* Box 65.

17    Klein to Bundy, August 7, 1963. JFKLM. *NSF-Regional Security.* Box 225.

18    Victor Levant, *Quiet Complicity*, p. 47.

19    Bothwell, "The Further Shore," p. 104.

20    House of Commons, *Debates.* March 8, 1962.

21    Dallek, *An Unfinished Life*, p. 450.

22    Martin, *The Presidents and the Prime Ministers*, p. 222.

23    Bundy to Butterworth, May 21, 1963. JFKLM. *NSF.* Countries Files: Canada. Box 18A. File 5.

24    Bundy to Secretary of State, May 13, 1963. JFKLM. *NSF.* Countries Files: Canada. Box 18A. File 5.

25    Butterworth to Bundy, May 27, 1963. JFKLM. *NSF.* Countries Files: Canada. Box 18A. File 5.

26   English, *The Worldly Years*, p. 270.

27   Nash, *Kennedy and Diefenbaker*, p. 308.

28   *Ottawa Citizen*, May 13, 1963.

29   *Washington Post*, May 16, 1963.

30   Nash, *Kennedy and Diefenbaker*, p. 279.

31   Ibid., p. 280.

32   Walter L. Gordon, *Walter Gordon*, p. 138.

33   House of Commons, *Debates*. June 13, 1963.

34   House of Commons, *Debates*. June 15, 1963.

35   English, *The Worldly Years*, p. 274.

36   Harry G. Johnson, "The Ottawa-Washington Troubles," p. 26.

37   *New York Times*, June 24, 1963.

38   J. L. Granatstein, "When Push Comes to Shove: Canada and the United States," in Thomas G. Paterson (ed.), *Kennedy's Quest for Victory*, p. 101.

39   State Department to the Embassy in Canada, June 28, 1963. JFKLM. *FRUS*. Vol. 13.

40   J. L. Granatstein, "When Push Comes to Shove: Canada and the United States," in Thomas G. Paterson (ed.), *Kennedy's Quest for Victory*, p. 102.

41   Memorandom for File, June 21, 1963. LAC. *Robinson Papers*. MG31. E31. Vol. 12.

42   Ibid.

43   Ritchie, *Storm Signals*, p. 52.

44   State Department to the Embassy in Canada, June 28, 1963. JFKLM. *FRUS*. Vol. 13

45   Memorandum of Conversation, Robinson and Armstrong, June 21, 1963. JFKLM. *NSF*. Countries Files: Canada. Box 18A. File 5.

46   Klein to Bundy, June 21, 1963. JFKLM. *NSF*. Countries Files: Canada. Box 18A. File 5.

47   Pearson, *Mike*. Vol. 3, p. 107.

48   House of Commons, *Debates*. June 19, 1963.

49   *Globe and Mail*, June 21, 1963.

50   Cohen, *Lester B. Pearson*, p. 152.

51   Butterworth to Secretary of State, June 20, 1963. JFKLM. *NSF*. Countries Files: Canada. Box 18A. File 5.

52   David McClelland and Dean Acheson (eds.), *Among Friends*, p. 250.

53   Rusk and Ball, Telcon, July 19, 1963. JFKLM. *Ball Papers*. Box 2. File: Canada.

54   Bundy and Ball, Telcon, July 19, 1963. JFKLM. *Ball Papers*. Box 2. File: Canada.

55   Rusk and Ball, Telcon, July 19, 1963. JFKLM. *Ball Papers*. Box 2. File: Canada.

56   Gordon, *Walter Gordon*, p. 158.

57   Ibid., p. 159.

58   Ibid., p. 160.

59   Ibid.

60   Ball and Kaysen, Telcon, October 14, 1963. JFKLM. *Ball Papers*. Box 2. File: Canada.

61   George Ball, *The Discipline of Power*, p. 113.

62   Dimitry Anastakis, *Auto Pact*, pp. 24–25.

63   Vincent W. Bladen, *Report of the Royal Commission on the Automotive Industry*. See executive summary.

64   Dillon and Ball, Telcon, October 31, 1963. JFKLM. *Ball Papers*. Box 2. File: Canada.

65   Ball and Kaysen, Telcon, October 31, 1963. JFKLM. *Ball Papers*. Box 2. File: Canada.

66   Dillon and Ball, Telcon, November 5, 1963. JFKLM. *Ball Papers*. Box 2. File: Canada.

67   Dillon and Ball, Telcon, October 31, 1963. JFKLM. *Ball Papers*. Box 2. File: Canada.

68   Dillon and Ball, Telcon, November 5, 1963. JFKLM. *Ball Papers*. Box 2. File: Canada.

69   Roosevelt and Ball, Telcon, November 5, 1963. JFKLM. *Ball Papers*. Box 2. File: Canada.

70   Ball and Dillon, Telcon, November 5, 1963. JFKLM. *Ball Papers*. Box 2. File: Canada.

71   State Department to U.S. Embassy Ottawa, November 8, 1963. JFKLM. *NSF*. Countries File: Canada. Box 19.

72   Gary Marcuse, "Labour's Cold War," p. 200.

73   Peter Edwards, *Waterfront Warlord*, p. 9.

74   William Kaplan, *Everything That Floats*, p. 67.

75   House of Commons, *Debates*. May 2, 1963.

76   Nash, *Kennedy and Diefenbaker*, p. 311.

77   Ball and Bundy, Telcon, May 24, 1963. JFKLM. *Ball Papers*. Box 2. File: Canada.

78   T. G. Norris, *Report of an Industrial Inquiry Commission Concerning Matters Related to the Disruption of Shipping on the Great Lakes, the St. Lawrence River System and Connecting Waters*, pp. 296–99.

79   Dallek, *An Unfinished Life*, p. 483.

80   Archie Robinson, *George Meany and His Times*, p. 23.

81   General Colour on Hyannisport Meeting, May 15, 1963. LAC. *Robinson Papers*. MG31. E31. Vol. 12.

82   Pearson and Kennedy, Telcon, October 21, 1963. JFKLM. *POF*. Digital File: POFTPH-27B.

83   Wirtz and Ball, Telcon, May 24, 1963. JFKLM. *Ball Papers*. Box 2. File: Canada.

84   Kaplan, *Everything That Floats*, p. 140.

85   Robertson to Minister and Deputy Minister of Labour, October 9, 1963. LAC. *Robinson Papers*. MG31. E31. Vol. 12.

86   Wirtz to Kennedy, October 12, 1963. JFKLM. *NSF*. Countries Files: Canada. Box 19. File 6.

87 Wirtz Press Conference, October 10, 1963. JFKLM. *POF.* Digital File: JFKPOF-082-004.

88 Kennedy and Pearson, Telcon, October 12, 1963. JFKLM. *POF.* Digital File: JFKPOF-TPH-2C.

89 Edwards, *Waterfront Warlord*, p. 155.

90 Kennedy and Pearson, Telcon, October 21, 1963. JFKLM. *POF.* Digital File: JFKPOF-TPH-27B.

91 House of Commons, *Debates.* October 21, 1963.

92 *Globe and Mail*, October 22, 1963.

93 Robinson to Ritchie, October 28, 1963. LAC. *Robinson Papers.* MG31. E31. Vol. 12.

94 Pearson and Kennedy, Telcon, October 2, 1963. JFKLM. *POF.* Digital File: JFKPOF-TPH-27C.

95 Memorandum to the President: Re the Canadian Maritime Situation, November 5, 1963. JFKLM. *NSF.* Countries File: Canada. Box 19.

96 McKillop, *Pierre Berton*, p. 421.

# FOURTEEN: MYTHS, MOURNING, AND THE ROAD TAKEN

1 John F. Kennedy, "Commencement Address at American University, Washington, D.C.," June 10, 1963. JFKLM. *Kennedy Papers. POF.* Digital File: JFKPOF-045-002.

2 Ibid.

3 Kennedy to Pearson, August 2, 1963. JFKLM. *Kennedy Papers. NSF.* Countries File: Canada. Box 20. File 6.

4 John F. Kennedy, "Radio and Television Report to the American People on Civil Rights," June 11, 1963. JFKLM. *Kennedy Papers. POF.* Digital File: JFKPOF-045-005.

5 Thurston Clarke, *JFK's Last Hundred Days*, p. 9.

6 Bothwell, "The Further Shore," p. 105.

7 Christine Bragg, *Vietnam, Korea and US Foreign Policy 1945–75*, p. 1.

8 Clarke, *JFK's Last Hundred Days*, p. 17.

9 Ibid.

10 John F. Kennedy, "Speech to Fort Worth Chamber of Commerce," November 22, 1963. JFKLM. *Kennedy Papers. POF.* Digital File: JFKPOF-048-021.

11 Ibid.

12. Clarke, *JFK's Last Hundred Days*, p. 340.

13 Bob Schieffer, "JFK's back brace may have cost him his life, doctor says." CBS News, November 19, 2013. www.cbsnews.com/news/jfks-backbrace-may-have-cost-him-his-life-doctor-says/, March 19, 2014.

14    James S. Wolfe, *The Kennedy Myth*, p. 237.

15    Clarke, *JFK's Last Hundred Days*, pp. 349–51.

16    Edward P. Comentale, Stephen Watt, and Skip Willman, (eds.), *Ian Fleming and James Bond*, p. 177

17    Paul Simpson (ed.), *The Rough Guide to James Bond*, p. 243.

18    Penelope Rowlands, *The Beatles Are Here!*, p. 7.

19    Dallek, *An Unfinished Life*, p. 637.

20    Clarke, *JFK's Last Hundred Days*, p. 275.

21    Ibid.

22    Ibid., p. 636.

23    George Radwanski, *Trudeau*, p. 115.

24    Clint Hill and Lisa McCubbin, *Mrs. Kennedy and Me*, p. 302.

25    Ritchie to External Affairs, November 27, 1963. LAC. *Robinson Papers*. MG31. E31. Vol. 12.

26    Ibid.

27    Rusk to Johnson, "Western Europe and Canada," December 12, 1963. JFKLM. *FRUS*, 1961–1963. Vol. XIII. Document 455.

28    Lester B. Pearson, "Good Neighborhood," p. 158.

29    Greg Donaghy, *Tolerant Allies*, p. 126.

30    English, *The Worldly Years*, p. 357.

31    Roger Frank Swanson, (ed.), *Canadian-American Summit Diplomacy, 1923–1973*, p. 234.

32    John Clearwater, *American Nuclear Weapons in Canada*, p. 25.

33    Johnson to Pearson, March 14, 1964. LAC. *Pearson Papers*. R7581-14-9-E. Vol. 322.

34    Hellyer to Chiefs of Staff, March 16, 1964. Cited in Clearwater, *American Nuclear Weapons in Canada*, p. 26.

35    Clearwater, *American Nuclear Weapons in Canada*, p. 26.

36    Anastakis, *Auto Pact*, p. 60.

37    Brubeck to the President, November 19, 1963. JFKLM. *Brubeck Papers*. Box 381. File 11.

38    Robertson to Kent and Dier, January 27, 1964. LAC. *Robinson Papers*. MG31. E31. Vol. 12.

39    Canadian Auto Parts, August 31, 1964. JFKLM. *Dillon Papers*. Box 22C.

40    Donaghy, *Tolerant Allies*, p. 37–67.

41    Gordon, *Walter Gordon*, p. 169.

42    Ibid.

43   Pearson, *Mike*. Vol. 3, 138.

44   Costas Melakopides, *Pragmatic Idealism*, p. 71.

45   Pearson, *Mike*. Vol. 3, p. 142.

46   Livingston Merchant and Arnold Heeney, *Canada and the United States*. See especially the executive summary and Recommendations 54 and 55.

47   Ibid.

48   Steven Kendall Holloway, *Canadian Foreign Policy*, p. 146.

49   George Grant, *Lament for a Nation*, p. 7.

50   Ibid., p. 12.

51   Stephen Azzi, *Walter Gordon and the Rise of Canadian Nationalism*, p. 88.

52   Norman Hillmer (ed.), *Pearson*, p. 104.

53   Grant, *Lament for a Nation*, p. 17.

54   *Globe and Mail*, September 1, 2007.

# B I B L I O G R A P H Y

---

## ARCHIVAL SOURCES

### LIBRARY AND ARCHIVES CANADA–OTTAWA (LAC)

Arnold Heeney Papers

Department of External Affairs Papers (DEA)

Donald Fleming Papers

Douglas S. Harkness Papers

George Pearkes Papers

Gladstone Murray Papers

H. Basil Robinson Papers

House of Commons Debates

Howard Green Papers

John Diefenbaker Papers

Lester Pearson Papers

Louis St. Laurent Papers

Privy Council Office fonds (PCO)

Robert B. Bryce Papers

Tom Kent Papers

### JOHN F. KENNEDY LIBRARY AND MUSEUM–BOSTON (JFKLM)

Dean Rusk Papers

Douglas Dillon Papers

Foreign Relations United States Files (FRUS)

George Ball Papers

John K. Galbraith Papers

John F. Kennedy Papers

   National Security Files (NSF)

   Pre-Presidential Papers (PPP)

   President's Office Files (POF)

McGeorge Bundy Papers

Robert McNamara Papers

William H. Brubeck Papers

UNIVERSITY OF SASKATCHEWAN, UNIVERSITY ARCHIVES & SPECIAL COLLECTIONS SASKATOON (USKUASC)

Diefenbaker Papers

## NEWSPAPERS AND MAGAZINES

*Atlantic*

*Boston Globe*

*Globe and Mail*

*Guelph Mercury*

*Halifax Chronicle-Herald*

*Life*

*Maclean's*

*Montreal Gazette*

*Montreal Star*

*New York Times*

*New York Herald*

*Ottawa Citizen*

*Peterborough Examiner*

*Saturday Evening Post*

*Saturday Review*

*Star Phoenix*

*Toronto Star*

*Washington Post*

*Winnipeg Free Press*

## SECONDARY SOURCES

Anastakis, Dimitry. *Auto Pact: Creating a Borderless North American Auto Industry, 1960–1971*. Toronto: University of Toronto Press, 2005.

Axworthy, Thomas S. "An Independent Canada in a Shared North America: Must We Be in Love or Will an Arranged Marriage Do?" *International Journal* 59, no. 4 (Autumn2004): 761–82.

Azzi, Stephen. *Walter Gordon and the Rise of Canadian Nationalism*. Kingston-Montreal: McGill-Queen's University Press, 1999.

Ball, George. *The Discipline of Power: Essentials of a Modern World Structure*. London: Bodley Head, 1968.

Baxter, R.R. *Documents on the St. Lawrence Seaway: A Selection of Documents.* London: Stevens and Sons, 1960.

Beigie, Carl E. *The Canadian-U.S. Automotive Agreement: An Evaluation.* Washington: National Planning Association, 1970.

Berding, Andrew H. *Dulles on Diplomacy.* Princeton: D. Van Nostrand Company, Inc., 1965.

Bernstein, Barton. "The Cuban Missile Crisis: Trading the Jupiters in Turkey." *Political Science Quarterly* 95, no. 1 (Spring 1980): 97–125.

Beschloss, Michael R. *The Crisis Years: Kennedy and Khrushchev, 1960–1963.* New York: HarperCollins, 1991.

Bladen, Vincent W. *Report of the Royal Commission on the Automotive Industry.* Ottawa: Queen's Printer, 1961.

Blanchette, Arthur E. *Canadian Foreign Policy, 1945–2000: Major Documents and Speeches.* Toronto: Dundurn, 2000.

Bliss, Michael. *Northern Enterprise: Five Centuries of Canadian Business.* Toronto: McClelland & Stewart, 1987.

Bordo, Michael, Tamara Gomes, and Lawrence Schembri. "Canada and the IMF: Trailblazer or Prodigal Son?" Bank of Canada Discussion Paper 2009-1. Ottawa: Bank of Canada, 2009.

Bothwell, Robert. *Alliance and Illusion: Canada and the World, 1945–1984.* Vancouver: University of British Columbia Press, 2007

———. "The Canadian Isolationist Tradition." *International Journal* 54, no. 1 (Winter 1998–99): 76–87.

———. "The Further Shore: Canada and Vietnam." *International Journal* 56, no. 1 (Winter 2000–01): 89–114.

———. "Journey to a Small Country: Only in Canada You Say? Pity." *International Journal* 50, no. 1 (Winter 1994–95): 128–39.

Bothwell, Robert, Ian M. Drummond, and John English. *Canada Since 1945: Power, Politics and Provincialism.* Toronto: University of Toronto Press, 1989.

Bow, Brian. "Parties and Partisanship in Canadian Defence Policy." *International Journal* 64, no. 1 (Winter 2008–09): 67–88.

———. *The Politics of Linkage: Power, Interdependence, and Ideas in Canada-US Relations.* Vancouver: University of British Columbia Press, 2009.

Bow, Brian and David Black. "Does Politics Stop at the Water's Edge in Canada? Party and Partisanship in Canadian Foreign Policy." *International Journal* 64, no. 1 (Winter 2008–09), pp. 7–27.

Bradlee, Benjamin C. *Conversations with Kennedy.* New York: Pocket Books, 1975.

Bragg, Christine. *Vietnam, Korea and US Foreign Policy, 1945–75*. London: Harcourt Education, 2005.

Brecher, Irving and S.S. Reisman. *Canada-United States Economic Relations*. Ottawa: Queen's Printer for Royal Commission on Canada's Economic Prospects, 1957.

Brewster, Hugh. "Meeting Jackie: A Canadian Encounters Camelot." *Zoomer*, November 21, 2013.

Bricker, Darrell and John Ibbitson. *The Big Shift: The Seismic Change in Canadian Politics, Business, and Culture and What It Means for Our Future*. Toronto: HarperCollins Publishers Ltd., 2013.

Browne, Stephen H. *Edmund Burke and the Discourse of Virtue*. Tuscaloosa: University of Alabama Press, 1993.

Bryden, Penny E. *Planners and Politicians: Liberal Politics and Social Policy, 1957–1968*. Kingston-Montreal: McGill-Queen's University Press, 1997.

Bundy, McGeorge. *Danger and Survival: Choices About the Bomb in the First Fifty Years*. New York: Random House, 1988.

Burch, Andrew. *Give Me Shelter: The Failure of Canada's Cold War Civil Defence*. Vancouver: University of British Columbia Press, 2012.

Burke, Edmund. *Reflections on the Revolution in France, 1790*. London: J.M. Dent and Sons, 1910.

Caiden, N. "The Canadian General Election of 1962." *Australian Quarterly* 34, no. 3 (September 1962): 72–82.

Calvocoressi, Peter. *World Politics Since 1945*. London: Longman Publishing, 1991.

Campagna, Palmiro. *Storms of Controversy: The Secret Avro Arrow Files Revealed*. 4th ed. Toronto: Stoddart Publishing, 2010.

Chapnick, Adam. *Canada's Voice: The Public Life of John Wendell Holmes*. Vancouver: University of British Columbia Press, 2009.

———. "The Golden Age: A Canadian Foreign Policy Paradox." *International Journal* 64, no. 1 (Winter 2008–09): 205–21.

———. "The Middle Power." *Canadian Foreign Policy* 7, no. 2 (Winter 1999): 73–82.

———. *The Middle Power Project: Canada and the Founding of the United Nations*. Vancouver: University of British Columbia Press, 2005.

Clark, Joe. *How We Lead: Canada in a Century of Change*. Toronto: Random House Canada, 2013.

Clarke, Thurston. *JFK's Last Hundred Days: The Transformation of the Man and the Emergence of a Great President*. New York: Penguin Group, 2013.

Clearwater, John. *American Nuclear Weapons in Canada*. Toronto: Dundurn Press, 1999.

Cohen, Andrew. *Lester B. Pearson*. Toronto: Penguin Group, 2008.

————. *While Canada Slept: How We Lost Our Place in the World*. Toronto: McClelland &Stewart, 2003.

Collier, Peter and David Horowitz. *The Kennedys: The American Drama*. New York: Summit Books, 1984.

Comentale, Edward P., Stephen Watt, and Skip Willman, eds. *Ian Fleming and James Bond: The Cultural Politics of 007*. Bloomington: Indiana University Press, 2005.

Committee on Foreign Relations. *St. Lawrence Seaway Manual: A Compilation of Documents on the Great Lakes Seaway Project and Correlated Power Development*. 83rd Congress, 2nd Session, Senate Document 165. Washington, DC: United States Printing Office, 1955.

Cook, Ramsay. "Policy and the Election: An Uncertain Trumpet" *International Journal*, Vol. 18, No. 3 (Summer, 1963), pp. 374-380.

Coombes, Howard G. and Richard Goett. "Supporting the Pax Americana: Canada's Military in the Cold War." In *Perspectives on the Canadian Way of War, Serving the National Interest*, edited by Lieutenant Colonel Bernd Horn, 265–96. Toronto: Dundurn Press, 2006.

Cooper, Andrew. *Canadian Foreign Policy: Old Habits and New Directions*. Scarborough, ON: Prentice-Hall Allyn and Bacon Canada, 1997.

Costigliola, Frank. "The Pursuit of Atlantic Community: Nuclear Arms, Dollars, and Berlin." In *Kennedy's Quest for Victory: American Foreign Policy, 1961–1963*, edited by Thomas G. Paterson, 24–56. New York: Oxford University Press, 1989.

Creighton, Donald. *John A. Macdonald: The Old Chieftain*. Toronto: The Macmillan Company of Canada, 1952.

————. *John A. Macdonald: The Young Politician*. Toronto: The Macmillan Company of Canada, 1952.

Dallek, Robert. *Flawed Giant: Lyndon Johnson and His Times, 1961–1973*. New York: Oxford University Press, 1998.

————. *An Unfinished Life: John F. Kennedy, 1917–1963*. Boston: Little, Brown and Company, 2003.

Dart, Ron. *The Red Tory Tradition: Ancient Roots, New Routes*. Dewdney, BC: Synaxis Press, 1999.

Dempson, Peter. *Assignment Ottawa: Seventeen Years in the Press Gallery*. Toronto: University of Toronto Press, 1968.

DeVolpi, A., Vladimir E. Minkov, Vadim A. Simonenko, and George S. Stanford. *Nuclear Shadowboxing: Cold War Redux, Volume 1*. Kalamazoo, MI: Fidlar Doubleday, 2004.

Dickey, John Sloan. "The Relationship in Rhetoric and Reality: Merchant-Henney Revisited." *International Journal* 27, no. 2 (Spring 1972): 172–84.

Diebold, William. "Canada and the United States: Twenty-Five Years of Economic Relations." *International Journal* 39, no. 2 (Spring 1984): 389–409.

Diefenbaker, John G. *One Canada—Memoirs of the Right Honourable John G. Diefenbaker: The Crusading Years, 1895 to 1956.* Toronto: Macmillan of Canada, 1975.

———. *One Canada—Memoirs of the Right Honourable John G. Diefenbaker: The Tumultuous Years, 1962 to 1967.* Toronto: Macmillan of Canada, 1977.

———. *One Canada—Memoirs of the Right Honourable John G. Diefenbaker: The Years of Achievement, 1956 to 1962.* Toronto: Macmillan of Canada, 1976.

Dinerstein, Herbert S. *The Making of a Missile Crisis: October 1962.* Baltimore: Johns Hopkins University Press, 1976.

Divine, Robert A. *The Cuban Missile Crisis.* Chicago: Quadrangle, 1971.

Dobbs, Michael. *One Minute to Midnight: Kennedy, Khrushchev, and Castro on the Brink of Nuclear War.* New York: Alfred A. Knopf, 2008.

Dobell, P.C. "A Matter of Balance." *International Journal* 28, no. 4 (Spring 1973): 315–24.

———. "Negotiating with the United States." *International Journal* 36, no. 1 (Winter 1980–81): 185–207.

Donaghy, Greg, ed. *Canada and the Early Cold War, 1943–1957.* Ottawa: Department of Foreign Affairs and International Trade, 1998.

———. "A Continental Philosophy: Canada, the United States and the Negotiation of the Auto Pact, 1963–1965." *International Journal* 53, no. 3 (Summer 1998): 441–64.

———. *Tolerant Allies: Canada and the United States, 1963–1968.* Kingston-Montreal: McGill-Queen's University Press, 2002.

Donaghy, Greg and Michael Stevenson. "The Limits of Alliance: Solidarity and Canadian Wheat Exports to China, 1950–1963." *Agricultural History* 83, no. 1 (Winter 2009): 29–50.

Dosman, Edgar. "Canada-Cuba Relations: The Other Good Neighbor Policy." *Journal of Interamerican Studies and World Affairs* 41, no. 1 (Spring 1999): 109–12.

Dyer, Gwynne. *Canada in the Great Power Game, 1914–2014.* Toronto: Random House. 2014.

Duffy, John, *Fights of Our Lives.* Toronto: Harper Collins, 2002.

Eayrs, James. "Defining A New Place for Canada in the Hierarchy of World Power." *International Perspectives* (May/June 1975): 15–24.

———. *In Defence of Canada, Volume 1.* Toronto: University of Toronto Press, 1964.

Edmond, C.M.G., et al. *Royal Commission on Canada's Economic Prospects: Preliminary Report, December 1956.* Hull: Queen's Printer, 1956.

Edwards, Peter. *Waterfront Warlord. The Life and Violent Times of Hal C. Banks.* Toronto: Key Porter Books, 1987.

Eisenhower, Dwight D. *Eisenhower Diaries.* Edited by Robert H. Ferrell. New York: W.W. Norton and Company, 1981.

Eisenhower, Dwight D. *Waging Peace, 1956–1961*. New York: Doubleday, 1965.

Eisenhower, Dwight D. *Eisenhower Papers. Public Papers of the Presidents of the United States, 1953. Containing the Public Messages, Speeches, and Statements of the President January 20 to December 31, 1953*. Washington: Office of the Federal Register National Archives and Records Service, 1960.

English, John. *Shadow of Heaven, Volume One: The Life of Lester Pearson, 1897–1948*. Toronto: Lester & Orpen Dennys, 1989.

———. *The Worldly Years: The Life of Lester Pearson 1949–1972*. Toronto: Alfred A. Knopf Canada, 1992.

Fairclough, Ellen Louks. *Saturday's Child: Memoirs of Canada's First Female Cabinet Minister*. Toronto: University of Toronto Press, 1995.

Fetzer, James, "Clinging to Containment: China Policy," In *Kennedy's Quest for Victory: American Foreign Policy, 1961–1963*, edited by Thomas G. Paterson, 178–97. New York: Oxford University Press, 1989.

Fleming, Donald M. *So Very Near: The Political Memoirs of the Honourable Donald M. Fleming, Volume 1: The Rising Years*. Toronto: McClelland & Stewart, 1985.

Frankel, Max. *High Noon in the Cold War: Kennedy, Khrushchev, and the Cuban Missile Crisis*. New York: Ballantine Books, 2004.

Freedman, Lawrence. *Kennedy's Wars: Berlin, Cuba, Laos, and Vietnam*. New York: Oxford University Press, 2000.

Friesen, Gerald. *Citizens and Nation: An Essay on History, Communications and Canada*, Toronto: University of Toronto Press, 2000.

Fergusson, James G. *Canada and Ballistic Missile Defence, 1954–2009: Déjà Vu All Over Again*. Seattle: University of Washington Press, 2010.

Gardner, Lloyd C. and Ted Gittinger, eds. *The Search for Peace in Vietnam, 1964–1968*. College Station: Texas A&M University Press, 2004.

Garrity, Patrick J. "Warnings of a Parting Friend." *The National Interest* 45 (Fall 1996): 14–26.

George, Alice L. *Awaiting Armageddon: How Americans Faced the Cuban Missile Crisis*. Chapel Hill: University of North Carolina Press, 2003.

———. *The Cuban Missile Crisis: The Threshold of Nuclear War*. New York: Routledge, 2014.

Ghent, Jocelyn Maynard. "Canada, the United States and the Cuban Missile Crisis." *Pacific Historical Review* 48, no. 2 (May 1979): 159–84.

———. "Did He Fall or Was He Pushed? The Kennedy Administration and the Collapse of the Diefenbaker Government." *International History Review* 1, no. 2 (April 1979): 246–70.

Glazov, Jamie. *Canadian Policy toward Khrushchev's Soviet Union*. Kingston-Montreal: McGill-Queen's University Press, 2002.

Gleijeses, Piero. *Conflicting Missions: Havana, Washington and Africa, 1959–1976.* Chapel Hill: University of North Carolina Press, 2002.

Goduti, Phillip A. *Robert F. Kennedy and the Shaping of Civil Rights, 1960–1964.* Jefferson. NC: McFarland and Company, 2012.

Gordon, Walter L. *Walter Gordon: A Political Memoir.* Toronto: McClelland & Stewart, 1977.

Granatstein, Jack. "The Anglocentrism of Canadian Diplomacy." In *Canadian Culture: International Dimensions*, edited by Andrew Fenton Cooper. Waterloo: Centre on Foreign and Federalism, 1985.

———. *Canada, 1957–1967: The Years of Uncertainty and Innovation.* Toronto: McClelland & Stewart, 1986.

———. *How Britain's Weakness Forced Canada into the Arms of the Americans: The 1988 Joanne Goodman Lectures.* Toronto: University of Toronto Press, 1989.

———. "When Push Came to Shove: Canada and the United States." In *Kennedy's Quest for Victory: American Foreign Policy, 1961–1963*, edited by Thomas G. Paterson, 86–104. New York: Oxford University Press, 1989.

Grant, George. *Lament for a Nation. The Defeat of Canadian Nationalism.* Kingston-Montreal: McGill-Queen's University Press, 2005.

Groves, Leslie R. *Now It Can Be Told: The Story of the Manhattan Project.* New York: Harper and Brothers, 1962.

Guhin, Michael A. *John Foster Dulles: A Statesman and His Times.* New York: Columbia University Press, 1972.

Gwyn, Richard. *The Man Who Made Us: The Life and Times of John A. Macdonald.* Toronto: Random House, 2009.

Halberstam, David. *The Best and the Brightest.* New York: Random House, 1972.

Hamilton, Nigel. *JFK: Reckless Youth.* New York: Random House, 1995.

Hart, Michael. *A Trading Nation: Canadian Trade Policy from Colonialism to Globalism.* Vancouver: University of British Columbia Press, 2002.

Haydon, Peter. "Canadian Involvement in the Cuban Missile Crisis Reconsidered." *Northern Mariner/Le marin du nord* XVII, no. 2 (April 2007): 39–65.

———. *The 1962 Cuban Missile Crisis: Canada's Involvement Reconsidered.* Toronto: Canadian Institute of International Studies, 1993.

Head, Ivan and Pierre Trudeau. *The Canadian Way: Shaping Canada's Foreign Policy, 1968–1984.* Toronto: McClelland & Stewart, 1995.

Healy, Paul. "The Senate's Gay Young Bachelor." *Saturday Evening Post*, June 13, 1953.

Heeney, Arnold. *The Things That Are Caesar's: Memoirs of a Canadian Public Servant.* Toronto: University of Toronto Press, 1972.

Hellyer, Paul. *Damn the Torpedos: My Fight to Unify Canada's Armed Forces.* Toronto: McClelland & Stewart, 1990.

Hersh, Seymour M. *The Dark Side of Camelot.* Boston: Little, Brown and Company, 1997.

Hershberg, James. G. "Before the Missiles of October: Did Kennedy Plan a Military Strike against Cuba?" In *The Cuban Missile Crisis Revisited*, edited by James A. Nathan, 237–80. New York: St. Martin's, 1992.

Hill, Clint and Lisa McCubbin. *Mrs. Kennedy and Me: An Intimate Memoir.* New York: Simon and Schuster, 2012.

Hilliker, John. *Canada's Department of Foreign Affairs, Volume 1.* Kingston-Montreal: McGill-Queen's University Press, 1990.

———. "The Politicians and the 'Personalities': The Diefenbaker Government and the Conduct of Canadian External Relations." Historical Papers/Communications historiques, Volume 19, Number 1, 1984, 151–67.

Hillmer, Norman, ed. *Pearson: The Unlikely Gladiator.* Kingston-Montreal: McGill-Queen's University Press, 1999.

———. "Reflections on the Unequal Border." *International Journal* 60, no. 2 (Spring 2005): 331–40.

Hillmer, Norman and Adam Chapnick. "Introduction: An Abundance of Nationalisms." In *Canadas of the Mind: The Making and Unmaking of Canadian Nationalisms in the Twentieth Century.* Edited by Norman Hillmer and Adam Chapnick, 3–14. Kingston-Montreal: McGill-Queen's University Press, 2007.

Hillmer, Norman and Jack Granastein. *Empire to Umpire.* Toronto: Copp Clark Longman, 1994.

Holloway, Steven Kendall. *Canadian Foreign Policy: Defining the National Interest.* Toronto: University of Toronto Press, 2009.

Holmes, John W. "Canada in Search of Its Role." *Foreign Affairs* 41, no. 4 (July 1963: 659–72.

———. *Life with Uncle: The Canadian-American Relationship.* Toronto: University of Toronto Press, 1981.

———. "The Unquiet Diplomat: Lester B. Pearson." *International Journal* 62, no. 2 (Spring 2007): 289–309.

Horne, Alistair. *Harold Macmillan, Volume 2.* New York: Viking Press, 1989.

House, Jonathan M. *A Military History of the Cold War, 1944–1962.* Norman: University of Oklahoma Press, 2012.

Ignatieff, George. *The Making of a Peacemonger: The Memoirs of George Ignatieff.* Toronto: University of Toronto Press, 1985.

Jeanes, Ike. *Forecast and Solution: Grappling with the Nuclear—A Trilogy for Everyone.* Blacksburg, VA: Pocahontas Press, 1996.

Jockel, Joseph T. *Canada in NORAD, 1957–2007: A History*. Kingston-Montreal: McGill-Queen's University Press, 2007.

———. *No Boundaries Upstairs: Canada, the United States and the Origins of North American Air Defence, 1945–1958*. Vancouver: University of British Columbia Press, 1987.

Johnson, Harry G. "The Ottawa-Washington Troubles." *Challenge* 12, no. 9 (June 1964): 25–7.

Johnson, Paul. "The Myth of American Isolationism." *Foreign Policy* 74, no. 3 (May/June 1995): 159–64.

Kalser, David. *American Tragedy: Kennedy, Johnson and the Origins of the Vietnam War*. Cambridge, MA: Harvard University Press, 2000.

Kaplan, William. *Everything That Floats: Pat Sullivan, Hal Banks, and the Seamen's Unions of Canada*. Toronto: University of Toronto Press, 1987.

Keirstead, B.S. *Canada and World Affairs: September 1951 to October 1953*. Toronto: Oxford University Press, 1956.

Kempe, Frederick. *Berlin 1961: Kennedy, Khrushchev, and the Most Dangerous Place on Earth*. New York, Putnam and Sons, 2011.

Kennan, George. "The Success of Soviet Conduct." *Foreign Affairs* 25, no. 4 (July 1949): 566–82.

Khan, Rais A. "Canada: An Emerging World Leader." *Pakistan Horizon* 22, no. 4 (Fourth Quarter 1969): 308–20.

John F. Kennedy. "The Terrain of Today's Statecraft." *Saturday Review*, August 1, 1959.

———. *Profiles in Courage*. Memorial Edition. New York: Harper and Row, 1968.

———. *Why England Slept*. New York: Wilfred Funk, Inc., 1961.

Kirk, John M. and Peter McKenna. *Canada-Cuba Relations: The Other Good Neighbor Policy*. Gainsville: Florida University Press, 1997.

Kissinger, Henry. *White House Years*. New York: Little Brown and Company, 1979.

Lavin, Franklin L. "Isolationism and U.S. Foreign Policy." *The Brown Journal of World Affairs* 3, no. 1 (Winter/Spring 1996): 271–77.

Lennox, Patrick. *At Home and Abroad: The Canada-US Relationship and Canada's Place in the World*. Vancouver: University of British Columbia Press, 2009.

Lettner, Howard, H. "Foreign Policy Decision Making: The Case of Canada and Nuclear Weapons." *World Politics* 29, no. 1 (October 1976): 29–66.

Levant, Victor. *Quiet Complicity: Canada's Involvement in the Vietnam War*. Toronto: Between the Lines, 1986.

Lindley-French, Julian and Neil Macfarlane. *The North Atlantic Treaty Organization: The Enduring Alliance*. New York: Routledge, 2007.

Locker, Anne and Christian Nuenlist. "Reinventing NATO: Canada and the Multilateralization of Détente, 1962–1966." *International Journal* 58, no. 2 (Spring 2003): 283–302.

Luxenberg, Alan. "Did Eisenhower Push Castro into the Arms of the Soviets?" *Journal of International Studies and World Affairs* 30, no. 1 (Spring 1988): 37–71.

Lyon, Peyton V. *Canada in World Affairs, 1961–1963.* Toronto: Oxford University Press, 1968.

Macfarlane, Daniel. "Courting War over a Rubber Stamp: Canada and the 1961 Berlin Wall Crisis." *International Journal* 63, no. 3 (Summer 2008): 751–68.

MacLaren, Roy. *Commissions High: Canada in London, 1870–1971.* Kingston-Montreal: McGill-Queen's University Press, 2006.

MacLennan, Christopher. *Toward the Charter: Canadians and the Demand for a National Bill of Rights, 1929–1960.* Kingston-Montreal: McGill-Queen's University Press, 2003.

Macmillan, Harold. *At the End of the Day.* London and New York: Macmillan Press, 1973.

———. *Pointing the Way.* London and New York: Macmillan Press, 1972.

———. *Riding the Storm, 1956–1959.* London and New York: Macmillan Press, 1971.

Mahant, Edelgard and Graeme S. Mount. *Invisible and Inaudible in Washington: American Policies Toward Canada.* Vancouver: University of British Columbia Press, 1999.

Maloney, Sean. *Learning to Love the Bomb: Canada's Nuclear Weapons in the Cold War.* Washington, DC: Potomac Books, 2007.

Mann, Martin. "Plain Facts About Fall Out Shelters." *Popular Science*, December 1961, 56–60.

Marcuse, Gary. "Labour's Cold War: The Story of a Union That Was Not Purged." *Labour/Le Travail* 22 (Fall 1988): 199–210.

Marks III, Frederick W. *Power and Peace: The Diplomacy of John Foster Dulles.* Westport, CT: Praeger Press, 1993.

Martin, Lawrence. *The Presidents and the Prime Ministers—Washington and Ottawa Face to Face: The Myth of Bilateral Bliss, 1867–1982.* Toronto: Doubleday Canada, 1982.

Martin, Ralph and Ed Plaut. *Front Runner, Dark Horse.* Garden City, NY: Doubleday, 1960.

Mayer, Michael S. *The Eisenhower Years.* New York: Infobase Publishing, 2010.

McClelland, David and Dean Acheson, eds. *Among Friends: Personal Letters of Dean Acheson.* New York: Dodd Mead, 1980.

McKercher, Asa. "Dealing with Diefenbaker: Canada-US Relations 1958." *International Journal* 66, no. 4 (Autumn 2011): 1,043–60.

———. "A 'Half-Hearted Response'?: Canada and the Cuban Missile Crisis, 1962." *International History Review* 33, no. 2 (June 2011): 335–52.

———. "'The Most Serious Problem'?: Canada-US Relations and Cuba, 1962." *Cold War History* 12, no. 1 (March 2012): 69–88.

———. "Southern Exposure: Diefenbaker, Latin America, and the Organization of American States." *Canadian Historical Review* 93, no. 1 (March 2012) 57–80.

McKillop, A.B. *Pierre Berton: A Biography.* Toronto: McClelland & Stewart, 2008.

McLin, Jon B. *Canada's Changing Defence Policy, 1957–1963*. Baltimore: Johns Hopkins Press, 1967.

McIllory, Thad, *Private Letters of a Private Man: The Family Letters of John G. Diefenbaker*. Toronto: Doubleday, 1985.

McMahon, Patricia. *Essence of Indecision: Diefenbaker's Nuclear Policy, 1957–1963*. Kingston-Montreal: McGill-Queen's University Press, 2009.

Meisel, John. *The Canadian General Election of 1957*. Toronto: University of Toronto Press, 1962.

Melakopides, Costas. *Pragmatic Idealism: Canadian Foreign Policy, 1945–1995*. Kingston-Montreal: McGill-Queen's University Press, 1998.

Merchant, Livingston and Arnold Heeney. *Canada and the United States: Principles for Partnership*. Ottawa: Queen's Printer, 1965.

Miller, Merle. *Plain Speaking: An Oral Biography of Harry S. Truman*. New York: Berkley Publishing Corporation, 1973.

Minifie, James. *Peacemaker or Powedermonkey*. Toronto: McClelland & Stewart, 1960.

Molinaro, Dennis. "Calculated Diplomacy: John Diefenbaker and the Origins of Canada's Cuba Policy." In *Our Place in the Sun: Canada and Cuba in the Castro Era*, edited by Robert Anthony Wright and Lana Vylie, 75–95. Toronto: University of Toronto Press, 2009.

Morley, Morris. H. "The United States and the Global Economic Blockade of Cuba: A Study in Political Pressures on America's Allies." *Canadian Journal of Political Science* 17, no. 1 (March 1984): 25–48.

Moss, Walter. *A History of Russia, Volume 2*. London: Anthem Press, 2005.

Mulroney, Brian. *Memoirs*. Toronto: McClelland & Stewart, 2007.

Munton, Don. "Going Fission: Tales and Truths about Canada's Nuclear Weapons." *International Journal* 51, no. 3 (Summer 1996): 506–28.

———. "Myths of the Golden Age." *Canadian Foreign Policy* 12, no. 1 (Spring 2005): 175–77.

Munton, Don and David A. Welch. *The Cuban Missile Crisis: A Concise History*. New York: Oxford University Press, 2007.

Nasaw, David. *The Patriarch. The Remarkable Life and Turbulent Times of Joseph P. Kennedy*. New York: Penguin Press, 2012.

Nash, Knowlton. *Kennedy and Diefenbaker: The Feud That Helped Topple a Government* Toronto: McClelland & Stewart, 1990.

Nash, Phillip. *The Other Missiles of October: Eisenhower, Kennedy, and the Jupiters, 1957–1963*. London: University of North Carolina Press, 1997.

Nathan, James A. *Anatomy of the Cuban Missile Crisis*. Westport, CT: Greenwood Press, 2001.

Neufeld, Mark, "Hegemony and Foreign Policy Analysis: The Case of Canada as Middle Power." *Political Economy* 48 (Autumn 1995): 7–29.

Newman, Peter C. *Here Be Dragons: Telling Tales of People, Passion and Power*. Toronto: McClelland & Stewart, 2004.

———. *Renegade in Power: The Diefenbaker Years* Toronto: McClelland & Stewart, 1963.

Newton, Jim. *Eisenhower: The White House Years*. New York: Random House, 2011.

Nicholson, Patrick. *Vision and Indecision*. Don Mills, ON: Longmans, 1968.

Nixon, Richard. *RN: The Memoirs of Richard Nixon, Volume One*. New York: Warner Books, 1978.

Norris. G.T. *Report of an Industrial Inquiry Commission Concerning Matters Related to the Disruption of Shipping on the Great Lakes, the St. Lawrence River System and Connecting Waters*. Ottawa: Queen's Printer, 1963.

Nutter, John Jacob. *The CIA's Black Ops: Covert Action, Foreign Policy, and Democracy*. New York: Prometheus Books, 2000.

Nye, Joseph S. Jr. "Transnational Relations and Interstate Conflicts: An Empirical Analysis." *International Organization* 28, no. 4 (Autumn 1974): 961–96.

O'Donnell, Kenneth P. and David R. Powers with Joe McCarthy. *Johnny We Hardly Knew Ye: Memories of John Fitzgerald Kennedy*. New York: Little Brown & Company, 1972.

Ogelsby, J.C.M. "Canada and the Pan American Union: Twenty Years On." *International Journal* 24, no. 3 (Summer 1969): 571–89.

Parmet, Herbert S. "The Kennedy Myth and American Politics." *History Teacher* 24, no. 1 (November 1990): 31-39.

Thomas Paterson, "Introduction: John F. Kennedy's Quest for Victory and Global Crisis," in *Kennedy's Quest for Victory: American Foreign Policy, 1961-1963*, edited by Thomas Paterson, 3–23. New York: Oxford University Press, 1989.

———— "Fixation with Cuba: The Bay of Pigs, Missile Crisis, and Covert War Against Fidel Castro." In *Kennedy's Quest for Victory: American Foreign Policy, 1961-1963*, edited by Thomas Paterson, 123–55. New York: Oxford University Press, 1989.

Pearson, Geoffrey A.H. *Seize the Day: Lester B. Pearson and Crisis Diplomacy*. Ottawa: Carleton University Press, 1993.

Pearson, Lester B. "Good Neighborhood. "*Foreign Affairs* 43, no. 2 (January 1965): 151–61.

———. *Mike: The Memoirs of the Right Honourable Lester B. Pearson, Volume 1, 1897–1948*. Toronto: University of Toronto Press, 1972.

———. *Mike: The Memoirs of the Right Honourable Lester B. Pearson, Volume 2, 1948–1957*. Toronto: University of Toronto Press, 1973.

Pearson, Lester B., John A. Munro, and Alex I. Inglis, ed. *Mike. The Memoirs of the Right Honourable Lester B. Pearson, Volume 3, 1957–1968*. Toronto: University of Toronto Press, 1975.

Perras, Galen Roger. *Franklin Roosevelt and the Origins of the Canadian-American Security Alliance, 1933-1945: Necessary, But Not Necessary Enough*. Westport, CT: Greenwood Press, 1998.

Plokhy, S.M. *Yalta: The Price of Peace*. New York: Viking Press, 2010.

Polmar, Norman. *DEFCON-2: Standing on the Brink of Nuclear War During the Cuban Missile Crisis*. Hoboken, NJ: Wiley, 2006.

Powaski, Ronald E. *March to Armageddon: The United States and the Nuclear Arms Race, 1939 to the Present*. New York: Oxford University Press, 1987.

Preble, Christopher A. *John F. Kennedy and the Missile Gap*. DeKalb: Northern Illinois University Press, 2004.

———. "Who Ever Believed the Missile Gap?: John F. Kennedy and the Politics of National Security." *Presidential Studies Quarterly* 33, no. 4 (December 2003): 801–26.

Press, Daryl G. *Calculating Credibility: How Leaders Assess Military Threats*. London: Cornell University Press, 2005.

Radwanski, George. *Trudeau*. Toronto: Macmillan of Canada, 1978.

Rafferty, Kirsten. "An Internationalist Reinterpretation of Cold War Alliance Systems: Insights for Alliance Theory." *Canadian Journal of Political Science* 36, no. 2 (June 2003): 341–62.

Reeves, Richard. *President Kennedy: Profile of Power*. New York: Simon & Schuster, 1993.

Regehr, Ernie. *Arms Canada: The Deadly Business of Military Exports*. Toronto: James Lorimer and Company, 1987.

Regenstreif, Peter. *The Diefenbaker Interlude: Parties and Voting in Canada*. Don Mills, ON: Longmans, 1965.

Reid, Escott. *Radical Mandarin: The Memoirs of Escott Reid*. Toronto: University of Toronto Press, 1989.

Ritcher, Andrew. *Avoiding Armageddon: Canadian Military Strategy and Nuclear Weapons, 1950–63*. Vancouver: University of British Columbia Press, 2002.

Ritchie, Charles. *Storm Signals: More Undiplomatic Diaries, 1962–1971*. Toronto: Macmillan of Canada, 1983.

Robinson, Archie. *George Meany and His Times: A Biography*. New York: Simon and Schuster, 1981.

Robinson, H. Basil. *Diefenbaker's World: A Populist in Foreign Affairs*. Toronto: University of Toronto Press, 1989.

Rochlin, James Francis. *Discovering the Americas: The Evolution of Canadian Foreign Policy Toward Latin America*. Vancouver: University of British Columbia Press, 1994.

Rose, Lisle Abbot, *Power at Sea, A Violent Peace, 1946–2006*. Columbia: University of Missouri Press, 2007.

Rowlands, Penelope. *The Beatles Are Here!: 50 Years after the Band Arrived in America, Writers, Musicians and other Fans Remember*. New York: Workman Publishing, 2014.

Rubin, Gretchen. *Forty Ways to Look at JFK*. New York: Ballantine Books, 2005.

Savranskaya, Svetlana. "New Sources on the Role of Soviet Submarines in the Cuban Missile Crisis." *Journal of Strategic Studies* 28, no. 2 (April 2005): 233–59.

Schieffer, Bob, "JFK's back brace may have cost him his life, doctor says." *CBS News*, November 19, 2013. www.cbsnews.com/news/jfks-backbrace-may-have-cost-him-his-life-doctor-says/, March 19, 2014.

Schoenbaum, Thomas J. *Waging Peace and War: Dean Rusk in the Truman, Kennedy and Johnson Years.* New York: Simon and Schuster, 1988.

Schuyler, George, W. "Perspectives on Canada and Latin America: Changing Context . . . Changing Policy?" *Journal of Interamerican Studies and World Affairs* 33, no. 1 (Spring 1991): 19–58.

Schlesinger, Arthur, Jr. "Back to the Womb? Isolationism's Renewed Threat." *Foreign Affairs* 74, no. 1 (July/August 1995): 2–8.

———. *A Thousand Days, John F. Kennedy in the White House.* Boston: Houghton Mifflin, 1965.

Sidey, Hugh. *Prelude to Leadership: The European Diary of John F. Kennedy—Summer 1945.* Washington, DC: Regnery, 1995.

Sigler, John H. and Dennis Goresky. "Public Opinion on United States-Canadian Relations." *International Organization* 28, no. 4 (Autumn 1974): 637–68.

Simpson, Paul, ed. *The Rough Guide to James Bond.* London: Penguin Books, 2002.

Sorensen, Theodore. *Kennedy.* New York: Bantam Books, 1965.

Soward, F.H. "On Becoming and Being a Middle Power." *Pacific Historical Review* 32, no. 2 (May 1963): 111–36.

Smith, Cameron. *Unfinished Journey: The Lewis Family.* Toronto: University of Toronto Press, 1989.

Smith, Denis. *Gentle Patriot: A Political Biography of Walter Gordon.* Toronto: Hurtig Publishers, 1973.

———. *Rogue Tory: The Life and Legend of John G. Diefenbaker.* Toronto: Mcfarlane Walter & Ross, 1995.

Smith, Jean Edward. *Eisenhower in War and Peace.* New York: Random House, 2012.

Spencer, Dick. *Trumpets and Drums: John Diefenbaker on the Campaign Trail.* Vancouver: Greystone Books, 1994.

Spencer, R.A. "Triangle into Treaty: Canada and the Origins of NATO." *International Journal* XIV (1959): 87–98.

St. Laurent, Louis. "Foundations of Canadian Policy in World Affairs." In *Canadian Foreign Policy, 1945–1954: Selected Speeches and Documents*, edited by R.A. MacKay, 388–99. Toronto: McClelland & Stewart, 1971.

Stacey, C.P. *Canada and the Age of Conflict, Volume 2: The Mackenzie King Era.* Toronto: University of Toronto Press, 1981.

Stagg, Ronald. *The Golden Dream: A History of the St. Lawrence Seaway*. Toronto: Dundurn Press, 2010.

Stairs, Denis. *The Diplomacy of Restraint: Canada, the Korean War and the United States*. Toronto: University of Toronto Press, 1974.

Steinnes, Kristian. "The European Challenge: Britain's EEC Application in 1961." *Contemporary European History* 7, no. 1 (March 1998): 61–79.

Stern, Sheldon. *Averting the Final Failure: John F. Kennedy and the Secret Cuban Missile Crisis Meetings*. Stanford: Stanford University Press, 2003.

———. *The Cuban Missile Crisis in American Memory: Myths versus Reality*. Stanford: Stanford University Press, 2012.

———. *The Week the World Stood Still: Inside the Cuban Missile Crisis*. Stanford: Stanford University Press, 2005.

Story, Donald C. and R. Bruce Shepard, eds. *The Diefenbaker Legacy: Canadian Politics, Law and Society Since 1957*. Regina, SK: Canadian Great Plains Research Centre, 1988.

Stuart, Reginald C. *Dipersed Relations: Americans and Canadians in Upper North America*. Washington, DC: Woodrow Wilson Center Press, 2007.

Stursberg, Peter. *Leadership Gained, 1956–1962*. Toronto: University of Toronto Press, 1975.

———. *Leadership Lost, 1962–1967*. Toronto: University of Toronto Press, 1976.

———. *Lester Pearson and the American Dilemma*. Toronto: Doubleday Canada, 1980.

———. *Lester Pearson and the Dream of Unity*. Toronto: Doubleday Canada, 1978.

Swanson, Roger Frank, ed. *Canadian-American Summit Diplomacy, 1923–1973*. Toronto: McClelland & Stewart, 1975.

Taylor, Charles. *Radical Torys: The Conservative Tradition in Canada*. Toronto: House of Anansi Press, 2006.

Thomas, Scott G. *A New World to Be Won: John Kennedy, Richard Nixon, and the Tumultuous Year of 1960*. Westport, CT: Praeger Press, 2011.

Thompson, John Herd and Stephen J. Randall. *Canada and the United States: Ambivalent Allies*. Athens: University of Georgia Press, 2002.

Thomson, Alex. *U.S. Policy Towards Apartheid South Africa, 1948–1994: Conflict of Interests*. Basingstoke: Palgrave-Macmillan, 2008.

Thordarson, Bruce. *Lester Pearson: Diplomat and Politician*. Toronto: Oxford University Press, 1974.

———. "Posture and Policy: Leadership in Canada's External Affairs." *International Journal* 31, no. 4 (Autumn 1976): 666–91.

Troy, Gil and Ian L. MacDonald. "US Presidents and Canadian Prime Ministers: Good Vibes, or Not." *Policy Options* (March 2011): 27–35.

Trudeau, Pierre Elliott. *Memoirs*. Toronto: McClelland & Stewart, 1993.

Van Dusen, Thomas. *The Chief.* Toronto: McGraw-Hill, 1968.

Vincent, Bladen W. *Report of the Royal Commission on the Automotive Industry*. Ottawa: Queen's Printer, 1961.

Ward, Stuart. "Kennedy, Britain and the European Community." In *John F. Kennedy and Europe*, edited by Douglas Brinkley and Richard T. Griffiths, 317–32. Baton Rouge: Louisiana State University Press, 1999.

Warnock, John. *Partner to Behemoth: The Military Policy of a Satellite Canada*. Toronto: New Press, 1970.

Warren, Spencer. *Churchill's Iron Curtain Speech Fifty Years Later*. Columbia: University of Missouri Press, 1999.

Whitaker, Reg and Gary Marcuse. *Cold War Canada: The Making of a National Insecurity State, 1945–1957*. Toronto: University of Toronto Press, 1996.

White, Theodore, *The Making of the President 1960*. New York: Athenaeum Press, 1961.

Wiebes, Cees and Bert Zeeman. "Political Consultation during International Crises: Small Powers in NATO." In *NATO After Forty Years*, edited by Lawrence Kaplan, S.V Papacsma, Mark Rubin, and Ruth Young. Wilmington, DE: Scholarly Resources, 1990.

Wills, Garry. *Nixon Agonistes: The Crisis of the Self-Made Man*. Boston: Houghton Mifflin, 1970.

Willoughby, William. *The St. Lawrence Waterways: A Study in Politics and Diplomacy*. Madison: University of Wisconsin Press, 1961.

Winters, Francis, X. *The Year of the Hare: America in Vietnam, January 25, 1963–February 15, 1964*. Athens: University of Georgia Press, 1997.

Wofford, Harris. *Of Kennedy and Kings*. New York: Farrar, Straus & Giroux, 1980.

Wolfe, James S. *The Kennedy Myth: American Civil Religion in the Sixties*. Bloomington, IN: AuthorHouse, 2013.

Wolk, Herman. "The New Look." *Air Force Magazine*, August 2003.

Wolman, William. "Canada at the Crossroads." *Challenge* 10, no. 1 (October 1961): 39–41.

Wright, Robert. *Three Nights in Havana: Pierre Trudeau, Fidel Castro and the Cold War World*. Toronto: Harper Perennial, 2007.

Wrong, Dennis H. "Canadian Politics in the Sixties." *Political Science Quarterly* 78, no. 1 (March 1963): 1–12.

Wyatt, Daniel. *The Last Flight of the Arrow*. Toronto: Random House, 1990.

Zorbas, Jason Gregory. *Diefenbaker and Latin America: The Pursuit of Canadian Autonomy*. Newcastle Upon Tyne: Cambridge Scholars Publishing, 2011.

# ACKNOWLEDGEMENTS

---

I am indebted to a number of people who made this book possible. It began with my mother spurring my love of reading and history and my grandfather's gentle wit teaching me wordplay and the pleasure of a well-spun story.

Thank you to the knowledgeable professionals at Trent University's Bata Library who helped me gather books from collections far and wide. Thank you to the gifted archivists at the Library and Archives Canada in Ottawa, the John F. Kennedy Presidential Library and Museum in Boston, and the University of Saskatchewan Archives in Saskatoon. I was warmly welcomed and thoughtfully helped to locate the papers I needed, and pointed to documents made recently available to researchers. I was impressed by the dedication of those who guided me through the Kennedy Museum and Diefenbaker Canada Centre. I was thrilled to slip beneath the velvet ropes to sit at Bobby Kennedy's desk and at Diefenbaker's place at the Cabinet table.

The team at Knopf Canada is exceptional. Publisher Anne Collins offered her faith and support, senior editor Craig Pyette helped shepherd and shape the book, and copy editor Linda Pruessen sharpened my prose. Many thanks also to proofreader Tilman Lewis. I am grateful as well to those whose talents in design, marketing, and promotion at Penguin Random House in Canada and the United States helped the book find its audience.

My literary agent, Daphne Hart, continues to impress me with her hard work and dedicated efforts on my behalf.

Three talented and respected scholars read an early draft of the manuscript and offered insightful suggestions and welcome corrections. I sincerely thank Greg Donaghy, head of the Historical Section in the Department of Foreign Affairs, Trade and Development, and adjunct professor in the Department of History at St. Jerome's University; Joseph Jockel, professor of Canadian Studies at St. Lawrence University; and Adam Chapnick, deputy director of education at the Canadian Forces College and a professor of defence studies at the Royal Military College of Canada.

I thank Jennifer, Kenzie, Anna, and especially my dear wife, Sue. They carried on when I was gone on research trips and speaking engagements or squirrelled away in my office. They gently teased me back when my eyes betrayed that I was in the same room but had somehow wandered off to the 1960s.

# INDEX

JOHN BOYKO is the author of five previous books, including the critically acclaimed *Blood and Daring: How Canada Fought the American Civil War and Forged a Nation* and *Bennett: The Rebel Who Challenged and Changed a Nation.* Called by the *Globe and Mail* "a distinguished scholar of Canadian political history" and praised by the *Winnipeg Free Press* for his "encyclopedic knowledge of Canadian history," John Boyko has earned degrees from Queen's, Trent, and McMaster universities. He is a former dean of history and currently an administrator at Lakefield College School, and an op-ed contributor to newspapers across Canada. He lives in Lakefield, Ontario.